THE NORTON 

Fifth Edition

On writing
pp. 19, 21
Incorporate in
syllabus?

Also by Thomas Cooley

The Norton Guide to Writing

Huckleberry Finn, *Second Edition*

A Norton Critical Edition

The Norton Sampler

Short Essays for Composition

Fifth Edition

Thomas Cooley

The Ohio State University

W · W · Norton & Company

New York London

Printed in the United States of America.
Fifth Edition

The text of this book is composed in Berkeley Old Style
with the display set in Gill Sans.
Composition by Vail Composition.
Manufacturing by Maple-Vail Book Manufacturing Group.
Cover illustration: by Matthew Pfleghaar, 1997/Nonstock.

Library of Congress Cataloging-in-Publication Data
The Norton sampler : short essays for composition / [edited by] Thomas
Cooley.—5th ed.
p. cm.
ISBN 0-393-97090-6 (pbk.)
1. College readers. 2. English language—Rhetoric. 3. Essays.
I. Cooley, Thomas, 1942–
PE1417.N6 1997
808′.0427—dc20 96-24245

W. W. Norton & Company, Inc., 500 Fifth Avenue, New York, N.Y. 10110
http://www.wwnorton.com
W. W. Norton & Company Ltd., 10 Coptic Street, London WC1A 1PU

1 2 3 4 5 6 7 8 9 0

Lee K. Abbott: "The True Story of Why I Do What I Do." First appeared in *Puerto del Sol* magazine. Copyright © 1987 by Lee K. Abbott. Reprinted by permission of the author.

Diane Ackerman: "Anosmia." From *A Natural History of the Senses* by Diane Ackerman. Copyright © 1990 by Diane Ackerman. Reprinted by permission of Random House, Inc.

Isaac Asimov: "What Do You Call a Platypus?" From the March / April 1971 issue of *National Wildlife*. Reprinted by permission of The Estate of Isaac Asimov, c/o Ralph M. Vicinanza, Ltd.

Russell Baker: "A Nice Place to Visit." Copyright © 1980 by The New York Times Company. Reprinted by permission.

Bruce Catton: "Grant and Lee: A Study in Contrasts." From *The American Story*, edited by Earl Schenck Miers. Copyright U.S. Capitol Historical Society, all rights reserved.

Judith Ortiz Cofer: "More Room." Reprinted with permission from the publisher of *Silent Dancing: A Partial Remembrance of a Puerto Rican Childhood*, by Judith Ortiz Cofer (Houston: Arte Publico Press-University of Houston, 1990).

Debi Davis: "Body Imperfect." First appeared in *The Norton Textra Extra*, February 1992, Vol. 1, No. 2. Used by permission of W. W. Norton & Company, Inc.

Alan M. Dershowitz: "Shouting 'Fire!' " From *The Atlantic Monthy*. Reprinted by permission of the author.

Jared Diamond: "Who Killed Easter Island?" Copyright © 1995 by The Walt Disney Company. Reprinted with permission of *Discover* magazine. (Originally titled "Easter's End.")

Joan Didion: "On Keeping a Notebook." From *Slouching Towards Bethlehem* by Joan Didion. Copyright © 1968 by Joan Didion. Reprinted by permission of Farrar, Straus & Giroux, Inc.

Annie Dillard: Excerpt from *Holy the Firm* by Annie Dillard. Copyright © 1977 by Annie Dillard. Reprinted by permission of HarperColllins Publishers, Inc. "How I Wrote the Moth Essay—and Why," and journal selections containing earlier versions of "Transfiguration" (editor's title). Reprinted by permission of the author and Blanche C. Gregory, Inc. Copyright © 1985 by Annie Dillard.

Beverly Dipo: "No Rainbows, No Roses." Copyright © 1989, from *Student Writers At Work and in the Company of Others: The Bedford Prizes*, Third Edition, by Nancy Sommers and Donald McQuade. Reprinted with permission of St. Martin's Press, Inc.

Barbara Ehrenreich: "Maintaining the Crime Supply." From *The Snarling Citizen: Essays* by Barbara Ehrenreich. Copyright © 1995 by Barbara Ehrenreich. Reprinted by permission of Farrar, Straus & Giroux, Inc.

Louis Erdrich: "Skunk Dreams." From *The Bluejay's Dance* by Louis Erdrich. Copyright © 1993 by Louise Erdrich. Reprinted by permission of HarperCollins Publishers, Inc.

Kitty Burns Florey: "Ticky-Tacky." From *House Beautiful*, November 1995. Copyright © 1995 by *House Beautiful*, The Hearst Corporation. Reprinted by permission from the publisher.

Henry Louis Gates, Jr.: "A Giant Step." From "About Men," December 9, 1990, *The New York Times Magazine*. Copyright © 1990 by The New York Times Company. Reprinted by permission.

Nikki Giovanni: "On Holidays and How to Make Them Work." From *Sacred Cows . . . and Other Edibles* by Nikki Giovanni. Copyright © 1988 by Nikki Giovanni. Reprinted by permission of William Morrow & Company, Inc.

Ellen Goodman: "The Maidenform Woman Administers Shock Treatment." © 1989 by The Boston Globe Newspaper Co. / Washington Post Writers Group. Reprinted with permission.

Gordon Grice: "Caught in the Widow's Web." Copyright © 1996 by Gordon Grice. From *Harper's* Magazine, February 1996. Originally published in an expanded version as "The Black Widow" in the Fall issue of *The High Plains Literary Review*. Reprinted by permission of the author.

Ann Hodgman: "No Wonder They Call Me a Bitch." Copyright © 1993. Reprinted by permission of *SPY* magazine.

Garrison Keillor: "How to Write a Letter." Copyright © 1986 by Garrison Keillor. From *We Are Still Married*, published by Viking Penguin Inc. Reprinted by permission of International Paper pany. (Originally titled "How to Write a Personal Letter.")

Cherokee Paul McDonald: "A View from the Bridge." Reprinted by permission of the author and Jay Garon-Brooke Associates, Inc.

Joyce Maynard: "Four Generations." Copyright © 1979 by Joyce Maynard. First appeared in *The New York Times*. Reprinted by permission of the author.

Mary E. Mebane: "The Back of the Bus." Copyright © 1981 by Mary Elizabeth Mebane. From *Mary* by Mary E. Mebane. Used by permission of Viking Penguin, a division of Penguin Books USA Inc.

Johnson C. Montgomery: "The Island of Plenty." First appeared in *Newsweek* magazine. Reprinted by permission of Nancy Montgomery Moyer.

Naomi Shihab Nye: "Double Vision in a New Old World" From *American Way*, January 1, 1993. Copyright © 1993 by Naomi Shihab Nye. Reprinted by permission of the author.

George Orwell: "Politics and the English Language," by George Orwell. Copyright © 1946 by Sonia Brownell Orwell and renewed 1974 by Sonia Orwell. Reprinted from *Shooting an Elephant and Other Essays* by permission of Harcourt Brace Jovanovich. Reprinted by permission of A. M. Heath & Company Ltd., the estate of Sonia Brownell Orwell, and Martin Secker & Warburg Ltd.

Alexander Petrunkevitch: "The Spider and the Wasp." From *Scientific American*, August 1952. Reprinted with permission. Copyright © 1952 by Scientific American, Inc. All rights reserved.

Anna Quindlen: "The War on Drinks." Copyright © 1991 by The New York Times Company. Reprinted by permission.
Kori Quintana: "The Price of Power: Living in the Nuclear Age." Reprinted from *Best Student Essays,* Vol. 2, No. 2, Fall 1990, University of New Mexico Student Publications.
Anne Raver: "Pulling Up Roots." From *Deep in the Green: An Exploration of Country Pleasures* by Anne Raver. Copyright © 1995 by Anne Raver. Reprinted by permission of Alfred A. Knopf, Inc.
Richard Rodriguez: "None of This Is Fair." Copyright © 1977 by Richard Rodriguez. Reprinted by permission of Georges Borchardt, Inc. for the author.
Cindy Schneider: "A Name Is Just a Name?" From W. W. Norton's *New Worlds of Literature* Essay Contest. Reprinted by permission of the author.
James Seilsopour: "I Forgot the Words to the National Anthem." Copyright © 1984. From *Student Writers at Work: The Bedford Prizes* by Nancy Sommers and Donald McQuade. Reprinted with permission of St. Martin's Press, Inc.
Randy Shilts: "Good AIDS, Bad AIDS." Copyright © 1991 by The New York Times Company. Reprinted by permission.
Jane Smiley: "Reflections on a Lettuce Wedge." First appeared in *The Hungry Mind Review,* Fall 1993. Copyright © 1993 by Jane Smiley. Reprinted by permission of the author.
Gary Soto: "Like Mexicans." From *Small Faces* by Gary Soto. Copyright © 1986 by Gary Soto. Used by permission of Delacorte Press, a division of Bantam Doubleday Dell Books for Young Readers.
Mary Talbot: "The Potato: How It Shaped the World." From *Newsweek* magazine, October 12, 1991. Copyright © 1991 by Newsweek, Inc. All rights reserved. Reprinted by permission.
Amy Tan: "Mother Tongue." Copyright © 1990 by Amy Tan. First appeared in *The Threepenny Review,* 1990. Reprinted by permission of the author and the Sandra Dijkstra Literary Agency.
Susan Allen Toth: "Cinematypes." Copyright © 1980 by Susan Allen Toth. First appeared in *Harper's* magazine. Reprinted by permission of the author.
Roger Verhulst: "Being Prepared in Suburbia." Originally published by *Newsweek* magazine. Copyright © 1992 by Ad Cetera Communications, Inc. Reprinted by permission.
Eric A. Watts: "The Color of Success." First appeared in *The Brown Alumni Monthly,* April 1992. Copyright © 1992 by Eric Watts. Reprinted by permission of the author.
Philip Weiss: "How to Get Out of a Locked Trunk." Originally published in *Harper's* magazine. Copyright by Philip Weiss. Reprinted by permission of the author.
E. B. White: "Once More to the Lake." From *Essays of E. B. White*. Copyright © 1944 by E. B. White. Reprinted by permission of HarperCollins Publishers.
James Q. Wilson: "Reasonable Search and Seizure." Copyright by James Q. Wilson. Reprinted by permission of the author.
Virginia Woolf: "The Death of the Moth." From *The Death of the Moth and Other Essays* by Virginia Woolf. Published by The Hogarth Press. Copyright © 1942 by Harcourt Brace Jovanovich, and renewed 1970 by Marjorie T. Parsons, Executrix, reprinted by permission of the publisher.
Lynn Woolsey: "Reinvent Welfare, Humanely." From *The New York Times,* January 22, 1994. Copyright © 1994 by The New York Times Company. Reprinted by permission.

Contents

Thematic Table of Contents *xvii*

Preface *xxiv*

Introduction *3*

The Writing Process *7*

Annie Dillard, Transfiguration *9*

"And that is why I believe those hollow crisps on the bathroom floor are moths. I think I know moths, and fragments of moths, and chips and tatters of utterly empty moths, in any state. How many of you, I asked the people in my class, which of you want to give your lives and be writers?"

Annie Dillard, How I Wrote the Moth Essay—and Why *15*

"Walking back to my desk, where I had been answering letters, I realized that the burning moth was a dandy visual focus for all my recent thoughts about an empty, dedicated life. Perhaps I'd try to write a short narrative about it."

Narration

Exposition

Description

Persuasion and Argumentation

Randy Shilts, GOOD AIDS, BAD AIDS 358
"With those words, she seemed to be separating those who don't deserve AIDS from those who do. These were troubling words."

Anna Quindlen, THE WAR ON DRINKS 362
". . . [It] is not just that they make drinking seem cool, but that they make it seem inevitable, as though parties would not take place, Christmas never come, success be elusive without a bottle."

Chief Seattle, REPLY TO THE U.S. GOVERNMENT 367
"Let him be just and deal kindly with my people, for the dead are not powerless. Dead, did I say? There is no death, only a change of worlds."

Writers on the Writing Process
ROGER VERHULST 374

ESSAYS FOR FURTHER READING: COMBINING THE MODES 378

Jonathan Swift, A MODEST PROPOSAL 381
"I have been assured by a very knowing American of my acquaintance in London, that a young healthy child well nursed is at a year old a most delicious, nourishing, and wholesome food, whether stewed, roasted, baked, or boiled. . . ."

George Orwell, POLITICS AND THE ENGLISH LANGUAGE 390
"Political language—and with variations this is true of all political parties, from Conservatives to Anarchists—is designed to make lies sound truthful and murder respectable, and to give an appearance of solidity to pure wind. One can not change this all in a moment, but one can at least change one's own habits. . . ."

E. B. White, ONCE MORE TO THE LAKE 403
"I felt the same damp moss covering the worms in the bait can, and saw the dragonfly alight on the tip of my rod. . . . It was the arrival of this fly that convinced me beyond any doubt that everything was as it always had been, that the years were a mirage and that there had been no years."

Virginia Woolf, THE DEATH OF THE MOTH 410
"It was as if someone had taken a tiny bead of pure life and decking it as lightly as possible with down and feathers, had set it dancing and zigzagging to show us the true nature of life."

Thematic Table of Contents

Cultural Barriers

* Selection is accompanied by Writers on the Writing Process.

Death and Dying

Environment

Gender Issues

History

Home and Family

Humor and Satire

Language and Communication

Lifestyles

Memories of Youth

Overcoming Disability

Public Policy

Scientific and Nature Writing

Sociology and Anthropology

Sports and Leisure

Student Writing

The Writing Process

Preface to the Fifth Edition

In this Fifth Edition of the *Sampler,* fifteen of the selections are new, and they represent a wide range of voices. Along with more works by women and minorities and more student essays, however, I have tried to keep the selections, or at least authors, that readers of earlier editions found indispensable.

Thus I have kept Annie Dillard's remarks on "Transfiguration" at the front of the book, and many of the comments in "Writers on the Writing Process" will also be familiar. These are the sections at the end of each chapter in which professional and beginning writers explain how particular pieces in the collection were composed and, in general, how and why they write. Among the new voices in these sections are those of Nikki Giovanni, Barbara Ehrenreich, and Judith Ortiz Cofer, who granted an interview exclusively for the new *Sampler* on her essay, "More Room."

It was Edgar Allan Poe who said that a long poem does not exist. As editor of these readings for composition, I have kept in mind the unity of effect that Poe taught us to value. Most of the essays in this collection, therefore, are only two to four pages long, and even the longest can be easily read at a single sitting.

It is misleading to talk about unity, however, when one is dealing with a fragment. How do we tell our students about beginnings, middles, and ends or about an author's shapely rhetoric when the shape is actually an editor's? (I have found that even "classics" such as Alexander Petrunkevitch's "The Spider and the Wasp" are routinely reprinted with amputations.) It is the rhetoric of the short piece that our students are learning in beginning composition classes, and such pieces have their own unique rules of order. Thus I have taken pains to gather *complete* essays, or, in a few cases (indicated in the headnotes), *complete* chapters of books.

The organization of the *Sampler* remains essentially the same as before, though it represents but one way of proceeding, hardly the only way. The introductory chapter exposes the student to the writing process as a whole. The rest of the book is organized by the traditional modes of discourse. Narration comes first because these are personal narratives and many teachers like to begin a course by having students write about their own experience.

The next six chapters, the bulk of the book, illustrate strategies of exposition and can be taken up in any order, though here the plan has been to build from the simple (as I perceive it) to the more complex. For example: Chapter 5 ("Essays That Define") presents extended definitions that draw upon the techniques of classification and analysis discussed earlier.

Description is treated in a single chapter (Chapter 8) because this mode is seldom isolated from the others in practice; the teacher who requires more examples will find them throughout the collection. Chapters 9 and 10 are devoted to persuasion and argumentation, and they observe the classical division of persuasion into *logos, pathos,* and *ethos* (although I have not burdened the student with these terms). Some teachers will want to start here.

The questions after each selection are intended to help students understand what they are reading and especially to aid them in analyzing standard rhetorical strategies and techniques. The comparative questions—which invite students to make connections between essays—are an innovation; and so is the inclusion of student essays in full parity with those of the professionals. The "Essays for Further Reading" are more complicated, and generally longer, than the rest; but they too have been selected from a wide range of subjects.

Many people have had a hand in this fifth edition of the *Sampler,* and the editor wishes to thank them warmly here: Carol Hollar-Zwick, Julia Reidhead, Diane O'Connor, Hugh O'Neill, Kristin Sheerin, Shelly Perron, Kate Lovelady, and Marian Johnson—all of W. W. Norton; in a class by herself: Barbara Cooley; at Ohio State:

Lee K. Abbott, William Allen, Richard D. Altick, Daniel Barnes, Toni Bates, Morris Beja, Ellen Carter, David Citino, Rebecca Cline, Edward P. J. Corbett, Suellyn Duffey, John B. Gabel, Kim Gainer, Sara Garnes, Andrea Lunsford, Kitty Locker, Richard T. Martin, Terence Odlin, Frank O'Hare, Faye Purol, Dennis Quon, Barbara Rigney, Michael Rupright, Arnold Shapiro, Frances Shapiro, Amy Shuman, Clifford Vaida, Eric Walborn, Charles Wheeler, and Christian Zacher.

For the criticism and encouragement that guided me in the initial stages of writing, I wish to thank the following at other places: Judith Barnet, Cape Cod Community College; Richard Benston, Bakersfield College; Harry Brent, Rutgers University—Camden College of Arts and Sciences; Lois Bueler, Winona State University; Larry Carver, the University of Texas at Austin; John Cope, Western State College of Colorado; Charles B. Dodson, University of North Carolina at Wilmington; Betty Flowers, the University of Texas at Austin; Ramsey Fowler, Memphis State University; Barbara Goff, Rutgers University—Cook College; David Goslee, the University of Tennessee; William Gracie, Miami University; Joan Hartman, the College of Staten Island; Robert W. Hill, Clemson University; John Huxhold, Meramec Community College; Bernetta Jackson, Washington University; H. Gerald Joiner, Clayton Junior College; Russ Larson, Eastern Michigan University; Kristin Lauer, Fordham University; James MacKillop, Onondaga Community College; Catharine McCue, Framingham State College; John Mellon, University of Illinois at Chicago Circle; Tom Miles, West Virginia University; Robin Mitchell, Marquette University; James Murphy, California State University—Hayward; Elizabeth Penfield, University of New Orleans; Richard Poulsen, Brigham Young University; Kenn Sherwood Roe, Shasta College; Charles Schuster, the University of Iowa; Jayana Sheth, Baruch College; Susan Shreve, George Mason University; Lynne Shuster, Erie Community College; Donald Smith, University of New Haven; Tori Haring Smith, University of Illinois at Urbana-Champaign; Craig Snow, the University of Arizona; William Tucker, the University of North Carolina at Greensboro; John L. Vifian, Central Washington State College; and J. Peter Williams, County College of Morris.

The Norton Sampler

Fifth Edition

INTRODUCTION

Suppose that you went on a strenuous camping trip in the mountains, while all your friends decided to relax at the seashore. Suppose, also, that you got bored after two days without company and that you composed a letter inviting your best friend to forsake the surf and join you on the rocks. Your letter might contain the following elements:

—the story of your time on the road, your arrival in camp, and the events of the first two days, including an account of the skunk that got into your provisions;

—directions for getting there and a list of equipment, food, and clothes to bring;

—a description of your campsite, the yellow tent, the beautiful blue valley in the distance, and the crystal lake nearby;

—all the reasons why your friend should join you and why the mountains are preferable to the shore.

The four parts of your letter would conform to the four traditional MODES[1] (or "means") of writing: NARRATION, EXPOSITION, DESCRIPTION, and PERSUASION. The first part would be in the narrative mode. Narration is writing that tells a story; it records events, actions,

[1] Terms printed in small capitals are defined in the Glossary.

adventures. It tells, in short, what happened. The part of your letter that gives directions is exposition. This is informative writing, or writing that explains. In this book, exposition receives more attention than the other modes because it is the one you are likely to use most often in the years to come. Examinations, term papers, insurance claims, job and graduate school applications, sales reports, almost every scrap of practical prose you write over a lifetime, including your last will and testament, will demand expository skills.

The third part of your letter, of course, is description. This is the mode that captures how a person, thing, place, or idea looks, feels, sounds, or otherwise impresses the senses or the mind. The last part of your letter, the part designed to convince your friend to join you, is in the persuasive mode. Persuasion is writing that seeks assent, conveys advice, or moves the reader to action. In a sense, all writing is persuasion because the writer must convince the reader that what he or she says deserves to be heeded.

As our hypothetical letter to a friend suggests, the four modes of writing seldom appear in "pure" states. An accomplished writer is not likely to say, "Well I shall produce an expository definition today." The mode (or means) that a writer chooses will vary with his or her purpose (as in our letter). A writer may set out to define something and end up describing it or telling the story of its invention. Writers often mix the modes in actual practice, and you will find more than one essay in this collection that could be placed under a different heading.

Nevertheless, a single mode often dominates the others in any given essay. Furthermore, composing themes that largely narrate, explain, describe, or persuade is a valuable exercise toward learning to write well; and so is concentrating on a single strategy within a mode. A good piece of exposition, for example, may follow several methods of development; but before learning to combine, say, PROCESS ANALYSIS with DEFINITION it is useful to study each of these strategies independently. Therefore, the modes and strategies of writing have been separated in this book.

The narrative mode is exemplified in Chapter 1 (Essays in the First Person Singular). The next six chapters (2–7) give examples of the common strategies of exposition: CLASSIFICATION, PROCESS ANALYSIS, CAUSE AND EFFECT, DEFINITION, COMPARISON AND CONTRAST, METAPHOR and ANALOGY. Chapter 8 (Essays That Appeal to the Senses) is a collection of descriptive writing. Chapter 9 (Essays That Appeal to

Reason) and Chapter 10 (Essays That Appeal to Emotion and Ethics) present examples of the different strategies of persuasion. At the end of the book you will find a collection of Essays for Further Reading.

No one expects you to imitate word for word these highly finished productions of professional writers (though you may well emulate some of the student writing included here). But you can analyze standard rhetorical devices and techniques and so learn to use them in your own writing.

By RHETORIC, as the term will be applied in these pages, we mean "the art of using language effectively"—both in writing and in reading. A skilled writer is usually a skilled reader, in fact. The patterns of words on the written page (and of the sounds those words stand for) lodge themselves in the reader's head. When the writer puts pen to paper, therefore, he or she has a store of patterns to impose upon his or her own black marks. A writer learns some patterns of language by hearing them used orally. But others—such as the printed alphabet—can only be learned by reading.

The purpose of this collection of readings, then, is that set forth by Mark Twain in "The Art of Authorship." Attempting to analyze his own methods of composition, Twain found that "whenever we read a sentence and like it, we unconsciously store it away in our model-chamber; and it goes with a myriad of its fellows to the building, brick, by brick, of the eventual edifice which we call our style. And let us guess that whenever we run across other forms—bricks—whose color, or some other defect, offends us, we unconsciously reject these, and so one never finds them in our edifice."

This is a book of prose forms. Each essay offers proven rhetorical designs that you can store away in your "model-chamber," ready at hand whenever you have a verbal edifice to construct. Such a collection provides this further advantage over reading at random: the defective bricks have already been discarded for you.

THE WRITING PROCESS

WRITING is a little like baking bread. Before you can serve it, you must go through a busy process of sifting and blending. In the chapters to follow, you will get a taste of both the baking and the loaf. Essays by professional and student writers are accompanied in this collection by study questions asking you to probe their work. Many of these questions, you will notice, are about the finished product of the writer's labor, but many others address the process behind it. You will also find comments on the writing process by the writers themselves as they respond to inquiries from the editor about their methods.

Many professional writers learn the art of authorship as Mark Twain did—"unconsciously." Some writers, however, especially if they are also teachers of writing, can speak of their methods with a clarity that lifts the veil for us. One of these is the poet and essayist Annie Dillard, winner of the Pulitzer Prize for her prose narrative *Pilgrim at Tinker Creek*.

The best writing, says Dillard, does not tell the reader what to feel; it "evokes" a response. The ending of E. B. White's "Once More to the Lake," she notes, for example, "creates a sense of mortality without mentioning it." (White himself comments on that famous ending in Essays for Further Reading.) "Hemingway, I believe," says Dillard "taught us all this particular form of excellence; it distinguishes modern writing. All readers are sophisticated enough to grasp it—but not all writers are conscious enough to have noticed it: don't describe emotions!"

Evoking feelings instead of describing them is a key strategy in Dillard's own "Transfiguration," an essay about the writer's calling reprinted in the following pages. In an effort to "demystify" (her word) the writing process for you, Annie Dillard has written a second essay explaining how she composed the first. Going back to her notebooks and earliest recollections of the death of a moth, this newer essay about writing traces the composition of the earlier piece from its inception through revisions made after it had already appeared in print.

Once you have read "Transfiguration," but before you go on to "How I Wrote the Moth Essay—and Why," take a look at the questions in between. Typical of the study questions following all the essays in this collection, they will help you to understand the work Dillard is analyzing. Then turn to the author's comments on the process of writing it. Later, if you want more examples of essays built upon METAPHOR and ANALOGY,[1] you can read Chapter 7. Or, for an essay that treats the same natural object in a different light, you might try Virginia Woolf's classic, "The Death of the Moth," in Essays for Further Reading.

[1] Terms printed in small capitals are defined in the Glossary.

Annie Dillard

Transfiguration

Annie Dillard was born in Pittsburgh in 1945. She attended private school there and, later, Hollins College in Roanoke, Virginia, from which she received a master's degree in English literature in 1968. She lived in the Roanoke Valley from 1965 to 1975, when she moved to Puget Sound. In 1979, she returned to the East Coast. Dillard has written a book of poems, *Tickets for a Prayer Wheel* (1974); a prose narrative, *Pilgrim at Tinker Creek* (1974), which won a Pulitzer Prize; a short prose narrative, *Holy the Firm* (1977), from which "Transfiguration" (editor's title) is taken; a book of literary theory, *Living by Fiction* (1982); a collection of narrative essays, *Teaching a Stone to Talk* (1982); and *Encounters with Chinese Writers* (1984). "Transfiguration" originally appeared in a somewhat different version in *Harper's* under the title "The Death of a Moth." Other works by Annie Dillard include a memoir, *An American Childhood* (1987); *The Living* (1992); her first novel; and *Mornings Like This: Found Poems* (1995).

I live on northern Puget Sound, in Washington State, alone. I have a gold cat, who sleeps on my legs, named Small. In the morning I joke to her blank face, Do you remember last night? Do you remember? I throw her out before breakfast, so I can eat. 1

There is a spider, too, in the bathroom, with whom I keep a sort of company. Her little outfit always reminds me of a certain moth I helped to kill. The spider herself is of uncertain lineage, bulbous at the abdomen and drab. Her six-inch mess of a web works, works somehow, works miraculously, to keep her alive and me amazed. The web itself is in a corner behind the toilet, connecting tile wall to tile wall and floor, in a place where there is, I would have thought, scant traffic. Yet under the web are sixteen or so corpses she has tossed to the floor. 2

The corpses appear to be mostly sow bugs, those little armadillo creatures who live to travel flat out in houses, and die round. There is also a new shred of earwig, three old spider skins crinkled and clenched, and two moth bodies, wingless and huge and empty, moth bodies I drop to my knees to see. 3

Today the earwig shines darkly and gleams, what there is of him: a dorsal curve of thorax and abdomen, and a smooth pair of cerci[1] by which I knew his name. Next week, if the other bodies are any indication, he will be shrunken and gray, webbed to the floor with dust. The sow bugs beside him are hollow and empty of color, fragile, a breath away from brittle fluff. The spider skins lie on their sides, translucent and ragged, their legs drying in knots. And the moths, the empty moths, stagger against each other, headless, in a confusion of arching strips of chitin like peeling varnish, like a jumble of buttresses for cathedral domes, like nothing resembling moths, so that I should hesitate to call them moths, except that I have had some experience with the figure Moth reduced to a nub. 4

Two summers ago I was camping alone in the Blue Ridge Mountains in Virginia. I had hauled myself and gear up there to read, among other things, James Ramsey Ullman's *The Day on Fire,* a novel about Rimbaud that had made me want to be a writer when I was sixteen;[2] I was hoping it would do it again. So I read, lost, every day sitting under a tree by my tent, while warblers swung in the leaves overhead and bristle worms trailed their inches over the twiggy dirt at my feet; and I read every night by candlelight, while barred owls called in the forest and pale moths massed round my head in the clearing, where my light made a ring. 5

Moths kept flying into the candle. They would hiss and recoil, lost upside down in the shadows among my cooking pans. Or they would singe their wings and fall, and their hot wings, as if melted, would stick to the first thing they touched—a pan, a lid, a spoon—so that the snagged moths could flutter only in tiny arcs, unable to struggle free. These I could release by a quick flip with a stick; in the morning I would find my cooking stuff gilded with torn flecks of 6

[1]Plural of *cercus,* posterior "feeler" of an insect.

[2]French poet Arthur Rimbaud (1854–1891) himself began writing at age sixteen and produced his major work before he was twenty. Ullman's novel was published in 1958.

moth wings, triangles of shiny dust here and there on the aluminum. So I read, and boiled water, and replenished candles, and read on.

One night a moth flew into the candle, was caught, burnt dry, 7
and held. I must have been staring at the candle, or maybe I looked up when a shadow crossed my page; at any rate, I saw it all. A golden female moth, a biggish one with a two-inch wingspan, flapped into the fire, dropped her abdomen into the wet wax, stuck, flamed, frazzled and fried in a second. Her moving wings ignited like tissue paper, enlarging the circle of light in the clearing and creating out of the darkness the sudden blue sleeves of my sweater, the green leaves of jewelweed by my side, the ragged red trunk of a pine. At once the light contracted again and the moth's wings vanished in a fine, foul smoke. At the same time her six legs clawed, curled, blackened, and ceased, disappearing utterly. And her head jerked in spasms, making a spattering noise; her antennae crisped and burned away and her heaving mouth parts crackled like pistol fire. When it was all over, her head was, so far as I could determine, gone, gone the long way of her wings and legs. Had she been new, or old? Had she mated and laid her eggs, had she done her work? All that was left was the glowing horn shell of her abdomen and thorax—a fraying, partially collapsed gold tube jammed upright in the candle's round pool.

And then this moth-essence, this spectacular skeleton, began to 8
act as a wick. She kept burning. The wax rose in the moth's body from her soaking abdomen to her thorax to the jagged hole where her head should be, and widened into flame, a saffron-yellow flame that robed her to the ground like any immolating monk. That candle had two wicks, two flames of identical height, side by side. The moth's head was fire. She burned for two hours, until I blew her out.

She burned for two hours without changing, without bending or 9
leaning—only glowing within, like a building fire glimpsed through silhouetted walls, like a hollow saint, like a flame-faced virgin gone to God, while I read by her light, kindled, while Rimbaud in Paris burnt out his brains in a thousand poems, while night pooled wetly at my feet.

And that is why I believe those hollow crisps on the bathroom 10
floor are moths. I think I know moths, and fragments of moths, and chips and tatters of utterly empty moths, in any state. How many of you, I asked the people in my class, which of you want to give your lives and be writers? I was trembling from coffee, or cigarettes, or

the closeness of faces all around me. (Is this what we live for? I thought; is this the only final beauty: the color of any skin in any light, and living, human eyes?) All hands rose to the question. (You, Nick? Will you? Margaret? Randy? Why do I want them to mean it?) And then I tried to tell them what the choice must mean: you can't be anything else. You must go at your life with a broadax. . . . They had no idea what I was saying. (I have two hands, don't I? And all this energy, for as long as I can remember. I'll do it in the evenings, after skiing, or on the way home from the bank, or after the children are asleep. . . .) They thought I was raving again. It's just as well.

I have three candles here on the table which I disentangle from 11
the plants and light when visitors come. Small usually avoids them, although once she came too close and her tail caught fire; I rubbed it out before she noticed. The flames move light over everyone's skin, draw light to the surface of the faces of my friends. When the people leave I never blow the candles out, and after I'm asleep they flame and burn.

Questions

Understanding

1. What is the most important ANALOGY in Dillard's essay? What is she comparing to what?
2. What is Dillard referring to in paragraph 10 when she says, "I'll do it in the evening, after skiing, or on the way home from the bank . . ."?
3. At what cost does Dillard seem to think the writer does her (or his) work?
4. When Dillard draws an analogy between the moth and an "immolating monk" (par. 8) or a "flame-faced virgin" (par. 9), she gets beyond the realm of merely natural phenomena. Into what?
5. What is "miraculous" about the spider's web in paragraph 2? Of all nature as Dillard sees it? What miracle does she celebrate throughout the essay?
6. Why does Dillard refer to the corpses of the moths beneath the spider web in her bathroom?

7. What kind of beauty does Dillard have in mind when she refers to "the color of any skin in any light, and living, human eyes" (par. 10)?
8. What is the significance of the book Dillard is reading when the moth burns?

Strategies and Structure

1. When did you first realize that Dillard's essay draws an extended analogy between the writer and the moth? How does she introduce the comparison without saying flatly, "The writer is like . . ."?
2. How does Dillard's main analogy help to explain the kind of beauty the writer seeks? Her (or his) dedication to her art?
3. How does Dillard's main analogy convey her own sense of awe and wonder at the sacredness of the writer's calling?
4. What analogy is Dillard drawing in the line, "You must go at your life with a broadax . . ." (par. 10)?
5. What is the effect of Dillard's calling the moth "she" instead of "it"? Of Dillard's wondering whether the moth has finished her earthly work (par. 7)?
6. How effective do you find the specific details of the DESCRIPTION in paragraph 3? Explain your answer.
7. How does Dillard give the impression of seeing her world intently, as if through a magnifying glass?
8. In paragraph 9, moth and candle seem almost to be holding the night at bay. How does Dillard create this impression? How does she get across to us the sudden flare of the moth as it first hits the flame?
9. Dillard's analogies are developed through a personal NARRATIVE of the sort exemplified in Chapter 1. Which parts of her narrative are set in the present (the time at which she writes)? Where is she located physically in the present time?
10. In what *two* places is the past action of Dillard's narrative located? When does she return to the present?
11. How does Dillard achieve a welcome comic relief in paragraph 11?

Words and Figures of Speech

1. What is the effect of Dillard's including "like a jumble of buttresses for cathedral domes" in the list of SIMILES at the end of paragraph 4?

2. Look up *transfiguration* in your dictionary. What does it mean in religious terms? How does it apply to Dillard's essay?
3. Why do you think Dillard uses such technical terms as *thorax, cerci,* and *chitin* (par. 4)?
4. How effective do you find the phrase "scant traffic" in paragraph 2? What is the effect of the word *raving* in paragraph 10?
5. Why does Dillard capitalize *Moth* in paragraph 4?
6. Consult your dictionary as necessary for the following words: *lineage* (par. 2), *bulbous* (2), *dorsal* (4), *thorax* (4), *translucent* (4), *chitin* (4), *buttresses* (4), *gilded* (6), *replenished* (6), *essence* (8), *immolating* (8).

Comparing

1. They do not smell alike or belong to the same phylum, but Dillard's moth and Louise Erdrich's skunk ("Skunk Dreams," Essays for Further Reading) help to organize their respective essays in similar ways. What are some of them?
2. In a sense, Dillard's account of the death of a moth and Virginia Woolf's account of the same phenomenon (Essays for Further Reading) come to opposite conclusions. What are those conclusions? Explain the contrast.

Annie Dillard

How I Wrote the Moth Essay—and Why

Annie Dillard's essay on the death of a moth, reprinted in the preceding pages, is the kind of work that makes the reader itch to interrogate the absent author. Or burn, in this case. If only we could go to the source for an authoritative answer to a fundamental question: How was it done? In particular, the editor wanted to know from the author: When did you first think of comparing the writer to a burning moth? You mention Rimbaud and the moths, but when and how did it occur to you to put the two together? How did you come to the idea of writing as burning, a consuming and purifying act? Do you still define writing and the writer that way? How much revising did you do in this essay? In the book from which it is taken? Could you describe any struggle you recall with particular words, phrases, or images? What kind of audience did you have in mind? Why did you write the piece? Why do you write? What advice would you give to beginners? Annie Dillard's generous reply to these and many other questions about the process of composing the essay you have just read was "How I Wrote the Moth Essay—and Why," an essay on an essay.

It was November 1975. I was living alone, as described, on an island in Puget Sound, near the Canadian border. I was thirty years old. I thought about myself a lot (for someone thirty years old), because I couldn't figure out what I was doing there. What was my life about? Why was I living alone, when I am gregarious? Would I ever meet someone, or should I reconcile myself to all this solitude? I disliked celibacy; I dreaded childlessness. I couldn't even think of anything to write. I was examining every event for possible meaning.

I was then in full flight from success, from the recent fuss over a book of prose I'd published the previous year called *Pilgrim at Tinker Creek*. There were offers from editors, publishers, and Hollywood and network producers. They tempted me with world travel, film and TV work, big bucks. I was there to turn from literary and commercial success and to rededicate myself to art and to God. That's how I justified my loneliness to myself. It was a feeble justification and I knew it, because you certainly don't need to live alone either to write or to pray. Actually I was there because I had picked the place from an atlas, and I was alone because I hadn't yet met my husband.

My reading and teaching fed my thoughts. I was reading Simone Weil, *First and Last Notebooks*. Simone Weil was a twentieth-century French intellectual, born Jewish, who wrote some of the most interesting Christian theology I've ever read. She was brilliant, but a little nuts; her doctrines were harsh. "Literally," she wrote, "it is total purity or death." This sort of fanaticism attracted and appalled me. Weil had deliberately starved herself to death to call attention to the plight of French workers. I was taking extensive notes on Weil.

In the classroom I was teaching poetry writing, exhorting myself (in the guise of exhorting my students), and convincing myself by my own rhetoric: commit yourself to a useless art! In art alone is meaning! In sacrifice alone is meaning! These, then, were issues for me at that time: dedication, purity, sacrifice.

Early that November morning I noticed the hollow insects on the bathroom floor. I got down on my hands and knees to examine them and recognized some as empty moth bodies. I recognized them, of course, only because I'd seen an empty moth body already—two years before, when I'd camped alone and had watched a flying moth get stuck in a candle and burn.

Walking back to my desk, where I had been answering letters, I realized that the burning moth was a dandy visual focus for all my recent thoughts about an empty, dedicated life. Perhaps I'd try to write a short narrative about it.

I went to my pile of journals, hoping I'd taken some nice, specific notes about the moth in the candle. What I found disappointed me at first: that night I'd written a long description of owl sounds, and only an annoyed aside about bugs flying into the candle. But the next night, after pages of self-indulgent drivel, I'd written a fuller description, a description of the moth which got stuck in candle wax.

The journal entry had some details I could use (bristleworms on the ground, burnt moths' wings sticking to pans), some phrases (her body acted as a wick, the candle had 2 flames, the moth burned until I blew it out), and, especially, some verbs (hiss, recoil, stick, spatter, jerked, crackled).

Even in the journals, the moth was female. (From childhood reading I'd learned to distinguish moths by sex.) And, there in the journal, was a crucial detail: on that camping trip, I'd been reading about Rimbaud. Arthur Rimbaud—the French symbolist poet, a romantic, hotheaded figure who attracted me enormously when I was sixteen—had been young and self-destructive. When *he* was sixteen, he ran away from home to Paris, led a dissolute life, shot his male lover (the poet Verlaine), drank absinthe which damaged his brain, deranged his senses with drunkenness and sleeplessness, and wrote mad vivid poetry which altered the course of Western literature. When he was in his twenties, he turned his back to the Western world and vanished into Abyssinia as a gunrunner.

With my old journal beside me, I took up my current journal and scribbled and doodled my way through an account of my present life and the remembered moth. It went extraordinarily well; it was not typical. It seemed very much "given"—given, I think, because I'd asked, because I'd been looking so hard and so long for connections, meanings. The connections were all there, and seemed solid enough: I saw a moth burnt and on fire; I was reading Rimbaud hoping to rededicate myself to writing (this one bald statement of motive was unavoidable); I live alone. So the writer is like the moth, and like a religious contemplative: emptying himself so he can be a channel for his work. Of course you can reinforce connections with language: the bathroom moths are like a jumble of buttresses for cathedral domes; the female moth is like an immolating monk, like a hollow saint, a flame-faced virgin gone to God; Rimbaud burnt out his brains with poetry while night pooled wetly at my feet.

I liked the piece enough to rewrite it. I took out a couple of paragraphs—one about why I didn't have a dog, another that ran on about the bathroom spider. This is the kind of absurdity you fall into when you write about anything, let alone about yourself. You're so pleased and grateful to be writing at all, especially at the beginning, that you babble. Often you don't know where the work is going, so you can't tell what's irrelevant.

Jan 13.

while R out his brains

Kindling

Jan 3

Two summers ago I ~~was camped~~ was camping alone ~~on~~ in the Blue Ridge mountains in Virginia. I had hauled myself and gear up there to read, among other things, ~~in peace~~, James Ramsey Ullman's ~~novel~~ The Day on Fire, a novel about Rimbaud that had made a writer want to be ~~of me~~ when I was sixteen; I was hoping it would do it again. So I read every ~~all~~ day sitting under a tree by my tent, ~~pausing to eat four or five times and walk once or twice, and I read all night~~ every night while warblers swung in the leaves overhead and bristleworms trailed their inches over the twiggy dirt ~~ground~~ at my (side) feet; and I read every night by candlelight, while the barred owls called in the forest and pale moths massed in the clearing ~~near me, where my light made~~ round my head, ~~a ring by the woods~~. when my light made a ring.

~~The moths flew in~~ Moths kept flying into the candle. They would hiss ~~and spatter~~ and recoil, lost upside down in the shadows darkness among my cooking pans. Or they would singe their wings and fall and their ~~burnt~~ hot wings would stick, as if melted, to whatever the first thing they touched, a pan, a lid, a spoon, so that the snagged moths could struggle only in tiny arcs, unable to ~~tear~~ flutter free. These I could release ~~with~~ by a quick flip ~~by~~ with a stick; in the morning I would find my cooking stuff embossed with torn flecks of moth wings, little triangles of shiny dust here and there on the aluminum. So I read, and boiled water, and replenished candles, and read on.

One night one a female moth flew into the candle, was caught, burned dry and ~~stayed~~ held ~~burning~~. ~~and burned so fast~~ sizzled, dropped ~~ab~~ abdomen into the wet wax, stuck, flamed and fried in a second. Her wings burnt right off and disappeared in a thin, foul smoke, her legs ~~crackled~~ spattered and curled, her head ~~jerked~~ crackled and jerked (like small arms fire)

~~Her wings, tant wings~~ I must have been staring at the candle, or maybe I looked up when a shadow crossed my page; at any rate, I saw ~~the whole thing~~ it all.

It doesn't hurt much to babble in a first draft, so long as you have the sense to cut out irrelevancies later. If you are used to analyzing texts, you will be able to formulate a clear statement of what your draft turned out to be about. Then you make a list of what you've already written, paragraph by paragraph, and see what doesn't fit and cut it out. (All this requires is nerves of steel and lots of coffee.) Most of the time you'll have to add to the beginning, ensuring that it gives a fair idea of what the point might be, or at least what is about to happen. (Suspense is for mystery writers. The most inept writing has an inadvertent element of suspense: the reader constantly asks himself, where on earth is this going?) Usually I end up throwing away the beginning: the first part of a poem, the first few pages of an essay, the first scene of a story, even the first few chapters of a book. It's not holy writ. The paragraphs and sentences are tesserae—tiles for a mosaic. Just because you have a bunch of tiles in your lap doesn't mean your mosaic will be better if you use them all. In this atypical case, however, there were very few extraneous passages. The focus was tight, probably because I'd been so single-minded before I wrote it.

I added stuff, too, to strengthen and clarify the point. I added some speculation about the burning moth: had she mated and laid her eggs, had she done her work? Near the end I added a passage about writing class: which of you want to give your lives and become writers?

Ultimately I sent it to *Harper*'s magazine, which published it. The early drafts, and the *Harper*'s version, had a different ending, a kind of punch line that was a series of interlocking statements:

> I don't mind living alone. I like eating alone and reading. I don't mind sleeping alone. The only time I mind being alone is when something is funny; then, when I am laughing at something funny, I wish someone were around. Sometimes I think it is pretty funny that I sleep alone.

I took this ending out of the book version, which is the version you have. I took it out because the tone was too snappy, too clever;

OPPOSITE. *"With my old journal beside me, I took up my current journal and scribbled and doodled my way through an account of my present life and the remembered moth." Page from the first draft of "Transfiguration."*

in these were quickly, too.

The rip on thigh seam is 10" long. Oh, dear jeans.

Last night moths kept flying into the candle. They would hiss & spatter & recoil, lost upside down & flapping in the shadows among the pans on the table. Or – and this happened often, & again tonight – they'd burn their wings, & then their wings would stick to the next thing they'd touch – the edge of a pan, a lid . . . these I could free with a quick flip with a spoon or something.

Some, of course, burnt badly & couldn't get away. One moth flew in the near candle. Her wings burnt right off, her legs & head crackled and jerked. Her body was stuck upright in the wax; it must have been dry. Moths are dry. Because it acted as a wick, without burning itself, it drew up wax from the pool, and gave off a steady flame for two hours, until I blew ~~the candle~~ it out. That one candle had two flames. Brightened up my whole evening.

I was screaming to them last night. I got upset, & it was in my voice. Wonder what the neighbors thought: no! don't do it! please – no! So tonight I read in the lodge. After the B & O, I read upstairs on the couch.

Talked to Steve, at Contes w/ KK; talked to Richard twice, at noon, & now.

I don't know what those firm segmented multilegged invertebrates are, but they're all over the place up here. Bristleworms? They're hard on the outside, chitinous I guess. Anyway. One on the path today was on its side, struggling. A big spider of the harvestman sort, but w/ a big grey body, was all over it doing I know not what, & so was a fly.

it reduced everything to celibacy, which was really a side issue; it made the reader forget the moth; and it called too much attention to the narrator. The new ending was milder. It referred back to the main body of the text.

Revising is a breeze if you know what you're doing—if you can look at your text coldly, analytically, manipulatively. Since I've studied texts, I know what I'm doing when I revise. The hard part is devising the wretched thing in the first place. How do you go from nothing to something? How do you face the blank page without fainting dead away?

To start a narrative, you need a batch of things. Not feelings, not opinions, not sentiments, not judgments, not arguments, but specific objects and events: a cat, a spider web, a mess of insect skeletons, a candle, a book about Rimbaud, a burning moth. I try to give the reader a story, or at least a scene (the flimsiest narrative occasion will serve), and something to look at. I try not to hang on the reader's arm and bore him with my life story, my fancy self-indulgent writing, or my opinions. He is my guest; I try to entertain him. Or he'll throw my pages across the room and turn on the television.

I try to say what I mean and not "hide the hidden meaning." "Clarity is the sovereign courtesy of the writer," said J. Henri Fabre, the great French entomologist, "I do my best to achieve it." Actually, it took me about ten years to learn to write clearly. When I was in my twenties, I was more interested in showing off.

What do you do with these things? You juggle them. You toss them around. To begin, you don't need a well defined point. You don't need "something to say"—that will just lead you to reiterating clichés. You need bits of the world to toss around. You start anywhere, and join the bits into a pattern by your writing about them. Later you can throw out the ones that don't fit.

I like to start by describing something, by ticking off the five senses. Later I go back to the beginning and locate the reader in time and space. I've found that if I take pains to be precise about *things*, feelings will take care of themselves. If you try to force a reader's feelings through dramatic writing ("writhe," "ecstasy," "scream"), you make a fool of yourself, like someone at a party trying too hard to be liked.

OPPOSITE. *First encounter with the flaming moth: a page from Annie Dillard's journal, August–October 1974.*

I have piles of materials in my journals—mostly information in the form of notes on my reading, and to a lesser extent, notes on things I'd seen and heard during the day. I began the journals five or six years after college, finding myself highly trained for taking notes and for little else. Now I have thirty-some journal volumes, all indexed. If I want to write about arctic exploration, say, or star chemistry, or monasticism, I can find masses of pertinent data under that topic. And if I browse I can often find images from other fields that may fit into what I'm writing, if only as metaphor or simile. It's terrific having all these materials handy. It saves and makes available all those years of reading. Otherwise, I'd forget everything, and life wouldn't accumulate, but merely pass.

The moth essay I wrote that November day was an "odd" piece—"freighted with heavy-handed symbolism," as I described it to myself just after I wrote it. The reader must be startled to watch this apparently calm, matter-of-fact account of the writer's life and times turn before his eyes into a mess of symbols whose real subject matter is their own relationship. I hoped the reader wouldn't feel he'd been had. I tried to ensure that the actual, historical moth wouldn't vanish into idea, but would stay physically present.

A week after I wrote the first draft I considered making it part of the book *(Holy the Firm)* I had been starting. It seemed to fit the book's themes. (Actually, I spent the next fifteen months fitting the book to *its* themes.) In order to clarify my thinking I jotted down some notes:

moth in candle:
the poet—materials of world, of bare earth at feet, sucked up, transformed, subsumed to spirit, to air, to light
the mystic—not through reason
but through emptiness
the martyr—virgin, sacrifice, death with meaning.

I prefaced these notes with the comical word "Hothead."

It had been sheer good luck that the different aspects of the historical truth fit together so nicely. It had actually been on that particular solo camping trip that I'd read the Rimbaud novel. If it hadn't been, I wouldn't have hesitated to fiddle with the facts. I fiddled with one fact, for sure: I foully slandered my black cat, Small, by saying she was "gold"—to match the book's moth and little blonde burnt girl. I actually had a gold cat at that time, named Kindling. I figured no one would believe it. It was too much. In the book, as in real life, the cat was spayed.

This is the most personal piece I've ever written—the essay itself, and these notes on it. I don't recommend, or even approve, writing personally. It can lead to dreadful writing. The danger is that you'll get lost in the contemplation of your wonderful self. You'll include things for the lousy reason that they actually happened, or that you feel strongly about them; you'll forget to ensure that the *reader* feels anything whatever. You may hold the popular view that art is self-expression, or a way of understanding the self—in which case the artist need do nothing more than babble uncontrolledly about the self and then congratulate himself that, in addition to all his other wonderfully interesting attributes, he is also an artist. I don't (evidently) hold this view. So I think that this moth piece is a risky one to read: it seems to enforce these romantic and giddy notions of art and the artist. But I trust you can keep your heads.

Narration

One

Essays in the First Person Singular

NARRATION[1] is the story-telling mode of writing; it recounts actions and events; it answers the question, "What happened?" The essays in this chapter are written in the narrative mode. They are personal narratives in which each author records experiences from his or her private life.

One reason for beginning with personal narratives is suggested by Henry David Thoreau's famous opening words in *Walden:*

> In most books, the *I,* or first person, is omitted; in this it will be retained; that, in respect to egotism, is the main difference. We commonly do not remember that it is, after all, always the first person that is speaking. I should not talk so much about myself if there were anybody else whom I knew as well. . . . Moreover, I, on my side, require of every writer, first or last, a simple and sincere account of his own life. . . .

The common feature of these openly autobiographical selections is the controlling presence of a distinct personality—like yours. You may not think that you know yourself well, but whom do you know better?

Another reason for beginning with personal narratives is that

[1] Terms printed in small capitals are defined in the Glossary.

essays have always been personal. Our modern word *essay* comes from the French *essayer*, meaning "to try." An essay is your personal trial or attempt to grapple with a subject or problem. Yours and nobody else's. Another person addressing the same subject would necessarily speak in a different voice from a different perspective. Because they invited readers to listen in (like informal guests in the writer's living room), these modest attempts at self-expression became known as "personal" or "familiar" essays.

Any writer who gives an account of his or her own experiences must understand the difference between events and the telling of events. Think of actions as sounds for a moment—the sounds of a college band playing the national anthem. When the band strikes up "Oh, say can you see," your ear hears trombones, trumpets, and drums all in a single harmonious strain. If you were to look at the written parts of the different instruments in their music-holders, however, you would have to separate them. You might follow a single bar of trombone music, then race over to the trumpet section, then back to the drums. But you would be alternating between parts, as the readers of a book must do when his or her eyes move from left to right and down the printed page. Events in real life often occur simultaneously; in a written narrative, they must be printed in sequence.

The sequence of events in a narrative is called the PLOT; unlike random events in real life, the plot of a narrative must be controlled and directed by the narrator. So must the POINT OF VIEW. Point of view is the vantage from which a narrative is told. It is not a difficult concept to master if you think of the difference between watching a football game in the stadium and watching it on television. The camera controls your point of view on the screen; you see only what the camera focuses upon. In the stands, however, you are free to scan the entire field, to watch the quarterback or the line, to concentrate on the cheerleaders. Your point of view is determined by your eyes alone; your vantage is a high place above the total action.

In narration, point of view is controlled in part by the grammatical PERSON in which an author chooses to write. Many narratives are told "in the third person" or "from the third-person point of view." For example, you might write: "The tornado hit while George was playing cards; he had just drawn a third ace, but when he plunked it down, the table was gone." Here the narrator and George are different persons; the narrator does not say how George felt inside at the crucial moment; the story is told after the fact and from the outside (of George). The essays in this chapter are "first-person" narratives, the point of view you would adopt in an autobiography or an account of your adventures during the first day of your college career. Here the "I" is an actor in each drama, and we see the world of the narrative through the narrator's eyes.

Authors of narrative essays in the first person have great freedom: they may record their personal thoughts on anything that has happened to them. As attested by master essayist E. B. White (whose "Once More to the Lake" appears at the end of this volume), "There is one thing the essayist cannot do, though—he cannot indulge himself in deceit or in concealment, for he will be found out in no time." Modern readers of essays, like Thoreau, require a "simple and sincere account"—the sincerity that comes of personal integrity and the simplicity that comes from discipline. The essayist may wander at will, but may not ramble. He or she may be relaxed, even self-indulgent. But if the reader cannot follow along because the essayist writes obscurely or is dishonest, their partnership will be disbanded. And this is what a personal essay amounts to, finally—a friendly partnership between reader and author.

Joyce Maynard

Four Generations

Born in 1953, Joyce Maynard grew up in Durham, New Hampshire, where her father taught at the university. Maynard thus spent her adolescence in the 1960s, but she saw it as a time with no place for youth; at nineteen, while a sophomore at Yale, Maynard published her first book, *Looking Backward: A Chronicle of Growing Up Old in the Sixties* (1973). Since then, Maynard has produced three children, including the daughter so proudly displayed in "Four Generations," and a novel called *Baby Love* (1981). Her *Domestic Affairs: Enduring the Pleasures of Motherhood and Family Life* (1987) brings together Maynard's contributions, over a nine-year period, to the *New York Times*'s nationally syndicated "Hers" column. *Where Love Goes* (1995), a novel, carries the domestic affairs theme into the arena of single parenting. Maynard is also the author of *To Die For* (1992), a novel.

My mother called last week to tell me that my grandmother is dying. She has refused an operation that would postpone, but not prevent, her death from pancreatic cancer. She can't eat, she has been hemorrhaging, and she has severe jaundice. "I always prided myself on being different," she told my mother. "Now I *am* different. I'm yellow." 1

My mother, telling me this news, began to cry. So I became the mother for a moment, reminding her, reasonably, that my grandmother is eighty-seven, she's had a full life, she has all her faculties, and no one who knows her could wish that she live long enough to lose them. Lately my mother has been finding notes in my grandmother's drawers at the nursing home, reminding her, "Joyce's husband's name is Steve. Their daughter is Audrey." In the last few years she hadn't had the strength to cook or garden, and she's begun to say she's had enough of living. 2

My grandmother was born in Russia, in 1892—the oldest daugh- 3
ter in a large and prosperous Jewish family. But the prosperity didn't last. She tells stories of the pogroms and the cossacks who raped her when she was twelve. Soon after that, her family emigrated to Canada, where she met my grandfather.

Their children were the center of their life. The story I loved best, 4
as a child, was of my grandfather opening every box of Cracker Jack in the general store he ran, in search of the particular tin toy my mother coveted. Though they never had much money, my grandmother saw to it that her daughter had elocution lessons and piano lessons, and assured her that she would go to college.

But while she was at college, my mother met my father, who was 5
blue-eyed and blond-haired and not Jewish. When my father sent love letters to my mother, my grandmother would open and hide them, and when my mother told her parents she was going to marry this man, my grandmother said if that happened, it would kill her.

Not likely, of course. My grandmother is a woman who used to 6
crack Brazil nuts open with her teeth, a woman who once lifted a car off the ground, when there was an accident and it had to be moved. She has been representing her death as imminent ever since I've known her—twenty-five years—and has discussed, at length, the distribution of her possessions and her lamb coat. Every time we said goodbye, after our annual visit to Winnipeg, she'd weep and say she'd never see us again. But in the meantime, while every other relative of her generation, and a good many of the younger ones, has died (nursed usually by her), she has kept making knishes, shopping for bargains, tending the healthiest plants I've ever seen.

After my grandfather died, my grandmother lived, more than 7
ever, through her children. When she came to visit, I would hide my diary. She couldn't understand any desire for privacy. She couldn't bear it if my mother left the house without her.

This possessiveness is what made my mother furious (and then 8
guilt-ridden that she felt that way, when of course she owed so much to her mother). So I harbored the resentment that my mother—the dutiful daughter—would not allow herself. I—who had always performed specially well for my grandmother, danced and sung for her, presented her with kisses and good report cards—stopped writing to her, ceased to visit.

But when I heard that she was dying, I realized I wanted to go to 9

Winnipeg to see her one more time. Mostly to make my mother happy, I told myself (certain patterns being hard to break). But also, I was offering up one more particularly fine accomplishment: my own dark-eyed, dark-skinned, dark-haired daughter, whom my grandmother had never met.

I put on my daughter's best dress for our visit to Winnipeg, the way the best dresses were always put on me, and I filled my pockets with animal crackers, in case Audrey started to cry. I scrubbed her face mercilessly. On the elevator going up to her room, I realized how much I was sweating. 10

Grandma was lying flat with an IV tube in her arm and her eyes shut, but she opened them when I leaned over to kiss her. "It's Fredelle's daughter, Joyce," I yelled, because she doesn't hear well anymore, but I could see that no explanation was necessary. "You came," she said. "You brought the baby." 11

Audrey is just one, but she has seen enough of the world to know that people in beds are not meant to be so still and yellow, and she looked frightened. I had never wanted, more, for her to smile. 12

Then Grandma waved at her—the same kind of slow, finger-flexing wave a baby makes—and Audrey waved back. I spread her toys out on my grandmother's bed and sat her down. There she stayed, most of the afternoon, playing and humming and sipping on her bottle, taking a nap at one point, leaning against my grandmother's leg. When I cranked her Snoopy guitar, Audrey stood up on the bed and danced. Grandma wouldn't talk much anymore, though every once in a while she would say how sorry she was that she wasn't having a better day. "I'm not always like this," she said. 13

Mostly she just watched Audrey. Sometimes Audrey would get off the bed, inspect the get-well cards, totter down the hall. "Where is she?" Grandma kept asking. "Who's looking after her?" I had the feeling, even then, that if I'd said, "Audrey's lighting matches," Grandma would have shot up to rescue her. 14

We were flying home that night, and I had dreaded telling her, remembering all those other tearful partings. But in the end, I was the one who cried. She had said she was ready to die. But as I leaned over to stroke her forehead, what she said was, "I wish I had your hair" and "I wish I was well." 15

On the plane flying home, with Audrey in my arms, I thought about mothers and daughters, and the four generations of the family 16 that I know most intimately. Every one of those mothers loves and needs her daughter more than her daughter will love or need her some day, and we are, each of us, the only person on earth who is quite so consumingly interested in our child.

17 Sometimes I kiss and hug Audrey so much she starts crying—which is, in effect, what my grandmother was doing to my mother, all her life. And what makes my mother grieve right now, I think, is not simply that her mother will die in a day or two, but that, once her mother dies, there will never again be someone to love her in quite such an unreserved, unquestioning way. No one else who believes that, fifty years ago, she could have put Shirley Temple out of a job, no one else who remembers the moment of her birth. She will only be a mother, then, not a daughter anymore.

18 Audrey and I have stopped over for a night in Toronto, where my mother lives. Tomorrow she will go to a safe-deposit box at the bank and take out the receipt for my grandmother's burial plot. Then she will fly back to Winnipeg, where, for the first time in anybody's memory, there was waist-high snow on April Fool's Day. But tonight she is feeding me, as she always does when I come, and I am eating more than I do anywhere else. I admire the wedding china (once my grandmother's) that my mother has set on the table. She says (the way Grandma used to say to her, of the lamb coat), "Some day it will be yours."

QUESTIONS

Understanding

1. Who are the representatives of the four generations cited in Maynard's title? What do they have in common physically?
2. Why had Maynard stopped writing and visiting her Canadian grandmother before the last visit described here? Why does she go back to see the dying woman?
3. What does her treatment of Maynard's baby reveal about the grandmother? What does Maynard's presenting the baby as a proud "accomplishment" (par. 9) reveal about *her*?
4. How does Maynard treat her daughter when they are alone together?

5. With her own daughter, is Maynard breaking the generational pattern that has characterized her family for so long, or is she repeating it? Explain your answer.
6. Who seems to be more concerned with death here, the dying grandmother or the granddaughter? Why do you say so?
7. In Maynard's narrative, how does the grandmother's long-standing attitude toward her children and grandchildren resemble her attitude toward life when she is dying?

Strategies and Structure

1. Roughly how many years does Maynard's narrative span in all? Where does she mention the earliest years?
2. Most of Maynard's narrative tells what happened in the past, though not necessarily the distant past. After comparing the verb TENSES in paragraph 18 with those in paragraph 13, explain whether Maynard's visit to her dying grandmother is an event of the present or the past time of the narrative.
3. What events are taking place in the present time of Maynard's narrative?
4. "Four Generations" is both an account of events over time and a meditation upon their meaning. Point out passages in which Maynard comments directly on the meaning of events. How else does she give her narrative a sense of meditation or reflection?
5. By what carefully selected specific details does Maynard give us a picture of her grandmother in paragraphs 5 and 6? What physical characteristics and qualities of temperament do these details reveal? How does Maynard begin to characterize her grandmother in the very first paragraph of this essay?
6. By what specific details in paragraphs 13–15 does Maynard reveal the grandmother's state of mind in the presence of death? The granddaughter's?
7. How would you describe the *pace* of Maynard's narration in paragraphs 7–12? How does the length of the paragraphs here compare with that of other paragraphs in the narrative?
8. Why do you think Maynard breaks the text of her essay after paragraphs 3 and 15? Why do you suppose she puts the third paragraph, about her grandmother's distant past, before the break rather than after?

9. What is the effect of ending this narrative by referring to the wedding china (par. 18)?

Words and Figures of Speech

1. In paragraph 9, Maynard plans to present her daughter to her grandmother as an "accomplishment." Which single word in paragraph 8 names the quality in the grandmother that encourages "accomplishments" in her offspring?
2. What are the CONNOTATIONS of *consumingly* in paragraph 16? How does Maynard's treatment of her own daughter in paragraph 17 justify the use of this strong word?
3. Explain the difference in DENOTATION between *emigrated* (par. 3) and *immigrated.*
4. What is the effect of Maynard's choice of the word "reasonably" in paragraph 2?
5. Why does Maynard refer to "pogroms" in paragraph 3 instead of "persecution" or "discrimination"?
6. Consult your dictionary for any of these words that you don't know: *pancreatic* (par. 1), *hemorrhaging* (1), *jaundice* (1), *cossacks* (3), *coveted* (4), *elocution* (4), *imminent* (6), and *knishes* (6).
7. What is the difference in meaning between *imminent* (par. 6) and *eminent?*

Comparing

1. Compare and contrast Maynard's treatment of the generations and family continuity with Gary Soto's handling of the same theme in "Like Mexicans" (Chapter 6).
2. How does Maynard's account of handing down a tradition from mother to daughter *contrast* with E. B. White's account of a father and son in "Once More to the Lake" (Essays for Further Reading)?

Discussion and Writing Topics

1. Do you think Maynard was justified in not writing or visiting her grandmother when she was well? Why or why not?

2. Write an essay that gives an account of your own last visit with a relative or friend.
3. Write an essay about your family that tells about events and gestures (at a family reunion, perhaps) that show a family resemblance in spirit or behavior across several generations.

Mary E. Mebane

The Back of the Bus

Mary E. Mebane was born in 1933 in the Wildwood community near Durham, North Carolina, a member of the last generation of Americans to endure legal segregation in the South. The daughter of a dirt farmer who sold junk to raise cash, she attended North Carolina College in Durham (graduating *summa cum laude*) and later the University of North Carolina at Chapel Hill, where she took the M.A. and Ph.D. degrees. Now a resident of Milwaukee, she has taught writing at the University of Wisconsin (Milwaukee campus) and at South Carolina State College. In 1971 on the Op-Ed page of the *New York Times,* Mebane described a bus ride from Durham to Orangeburg, S.C., that "realized for me the enormousness of the change" in the lives of black Americans since the Civil Rights Act of 1964, when legal segregation was overturned. That bus ride was the germ of two autobiographical volumes, *Mary* (1981) and *Mary, Wayfarer* (1983). "The Back of the Bus" (editor's title) is a complete chapter from the earlier book. The author herself explains how and why she wrote it in an interview following the study questions on her essay.

1 Historically, my lifetime is important because I was part of the last generation born into a world of total legal segregation in the Southern United States. When the Supreme Court outlawed segregation in the public schools in 1954, I was twenty-one. When Congress passed the Civil Rights Act of 1964, permitting blacks free access to public places, I was thirty-one. The world I was born into had been segregated for a long time—so long, in fact, that I never met anyone who had lived during the time when restrictive laws were not in existence, although some people spoke of parents and others who had lived during the "free" time. As far as anyone knew, the laws as they then existed would stand forever. They were meant to—and

did—create a world that fixed black people at the bottom of society in all aspects of human life. It was a world without options.

Most Americans have never had to live with terror. I had had to live with it all my life—the psychological terror of segregation, in which there was a special set of laws governing your movements. You violated them at your peril, for you knew that if you broke one of them, knowingly or not, physical terror was just around the corner, in the form of policemen and jails, and in some cases and places white vigilante mobs formed for the exclusive purpose of keeping blacks in line. 2

It was Saturday morning, like any Saturday morning in dozens of Southern towns. 3

The town had a washed look. The street sweepers had been busy since six o'clock. Now, at eight, they were still slowly moving down the streets, white trucks with clouds of water coming from underneath the swelled tubular sides. Unwary motorists sometimes got a windowful of water as a truck passed by. As it moved on, it left in its wake a clear stream running in the gutters or splashed on the wheels of parked cars. 4

Homeowners, bent over industriously in the morning sun, were out pushing lawn mowers. The sun was bright, but it wasn't too hot. It was morning and it was May. Most of the mowers were glad that it was finally getting warm enough to go outside. 5

Traffic was brisk. Country people were coming into town early with their produce; clerks and service workers were getting to the job before the stores opened at ten o'clock. Though the big stores would not be open for another hour or so, the grocery stores, banks, open-air markets, dinettes, were already open and filling with staff and customers. 6

Everybody was moving toward the heart of Durham's downtown, which waited to receive them rather complacently, little knowing that in a decade the shopping centers far from the center of downtown Durham would create a ghost town in the midst of the busiest blocks on Main Street. 7

Some moved by car, and some moved by bus. The more affluent used cars, leaving the buses mainly to the poor, black and white, though there were some businesspeople who avoided the trouble of trying to find a parking place downtown by riding the bus. 8

I didn't mind taking the bus on Saturday. It wasn't so crowded. 9

At night or on Saturday or Sunday was the best time. If there were plenty of seats, the blacks didn't have to worry about being asked to move so that a white person could sit down. And the knot of hatred and fear didn't come into my stomach.

10 I knew the stop that was the safety point, both going and coming. Leaving town, it was the Little Five Points, about five or six blocks north of the main downtown section. That was the last stop at which four or five people might get on. After the stop, the driver could sometimes pass two or three stops without taking on or letting off a passenger. So the number of seats on the bus usually remained constant on the trip from town to Braggtown. The nearer the bus got to the end of the line, the more I relaxed. For if a white passenger got on near the end of the line, often to catch the return trip back and avoid having to stand in the sun at the bus stop until the bus turned around, he or she would usually stand if there were not seats in the white section, and the driver would say nothing, knowing that the end of the line was near and that the standee would get a seat in a few minutes.

11 On the trip to town, the Mangum Street A&P was the last point at which the driver picked up more passengers than he let off. These people, though they were just a few blocks from the downtown section, preferred to ride the bus downtown. Those getting on at the A&P were usually on their way to work at the Duke University Hospital—past the downtown section, through a residential neighborhood, and then past the university, before they got to Duke Hospital.

12 So whether the driver discharged more passengers than he took on near the A&P on Mangum was of great importance. For if he took on more passengers than got off, it meant that some of the newcomers would have to stand. And if they were white, the driver was going to have to ask a black passenger to move so that a white passenger could sit down. Most of the drivers had a rule of thumb, though. By custom the seats behind the exit door had become "colored" seats, and no matter how many whites stood up, anyone sitting behind the exit door knew that he or she wouldn't have to move.

13 The disputed seat, though, was the one directly opposite the exit door. It was "no-man's-land." White people sat there, and black people sat there. It all depended on whose section was fuller. If the back section was full, the next black passenger who got on sat in the no-man's-land seat; but if the white section filled up, a white person

would take the seat. Another thing about the white people: they could sit anywhere they chose, even in the "colored" section. Only the black passengers had to obey segregation laws.

On this Saturday morning Esther and I set out for town for our 14
music lesson. We were going on our weekly big adventure, all the way across town, through the white downtown, then across the railroad tracks, then through the "colored" downtown, a section of run-down dingy shops, through some fading high-class black neighborhoods, past North Carolina College, to Mrs. Shearin's house.

We walked the two miles from Wildwood to the bus line. Though 15
it was a warm day, in the early morning there was dew on the grass and the air still had the night's softness. So we walked along and talked and looked back constantly, hoping someone we knew would stop and pick us up.

I looked back furtively, for in one of the few instances that I 16
remembered my father criticizing me severely, it was for looking back. One day when I was walking from town he had passed in his old truck. I had been looking back and had seen him. "Don't look back," he had said. "People will think that you want them to pick you up." Though he said "people," I knew he meant men—not the men he knew, who lived in the black community, but the black men who were not part of the community, and all of the white men. To be picked up meant that something bad would happen to me. Still, two miles is a long walk and I occasionally joined Esther in looking back to see if anyone we knew was coming.

Esther and I got to the bus and sat on one of the long seats at the 17
back that faced each other. There were three such long seats—one on each side of the bus and a third long seat at the very back that faced the front. I liked to sit on a long seat facing the side because then I didn't have to look at the expressions on the faces of the whites when they put their tokens in and looked at the blacks sitting in the back of the bus. Often I studied my music, looking down and practicing the fingering. I looked up at each stop to see who was getting on and to check on the seating pattern. The seating pattern didn't really bother me that day until the bus started to get unusually full for a Saturday morning. I wondered what was happening, where all these people were coming from. They got on and got on until the white section was almost full and the black section was full.

There was a black man in a blue windbreaker and a gray porkpie 18
hat sitting in no-man's-land, and my stomach tightened. I wondered

what would happen. I had never been on a bus on which a black person was asked to give a seat to a white person when there was no other seat empty. Usually, though, I had seen a black person automatically get up and move to an empty seat farther back. But this morning the only empty seat was beside a black person sitting in no-man's-land.

The bus stopped at Little Five Points and one black got off. A 19
young white man was getting on. I tensed. What would happen now? Would the driver ask the black man to get up and move to the empty seat farther back? The white man had a businessman's air about him: suit, shirt, tie, polished brown shoes. He saw the empty seat in the "colored" section and after just a little hesitation went to it, put his briefcase down, and sat with his feet crossed. I relaxed a little when the bus pulled off without the driver saying anything. Evidently he hadn't seen what had happened, or since he was just a few stops from Main Street, he figured the mass exodus there would solve all the problems. Still, I was afraid of a scene.

The next stop was an open-air fruit stand just after Little Five 20
Points, and here another white man got on. Where would he sit? The only available seat was beside the black man. Would he stand the few stops to Main Street or would the driver make the black man move? The whole colored section tensed, but nobody said anything. I looked at Esther, who looked apprehensive. I looked at the other men and women, who studiously avoided my eyes and everybody else's as well, as they maintained a steady gaze at a far-distant land.

Just one woman caught my eye; I had noticed her before, and I 21
had been ashamed of her. She was a stringy little black woman. She could have been forty; she could have been fifty. She looked as if she were a hard drinker. Flat black face with tight features. She was dressed with great insouciance in a tight boy's sweater with horizontal lines running across her flat chest. It pulled down over a nondescript skirt. Laced-up shoes, socks, and a head rag completed her outfit. She looked tense.

The white man who had just gotten on the bus walked to the seat 22
in no-man's-land and stood there. He wouldn't sit down, just stood there. Two adult males, living in the most highly industrialized, most technologically advanced nation in the world, a nation that had devastated two other industrial giants in World War II and had flirted with taking on China in Korea. Both these men, either of whom could have fought for the United States in Germany or Korea, faced

each other in mutual rage and hostility. The white one wanted to sit down, but he was going to exert his authority and force the black one to get up first. I watched the driver in the rearview mirror. He was about the same age as the antagonists. The driver wasn't looking for trouble, either.

"Say there, buddy, how about moving back," the driver said, meanwhile driving his bus just as fast as he could. The whole bus froze—whites at the front, blacks at the rear. They didn't want to believe what was happening was really happening. 23

The seated black man said nothing. The standing white man said nothing. 24

"Say, buddy, did you hear me? What about moving on back." The driver was scared to death. I could tell that. 25

"These is the niggers' seats!" the little lady in the strange outfit started screaming. I jumped. I had to shift my attention from the driver to the frieze of the black man seated and white man standing to the articulate little woman who had joined in the fray. 26

"The government gave us these seats! These is the niggers' seats." I was startled at her statement and her tone. "The president said that these are the niggers' seats!" I expected her to start fighting at any moment. 27

Evidently the bus driver did, too, because he was driving faster and faster. I believe that he forgot he was driving a bus and wanted desperately to pull to the side of the street and get out and run. 28

"I'm going to take you down to the station, buddy," the driver said. 29

The white man with the briefcase and the polished brown shoes who had taken a seat in the "colored" section looked as though he might die of embarrassment at any moment. 30

As scared and upset as I was, I didn't miss a thing. 31

By that time we had come to the stop before Main Street, and the black passenger rose to get off. 32

"You're not getting off, buddy. I'm going to take you downtown." The driver kept driving as he talked and seemed to be trying to get downtown as fast as he could. 33

"These are the niggers' seats! The government plainly said these are the niggers' seats!" screamed the little woman in rage. 34

I was embarrassed at the use of the word "nigger" but I was proud of the lady. I was also proud of the man who wouldn't get up. 35

The bus driver was afraid, trying to hold on to his job but plainly not willing to get into a row with the blacks. 36

The bus seemed to be going a hundred miles an hour and everybody was anxious to get off, though only the lady and the driver were saying anything. 37

The black man stood at the exit door; the driver drove right past the A&P stop. I was terrified. I was sure that the bus was going to the police station to put the black man in jail. The little woman had her hands on her hips and she never stopped yelling. The bus driver kept driving as fast as he could. 38

Then, somewhere in the back of his mind, he decided to forget the whole thing. The next stop was Main Street, and when he got there, in what seemed to be a flash of lightning, he flung both doors open wide. He and his black antagonist looked at each other in the rearview mirror; in a second the windbreaker and porkpie hat were gone. The little woman was standing, preaching to the whole bus about the government's gift of these seats to the blacks; the man with the brown shoes practically fell out of the door in his hurry; and Esther and I followed the hurrying footsteps. 39

We walked about three doors down the block, then caught a bus to the black neighborhood. Here we sat on one of the two long seats facing each other, directly behind the driver. It was the custom. Since this bus had a route from a black neighborhood to the downtown section and back, passing through no white residential areas, blacks could sit where they chose. One minute we had been on a bus in which violence was threatened over a seat near the exit door; the next minute we were sitting in the very front behind the driver. 40

The people who devised this system thought that it was going to last forever. 41

QUESTIONS

Understanding

1. Why does Mary Mebane claim a national significance for the events of her private life in "The Back of the Bus"?

2. Mebane's essay recalls events that occurred during her youth under "legal segregation." Was it *written* before or after *de*segregation? How do you know?
3. Why did the bus driver of Mebane's essay threaten to drive to the police station? What was his official duty under the segregation code?
4. Why do you suppose the businessman with the briefcase and brown shoes chose to take the separate seat in the back of the bus instead of the place on the bench across from the exit? Was he upholding or violating segregation by doing so?
5. With what emotion in particular did young Mary and her sister react to the confrontation they witnessed that May morning in Durham?
6. Who are the "people" to whom Mebane refers in paragraph 41?

Strategies and Structure

1. The bulk of Mebane's essay is a personal NARRATIVE. Where does the narrative part begin? Where does it end?
2. Mebane interrupts her account of a particular Saturday to supply information of a more general sort in paragraphs 10–13. What is she explaining to the reader, and why is this information necessary?
3. What is young Mary's role throughout the bus ride? In which paragraph is it defined most clearly?
4. Point out several paragraphs or passages that seem to be told from young Mary's POINT OF VIEW. Indicate several others that come from the point of view of the adult author looking back at an event in her youth. Besides time, what is the main difference in their perspectives?
5. What is the effect of Mebane's referring to the black passenger who confronts the bus driver as "the windbreaker and porkpie hat" (par. 39)? Point to other examples of such objectifying in her essay. Whose point of view do they help to capture?
6. Why do you think Mebane begins her narrative with the street sweepers who doused the pavement on the morning of Mary's ride and with the homeowners who dreamily put their yards in order?
7. How does the bus in Mebane's narrative serve to objectify the segregation laws? Why, historically, might a bus have been a likely place for racial segregation to be challenged?
8. How does Mebane use the increasing speed of the Durham bus to confirm what she has to say about the precariousness of the "system" (par. 41)?

9. Mary gets on the bus in paragraph 17. The strangely dressed woman screams out in paragraph 26. Who is the only person on the bus to speak in between? Do you think that the bus young Mary rode was in reality so still? Why might the author exaggerate the silence in an artful retelling of the event?

Words and Figures of Speech

1. Why does the author refer to the seat across from the exit as a "no-man's land" (par. 13)? Where did the term originate?
2. In the terminology of architecture, what is a "frieze" (par. 26)? Why is the METAPHOR appropriate here?
3. Look up *insouciance* (par. 21) in your dictionary. How does the word prepare you for the rebellious behavior of the "stringy" little woman?
4. A word like *insouciance* would not have been in the speaking vocabulary of a girl so young as Mary: it belongs, rather, to the writing vocabulary of the mature author. Pick out other words and phrases in Mebane's essay that young Mary could not have been expected to know.
5. In the interview following these study questions, Mary Mebane says that she composes early drafts of her writing partly in "black dialect." What traces of black or "Southern" speech can you detect in the finished product?
6. Why do you suppose Mebane elected to publish her account largely in what is called Standard Edited English? Why not cast the whole essay in the language of a particular race or region?
7. What are the two possible meanings of *scene* (par. 19)? How might Mebane's essay be said to illustrate both meanings?
8. Which of the many meanings of *articulate* (par. 26) in your dictionary best fits the woman who screams back at the bus driver?

Comparing

1. Where and how does the girl in "The Back of the Bus" show signs of "acting white," as defined by Eric A. Watts in "The Color of Success" (Chapter 2)? Why do these two authors appear to condone such behavior?
2. How does the way "The Back of the Bus" is told compare with the way Judith Ortiz Cofer speaks in "More Room" (Chapter 7)?

Discussion and Writing Topics

1. "The Back of the Bus" is more than a personal experience essay. How effective do you find it as a political statement? Explain your answer.
2. Describe a bewildering bus, train, plane, or other trip you made in the past from the standpoint of your present insight and maturity.
3. Spend a few hours in a public bus station observing and (unobtrusively) taking notes. Write an essay on the experience in which you use the physical place to help capture a slice of the social or political life of your town, city, or school.
4. Write about a trip you have repeated, a movie you have seen more than once, a person who has returned into your life, or some other recurring experience. Use the *difference* between the two experiences to illustrate a significant change in yourself or in your world.

Richard Rodriguez

None of This Is Fair

Although he holds a Ph.D. in English from Berkeley, Richard Rodriguez is not a university professor, for reasons touched upon in "None of This Is Fair." A journalist and writer instead, he contributes often to the *Los Angeles Times* and *Harper's Magazine*. He is also an associate editor for the Pacific News Service in his native San Francisco. Author of *Hunger of Memory: The Education of Richard Rodriguez* (1982), from which this essay is adapted, Rodriguez probes his deepest memories of Mexico in *Days of Obligation: An Argument with My Father* (1992).

My plan to become a professor of English—my ambition during long years in college at Stanford, then in graduate school at Columbia and Berkeley—was complicated by feelings of embarrassment and guilt. So many times I would see other Mexican-Americans and know we were alike only in race. And yet, simply because our race was the same, I was, during the last years of my schooling, the beneficiary of their situation. Affirmative Action programs had made it all possible. The disadvantages of others permitted my promotion; the absence of many Mexican-Americans from academic life allowed my designation as a "minority student." 1

For me opportunities had been extravagant. There were fellowships, summer research grants, and teaching assistantships. After only two years in graduate school, I was offered teaching jobs by several colleges. Invitations to Washington conferences arrived and I had the chance to travel abroad as a "Mexican-American representative." The benefits were often, however, too gaudy to please. In three published essays, in conversations with teachers, in letters to politicians and at conferences, I worried the issue of Affirmative Action. Often I proposed contradictory opinions. Though consistent was the 2 admission that—because of an early, excellent education—I was no longer a principal victim of racism or any other social oppression. I said that but still I continued to indicate on applications for financial aid that I was a Hispanic-American. It didn't really occur to me to say anything else, or to leave the question unanswered.

Thus I complied with and encouraged the odd bureaucratic logic of Affirmative Action. I let government officials treat the disadvantaged condition of many Mexican-Americans with my advancement. Each fall my presence was noted by Health, Education, and Welfare department statisticians. As I pursued advanced literary studies and learned the skill of reading Spenser and Wordsworth and Empson, I would hear myself numbered among the culturally disadvantaged. Still, silent, I didn't object. 3

But the irony cut deep. And guilt would not be evaded by averting my glance when I confronted a face like my own in a crowd. By late 1975, nearing the completion of my graduate studies at Berkeley, I was so wary of the benefits of Affirmative Action that I feared my inevitable success as an applicant for a teaching position. The months of fall—traditionally that time of academic job-searching—passed without my applying to a single school. When one of my professors chanced to learn this in late November, he was astonished, then furious. He yelled at me: Did I think that because I was a minority student jobs would just come looking for me? What was I thinking? Did I realize that he and several other faculty members had already written letters on my behalf? Was I going to start acting like some other minority students he had known? They struggled for success and then, when it was almost within reach, grew strangely afraid and let it pass. Was that it? Was I determined to fail? 4

I did not respond to his questions. I didn't want to admit to him, and thus to myself, the reason I delayed. 5

I merely agreed to write to several schools. (In my letter I wrote: "I cannot claim to represent disadvantaged Mexican-Americans. The very fact that I am in a position to apply for this job should make that clear.") After two or three days, there were telegrams and phone calls, invitations to interviews, then airplane trips. A blur of faces and the murmur of their soft questions. And, over someone's shoulder, the sight of campus buildings shadowing pictures I had seen years before when I leafed through Ivy League catalogues with great expectations. At the end of each visit, interviewers would smile and wonder if I had any questions. A few times I quietly wondered what 6 advantage my race had given me over other applicants. But that was an impossible question for them to answer without embarrassing me. Quickly, several persons insisted that my ethnic identity had given me no more than a "foot inside the door"; at most, I had a "slight edge" over other applicants. "We just looked at your dossier with extra care and we like what we saw. There was never any question of having to alter our standards. You can be certain of that."

In the early part of January, offers arrived on stiffly elegant station- 7
ery. Most schools promised terms appropriate for any new assistant professor. A few made matters worse—and almost more tempting—by offering more: the use of university housing; an unusually large starting salary; a reduced teaching schedule. As the stack of letters mounted, my hesitation increased. I started calling department chairmen to ask for another week, then 10 more days—"more time to reach a decision"—to avoid the decision I would need to make.

At school, meantime, some students hadn't received a single job 8
offer. One man, probably the best student in the department, did not even get a request for his dossier. He and I met outside a classroom one day and he asked about my opportunities. He seemed happy for me. Faculty members beamed. They said they had expected it. "After all, not many schools are going to pass up getting a Chicano with a Ph.D. in Renaissance literature," somebody said laughing. Friends wanted to know which of the offers I was going to accept. But I couldn't make up my mind. February came and I was running out of time and excuses. (One chairman guessed my delay was a bargaining ploy and increased his offer with each of my calls.) I had to promise a decision by the 10th; the 12th at the very latest.

On the 18th of February, late in the afternoon, I was in the office 9
I shared with several other teaching assistants. Another graduate student was sitting across the room at his desk. When I got up to leave, he looked over to say in an uneventful voice that he had some big news. He had finally decided to accept a position at a faraway university. It was not a job he especially wanted, he admitted. But he had to take it because there hadn't been any other offers. He felt trapped, and depressed, since his job would separate him from his young daughter.

I tried to encourage him by remarking that he was lucky at least 10
to have found a job. So many others hadn't been able to get anything. But before I finished speaking I realized that I had said the wrong thing. And I anticipated his next question.

"What are your plans?" he wanted to know. "Is it true you've gotten an offer from Yale?" 11

I said that it was. "Only, I still haven't made up my mind." 12

He stared at me as I put on my jacket. And smiling, then unsmiling, he asked if I knew that he too had written to Yale. In his case, however, no one had bothered to acknowledge his letter with even a postcard. What did I think of that? 13

He gave me no time to answer. 14

"Damn!" he said sharply and his chair rasped the floor as he pushed himself back. Suddenly, it was to *me* that he was complaining. "It's just not right, Richard. None of this is fair. You've done some good work, but so have I. I'll bet our records are just about equal. But when we look for jobs this year, it's a different story. You get all of the breaks." 15

To evade his criticism, I wanted to side with him. I was about to admit the injustice of Affirmative Action. But he went on, his voice hard with accusation. "It's all very simple this year. You're a Chicano. And I am a Jew. That's the only real difference between us." 16

His words stung me: there was nothing he was telling me that I didn't know. I had admitted everything already. But to hear someone else say these things, and in such an accusing tone, was suddenly hard to take. In a deceptively calm voice, I responded that he had simplified the whole issue. The phrases came like bubbles to the tip of my tongue: "new blood"; "the importance of cultural diversity"; "the goal of racial integration." These were all the arguments I had proposed several years ago—and had long since abandoned. Of course the offers were unjustifiable. I knew that. All I was saying amounted to a frantic self-defense. I tried to find an end to a sentence. My voice faltered to a stop. 17

"Yeah, sure," he said. "I've heard all that before. Nothing you say really changes the fact that Affirmative Action is unfair. You see that, don't you? There isn't any way for me to compete with you. Once there were quotas to keep my parents out of certain schools; now there are quotas to get you in and the effect on me is the same as it was for them." 18

I listened to every word he spoke. But my mind was really on something else. I knew at that moment that I would reject all of the offers. I stood there silently surprised by what an easy conclusion it was. Having prepared for so many years to teach, having trained 19 myself to do nothing else, I had hesitated out of practical fear. But now that it was made, the decision came with relief. I immediately knew I had made the right choice.

My colleague continued talking and I realized that he was simply 20
right. Affirmative Action programs *are* unfair to white students. But as I listened to him assert his rights, I thought of the seriously disadvantaged. How different they were from white, middle-class students who come armed with the testimony of their grades and aptitude scores and self-confidence to complain about the unequal treatment they now receive. I listen to them. I do not want to be careless about what they say. Their rights are important to protect. But inevitably when I hear them or their lawyers, I think about the most seriously disadvantaged, not simply Mexican-Americans, but of all those who do not ever imagine themselves going to college or becoming doctors: white, black, brown. Always poor. Silent. They are not plaintiffs before the court or against the misdirection of Affirmative Action. They lack the confidence (my confidence!) to assume their right to a good education. They lack the confidence and skills a good primary and secondary education provides and which are prerequisites for informed public life. They remain silent.

The debate drones on and surrounds them in stillness. They are 21
distant, faraway figures like the boys I have seen peering down from freeway overpasses in some other part of town.

QUESTIONS

Understanding

1. As interpreted by Rodriguez, what is the "odd bureaucratic logic" (par. 3) of Affirmative Action?
2. Does he think that Affirmative Action was not "fair" only in his case or in general? Please explain.
3. What choices did Rodriguez have when schools asked him to declare his "status" as a minority student?
4. Why, apparently, did Rodriguez decide not to take an academic job immediately after graduate school?

Strategies and Structure

1. Rodriguez does not tell us directly why he decided against taking an academic job. How and how much do we learn about his motives?
2. In the scene that takes place in the office on "the 18th of February" (par. 9), Rodriguez dismisses his own arguments for why he has accepted the benefits of Affirmative Action. Does this gesture make you more sympathetic toward him in his quandary? or less? Why?
3. How does Rodriguez use the calendar to help build suspense about his future? In which paragraph does he resolve that suspense?
4. Rodriguez presents himself as listening carefully to the eloquent arguments of his colleagues in graduate school. Why don't they (and we) hear the counter arguments of the "seriously disadvantaged" (par. 20)?
5. What *do* we hear from them? How compelling do you find this "argument"?
6. Why do you think Rodriguez ends with the reference to boys "peering down from freeway overpasses" (par. 21)? How would his essay have been different without this last paragraph?

Words and Figures of Speech

1. What is the complete antecedent of the pronoun *this* in Rodriguez's title?
2. What are the CONNOTATIONS of *drones* (par. 21)? For whom, according to Rodriguez, are the niceties of academic "debate" over Affirmative Action a droning, meaningless sound?
3. To whom, exactly, is Rodriguez comparing the boys (par. 21) in the SIMILE with which he ends? How telling do you find the likeness?

Comparing

1. How does Mary Mebane's treatment of the clash between passenger and driver ("The Back of the Bus," immediately preceding Rodriguez's essay) compare with Rodriguez's handling of the conflict between himself and his colleague?

2. Henry Louis Gates, Jr.'s "A Giant Step" (Chapter 4) is also about the life of a minority student. How and why does this essay differ from Rodriguez's in TONE?
3. By comparison with Rodriguez, how does Gary Soto ("Like Mexicans," Chapter 6) portray relationships between Hispanic-Americans and non-Hispanics?

Discussion and Writing Topics

1. Was Rodriguez justified in taking such advantages as his minority status afforded him in school? Why or why not?
2. How might his burden of "guilt" (par. 1) be seen as one of the "unfair" aspects of the way Affirmative Action is practiced?
3. How do you think "Affirmative Action" should be defined and administered?

Lee K. Abbott

The True Story of Why I Do What I Do

Born in the Panama Canal Zone, Lee K. Abbott grew up in a military family. "The True Story of Why I Do What I Do" is about how young Abbott, still in his teens, was pulled toward a life of writing by his stormy relationship with his father, a general officer who retired to New Mexico, which is the setting for this essay (first published in *Puerto del Sol*) and of many of Lee Abbott's short stories and other writings. Director of the creative writing program at The Ohio State University, Abbott is the author of the award-winning collection of stories *The Heart Never Fits Its Wanting* (1981), *Love Is a Crooked Thing* (1986), *Strangers in Paradise* (1987), and, most recently, *Dreams of Distant Lives* (1989). He often returns to New Mexico to write and to experience a change of elevation.

All stories are true stories, especially the artful lies we invent to satisfy the wishful thinker in us, for they present to us, in disguise often and at great distance, the way we are or would want to be. Told to us in a lingo as unique as a fingerprint, they address our up-and-down, our here-and-now. They come, I think, from a desire, as irresistable as love itself, to fix on the page a moment, suffered or made up, when something—one puny thing or idea or person—revealed itself and so turned off the Boom-Boom-Boom which usually deafens us to ourselves. Happily-ended or not, stories are the truth we leave behind, like crumbs, to say how we've come and what was there to see. 1

To be inspirational, as high-minded and upward-looking as the foolish half of me mostly aims to be, I have to tell you about my father—as crazed, driven and cross-hearted a hero as I have ever known. His analogues have appeared in dozens of my stories: he's 2 the gentleman, in golf togs or business suit, throwing the epic tantrum, careening hither and thither in a men's locker or banker's office; he's the one, in the fiction I invent, with the outraged moral intelligence, the one who hectors and harangues, the one telling another (usually me, you can guess) how to behave and when to beware and what is likely to be the dry end of things we love.

In fiction, he is imperious, forbidding as a Puritan God, sharp-minded as an out-of-town lawyer, stiff as pig bristle, wiry and unforgiving; in fiction, the made-up landscape I am a sometime citizen in, he suffers and is redeemed (or he is not), does the wrong thing and is shamed (or is not), comes to insight and is crushed (or is not). In fiction, given its unities and shape and its epiphanies, I comprehend my father. I know exactly what he meant when he told me that you could tell a gentleman by his handshake and his shoeshine. I know, and can articulate, what significance there is in the properly mowed lawn, what wisdom there is in the order of dried dishes. In fiction, I know—maybe as Flannery O'Connor did—why the heathen rage. 3

In life, however—which, messy and improbable and ephemeral, is not good fiction—I had no idea what made his world spin round and round. The facts were clear to me, not the flesh. He went to Dartmouth, I knew. He pole-vaulted cross-handed. One brother died on the Bataan Death March; his sister in a boating accident on Lake Sasebo in Maine. His father went blind in the last years of his life; his mother squandered an inheritance of at least one million dollars. He was a roué, I heard, a slick-haired rake who hung out on the pier at Old Orchard Beach and went down to Miami in the winter. He married my mother, the over-pampered daughter of a Canadian insurance executive, in Harligen, Texas, while he was at gunnery school in WWII. They lived in Panama, where I was born. He ran the National Guard in Illinois, where my brother was born. He played one year of professional golf. He became a career military man, went to England, Korea, Germany, resigned his commission twice because somebody, or something, infuriated him. 4

If it is true, as Willa Cather says, that the "basic material a writer works with is acquired before the age of fifteen," then by the time I was a sophomore in high school in Las Cruces, New Mexico, already telling my teachers and myself that I was going to be a writer, the material I had acquired I'd got from him: a duke's mixture of soirées, of country clubs and officers' clubs, of colorful *compadres* named Red and Goonch and Uncle Inches—the whole of it tragic and tearful 5 to the aggressively poetic kid I was then. My mother was a drunk, institutionalized when I was twelve; my father was a drinker. He had psoriasis on his knobby knees and knobby elbows, he smoked like the dickens, he threw a wedge at the TV, he dressed in pink polka dots for the Club Championship, he banished me to my room forever, he expected my brother and me to know the truth and speak it invariably—this was my material, a hodgepodge of goo and muck and human blah-blah-blah the responsibility for which I was absolutely unaware of until the inspirational summer afternoon I am partly here to yap about.

Once upon a time (Isn't this the rhetoric, in truth, that opens every fairy tale we survive and want to write about?), my father and I found ourselves alone at home. I want to say it was a Sunday, for in my memory the day, if not the events themselves, have a liturgical, quasi-holy "feel." In my memory, that attic atop the shoulders where everything truly felt is found, there is that Sunday light, crooked and mote-filled and lazy, and that Sunday time, heavy and ever in danger of wobbling to a halt. My father, in his Bermuda shorts and golf shirt, is in the TV room, drinking the rum thing he preferred; he had the habit, annoying I think now, of dumping his half-used ice cubes back in the freezer, a habit the girl who became my wife told me was disgusting every time I made her a Coke and it tasted like hooch. I am in the living room, I think, listening to records; more likely, I am reading—*Sports Illustrated,* the *National Geographic, Life* magazine. 6

My taste in those days ran to the quick, the immediate—prose of the slash-and-burn kind. *Mila 18* by Leon Uris, *The Naked and the Dead* (still an excellent book, by the way), Alistair MacClean's high-seas adventures. I saw myself writing a book like those one day—a book, conceived out of testosterone and *Nugget*-style macho, a book as pithy and direct as a dust jacket blurb: "Mr. Abbott," the endorsement would run, "writes like an assassin. He's the 'Aaarrgghh' the yellow yammer when they spy the vast What-Not opening to greet them." I had, I thought then, no experience (this was long before I realized that Henry James was correct when he said that "experience was an atmosphere of the mind"). I was just a kid, after all. Skinny, with a flattop and fifteen pimples, half my mind tilted toward girls, the other half tilted toward glory (which would, in the reasoning I was the victim of, get me girls). 7

The hours passed that Sunday afternoon as they always do when 8

I cast myself back into the dangerous tides that are my past: the clock above the antique writing desk chiming on the quarter-hour, the father wandering between the refrigerator and liquor cabinet, Pee Wee Reese or Dizzy Dean saying in the TV room what the Dodgers were doing; the son in another room cobbling together in his fertile but screwy imagination a tale of swashbuckling and hair-raising, a narrative of guns and grateful bimbos and nick-of-time derring-do. We were in our elements, him and me: one, the older, tuned to the stupid clatter of the exterior world; the other, the younger flesh of him, tuned to the twilight interior world of fetch-and-keep, of fantasy. Then he burst into the living room, eyed me as if wondering for the last time whether I was up to the burden he was about to pitch my way, and said, a little drunkenly, "Come with me."

He had been thinking about himself, it is clear now. An inventory, 9
check mark after check mark after check mark, had been taken: three heart attacks, a fist-sized hunk of his lung removed at William Beaumont General Hospital in Ft. Bliss, the yips on the putting green, Homeric-like anger, frustration at a life twisted which-away, hopes high as heaven he believed in, bitterness at being less than the hero he'd promised himself he'd be. I didn't know this at the time I followed him outdoors and into the utility rooms at the end of the carport. I knew only that he was semi-sloshed. I knew only that he was fifty-six years old, gray-headed and tough. I knew he hated going to work at the post office, his job in those days, where he supervised and inspected and, unhappiest of all for him, had to tattle on those who stole money or stamps or swiped somebody's *Playboy* magazine.

"See this, Kit?" he said. He was standing in the center of the utility 10
room, lawn mower here, gas can there, the walls hung with tools I never got the sense of. Golf clubs were in there, a bucket of practice balls, cans of oil, greasy rags, a hoe, a rake, a cheap hardware store of goodies that smelled old and used and too sweet. "You want to be a writer, huh?" he said, sweeping his arms, then pulling me after him. He snarled the word; it was a sound which scorned ignorance and innocence. Against the wall, high as the ceiling, were stacked his footlockers and steamer trunks, from the Army of the United States and from the regiments that were the families of his own father, innkeeper Lyman Kittredge Abbott of Portland, Maine. I like to think now that I knew we were coming to something, my father

and me, that he was going to say words to me, and I, perhaps for the first time, was going to understand him precisely. I like to think now that I was smart enough to know that I was in the presence of a truth grander than the two of us, a truth the price of which we go paying forever, a truth more dire than the knowing that we die and do not rise. This is the moment, I like to think of myself thinking then, when you discover how hard the world is, when what you've cleaved to is cleaved from you with a broadaxe.

Then he assaulted those lockers and trunks. In a fury, huffing and puffing, he snatched them down, one by one, hollering "Timber!" when the uppermost went tumbling. They crashed and banged, and I tried backing up a little, as he flung one behind him and scrambled over another to reach a third. He was hollering, you have to know, all the New England notes of his voice echoing in that now cramped room, and maybe I was some scared. This was the temper I'd witnessed elsewhere—on the golf course, behind the wheel of his Ford, in the living room when someone in the big world made a ding-a-ling out of himself. But there was more than anger here: there was pain, the particular kind of which was personal and buried deep in his bones, pain for which there is no Latin name or medicine or machine, other than fiction, to account for. 11

"Write it all down!" he was shouting. "Write it all goddam down!" 12

And it was here, from a certain X-spot in the world, 1855 Cruse, that my father, teetering from booze and the awful weight of his own life, was taking seriously, in a manner I couldn't yet, what purpose writing ought to have. Here it is, he was in effect saying. Crated and stored, catalogued and preserved, year by used-up year, place by rotten place. Here it is: the come and go of it, the building and collapse of it, the joy and weep of it. Here it is, he was saying. All the tissues and nerves and human jingle-jangle, that want and excess of it, the rigamarole and whirling, damaged creatures we are. And all you have to do, son and boy, is write it down. Write it all goddam down. 13

This, I submit, is the inspirational part. If we write for any larger purpose than a simple good time—and, believe me, there is nothing at all wrong with a good time—it is, I think, because we all feel, less and more, the obligation we have to our fathers, to our mothers, to all the folks, linked by biology or not, who have raised us; an obligation, as essential to our moral natures as our hearts are to long life, 14 to the places we were raised in and in the knowledge we learned there. We want, I hope, because there is no other way to do it, to write it down, to transform it, to set it straight. At our best, we do not write for the money alone, though money is nice; nor do we write for fame, though fame is likewise nice. We write, beginner and professional alike, because, though half-frightened, we want to know what is in the trunks and lockers we lug forward through time, what vital secrets they can be sprung to reveal.

QUESTIONS

Understanding

1. Lee Abbott is explaining here not only why he became a writer but also why writers in general write. Why do they, according to his "story"?
2. What is the "Boom-Boom-Boom" (par. 1) of life that, says Abbott, "usually deafens us to ourselves"?
3. Is the younger version of himself in Abbott's essay deafened or invigorated by the noises he hears in the garage? Please explain your answer.
4. Where has young Abbott been when his father drags him away? Abbott's father has been in the TV room. What temperamental difference between father and son do these "habitats" reveal?
5. Why does the father in Abbott's account challenge the son to write down his / their life? Why doesn't the father do it himself?
6. Why is Abbott's father often so angry? What's in all those trunks?

Strategies and Structure

1. The "effect" that Abbott is explaining here is his choice of vocation. Why do you suppose his analysis of the causes takes the form of a story?
2. Should Abbott have stated his reasons for becoming a writer more directly here? Why or why not?

3. To what extent does the story Abbott tells confirm what he says (for example in pars. 1 and 14) about the function of stories?
4. Why do you think Abbott gives the big day a Sunday silence? Why does he mention the tools and other unfamiliar aspects of the garage?
5. What impression about his father's life do you get from the details Abbott cites in paragraph 4? Why do you think he confines such facts to relatively few paragraphs in the essay as a whole?
6. This is a retrospect: the speaker looks back upon his earlier self. Why is such a perspective necessary for explaining the full effects of the events that it reveals to us?

Words and Figures of Speech

1. Good writers, says Abbott, use "a lingo as unique as a fingerprint" (par. 1). Point out other words and phrases like *lingo* that characterize Abbott's unique style throughout this essay.
2. Why do you think Abbott uses the phrase "I submit" in paragraph 14? Where has he spoken earlier about being "inspirational"?
3. How does Abbott characterize (par. 7) his youthful idea of a good writing style? How does his mature style, as illustrated by this essay, compare with it?
4. To what are the lockers and trunks of paragraphs 10 and 11 being compared, METAPHORICALLY?
5. Why do you think Abbott ALLUDES to two other writers in paragraphs 3 and 5? Does it matter that they are women? What raging "heathen" is Abbott himself writing about?

Comparing

1. Annie Dillard's "Transfiguration" (The Writing Process) is also about the writer's vocation. What does Abbott's view of their mutual calling have in common with hers?
2. Compare and contrast "The True Story of Why I Do What I Do" with E. B. White's "Once More to the Lake" as essays about father-son relationships.

Discussion and Writing Topics

1. What are some of the differences between a person's life and an *account* (Abbott's "story") of that life?
2. Write about an incident or person in your past that has made you think deeply about your vocation in life.
3. Describe a moment at home (or elsewhere) when another member of your family revealed a depth (or dearth) of character that surprised you.

Writers on the Writing Process

An Interview with Mary E. Mebane

EDITOR: How old is the girl in "The Back of the Bus"? 1

MEBANE: I was in the tenth grade—about fifteen or sixteen. 2

EDITOR: The book in which it first appeared was published in 1981. 3
When was the essay *written?*

MEBANE: The piece was finished in the summer of 1972. It took that 4
long to find a publisher for the book. I was about ready to give up.

EDITOR: When did you first get the idea of writing about buses? 5

MEBANE: In 1970. It was August, and I was riding a Trailways bus 6
from Durham, N.C., where I was born, to Orangeburg, S.C. I'm a great bus rider, have been for years. I recommend it for anyone who wants to really see the country.

EDITOR: What caused you to write about the experience? 7

MEBANE: The first time I went to Orangeburg was in June 1965. My 8
brother drove me down from Durham at night. It was around two in the morning when we crossed the line into South Carolina. Riding the bus down in daylight was unthinkable then, and yet here I was only five years later crossing the North Carolina line in a public bus. My stomach tightened slightly. The driver started laying into a black teenager, something about a ticket. They went back and forth, back and forth, and then the white driver just stopped arguing. I smiled to myself and relaxed. And we took the

bus in silence on down to Orangeburg. A decade earlier the bus driver would have been an enforcer of the segregation laws like the driver of teenage Mary's bus, and every black passenger on the bus would have been terrified. That difference between then and now was the germ of two essays I later wrote, the piece in *The Norton Sampler* and an earlier piece that appeared in the *New York Times* in January 1971.

EDITOR: The earlier essay was "The Black and White Bus Lines." When did you compose it? 9

MEBANE: Soon after the bus reached Orangeburg, within a month. It describes bus travel in the present after desegregation. A lot of people read the piece in the *Times,* and I was encouraged to do more. 10

EDITOR: What was your purpose for writing about young Mary's wild ride in Durham many years ago? 11

MEBANE: I wanted to show what it was like to live under legal segregation *before* the Civil Rights Act of 1964. 12

EDITOR: When did your experience as a girl riding a bus first come back to you as the way to show this? 13

MEBANE: Before the Trailways reached Orangeburg. My mind is constantly linking the past and the present: that's the way I see the world. 14

EDITOR: Why a bus, why not some other place? 15

MEBANE: The bus was the one place where the segregation laws might be challenged. Not in the bus station because blacks sat in a separate section; not in a white restaurant or restroom because they were off-limits. In a movie house you went in a separate entrance and walked upstairs. The segregation laws were enforced by space. The bus just had a sign: "Whites, please sit from the front. Colored, please sit from the rear." Only on a bus were the two cultures in close proximity in the same space. 16

EDITOR: So the bus serves in your essay as an enclosed space for the action to take place in, like a stage? 17

MEBANE: Yes. I often think in play terms when I write. The man in the porkpie hat was the bus driver's antagonist. 18

EDITOR: Why were the people on the bus so deathly silent before the "articulate" little woman started screaming? 19

MEBANE: They were all scared to death. The white passengers, too. The man in the brown shoes looked like a businessman, an orderly person from an orderly world. When he walked onto that 20 bus, I think for a second he saw the horror of a society that perpetuated racial segregation. When the bus stopped, everybody scattered like a yardful of chickens.

EDITOR: Why did you mention the truck that washes the street clean on the morning of Mary's ride? Why not launch right into the adventure instead of beginning the account this way? 21

MEBANE: To me the street washing was a sign of normality and ordinary routine. The reader is about to see an ugly scene. Terror is more terrifying when it strikes innocence. 22

EDITOR: Is "The Back of the Bus" inspired, then, by your recollection of physical terror? 23

MEBANE: And psychological terror. The police used to meet the bus whenever it pulled into the station. Two in the morning, three in the morning. They didn't have to do anything. They were enforcing segregation by their mere presence. When I heard the teenage boy talk back to the driver of the Orangeburg bus, I started trying to think of other acts of resistance I had seen. I came to recall the man in the porkpie hat because he was the only case of direct resistance I had actually witnessed before desegregation. 24

EDITOR: Is conflict a good subject, in general, to write about? 25

MEBANE: Especially if it's resolved. The conflict between the black man and the driver was resolved when the driver decided to forget the whole thing and flung open the door. I can give you an example of an incident that never developed into a conflict situation. When I became old enough to vote I went to register at the Braggtown schoolhouse in Durham county. As I went in the building, I met neighbors of mine coming out. They were black. Inside I stood for some time with the white people going into the principal's office. When I got to the counter, the woman didn't look at me, but she told me everybody had to write his name on a list. Now a number of white people had registered in between, but the name immediately above mine on the list was my neighbor's. It was a segregated list. 26

EDITOR: Did you ever write about that incident? 27

MEBANE: I wouldn't be able to write about it effectively because nothing happened. There was only a potential conflict, and so it was never resolved. 28

EDITOR: Can you give an example of the kind of incident that does make good writing material, like the incident you witnessed as a girl riding the bus in Durham? 29

MEBANE: I wrote this one up recently, but it hasn't been published 30 yet. I was walking down Wisconsin [a major street in Milwaukee] in front of McDonald's one Sunday when this black woman of about thirty stopped and admired my hat. She was as sleek and stylish as a fashion model flashing down the runway. She walked on down the street toward Gimbel's and the river. I was waiting for the bus. I heard declaiming in the street, and I looked up. It was the sleek woman. I realized then that she was deranged. What had happened in her life, I wondered, that a woman who looked to be on top of the world had been hurt so badly that she was driven crazy? It was the contrast between the way she looked and the way she actually was that made this woman something to write about for me.

EDITOR: I want to ask you a question now about language. You say that the little woman who started screaming on Mary's bus was dressed with great "insouciance." A word like that would not have been in young Mary's vocabulary. When did such words occur to you for reporting her experience? 31

MEBANE: *Insouciance* is part of my adult writing vocabulary. It got there from reading. I first thought of the way the woman looked and tried to get the visual image down on paper. The formal word for how her appearance had affected me came later, as I was polishing the piece. I compose at the typewriter. It has to be an electric to keep up with my thoughts. When I have the germ of an essay, I try to recall everything connected with it. I type, type, type—to get it all down. This is the fruitcake effect. Put in all the concrete details you can think of. Later you can take out anything that doesn't fit. I leave plenty of space between each line and in the margins for rewriting. Often I begin to write in a mixture of formal, "literary" language and black idiom. Certain black words and phrases can cut right to the heart of a situation. They can turn tragic experiences into humor and make it bearable. At the start I can sound like Richard Pryor—without the profanity. Then I come back and insert words like *insouciance*. I love literary language, too, and I am writing for a general audience. But black readers like my writing, I think, because I can express the pain. What happened to teenage Mary was painful to remember, yet I can bear to retell it because of the man in the porkpie hat. He resisted and won. 32

EDITOR: So did the "articulate" woman. Is writing a liberating form of articulation for you, too? 33

MEBANE: Absolutely. I didn't start writing until my late thirties, 34 didn't have much success till my forties. Then people read my work and started talking or writing to me about it, and I realized I was articulating many aspects of human experience for us both, reader and writer. I can live when I can write.

Writing Topics for Chapter One
Essays in the First Person Singular

1. Write an autobiography in which you give a chronological account of the formative events of your life.
2. Which aspects of college have you found most different from high school? Which have you found especially shocking or liberating? Tell the story of your adjustment to a new environment.
3. Have you had a religious or intellectual experience that has *changed* your life? Try to recapture it.
4. Do you have a special skill or talent? Relate how it has served you in past challenges or emergencies.
5. Recount your reaction to the news of a relative's or close friend's death.
6. Describe your reaction to one of the following: an athletic event; an election or political rally; a meeting with a famous person; an impressive building or natural scene; an accident.
7. Recall a childhood journey that you find unusually memorable. Organize your account around the stages of the journey.
8. From your own perspective, tell the story of a family reunion you have attended. Pay special attention to the oldest family members.
9. How do you expect to act at the tenth anniversary of your high school graduating class? The twentieth? Describe the scene.

Exposition

Two

Essays That Classify and Divide

When we divide a group of similar objects, we separate them from one another. For example, a physiologist divides human beings according to body types: mesomorph (muscular and bony), ectomorph (skinny), and endomorph (soft and fleshy). When we CLASSIFY[1] an object, we place it within a group of similar objects. The zoologist puts a monkey and a man in the order Primates because both mammals have nails and apposable thumbs. A librarian classifies Mark Twain's *Adventures of Huckleberry Finn* along with Herman Melville's *Moby-Dick* because both are works of prose fiction by nineteenth-century American authors. Shakespeare's *Macbeth* would go into a different class, however, because its distinguishing features are different. The technical definition of a class is a group with the same distinguishing features.

The simplest classification systems divide things into those that exhibit a set of distinguishing features and those that do not. A doctor conducting genetic research among identical male twins would divide the human race first into Males and Females; then he would subdivide the Males into Twins and Non-Twins; and finally he would subdivide the Twins into the categories, Identical and Nonidentical.

[1] Terms printed in small capitals are defined in the Glossary.

The doctor's simple system has limited uses, but it resembles even the most complicated systems in one respect. The categories do not overlap. They are mutually exclusive. A classification system is useless if it "cross-ranks" items. Suppose, for example, that we classified all birds according to the following categories: Flightless, Nocturnal, Flat-billed, Web-Footed. Our system might work well enough for owls (nocturnal), but where would a duck (flat-billed, web-footed) fit? Or a penguin (flightless, web-footed)? A system of classifying birds must have one and only one pigeonhole for pigeons. Otherwise it makes a distinction that does not distinguish, a flaw as serious as failing to make a distinction that really does exist. Our faulty system would not differentiate between a penguin and an ostrich since both are flightless, but a naturalist would see a big difference between the two.

The distinguishing features of a class must set its members apart from those of other classes or subclasses. How the features of a given class are defined, however, will vary with who is doing the classifying and for what purpose. A teacher divides a group of thirty students according to scholarship: types *A, B, C, D,* and *F.* A basketball coach would divide the same group of students into forwards, guards, and centers. The director of a student drama group would have an entirely different set of criteria. All three sets are valid for the purposes they are intended to serve. And classification must serve some larger purpose, or it becomes an empty game.

When you write a classification theme, keep your purpose firmly in mind. Are you classifying teachers in order to decide what a good teacher is? To demonstrate that different kinds of teachers can be equally instructive? To explain why some teachers fail? Return often to your reasons and conclusions, for classification is a method of organization that should propose as well as arrange.

The following paragraph from an essay on lightning by Richard Orville goes well beyond merely dividing its subject into three categories:

> There are several types of lightning named according to where the discharge takes place. Among them are intracloud lightning, by far the most common type, in which the flash occurs within the thundercloud; air-discharge lightning, in which the flash occurs between the cloud and the surrounding air; and cloud-to-ground lightning, in which the discharge takes place between the cloud and the ground.

This short paragraph names the types of lightning. But it also suggests a basis for defining all three types ("according to where the discharge takes place"); it defines them on that basis; it tells us that intracloud lightning is the commonest type; and it sets up all that follows.

In the next paragraphs of his essay, Orville explains what causes the three kinds of lightning; how much electrical power they generate; how scientists study them, and where such familiar names as "forked, streak, heat, hot, cold, ribbon, and bead" lightning fit into these categories. After discussing the related topic of thunder, Orville ends by explaining why we need to know as much as possible about his subject. The final sentence of his essay reads: "In the end, we hope that our effort will bring the goal of lightning prediction, and perhaps limited control, within the realm of applied technology."

The author of our example has taken the trouble to study lightning, classify it, and explain his system to us because human life and property may depend upon such efforts in the future. You may not be writing about life-and-death matters, but your theme should explain why a particular system of classification is valid, what we can learn from it, and what good that knowledge can do.

Susan Allen Toth

CINEMATYPES

A native of Iowa, Susan Allen Toth went to school at Smith College, Berkeley, and the University of Minnesota (Ph.D., 1969). She is now a professor of English at Macalester College in St. Paul, where she teaches and does research in American regionalist fiction, women's studies, and geography in literature. She is the author of *Blooming: A Small-Town Girlhood* (1981), *Ivy Days: Making My Way out East* (1984), *How to Prepare for Your High School Reunion* (1990), and *My Love Affair with England* (1992). "Cinematypes" was first printed in *Harper's Magazine* with the subtitle "Going to the Movies." It classifies films, but Toth's wistful essay in classification is mainly about other types, one of whom was born in 1940 and has been going to the movies (the same ones) almost ever since. The author describes the composition of "Cinematypes" at the end of this chapter.

Aaron takes me only to art films. That's what I call them, anyway: strange movies with vague poetic images I don't always understand, long dreamy movies about a distant Technicolor past, even longer black-and-white movies about the general meaninglessness of life. We do not go unless at least one reputable critic has found the cinematography superb. We went to *The Devil's Eye*,[1] and Aaron turned to me in the middle and said, "My God, this is *funny*." I do not think he was pleased. 1

When Aaron and I go to the movies, we drive our cars separately and meet by the box office. Inside the theater he sits tentatively in his seat, ready to move if he can't see well, poised to leave if the film is disappointing. He leans away from me, careful not to touch the bare flesh of his arm against the bare flesh of mine. Sometimes he 2

[1] 1960 satiric comedy by Swedish director Ingmar Bergman, generally known for the starkness and seriousness of his films.

leans so far I am afraid he may be touching the woman on his other side. If the movie is very good, he leans forward, too, peering between the heads of the couple in front of us. The light from the screen bounces off his glasses; he gleams with intensity, sitting there on the edge of his seat, watching the screen. Once I tapped him on the arm so I could whisper a comment in his ear. He jumped.

After *Belle de Jour*[2] Aaron said he wanted to ask me if he could stay overnight. "But I can't," he shook his head mournfully before I had a chance to answer, "because I know I never sleep well in strange beds." Then he apologized for asking. "It's just that after a film like that," he said, "I feel the need to assert myself." 3

Pete takes me only to movies that he thinks have redeeming social value. He doesn't call them "films." They tend to be about poverty, war, injustice, political corruption, struggling unions in the 1930s, and the military-industrial complex. Pete doesn't like propaganda movies, though, and he doesn't like to be too depressed, either. We stayed away from *The Sorrow and the Pity;* it would be, he said, just too much. Besides, he assured me, things are never that hopeless. So most of the movies we see are made in Hollywood. Because they are always topical, these movies offer what Pete calls "food for thought." When we saw *Coming Home,*[3] Pete's jaw set so firmly with the first half-hour that I knew we would end up at Poppin' Fresh Pies afterward. 4

When Pete and I go to the movies, we take turns driving so no one owes anyone else anything. We leave the car far from the theater so we don't have to pay for a parking space. If it's raining or snowing, Pete offers to let me off at the door, but I can tell he'll feel better if I go with him while he finds a spot, so we share the walk too. Inside the theater Pete will hold my hand when I get scared if I ask him. He puts my hand firmly on his knee and covers it completely with his own hand. His knee never twitches. After a while, when the scary part is past, he loosens his hand slightly and I know that is a signal to take mine away. He sits companionably close, letting his jacket 5

[2] Sensual 1967 movie by Spanish director Luis Buñuel, in which the glamorous actress Catherine Deneuve plays the role of a prostitute.

[3] *The Sorrow and the Pity:* 1972 documentary by Marcel Ophuls about France during the Nazi occupation. *Coming Home:* 1978 film of a wounded Vietnam veteran returning home.

just touch my sweater, but he does not infringe. He thinks I ought to know he is there if I need him.

One night, after *The China Syndrome,*[4] I asked Pete if he wouldn't like to stay for a second drink, even though it was past midnight. He thought a while about that, considering my offer from all possible angles, but finally he said no. Relationships today, he said, have a tendency to move too quickly. 6

Sam likes movies that are entertaining. By that he means movies that Will Jones in the *Minneapolis Tribune* loved and either *Time* or *Newsweek* rather liked; also movies that do not have sappy love stories, are not musicals, do not have subtitles, and will not force him to think. He does not go to movies to think. He liked *California Suite* and *The Seduction of Joe Tynan,*[5] though the plots, he said, could have been zippier. He saw it all coming too far in advance, and that took the fun out. He doesn't like to know what is going to happen. "I just want my brain to be tickled," he says. It is very hard for me to pick out movies for Sam. 7

When Sam takes me to the movies, he pays for everything. He thinks that's what a man ought to do. But I buy my own popcorn, because he doesn't approve of it; the grease might smear his flannel slacks. Inside the theater, Sam makes himself comfortable. He takes off his jacket, puts one arm around me, and all during the movie he plays with my hand, stroking my palm, beating a small tattoo on my wrist. Although he watches the movie intently, his body operates on instinct. Once I inclined my head and kissed him lightly just behind his ear. He beat a faster tattoo on my wrist, quick and musical, but he didn't look away from the screen. 8

When Sam takes me home from the movies, he stands outside my door and kisses me long and hard. He would like to come in, he says regretfully, but his steady girlfriend in Duluth wouldn't like it. When the *Tribune* gives a movie four stars, he has to save it to see with her. Otherwise her feelings might be hurt. 9

I go to some movies by myself. On rainy Sunday afternoons I often sneak into a revival house or a college auditorium for old Technicolor musicals, *Kiss Me Kate, Seven Brides for Seven Brothers, Calam-* 10

[4] 1979 movie warning against the dangers of nuclear power plants.
[5] Popular 1979 movies, both starring Alan Alda, among others.

ity Jane, even, once, *The Sound of Music.* Wearing saggy jeans so I can prop my feet on the seat in front, I sit toward the rear where no one can see me. I eat large handfuls of popcorn with double butter. Once the movie starts, I feel completely at home. Howard Keel and I are old friends; I grin back at him on the screen. I know the sound tracks by heart. Sometimes when I get really carried away I hum along with Kathryn Grayson, remembering how I once thought I would fill out a formal like that. I am rather glad now I never did. Skirts whirl, feet tap, acrobatic young men perform impossible feats, and then the camera dissolves into a dream sequence I know I can comfortably follow. It is not, thank God, Bergman.

If I can't find an old musical, I settle for Hepburn and Tracy, 11
vintage Grant or Gable, on adventurous days Claudette Colbert or James Stewart. Before I buy my ticket I make sure it will all end happily. If necessary, I ask the girl at the box office. I have never seen *Stella Dallas* or *Intermezzo.*[6] Over the years I have developed other peccadilloes: I will, for example, see anything that is redeemed by Thelma Ritter. At the end of *Daddy Long Legs* I wait happily for the scene when Fred Clark, no longer angry, at last pours Thelma a convivial drink. They smile at each other, I smile at them, I feel they are smiling at me. In the movies I go to by myself, the men and women always like each other.

QUESTIONS

Understanding

1. Toth is classifying not movies, but what or whom exactly?
2. Toth names representatives of three types. Which one would you characterize as a protective companion? Which one seems most intense? Which represents the provincial, boy-next-door type?
3. Who represents the fourth type in Toth's classification system? How would you characterize this person?

[6] Two 1930s tearjerkers.

4. What kind of movies does Toth herself prefer? What does she think of the kinds of movies her male friends take her to?
5. How strong are the personal attachments between Toth and her dates? How do they end differently from the movies she likes to see?
6. Why do Toth's friends only take her to the kinds of movies *they* like? What does this habit reveal about them?

Strategies and Structure

1. Toth describes her relationship with Aaron in three paragraphs. The first tells the kind of movie he prefers; the second describes how he behaves toward her when they go to the movies; the third describes "afterwards." To what extent does this pattern hold for the next two "cinematypes" she describes?
2. Toth devotes one paragraph to her kind of movie and a second paragraph to how she behaves when she goes to the movie alone. Why doesn't she include a third paragraph at the end?
3. Toth is sensitive to "signals" (par. 5). What signal do the characters give each other in her favorite movies but not in real life?
4. Who drives when Toth goes or is taken to the movies? How do these details about transportation help characterize her companions and her relationships with them? Point out other similar concrete details (such as the references to popcorn) by which Toth deftly pictures her types.
5. Toth says Pete will hold her hand "when I get scared if I ask him" (par. 5). What role is she playing here? Where else in the essay does she seem to act the same way?
6. Films project images by bathing them in an intense light that seems to flicker as the frames shift. What influence of cinematic technique upon Toth's presentation of her types can you detect in paragraphs 2, 5, and 8?

Words and Figures of Speech

1. With both Aaron and Pete, Toth "goes" to the movies. What verb does she use with Sam? Why the shift?
2. Given the personality she assumes here, why does Toth call what she sees "movies" instead of "films"? What are the differences in the CONNOTATIONS of the two terms?

3. What is an "art" film (par. 1)?
4. What does his use of the CLICHÉ "food for thought" (par. 4) reveal about Pete?
5. "Cinematography" (par. 1) is the technical name for the visual art of film making. How does Toth's use of such terms suggest another image of her besides the one she displays at the movies?
6. Consult your dictionary if you are ill at ease with any of the following: *tentatively* (par. 2), *propaganda* (4), *topical* (4), *companionably* (5), *infringe* (5), *tattoo* (8), *peccadilloes* (11), and *convivial* (11).

Comparing

1. Compare and contrast the personality of the speaker of "Cinematypes" with that of the speaker of Philip Weiss's "How to Get Out of a Locked Trunk" (Chapter 3). Which of Toth's categories does Weiss's persona come closest to fitting? Why do you say so?
2. How do both Toth and Joyce Maynard ("Four Generations," Chapter 1) give the impression of being *detached* from their subjects?

Discussion and Writing Topics

1. Movies, especially those made in Hollywood, are said to appeal to the American public as a form of wish fulfillment, of dreams-come-true. How does Toth's experience at the movies support or go against this observation? Your own experience?
2. In what ways, if any, do you find the "rules" of dates and dating to impose role-playing and "typing" upon the participants?
3. Classify dates you have had by type. Describe each type as vividly as you can by citing specific details, including bits of conversation, that dramatize the relationships. Be as objective or peevishly personal as you like.

Isaac Asimov

What Do You Call a Platypus?

Isaac Asimov (1920–1992) was born in Petrovichi, Russia, entered the United States at age three, and became a naturalized citizen in 1928. After attending undergraduate and graduate school at Columbia (Ph.D. in chemistry, 1948), he began teaching biochemistry at the Boston University School of Medicine. His almost five hundred books deal with an astounding range of subjects: biochemistry, the human body, ecology, mathematics, physics, astronomy, genetics, history, the Bible, and Shakespeare—to name only a few. Asimov's first real acclaim came with a short story, "Nightfall," in 1941; he continues to be best known, perhaps, for his science fiction, including *I, Robot* (1950); the *Foundation* trilogy (1951–53); and *The Caves of Steel* (1954). "What Do You Call a Platypus?" is an essay on taxonomy, the science of classification, that shows both the limitations of that science and how it can provide new knowledge of the world. After the study questions, you will find comments by Asimov himself on the process of writing this essay and his work in general.

In 1800, a stuffed animal arrived in England from the newly discovered continent of Australia. 1

The continent had already been the source of plants and animals never seen before—but this one was ridiculous. It was nearly two feet long, and had a dense coating of hair. It also had a flat rubbery bill, webbed feet, a broad flat tail, and a spur on each hind ankle that was clearly intended to secrete poison. What's more, under the tail was a single opening. 2

Zoologists stared at the thing in disbelief. Hair like a mammal! Bill and feet like an aquatic bird! Poison spurs like a snake! A single opening in the rear as though it laid eggs! 3

4 There was an explosion of anger. The thing was a hoax. Some unfunny jokester in Australia, taking advantage of the distance and strangeness of the continent, had stitched together parts of widely different creatures and was intent on making fools of innocent zoologists in England.

5 Yet the skin seemed to hang together. There were no signs of artificial joining. Was it or was it not a hoax? And if it wasn't a hoax, was it a mammal with reptilian characteristics, or a reptile with mammalian characteristics, or was it partly bird, or *what?*

6 The discussion went on heatedly for decades. Even the name emphasized the ways in which it didn't seem like a mammal despite its hair. One early name was *Platypus anatinus* which is Graeco-Latin[1] for "Flat-foot, ducklike." Unfortunately, the term, platypus, had already been applied to a type of beetle and there must be no duplication in scientific names. It therefore received another name, *Ornithorhynchus paradoxus,* which means "Birdbeak, paradoxical."

7 Slowly, however, zoologists had to fall into line and admit that the creature was real and not a hoax, however upsetting it might be to zoological notions. For one thing, there were increasingly reliable reports from people in Australia who caught glimpses of the creature alive. The *paradoxus* was dropped and the scientific name is now *Ornithorhynchus anatinus.*

8 To the general public, however, it is the "duckbill platypus," or even just the duckbill, the queerest mammal (assuming it is a mammal) in the world.

9 When specimens were received in such condition as to make it possible to study the internal organs, it appeared that the heart was just like those of mammals and not at all like those of reptiles. The egg-forming machinery in the female, however, was not at all like those of mammals, but like those of birds or reptiles. It seemed really and truly to be an egg-layer

10 It wasn't till 1884, however, that the actual eggs laid by a creature with hair were found. Such creatures included not only the platypus, but another Australian species, the spiny anteater. That was worth an excited announcement. A group of British scientists were meeting in Montreal at the time, and the egg-discoverer, W. H. Caldwell, sent them a cable to announce the finding.

[1]Combination of Greek and Latin; many scientific names put Latin endings on Greek roots.

It wasn't till the twentieth century that the intimate life of the 11
duckbill came to be known. It is an aquatic animal, living in Australian fresh water at a wide variety of temperatures—from tropical streams at sea level to cold lakes at an elevation of a mile.

The duckbill is well adapted to its aquatic life, with its dense fur, 12
its flat tail, and its webbed feet. Its bill has nothing really in common with that of the duck, however. The nostrils are differently located and the platypus bill is different in structure, rubbery rather than duckishly horny. It serves the same function as the duck's bill, however, so it has been shaped similarly by the pressures of natural selection.

The water in which the duckbill lives is invariably muddy at the 13
bottom and it is in this mud that the duckbill roots for its food supply. The bill, ridged with horny plates, is used as a sieve, dredging about sensitively in the mud, filtering out the shrimps, earthworms, tadpoles and other small creatures that serve it as food.

When the time comes for the female platypus to produce young, 14
she builds a special burrow, which she lines with grass and carefully plugs. She then lays two eggs, each about three quarters of an inch in diameter and surrounded by a translucent, horny shell.

These the mother platypus places between her tail and abdomen 15
and curls up about them. It takes two weeks for the young to hatch out. The new-born duckbills have teeth and very short bills, so that they are much less "birdlike" than the adults. They feed on milk. The mother has no nipples, but milk oozes out of pore openings in the abdomen and the young lick the area and are nourished in this way. As they grow, the bills become larger and the teeth fall out.

Yet despite everything zoologists learned about the duckbills, they 16
never seemed entirely certain as to where to place them in the table of animal classification. On the whole, the decision was made because of hair and milk. In all the world, only mammals have true hair and only mammals produce true milk. The duckbill and spiny anteater have hair and produce milk, so they have been classified as mammals.

Just the same, they are placed in a very special position. All the 17
mammals are divided into two subclasses. In one of these subclasses ("Prototheria" or "first-beasts") are the duckbill and five species of the spiny anteater. In the other ("Theria" or just "beast") are all the other 4,231 known species of mammals.

But all this is the result of judging only living species of mammals. 18

Suppose we could study extinct species as well. Would that help us decide on the place of the platypus? Would it cause us to confirm our decision—or change it?

Fossil remnants exist of mammals and reptiles of the far past, but 19
these remnants are almost entirely of bones and teeth. Bones and teeth give us interesting information but they can't tell us everything.

For instance, is there any way of telling, from bones and teeth 20
alone, whether an extinct creature is a reptile or a mammal?

Well, all living reptiles have legs splayed out so that the upper 21
part above the knee is horizontal (assuming they have legs at all). All mammals, on the other hand, have legs that are vertical all the way down. Again, reptiles have teeth that all look more or less alike, while mammals have teeth that have different shapes, with sharp incisors in front, flat molars in back, and conical incisors and premolars in between.

As it happens, there are certain extinct creatures, to which have 22
been given the name "therapsids," which have their leg bones vertical and their teeth differentiated just as in the case of mammals.—And yet they are considered reptiles and not mammals. Why? Because there is another bony difference to be considered.

In living mammals, the lower jaw contains a single bone; in rep- 23
tiles, it is made up of a number of bones. The therapsid lower jaw is made up of seven bones and because of that those creatures are classified as reptiles. And yet in the therapsid lower jaw, the one bone making up the central portion of the lower jaw is by far the largest. The other six bones, three on each side, are crowded into the rear angle of the jaw.

There seems no question, then, that if the therapsids are reptiles 24
they are nevertheless well along the pathway towards mammals.

But how far along the pathway are they? For instance, did they 25
have hair? It might seem that it would be impossible to tell whether an extinct animal had hair or not just from the bones, but let's see—

Hair is an insulating device. It keeps body heat from being lost 26
too rapidly. Reptiles keep their body temperature at about that of the outside environment. They don't have to be concerned over loss of heat and hair would be of no use to them.

Mammals, however, maintain their internal temperature at nearly 27
100° F. regardless of the outside temperature; they are "warm-blooded." This gives them the great advantage of remaining agile and active in cold weather, when the chilled reptile is sluggish. But then

the mammal must prevent heat loss by means of a hairy covering. (Birds, which also are warm-blooded, use feathers as an insulating device.)

With that in mind, let's consider the bones. In reptiles, the nostrils open into the mouth just behind the teeth. This means that reptiles can only breathe with their mouths empty. When they are biting or chewing, breathing must stop. This doesn't bother a reptile much, for it can suspend its need for oxygen for considerable periods. 28

Mammals, however, must use oxygen in their tissues constantly, in order to keep the chemical reactions going that serve to keep their body temperature high. The oxygen supply must not be cut off for more than very short intervals. Consequently mammals have developed a bony palate, a roof to the mouth. When they breathe, air is led above the mouth to the throat. This means they can continue breathing while they bite and chew. It is only when they are actually in the act of swallowing that the breath is cut off and this is only a matter of a couple of seconds at a time. 29

The later therapsid species had, as it happened, a palate. If they had a palate, it seems a fair deduction that they needed an uninterrupted supply of oxygen that makes it look as though they were warm-blooded. And if they were warm-blooded, then very likely they had hair, too. 30

The conclusion, drawn from the bones alone, would seem to be that some of the later therapsids had hair, even though, judging by their jawbones, they were still reptiles. 31

The thought of hairy reptiles is astonishing. But that is only because the accident of evolution seems to have wiped out the intermediate forms. The only therapsids alive seem to be those that have developed *all* the mammalian characteristics, so that we call them mammals. The only reptiles alive are those that developed *none* of the mammalian characteristics. 32

Those therapsids that developed some but not others seem to be extinct. 33

Only the duckbill and the spiny anteater remain near the border line. They have developed the hair and the milk and the singleboned lower jaw and the four-chambered heart, but not the nipples or the ability to bring forth live young. 34

For all we know, some of the extinct therapsids, while still having their many-boned lower jaw (which is why we call them reptiles instead of mammals), may have developed even beyond the duckbill 35 in other ways. Perhaps some late therapsids had nipples and brought forth living young. We can't tell from the bones alone.

If we had a complete record of the therapsids, flesh and blood, as 36
well as teeth and bone, we might decide that the duckbill was on the therapsid side of the line and not on the mammalian side.—Or are there any other pieces of evidence that can be brought into play?

An American zoologist, Giles T. MacIntyre, of Queens College, 37
has taken up the matter of the trigeminal nerve, which leads from the jaw muscles to the brain.

In all reptiles, without exception, the trigeminal nerve passes 38
through the skull at a point that lies between two of the bones making up the skull. In all mammals that bring forth living young, without exception, the nerve actually passes *through* a particular skull bone.

Suppose we ignore all the matter of hair and milk and eggs, and 39
just consider the trigeminal nerve. In the duckbill, does the nerve pass through a bone, or between two bones? It has seemed in the past that the nerve passed through a bone and that put the duckbill on the mammalian side of the dividing line.

Not so, says MacIntyre. The study of the trigeminal nerve was 40
made in adult duckbills, where the skull bones are fused together and the boundaries are hard to make out. In young duckbills, the skull bones are more clearly separated and in them it can be seen, MacIntyre says, that the trigeminal nerve goes between two bones.

In that case, there is a new respect in which the duckbill falls on 41
the reptilian side of the line and MacIntyre thinks it ought not to be considered a mammal, but as a surviving species of the otherwise long-extinct therapsid line.

And so, a hundred seventy years after zoologists began to puzzle 42
out the queer mixture of characteristics that go to make up the duckbill platypus—there is still argument as to what to call it.

Is the duckbill platypus a mammal? A reptile? Or just a duckbill 43
platypus?

QUESTIONS

Understanding

1. What are the chief distinguishing features of mammals as reported by Asimov? Of reptiles?
2. Which mammalian features does the platypus lack? Which reptilian characteristics does it possess?
3. How does the example of the platypus show the limitations of the zoological CLASSIFICATION system?
4. What new evidence does Asimov cite for reclassifying the platypus? How convincing do you find it? Why?

Strategies and Structure

1. Why do you think Asimov begins his case for reclassifying the platypus by recounting the confused history of how the animal got its name?
2. Why does it matter what we *call* a platypus? For what ultimate purpose is Asimov concerned with the creature's name?
3. Why does Asimov refer to extinct creatures beginning with paragraph 18? What is the function of the therapsids (par. 22) in his line of reasoning?
4. This essay in reclassification ends with three alternatives (par. 43). Why three instead of just two?
5. The logic of paragraph 32 depends upon an unstated assumption about the order of evolution. Which does Asimov assume came first, reptiles or mammals? How does this assumption influence his entire ARGUMENT? Is the assumption valid?

Words and Figures of Speech

1. Why was "paradoxical" (par. 6) an appropriate part of the platypus's name? How does it differ in precise usage from "ambiguous" and "ambivalent"?
2. Asimov refers to the "egg-forming machinery" (par. 9) of the female platypus. How technical is this term? What does it suggest about the audience for whom Asimov intends this essay?

3. What is meant by "the pressures of natural selection" (par. 12)?
4. Asimov's essay is an exercise in "taxonomy," although he does not use the word. What does it mean according to your dictionary?

Comparing

Asimov's essay has some features of a logical argument of the sort you will encounter in Chapter 9. What is he attempting to prove or disprove? When you read James Q. Wilson's "Reasonable Search and Seizure" in Chapter 9, compare the kind of evidence he uses to support his logical argument with the kind Asimov uses.

Discussion and Writing Topics

1. What would *you* call a platypus? Why?
2. Explain why a whale is classified as a mammal instead of a fish.
3. A classification system provides a means of arranging information about the known world. Using Asimov's train of thought or some other example, explain how classification systems also help us gain *new* knowledge.

Amy Tan

Mother Tongue

It was while composing *The Joy Luck Club* (1989), says the author of "Mother Tongue," that she learned to use in her writing all of the "Englishes" she had spoken since childhood to her mother, whose native language is Chinese. Some of them can also be heard in *The Kitchen God's Wife* (1991), *The Chinese Siamese Cat* (1994), and *The Hundred Secret Senses* (1995). Amy Tan lives in San Francisco.

I am not a scholar of English or literature. I cannot give you much more than personal opinions on the English language and its variations in this country or others, 1

I am a writer. And by that definition, I am someone who has always loved language. I am fascinated by language in daily life. I spend a great deal of my time thinking about the power of language—the way it can evoke an emotion, a visual image, a complex idea, or a simple truth. Language is the tool of my trade. And I use them all—all the Englishes I grew up with. 2

Recently, I was made keenly aware of the different Englishes I do use. I was giving a talk to a large group of people, the same talk I had already given to half a dozen other groups. The nature of the talk was about my writing, my life, and my book, *The Joy Luck Club*. The talk was going along well enough, until I remembered one major difference that made the whole talk sound wrong. My mother was in the room. And it was perhaps the first time she had heard me give a lengthy speech, using the kind of English I have never used with her. I was saying things like, "The intersection of memory upon imagination" and "There is an aspect of my fiction that relates to thus-and-thus"—a speech filled with carefully wrought grammatical phrases, burdened, it suddenly seemed to me, with nominalized forms, past perfect tenses, conditional phrases, all the forms of stan- 3 dard English that I had learned in school and through books, the forms of English I did not use at home with my mother.

Just last week, I was walking down the street with my mother, and I again found myself conscious of the English I was using, the English I do use with her. We were talking about the price of new and used furniture and I heard myself saying this: "Not waste money that way." My husband was with us as well, and he didn't notice any switch in my English. And then I realized why. It's because over the twenty years we've been together I've often used the same kind of English with him, and sometimes he even uses it with me. It has become our language of intimacy, a different sort of English that relates to family talk, the language I grew up with. 4

So you'll have some idea of what this family talk I heard sounds like, I'll quote what my mother said during a recent conversation which I videotaped and then transcribed. During this conversation, my mother was talking about a political gangster in Shanghai who had the same last name as her family's, Du, and how the gangster in his early years wanted to be adopted by her family, which was rich by comparison. Later, the gangster became more powerful, far richer than my mother's family, and one day showed up at my mother's wedding to pay his respects. Here's what she said in part: 5

"Du Yusong having business like fruit stand. Like off the street kind. He is Du like Du Zong—but not Tsung-ming Island people. The local people call putong, the river east side, he belong to that side local people. That man want to ask Du Zong father take him in like become own family. Du Zong father wasn't look down on him, but didn't take seriously, until that man big like become a mafia. Now important person, very hard to inviting him. Chinese way, came only to show respect, don't stay for dinner. Respect for making big celebration, he shows up. Mean gives lots of respect. Chinese custom. Chinese social life that way. If too important won't have to stay too long. He come to my wedding. I didn't see, I heard it. I gone to boy's side, they have YMCA dinner. Chinese age I was nineteen." 6

You should know that my mother's expressive command of English belies how much she actually understands. She reads the *Forbes* report, listens to *Wall Street Week,* converses daily with her stockbroker, reads all of Shirley MacLaine's books with ease—all kinds of things I can't begin to understand. Yet some of my friends tell me they understand 50 percent of what my mother says. Some say they understand 80 to 90 percent. Some say they understand 7 none of it, as if she were speaking pure Chinese. But to me, my mother's English is perfectly clear, perfectly natural. It's my mother tongue. Her language, as I hear it, is vivid, direct, full of observation and imagery. That was the language that helped shape the way I saw things, expressed things, made sense of the world.

Lately, I've been giving more thought to the kind of English my mother speaks. Like others, I have described it to people as "broken" or "fractured" English. But I wince when I say that. It has always bothered me that I can think of no way to describe it other than "broken," as if it were damaged and needed to be fixed, as if it lacked a certain wholeness and soundness. I've heard other terms used, "limited English," for example. But they seem just as bad, as if everything is limited, including people's perceptions of the limited English speaker. 8

I know this for a fact, because when I was growing up, my mother's "limited" English limited *my* perception of her. I was ashamed of her English. I believed that her English reflected the quality of what she had to say. That is, because she expressed them imperfectly her thoughts were imperfect. And I had plenty of empirical evidence to support me: the fact that people in department stores, at banks, and at restaurants did not take her seriously, did not give her good service, pretended not to understand her, or even acted as if they did not hear her. 9

My mother has long realized the limitations of her English as well. When I was fifteen, she used to have me call people on the phone to pretend I was she. In this guise, I was forced to ask for information or even to complain and yell at people who had been rude to her. One time it was a call to her stockbroker in New York. She had cashed out her small portfolio and it just so happened we were going to go to New York the next week, our very first trip outside California. I had to get on the phone and say in an adolescent voice that was not very convincing, "This is Mrs. Tan." 10

And my mother was standing in the back whispering loudly, "Why he don't send me check, already two weeks late. So mad he lie to me, losing me money." 11

And then I said in perfect English, "Yes, I'm getting rather concerned. You had agreed to send the check two weeks ago, but it hasn't arrived." 12

Then she began to talk more loudly. "What he want, I come to New York tell him front of his boss, you cheating me?" And I was trying to calm her down, make her be quiet, while telling the stockbroker, "I can't tolerate any more excuses. If I don't receive the check immediately, I am going to have to speak to your manager when I'm in New York next week." And sure enough, the following week there we were in front of this astonished stockbroker, and I was sitting there red-faced and quiet, and my mother, the real Mrs. Tan, was shouting at his boss in her impeccable broken English. 13

We used a similar routine just five days ago, for a situation that was far less humorous. My mother had gone to the hospital for an appointment, to find out about a benign brain tumor a CAT scan had revealed a month ago. She said she had spoken very good English, her best English, no mistakes. Still, she said, the hospital did not apologize when they said they had lost the CAT scan and she had come for nothing. She said they did not seem to have any sympathy when she told them she was anxious to know the exact diagnosis, since her husband and son had both died of brain tumors. She said they would not give her any more information until the next time and she would have to make another appointment for that. So she said she would not leave until the doctor called her daughter. She wouldn't budge. And when the doctor finally called her daughter, me, who spoke in perfect English—lo and behold—we had assurances the CAT scan would be found, promises that a conference call on Monday would be held, and apologies for any suffering my mother had gone through for a most regrettable mistake. 14

I think my mother's English almost had an effect on limiting my possibilities in life as well. Sociologists and linguists probably will tell you that a person's developing language skills are more influenced by peers. But I do think that the language spoken in the family, especially in immigrant families which are more insular, plays a large role in shaping the language of the child. And I believe that it affected my results on achievement tests, IQ tests, and the SAT. While my English skills were never judged as poor, compared to math, English could not be considered my strong suit. In grade school I did moderately well, getting perhaps B's, sometimes B-pluses, in English and scoring perhaps in the sixtieth or seventieth percentile on achievement tests. But those scores were not good enough to override the opinion that my true abilities lay in math and 15 science, because in those areas I achieved A's and scored in the ninetieth percentile or higher.

This was understandable. Math is precise; there is only one correct answer. Whereas, for me at least, the answers on English tests were always a judgment call, a matter of opinion and personal experience. Those tests were constructed around items like fill-in-the-blank sentence completion, such as, "Even though Tom was ______, Mary thought he was ______." And the correct answer always seemed to be the most bland combinations of thoughts, for example, "Even though Tom was shy, Mary thought he was charming," with the grammatical structure "even though" limiting the correct answer to some sort of semantic opposites, so you wouldn't get answers like, "Even though Tom was foolish, Mary thought he was ridiculous." Well, according to my mother, there were very few limitations as to what Tom could have been and what Mary might have thought of him. So I never did well on tests like that. 16

The same was true with word analogies, pairs of words in which you were supposed to find some sort of logical, semantic relationship—for example, "*Sunset* is to *nightfall* as ______ is to ______." And here you would be presented with a list of four possible pairs, one of which showed the same kind of relationship: *red* is to *stoplight, bus* is to *arrival, chills* is to *fever, yawn* is to *boring*. Well, I could never think that way. I knew what the tests were asking, but I could not block out of my mind the images already created by the first pair, "*sunset* is to *nightfall*"—and I would see a burst of colors against a darkening sky, the moon rising, the lowering of a curtain of stars. And all the other pairs of words—red, bus, stoplight, boring—just threw up a mass of confusing images, making it impossible for me to sort out something as logical as saying: "A sunset precedes nightfall" is the same as "a chill precedes a fever." The only way I would have gotten that answer right would have been to imagine an associative situation, for example, my being disobedient and staying out past sunset, catching a chill at night, which turns into feverish pneumonia as punishment, which indeed did happen to me. 17

I have been thinking about all this lately, about my mother's English, about achievement tests. Because lately I've been asked, as a writer, why there are not more Asian Americans represented in American literature. Why are there few Asian Americans enrolled in creative writing programs? Why do so many Chinese students go 18 into engineering? Well, these are broad sociological questions I can't begin to answer. But I have noticed in surveys—in fact, just last week—that Asian students, as a whole, always do significantly better on math achievement tests than in English. And this makes me think that there are other Asian-American students whose English spoken in the home might also be described as "broken" or "limited." And perhaps they also have teachers who are steering them away from writing and into math and science, which is what happened to me.

Fortunately, I happen to be rebellious in nature and enjoy the challenge of disproving assumptions made about me. I became an English major my first year in college, after being enrolled as pre-med. I started writing nonfiction as a freelancer the week after I was told by my former boss that writing was my worst skill and I should hone my talents toward account management. 19

But it wasn't until 1985 that I finally began to write fiction. And at first I wrote using what I thought to be wittily crafted sentences, sentences that would finally prove I had mastery over the English language. Here's an example from the first draft of a story that later made its way into *The Joy Luck Club,* but without this line: "That was my mental quandary in its nascent state." A terrible line, which I can barely pronounce. 20

Fortunately, for reasons I won't get into today, I later decided I should envision a reader for the stories I would write. And the reader I decided upon was my mother, because these were stories about mothers. So with this reader in mind—and in fact she did read my early drafts—I began to write stories using all the Englishes I grew up with: the English I spoke to my mother, which for lack of a better term might be described as "simple"; the English she used with me, which for lack of a better term might be described as "broken"; my translation of her Chinese, which could certainly be described as "watered down"; and what I imagined to be her translation of her Chinese if she could speak in perfect English, her internal language, and for that I sought to preserve the essence, but neither an English nor a Chinese structure. I wanted to capture what language ability tests can never reveal: her intent, her passion, her imagery, the rhythms of her speech and the nature of her thoughts. 21

Apart from what any critic had to say about my writing, I knew I had succeeded where it counted when my mother finished reading my book and gave me her verdict: "So easy to read." 22

QUESTIONS

Understanding

1. Into what two basic categories does the author of "Mother Tongue" divide "all the Englishes" (par. 2) that she uses in writing and speaking?
2. How many Englishes did Amy Tan learn at home from conversing with her mother, a native speaker of Chinese? How does she distinguish among them?
3. How does Tan define "standard" English (par. 3)? How and where did she learn it?
4. When and why did Tan switch from one set of Englishes to the other in her writing?
5. As a writer of many kinds of English, how did she know she had made the right choice among kinds? What standard of efficacy did she apply?

Strategies and Structure

1. Why do you think Amy Tan begins her essay with the disclaimer that she is "not a scholar" (par. 1) of the English language? How and how well does she otherwise establish her authority on the subject?
2. Tan first gives examples of "family talk" (par. 4) and only later classifies them (par. 21). Why do you think she follows this order? Why not give the categories first and *then* the specific examples?
3. What specific kind of home English, by Tan's classification, is represented by paragraph 6 of her essay?
4. Besides classifying and dividing Englishes, Tan is also telling stories about using them. In which paragraphs is she mostly classifying and dividing? In which is she mostly telling stories?
5. In which paragraphs is Tan advancing an argument about achievement tests? How does she use her different Englishes to show the limitations she finds in the tests?
6. Judging from the spacing between them, Tan intends her essay to be divided into three parts (pars. 1–7, 8–17, and 18–22). Why these divisions? How are they related to each other?
7. Why do you suppose Tan points out that her mother and her mother's stockbroker sometimes disagree on matters of finance?

Words and Figures of Speech

1. What are some of the obvious limitations of such terms as "broken" or "fractured" (par. 8) when used to refer to nonstandard forms of speech or writing?
2. As a class of language, do you find "simple" (par. 21) to be better or worse than "broken"? How about "watered down" (par. 21)?
3. Tan does not give a term for the kind of English she uses to represent her mother's "internal language" (par. 20). What name would you give it?
4. Explain the pun in Tan's title and in paragraph 7 of her essay.
5. By what standards, according to Tan, is "standard" English (par. 3) to be established and measured?

Comparing

1. How do Tan's views on the limits of achievement tests compare with George Orwell's on the political control of language in "Politics and the English Language" (Essays for Further Reading)?
2. Comment on "Mother Tongue" and Joyce Maynard's "Four Generations" (Chapter 1) as studies in mother-daughter relations.
3. Which (if any) of Tan's Englishes might Chief Seattle be said to use in his "Reply to the U.S. Government" (Chapter 10)?

Discussion and Writing Topics

1. How might "Mother Tongue" be read as an essay on the importance of "audience" in writing?
2. Does Tan's report of her performance on achievement tests show her to have more or less verbal aptitude than the tests themselves did? Please explain your answer.
3. How might Tan's episode on the phone with her mother's stockbroker be used to *refute* the claim that all Englishes are equal? To what extent is Tan making this claim when she says of her mother, "I believed that her English reflected the quality of what she had to say" (par. 9)?
4. Tan suggests that the more "insular" (par. 15) a family is, the more completely it will determine the language that is used by the children in the

family. How might her report of her own experience be seen to confirm this view with regard to "family talk" but not with regard to "standard English" of the kind in which much of Tan's essay is written?

5. What's wrong (if anything) with the sentence "That was my mental quandary in its nascent state" (par. 20)?
6. Why can literate people who grew up in different parts of China invariably communicate with each other in writing but not always when speaking?
7. How many different Englishes (or other languages) do you use—at home, school, elsewhere? How would you classify them? Would you be ashamed to use any of your languages outside the circumstances in which you usually do or did? Why?

Eric A. Watts

The Color of Success

Eric A. Watts attended a predominantly white high school in Springfield, Massachusetts, where he refused to conform to the racial stereotypes that his classmates and friends seemed bent upon perpetuating. When Watts wrote this essay about racial typing and false dichotomies, he was a sophomore at Brown University, leaning toward a major in philosophy. "The Color of Success" first appeared in the Brown *Alumni Monthly.*

When I was a black student at a primarily white high school, I occasionally confronted the stereotypes and prejudice that some whites aimed at those of my race. These incidents came as no particular surprise—after all, prejudice, though less prevalent than in the past, is ages old. 1

What did surprise me during those years was the profound disapproval that some of my black peers expressed toward my studious behavior. "Hitting the books," expressing oneself articulately, and, at times, displaying more than a modest amount of intelligence—these traits were derided as "acting white." 2

Once, while I was traveling with other black students, a young woman asked me what I thought of one of our teachers. My answer, phrased in what one might call "standard" English, caused considerable discomfort among my audience. Finally, the young woman exploded: "Eric," she said, "stop talking like a white boy! You're with us now!" 3

Another time, again in a group of black students, a friend asked how I intended to spend the weekend. When I answered that I would study, my friend's reaction was swift: "Eric, you need to stop all this studying; you need to stop acting so white." The others laughed in agreement. 4

Signithea Fordham's 1986 ethnographic study of a mostly black high school in Washington, D.C., *Black Students' School Success,* concluded that many behaviors associated with high achievement—speaking standard English, studying long hours, striving to get good grades—were regarded as "acting white." Fordham further concluded that "many black students limit their academic success so their peers won't think they are 'acting white'." 5

Frankly, I never took the "acting white" accusation seriously. It seemed to me that certain things I valued—hard work, initiative, articulateness, education—were not solely white people's prerogative. 6

Trouble begins, however, when students lower their standards in response to peer pressure. Such a retreat from achievement has potentially horrendous effects on the black community. 7

Even more disturbing is the rationale behind the "acting white" accusation. It seems that, on a subconscious level, some black students wonder whether success—in particular, academic success—is a purely white domain. 8

In his essay "On Being Black and Middle Class," in *The Content of Our Character* (1990), Shelby Steele, a black scholar at San Jose State University, argues that certain "middle-class" values—the work ethic, education, initiative—by encouraging "individualism," encourage identification with American society, rather than with race. The ultimate result is integration. 9

But, Steele argues, the racial identification that emerged during the 1960s, and that still persists, urges middle-class blacks to view themselves as an embattled minority: to take an adversarial stance toward the mainstream. It emphasizes ethnic consciousness over individualism. 10

Steele says that this form of black identification emerged in the civil-rights effort to obtain full racial equality, an effort that demanded that blacks present themselves (by and large) as a racial monolith: a single mass with the common experience of oppression. So blackness became virtually synonymous with victimization and the characteristics associated with it: lack of education and poverty. 11

I agree with Steele that a monolithic form of racial identification persists. The ideas of the black as a victim and the black as inferior have been too much entrenched in cultural imagery and too much enforced by custom and law not to have damaged the collective black psyche. 12

This damage is so severe that some black adolescents still believe that success is a white prerogative—the white "turf." These young people view the turf as inaccessible, both because (among other reasons) they doubt their own abilities and because they generally envision whites as, if not outspoken racists, people who are mildly interested in "keeping blacks down." 13

The result of identifying oneself as a victim can be, "Why even try? It's a white man's world." 14

Several years ago I was talking to an old friend, a black male. He justified dropping out of school and failing to look for a job on the basis of one factor: the cold, heartless, white power structure. When I suggested that such a power structure might indeed exist, but that opportunity for blacks was at an unprecedented level, he laughed. Doomed, he felt, to a life of defeat, my friend soon eased his melancholy with crack. 15

16

The most frustrating aspect of the "acting white" accusation is that its main premise—that academic and subsequent success are "white"—is demonstrably false. And so is the broader premise: that blacks are the victims of whites.

That academic success is "not black" is easily seen as false if one takes a brisk walk through the Brown University campus and looks at the faces one passes. Indeed, the most comprehensive text concerning blacks in decades, *A Common Destiny* (1989), states, "Despite large gaps . . . whether the baseline is the 1940s, 1950s, or 1960s, the achievement outcomes . . . of black schooling have greatly improved." That subsequent success in the world belongs to blacks as well as whites is exemplified today by such blacks as Jesse Jackson, Douglas Wilder, Norman Rice, Anne Wortham, Sara Lawrence Lightfoot, David Dinkins, August Wilson, Andrew Young. . . . 17

The idea of a victimized black race is slowly becoming outdated. Today's black adolescents were born after the *Brown v. Board of Education* decision of 1954; after the passage of the Civil Rights Act; after the Economic Opportunity Act of 1964. With these rulings and laws, whites' attitudes toward blacks have also greatly improved. Although I cannot say that my life has been free of racism on the part of whites, good racial relations in my experience have far outweighed the bad. I refuse to apologize for or retreat from this truth. 18

The result of changes in policies and attitudes has been to provide more opportunities for black Americans than at any other point in 19 their history. As early as 1978, William Julius Wilson, in *The Declining Significance of Race,* concluded that "the recent mobility patterns of blacks lend strong support to the view that economic class is clearly more important than race in predetermining . . . occupational mobility."

There are, of course, many factors, often socioeconomic, that still impede the progress of blacks. High schools in black neighborhoods receive less local, state, and federal support than those in white areas; there is evidence that the high school diplomas of blacks are little valued by employers. 20

We should rally against all such remaining racism, confronting particularly the economic obstacles to black success. But we must also realize that racism is not nearly as profound as it once was, and that opportunities for blacks (where opportunity equals jobs and acceptance for the educated and qualified) have increased. Furthermore, we should know that even a lack of resources is no excuse for passivity. 21

As the syndicated columnist William Raspberry (who is black) says, it is time for certain black adolescents to "shift their focus": to move from an identity rooted in victimization to an identity rooted in individualism and hard work. 22

Simply put, the black community must eradicate the "you're-acting-white" syndrome. Until it does, black Americans will never realize their potential. 23

QUESTIONS

Understanding

1. In high school, what specific "behaviors" (par. 5) did Eric A. Watts's "black peers" (par. 2) associate with "acting white" (par. 2)?
2. Eric Watts says that he, personally, never took the "accusation" of acting white too seriously when he was in high school. Why not? Has he changed his mind now that he is in college?
3. According to Watts (and the columnist William Raspberry, whom he quotes), what is the worst potential danger of "identifying oneself as a victim" (par. 14)?

4. So, if it is not white, what then, according to Eric Watts, is *the* color of success?

Strategies and Structure

1. Classifying human behavior strictly by race, says Eric Watts, is invalid. What reasons does he give for making this assertion, and how valid do you find them? Why?
2. As an essay in classifying (or, rather, declassifying), is "The Color of Success" about race or about success? Or both? Please explain your answer.
3. Eric Watts is not denying that people come in different colors. How then do his frequent references to "color" help him to call into question stereotypical ways of categorizing human beings and what they do?
4. An essay in classification and division, "The Color of Success" is also a PERSUASIVE argument (like those in Chapters 9 and 10). Does Watts make his points mostly through logical reasoning or by appealing to experience? Please explain your answer.
5. Why do you think Watts refers to the work of such scholars and researchers as Signithea Fordham (par. 5) and Shelby Steele (par. 9)? Do you think these appeals to authority bolster his argument? Why or why not?

Words and Figures of Speech

1. One of Watts's key terms is "success." How does he define it?
2. What does Eric Watts mean, apparently, by "standard" English (par. 3)? Cite several examples like the following that might help to define the standard he would appear to have in mind: "displaying more than a modest amount of intelligence" (par. 2), "caused considerable discomfort among my audience" (par. 3).
3. How well, would you say, does Watts himself use standard edited English? How does his use of language in this essay confirm (or deny) what he is saying about acting "white" or "black"?
4. What is a "syndrome" (par. 23)? How well does the term fit what Watts is describing?

Comparing

1. How well does Eric Watts's definition of success square with Richard Rodriguez's in "None of This Is Fair" (Chapter 1)?
2. Compare Eric Watts with Lynn Woolsey ("Reinvent Welfare, Humanely," Chapter 10) as writers who claim some special kind of knowledge about their subjects.

Discussion and Writing Topics

1. When Watts refers to "an old friend, a black male" (par. 15) as someone who dropped out of school, failed to look for a job, and became addicted to crack, is he implying that his friend was "acting black"? Please explain your answer.
2. If Eric Watts were not himself an African-American, would he have to change his tactics in an essay that came to the same conclusions as "The Color of Success" does? If so, how?
3. Eric Watts affirms that racial prejudice in America is "less prevalent" (par. 1) than in the past. Would you and your classmates agree or disagree with this statement? Why?

Isaac Asimov and Susan Allen Toth

Recovering the mental processes behind any piece of writing is difficult, even if attempted before the ink dries. The difficulty is greatly compounded, of course, for the prolific writer working over a period of many years; and no writer in America was more prolific than Isaac Asimov. When asked to explain how and why he wrote "What Do You Call a Platypus?" the author replied: "Your queries have succeeded in embarrassing me, but to answer your questions is almost impossible. You must understand that I have written, quite literally, 300 books and up to 3,000 shorter pieces. I am continually writing every day all day." 1

One among those thousands of shorter pieces whose composition Asimov recovered, in part, was his best-known science fiction story, "Nightfall." Asimov got the idea for the story from two sources available to any writer, not just the writer of fiction. They are the work of other writers and the suggestions of friends (including editors and teachers). 2

The other writer in this case was Ralph Waldo Emerson, who once exclaimed, "If the stars should appear one night in a thousand years, how would men believe and adore; and preserve for many generations the remembrance of the city of God." In 1941 Asimov's friend John W. Campbell, then editor of *Astounding Fiction,* mused over this passage and suggested that twenty-one-year-old Asimov 3 write about what would happen if the stars appeared to humankind only once in a thousand years.

"It was a crucial moment for me," Asimov recalls in his autobiographical narrative *In Memory Yet Green*. He had composed more than thirty stories at the time, but only three rated "three stars or better on my old zero-to-five scale." Taking off from his friend's suggestion, Asimov produced in twenty-one days the work that established him as a major writer of science fiction. (A letter from the author still bears the return address, "Nightfall, Inc.") 4

Asimov's first published work of nonfiction was a textbook, *Biochemistry and Human Metabolism* (1950). In his words, it was a "distressing failure." A collaboration with two other authors (whose writing styles clashed with Asimov's), the book nevertheless confirmed Asimov in the role he adopted in "What Do You Call a Platypus?" "I'm on fire to explain, and happiest when it's something reasonably intricate which I can make clear step by step." 5

Where did he get the urge to be an explainer? "It's the easiest way I can clarify things in my own mind." The "reasonably intricate" question that Asimov clarified for himself by the process of writing the "Platypus" essay was whether or not scientists were wrong to classify the duckbill as a mammal. What about the fossil record, the only record left by the platypus's prehistoric ancestors? Might it not show that the platypus had evolved from a reptile? Or even a bird? "What Do You Call a Platypus?" is a working out of this inquiry "step by step" on paper. 6

In Asimov's case the gap between urge and paper was unusually brief. Asked why many writers revise heavily instead of publishing their first drafts, Asimov protested: "I *do* always print the first words that pop into my head. I don't know how I decide a beginning or an ending or a title. I just sit down and type and that's that." (Asimov trained himself to type ninety words per minute, and over the last thirty years he produced an average of a book every month and a half.) He wrote quickly without revising, says Asimov, because after so much practice writing "comes as naturally as breathing to me." 7

Well aware that his method is not for beginning writers, Asimov was reluctant at first to have it reported: "it's not a good thing to tell students." But just as there is more than one way to classify a platypus, there is more than one way to write. Few writers have Asimov's "good fortune at being able to do it without [prior] thought," but many practicing writers discard the old formulas and outlines they 8 were once taught in school. The writing process is as idiosyncratic as the thinking process, and the right way to write is any way that works for the writer.

Although her methods are different, the author of "Cinematypes" writes out of the same motive that urges Asimov to explain: "I write," Toth says, "to give clarity and shape to my own feelings and perceptions of things—sometimes to rid my mental attic of old snapshots and bits of dialogue—and because I love to hear the sounds of words and the rhythm of sentences in my head." 9

She vividly recalls the feeling that prompted "Cinematypes": "As you might have guessed, I wrote this essay out of sheer frustration one day—shortly after attending a series of movies with three 'real-life' characters much like the ones described in the piece. I remember thinking, 'There *must* be better alternatives!' " 10

Toth turned her sense of frustration to conscious effect during the writing process. As her intention came clear, she aimed "to show *this is the way it was.*" To achieve this aim, she drew directly upon the experience of movie-going, but she was "not above changing details of 'reality' to make the real more real, if you see what I mean. (I'm sure I'd flay alive a student who wrote that last sentence.)" How much she altered the facts in the interests of truth is suggested by the reaction of one of her "types" to his portrait. "One of the models for a character in this essay didn't even recognize himself, which astonished—and delighted—me." 11

Toth's title for "Cinematypes" was originally "Going to the Movies"; "I think I had the title at the start of the piece," she says, "though I can't quite remember." Toth still likes her original title because "it was laconic, quiet, and left the reader free to draw his / her own conclusions about what the piece was about." Editors at *Harper's*, where "Cinematypes" first appeared, felt, however, that "Going to the Movies" was too "prosaic" and came up with the new title. 12

Toth is hardly down on editors, though. A trouble spot for her while composing "Cinematypes" was the ending. She labored over it "with lots of sweat, one rejected revision, tinkering with words and sentences, irritation & frustration & just wishing it were over with." Finally, Debbie McGill, whom Toth calls "an acute editor," suggested "an ending not quite as bitter and misanthropic as my first one." 13

The major revisions in Toth's essay came in the last section, but she revised throughout "substantially." How? "I worked hard on each 14 sentence to shorten, condense, and suggest as much as possible." As she revises, Toth strives "to understate and let the meaning emerge through carefully chosen detail and shadings of tone; I always worry about pounding my reader on the head. Much of the time I'm thinking to myself, 'It's awful, but funny. It's funny but awful.' "

What kind of audience did she have in mind as she composed 15
"Cinematypes"? She wrote it as she usually writes: "for an intelligent, open-minded reader of general education but familiar with books—someone who is not afraid of feelings—and who is alive to the nuances of irony."

And what of the "alternatives" she hoped to find? Are there less 16
obtuse "types" with which to stand before the marquee? "There are," says the former companion of Aaron, Pete, and Sam. "I no longer go to so many movies alone."

Writing Topics for Chapter Two
Essays That Classify and Divide

Write an essay on one of the following subjects that uses classification or division as its organizing principle. Remember that a good classification essay not only assigns members to a class but also gives interesting reasons for the divisions it makes and draws interesting conclusions about its subject:

1. Your teachers in high school or college
2. Blind dates
3. Drugs and drug-abusers
4. Moral codes
5. Fraternities or sororities
6. Neighborhoods, high schools, or churches in your hometown
7. Landlords in the campus area
8. Fast-food restaurants
9. Food in the dining facilities on your campus
10. Attitudes toward getting a college education
11. Cameras, bicycles, or motorcycles
12. Modern families
13. Movies you have seen in the last year

14. Television soap operas
15. Styles of rock, folk, country and western, or classical music
16. Ways of seeing (for the first time) a city, museum, or foreign country
17. Ways of reacting to personal disappointment or tragedy
18. Lifestyles among people under thirty

Three

ESSAYS THAT ANALYZE A PROCESS

Analysis breaks its object into components. It differs from CLASSIFICATION[1] by attending to a particular member of a class rather than the class in general. When we classify an artichoke, for example, we put it in the category of "thistlelike plants." When we analyze an artichoke, we pull apart an individual specimen and note that it is made up of layer upon layer of fibrous green scales. If we analyze the growth of an artichoke from a seed, we are analyzing a process (which tends to be in motion) rather than an object (which tends to be stable). Most how-to-do-it essays analyze processes, as do most accounts of how something works (a typewriter, a city transit system, gravity). The selections in this chapter are essays in PROCESS ANALYSIS.

In the following analysis, John McPhee tells how orange juice concentrate is made from fresh oranges:

As the fruit starts to move along a concentrate plant's assembly line, it is first culled. In what some citrus people remember as "the old fresh-fruit days," before the Second World War, about forty per cent of all oranges grown in Florida were eliminated at packinghouses and dumped in fields. Florida milk tasted like orangeade. Now, with the exception of split and rotten fruit, all of Florida's orange crop is used. Moving up a conveyer belt,

[1]Terms printed in small capitals are defined in the Glossary.

oranges are scrubbed with detergent before they roll on into juicing machines. There are several kinds of juicing machines, and they are something to see. One is called the Brown Seven Hundred. Seven hundred oranges a minute go into it and are split and reamed on the same kind of rosettes that are in the centers of ordinary kitchen reamers. The rinds that come pelting out the bottom are integral halves, just like the rinds of oranges squeezed in a kitchen. Another machine is the Food Machinery Corporation's FMC In-line Extractor. It has a shining row of aluminum teeth. When an orange tumbles in, the upper jaw comes crunching down on it while at the same time the orange is penetrated from below by a perforated steel tube. As the jaws crush the outside, the juice goes through the perforations in the tube and down into the plumbing of the concentrate plant. All in a second, the juice has been removed and the rind has been crushed and shredded beyond recognition.

From either machine, the juice flows on into a thing called the finisher, where seeds, rag, and pulp are removed. The finisher has a big stainless-steel screw that steadily drives the juice through a fine-mesh screen. From the finisher, it flows on into holding tanks. . . .

The first thing to notice about this analysis is that it combines several processes into one. McPhee describes the journey of fresh oranges from the time they enter the conveyor belt until the juice reaches the holding tanks. But because all companies do not use the same machines, he must digress to explain the differences between the Brown Seven Hundred and the In-line Extractor. The discussion returns from its divergent branches in the beginning of the second paragraph, "From either machine. . . ." McPhee picks up the flow so smoothly that we hardly notice any interruption; but, like many accounts of a complex process, his is a composite. The author has reduced the complexities to their elements and takes care of inconsistencies in brief asides to the reader. (The business of extracting "chilled juice" from fresh oranges is so different from making concentrate that McPhee has to describe it in a separate segment of his account.)

One aside in our example, however, has little to do with the process of making orange concentrate. This is the author's reference to the days before World War II when all Florida milk tasted like orangeade. To keep our interest, McPhee is laying out many things at once, including the history of change in Florida's citrus industry. Process analysis often draws upon other strategies of EXPOSITION and upon the other MODES OF DISCOURSE. When McPhee switches from what happened in "the old fresh-fruit days" to what happens "now," he slips into NARRATION. Process analysis might even be regarded as a specialized form of narration that tells what happens from one stage of a process to another. But the ultimate purpose of process analysis is to explain *how* rather than to tell *what.* And although process analysis often describes the parts of an operation, it focuses upon their function rather than their appearance (the business of DESCRIPTION).

Perhaps the most important lesson to be learned from McPhee's analysis is that he divides the process of making concentrate into stages: (1) culling, (2) scrubbing, (3) extracting, (4) straining, (5) storing. When you begin an essay in process analysis, make a list of the stages of the operation you are describing or the directions you are giving. Once you have a rough list of stages, make sure that they are separate and distinct. (McPhee does not isolate the movement of oranges up the conveyor belt as a stage because the conveyor is involved in more than one stage of the process of making concentrate.) When you are satisfied that none of the items on your list repeat others and that you have omitted no essential items, you are ready to decide upon the order in which your steps will be presented to the reader.

The usual order of a process analysis is chronological, beginning with the earliest stage of the process and ending with the last or with the finished product. If you are describing a cyclical rather than a linear process, however, you will have to break into the cycle at an arbitrary point, proceed through the cycle, and return to your starting place. For example, you might describe the circulation of the blood by starting as it leaves the heart, tracing it through the arteries and vessels, and concluding as it flows back into the heart. If the order of the process you are describing is controlled by a piece of mechanism, let that mechanism work for you. The first part of McPhee's analysis is organized as much by that conveyor belt as by time. Whatever order you choose, do not digress from it so long that the reader loses the sequence. Sequence is the backbone of process analysis, and it must be flexible yet strong.

Alexander Petrunkevitch

THE SPIDER AND THE WASP

Alexander Petrunkevitch (1875–1964), a native of Russia who came to the United States in his late twenties, was a world-renowned zoologist. After lecturing briefly at Harvard, he taught at Indiana University and then Yale for many years. Author of learned books on insects and a treatise in German on free will, he also translated poems by Byron (into Russian) and Pushkin (from Russian into English). Beginning in 1911, with an index to the species in Central and South America, Petrunkevitch devoted more than fifty years to the study of spiders. (His second book on amber spiders appeared in the year of his death.) "The Spider and the Wasp," which analyzes a natural process of life-out-of-death, is a product of that life-long fascination.

To hold its own in the struggle for existence, every species of animal must have a regular source of food, and if it happens to live on other animals, its survival may be very delicately balanced. The hunter cannot exist without the hunted; if the latter should perish from the earth, the former would, too. When the hunted also prey on some of the hunters, the matter may become complicated. 1

This is nowhere better illustrated than in the insect world. Think of the complexity of a situation such as the following: There is a certain wasp, *Pimpla inquisitor,* whose larvae feed on the larvae of the tussock moth. *Pimpla* larvae in turn serve as food for the larvae of a second wasp, and the latter in their turn nourish still a third wasp. What subtle balance between fertility and mortality must exist in the case of each of these four species to prevent the extinction of all of them! An excess of mortality over fertility in a single member of the group would ultimately wipe out all four. 2

This is not a unique case. The two great orders of insects, Hyme- 3 noptera and Diptera, are full of such examples of interrelationship. And the spiders (which are not insects but members of a separate order of arthropods) also are killers and victims of insects.

The picture is complicated by the fact that those species which are carnivorous in the larval stage have to be provided with animal food by a vegetarian mother. The survival of the young depends on the mother's correct choice of a food which she does not eat herself. 4

In the feeding and safeguarding of their progeny the insects and spiders exhibit some interesting analogies to reasoning and some crass examples of blind instinct. The case I propose to describe here is that of the tarantula spiders and their arch-enemy, the digger wasps of the genus *Pepsis*. It is a classic example of what looks like intelligence pitted against instinct—a strange situation in which the victim, though fully able to defend itself, submits unwittingly to its destruction. 5

Most tarantulas live in the Tropics, but several species occur in the temperate zone and a few are common in the southern U.S. Some varieties are large and have powerful fangs with which they can inflict a deep wound. These formidable looking spiders do not, however, attack man; you can hold one in your hand, if you are gentle, without being bitten. Their bite is dangerous only to insects and small mammals such as mice; for a man it is no worse than a hornet's sting. 6

Tarantulas customarily live in deep cylindrical burrows, from which they emerge at dusk and into which they retire at dawn. Mature males wander about after dark in search of females and occasionally stray into houses. After mating, the male dies in a few weeks, but a female lives much longer and can mate several years in succession. In a Paris museum is a tropical specimen which is said to have been living in captivity for 25 years. 7

A fertilized female tarantula lays from 200 to 400 eggs at a time; thus it is possible for a single tarantula to produce several thousand young. She takes no care of them beyond weaving a cocoon of silk to enclose the eggs. After they hatch, the young walk away, find convenient places in which to dig their burrows and spend the rest of their lives in solitude. Tarantulas feed mostly on insects and millepedes. Once their appetite is appeased, they digest the food for several days before eating again. Their sight is poor, being limited to sensing a change in the intensity of light and to the perception of moving objects. They apparently have little or no sense of hearing, 8 for a hungry tarantula will pay no attention to a loudly chirping cricket placed in its cage unless the insect happens to touch one of its legs.

But all spiders, and especially hairy ones, have an extremely delicate sense of touch. Laboratory experiments prove that tarantulas can distinguish three types of touch: pressure against the body wall, stroking of the body hair and riffling of certain very fine hairs on the legs called trichobothria. Pressure against the body, by a finger or the end of a pencil, causes the tarantula to move off slowly for a short distance. The touch excites no defensive response unless the approach is from above where the spider can see the motion, in which case it rises on its hind legs, lifts its front legs, opens its fangs and holds this threatening posture as long as the object continues to move. When the motion stops, the spider drops back to the ground, remains quiet for a few seconds and then moves slowly away. 9

The entire body of a tarantula, especially its legs, is thickly clothed with hair. Some of it is short and woolly, some long and stiff. Touching this body hair produces one of two distinct reactions. When the spider is hungry, it responds with an immediate and swift attack. At the touch of a cricket's antennae the tarantula seizes the insect so swiftly that a motion picture taken at the rate of 64 frames per second shows only the result and not the process of capture. But when the spider is not hungry, the stimulation of its hairs merely causes it to shake the touched limb. An insect can walk under its hairy belly unharmed. 10

The trichobothria, very fine hairs growing from disk-like membranes on the legs, were once thought to be the spider's hearing organs, but we now know that they have nothing to do with sound. They are sensitive only to air movement. A light breeze makes them vibrate slowly without disturbing the common hair. When one blows gently on the trichobothria, the tarantula reacts with a quick jerk of its four front legs. If the front and hind legs are stimulated at the same time, the spider makes a sudden jump. This reaction is quite independent of the state of its appetite. 11

These three tactile responses—to pressure on the body wall, to moving of the common hair and to flexing of the trichobothria—are so different from one another that there is no possibility of confusing them. They serve the tarantula adequately for most of its needs and enable it to avoid most annoyances and dangers. But they fail the spider completely when it meets its deadly enemy, the digger wasp *Pepsis*. 12

These solitary wasps are beautiful and formidable creatures. Most species are either a deep shiny blue all over, or deep blue with rusty wings. The largest have a wing span of about four inches. They live on nectar. When excited, they give off a pungent odor—a warning that they are ready to attack. The sting is much worse than that of a bee or common wasp, and the pain and swelling last longer. In the adult stage the wasp lives only a few months. The female produces but a few eggs, one at a time at intervals of two or three days. For each egg the mother must provide one adult tarantula, alive but paralyzed. The tarantula must be of the correct species to nourish the larva. The mother wasp attaches the egg to the paralyzed spider's abdomen. Upon hatching from the egg, the larva is many hundreds of times smaller than its living but helpless victim. It eats no other food and drinks no water. By the time it has finished its single gargantuan meal and become ready for wasphood, nothing remains of the tarantula but its indigestible chitinous skeleton. 13

The mother wasp goes tarantula-hunting when the egg in her ovary is almost ready to be laid. Flying low over the ground late on a sunny afternoon, the wasp looks for its victim or for the mouth of a tarantula burrow, a round hole edged by a bit of silk. The sex of the spider makes no difference, but the mother is highly discriminating as to species. Each species of *Pepsis* requires a certain species of tarantula, and the wasp will not attack the wrong species. In a cage with a tarantula which is not its normal prey the wasp avoids the spider, and is usually killed by it in the night. 14

Yet when a wasp finds the correct species, it is the other way about. To identify the species the wasp apparently must explore the spider with her antennae. The tarantula shows an amazing tolerance to this exploration. The wasp crawls under it and walks over it without evoking any hostile response. The molestation is so great and so persistent that the tarantula often rises on all eight legs, as if it were on stilts. It may stand this way for several minutes. Meanwhile the wasp, having satisfied itself that the victim is of the right species, moves off a few inches to dig the spider's grave. Working vigorously with legs and jaws, it excavates a hole 8 to 10 inches deep with a diameter slightly larger than the spider's girth. Now and again the wasp pops out of the hole to make sure that the spider is still there. 15

When the grave is finished, the wasp returns to the tarantula to complete her ghastly enterprise. First she feels it all over once more with her antennae. Then her behavior becomes more aggressive. She 16 bends her abdomen, protruding her sting, and searches for the soft membrane at the point where the spider's leg joins its body—the only spot where she can penetrate the horny skeleton. From time to time, as the exasperated spider slowly shifts ground, the wasp turns on her back and slides along with the aid of her wings, trying to get under the tarantula for a shot at the vital spot. During all this maneuvering, which can last for several minutes, the tarantula makes no move to save itself. Finally the wasp corners it against some obstruction and grasps one of its legs in her powerful jaws. Now at last the harassed spider tries a desperate but vain defense. The two contestants roll over and over on the ground. It is a terrifying sight and the outcome is always the same. The wasp finally manages to thrust her sting into the soft spot and holds it there for a few seconds while she pumps in the poison. Almost immediately the tarantula falls paralyzed on its back. Its legs stop twitching; its heart stops beating. Yet it is not dead, as is shown by the fact that if taken from the wasp it can be restored to some sensitivity by being kept in a moist chamber for several months.

After paralyzing the tarantula, the wasp cleans herself by dragging 17
her body along the ground and rubbing her feet, sucks the drop of blood oozing from the wound in the spider's abdomen, then grabs a leg of the flabby, helpless animal in her jaws and drags it down to the bottom of the grave. She stays there for many minutes, sometimes for several hours, and what she does all that time in the dark we do not know. Eventually she lays her egg and attaches it to the side of the spider's abdomen with a sticky secretion. Then she emerges, fills the grave with soil carried bit by bit in her jaws, and finally tramples the ground all around to hide any trace of the grave from prowlers. Then she flies away, leaving her descendant safely started in life.

In all this the behavior of the wasp evidently is qualitatively differ- 18
ent from that of the spider. The wasp acts like an intelligent animal. This is not to say that instinct plays no part or that she reasons as man does. But her actions are to the point; they are not automatic and can be modified to fit the situation. We do not know for certain how she identifies the tarantula—probably it is by some olfactory or chemo-tactile sense—but she does it purposefully and does not blindly tackle a wrong species.

On the other hand, the tarantula's behavior shows only confusion. 19
Evidently the wasp's pawing gives it no pleasure, for it tries to move

away. That the wasp is not simulating sexual stimulation is certain, because male and female tarantulas react in the same way to its advances. That the spider is not anesthetized by some odorless secretion is easily shown by blowing lightly at the tarantula and making it jump suddenly. What, then, makes the tarantula behave as stupidly as it does?

No clear, simple answer is available. Possibly the stimulation by the wasp's antennae is masked by a heavier pressure on the spider's body, so that it reacts as when prodded by a pencil. But the explanation may be much more complex. Initiative in attack is not in the nature of tarantulas; most species fight only when cornered so that escape is impossible. Their inherited patterns of behavior apparently prompt them to avoid problems rather than attack them. For example, spiders always weave their webs in three dimensions, and when a spider finds that there is insufficient space to attach certain threads in the third dimension, it leaves the place and seeks another, instead of finishing the web in a single plane. This urge to escape seems to arise under all circumstances, in all phases of life and to take the place of reasoning. For a spider to change the pattern of its web is as impossible as for an inexperienced man to build a bridge across a chasm obstructing his way. 20

In a way the instinctive urge to escape is not only easier but more efficient than reasoning. The tarantula does exactly what is most efficient in all cases except in an encounter with a ruthless and determined attacker dependent for the existence of her own species on killing as many tarantulas as she can lay eggs. Perhaps in this case the spider follows its usual pattern of trying to escape, instead of seizing and killing the wasp, because it is not aware of its danger. In any case, the survival of the tarantula species as a whole is protected by the fact that the spider is much more fertile than the wasp. 21

QUESTIONS

Understanding

1. In which paragraph does Petrunkevitch announce his main topic? When does he actually begin to discuss it? How do the wasp larvae of paragraph 2 anticipate his main "case"?

2. If the digger wasp's favorite kind of tarantula always loses the deadly struggle between them, why does that species not disappear?
3. What might happen to the digger wasp if it were a more prolific breeder? What delicate natural balance do spider and wasp together illustrate?
4. What opposing kinds of behavior do spider and wasp respectively represent?
5. The first half of paragraph 8 is a miniature process analysis. What process does it analyze?

Strategies and Structure

1. Petrunkevitch begins his process analysis with its end result and then returns to the first step, the wasp's hunt for her prey. What is that end result? In which paragraph is it explained?
2. Point out the six stages—from hunting to burying—into which Petrunkevitch analyzes the wasp's conquest of the spider.
3. Petrunkevitch enlarges the combat between spider and wasp to human scale by calling the wasp "her" and by referring to the wasp as the spider's "arch-enemy" (par. 5). Point out other similar techniques by which he minimizes the difference in scale between our world and the world of the insects.
4. Petrunkevitch's process analysis incorporates elements of the COMPARISON AND CONTRAST essay (Chapter 6). Does his comparison alternate point by point between spider and wasp, or does he concentrate on one for a while and then concentrate on the other? Explain your answer by referring to several specific passages.
5. Paragraph 12 is a TRANSITION paragraph. Which sentences look backward? Which look forward?
6. Which sentence in paragraph 19 sets up the remainder of the essay?
7. How does paragraph 4 fit in with the rest of Petrunkevitch's essay?

Words and Figures of Speech

1. Such words as *Hymenoptera, Diptera, arthropods,* and *trichobothria* (pars. 3, 9, 11) show that Petrunkevitch, a distinguished zoologist, was comfortable with the technical vocabulary of science; but this essay is sprinkled with nontechnical terms as well, for example: *wasphood* (par. 13),

pops out of the hole (15), *shot* (16), *prowlers* (17). Give several other examples of your own.

2. From the range of Petrunkevitch's DICTION, what conclusions can you draw about the make-up of the readership of *Scientific American,* the magazine in which this essay appeared?
3. Consult your dictionary for the exact meanings of any of the following words you cannot define precisely: *subtle* (par. 2), *carnivorous* (4), *progeny* (5), *instinct* (5, 18), *formidable* (6, 13), *appeased* (8), *tactile* (12), *pungent* (13), *gargantuan* (13), *chitinous* (13), *molestation* (15), *exasperated* (16), *secretion* (17, 19), *qualitatively* (18), *olfactory* (18), *simulating* (19), *anesthetized* (19).

Comparing

1. Compare and contrast Petrunkevitch's description of the behavior of spiders with Gordon Grice's in "Caught in the Widow's Web" (Essays for Further Reading). As an organizing device for their respective essays, which insect—Petrunkevitch's tarantula or Grice's black widow—more closely resembles the moth in Virginia Woolf's "The Death of the Moth" (Essays for Further Reading)? Please explain your answer.
2. In its treatment of the relationship between the human world and the insect world, how does the scale of Petrunkevitch's essay resemble that of Annie Dillard's "Transfiguration" (The Writing Process)?

Discussion and Writing Topics

1. Describe the process by which an insect or animal that you have observed feeds its young and starts them off in life.
2. Analyze the stages of maturation that bring a human being to adulthood.
3. Develop a parallel between two insects and two people (or types of people) with whom you are familiar.
4. Do you have a pet that has shown signs of true intelligence over and beyond mere instinct? Describe his or her behavior.

Garrison Keillor

How to Write a Letter

Born in Anoka, Minnesota, Garrison Keillor is the father of public radio's "Prairie Home Companion" and sole proprietor of mythical Lake Wobegon, "where all the men are good looking, all the women are strong, and all the children are above average." Though Keillor in recent years lived temporarily in New York City (and Europe), his tongue-in-cheek, lump-in-the-throat essays, stories, and letters still make him the voice of mid-America, as familiar in print as on the airwaves. *We Are Still Married* (from which "How to Write a Letter" is taken) is dedicated to Keillor's "classmate" Corrine Guntzel (1942–1986). She is the "Corrine," presumably, whom he addresses here. Keillor is also the author of a novel, *WLT* (1991), and *The Book of Guys* (1993).

We shy persons need to write a letter now and then, or else we'll dry up and blow away. It's true. And I speak as one who loves to reach for the phone, dial the number, and talk. I say, "Big Bopper here—what's shakin', babes?" The telephone is to shyness what Hawaii is to February, it's a way out of the woods, *and yet:* a letter is better. 1

Such a sweet gift—a piece of handmade writing, in an envelope that is not a bill, sitting in our friend's path when she trudges home from a long day spent among wahoos and savages, a day our words will help repair. They don't need to be immortal, just sincere. She can read them twice and again tomorrow: *You're someone I care about, Corinne, and think of often and every time I do you make me smile.* 2

We need to write, otherwise nobody will know who we are. They will have only a vague impression of us as A Nice Person, because, frankly, we don't shine at conversation, we lack the confidence to thrust our faces forward and say, "Hi, I'm Heather Hooten; let me 3 tell you about my week." Mostly we say "Uh-huh" and "Oh, really." People smile and look over our shoulder, looking for someone else to meet.

So a shy person sits down and writes a letter. To be known by another person—to meet and talk freely on the page—to be close despite distance. To escape from anonymity and be our own sweet selves and express the music of our souls. 4

Same thing that moves a giant rock star to sing his heart out in front of 123,000 people moves us to take ballpoint in hand and write a few lines to our dear Aunt Eleanor. *We want to be known.* We want her to know that we have fallen in love, that we quit our job, that we're moving to New York, and we want to say a few things that might not get said in casual conversation: *Thank you for what you've meant to me, I am very happy right now.* 5

The first step in writing letters is to get over the guilt of *not* writing. You don't "owe" anybody a letter. Letters are a gift. The burning shame you feel when you see unanswered mail makes it harder to pick up a pen and makes for a cheerless letter when you finally do. *I feel bad about not writing, but I've been so busy,* etc. Skip this. Few letters are obligatory, and they are *Thanks for the wonderful gift* and *I am terribly sorry to hear about George's death* and *Yes, you're welcome to stay with us next month,* and not many more than that. Write those promptly if you want to keep your friends. Don't worry about the others, except love letters, of course. When your true love writes, *Dear Light of My Life, Joy of My Heart, O Lovely Pulsating Core of My Sensate Life,* some response is called for. 6

Some of the best letters are tossed off in a burst of inspiration, so keep your writing stuff in one place where you can sit down for a few minutes and *(Dear Roy, I am in the middle of a book entitled* We Are Still Married *but thought I'd drop you a line. Hi to your sweetie, too)* dash off a note to a pal. Envelopes, stamps, address book, everything in a drawer so you can write fast when the pen is hot. 7

A blank white eight-by-eleven sheet can look as big as Montana if the pen's not so hot—try a smaller page and write boldly. Or use a note card with a piece of fine art on the front; if your letter ain't good, at least they get the Matisse. Get a pen that makes a sensuous line, get a comfortable typewriter, a friendly word processor—whichever feels easy to the hand. 8

Sit for a few minutes with the blank sheet in front of you, and meditate on the person you will write to, let your friend come 9 to mind until you can almost see her or him in the room with you. Remember the last time you saw each other and how your friend looked and what you said and what perhaps was unsaid between you, and when your friend becomes real to you, start to write.

Write the salutation—*Dear* You—and take a deep breath and 10
plunge in. A simple declarative sentence will do, followed by another and another and another. Tell us what you're doing and tell it like you were talking to us. Don't think about grammar, don't think about lit'ry style, don't try to write dramatically, just give us your news. Where did you go, who did you see, what did they say, what do you think?

If you don't know where to begin, start with the present moment: 11
I'm sitting at the kitchen table on a rainy Saturday morning. Everyone is gone and the house is quiet. Let your simple description of the present moment lead to something else, let the letter drift gently along.

The toughest letter to crank out is one that is meant to impress, 12
as we all know from writing job applications; if it's hard work to slip off a letter to a friend, maybe you're trying too hard to be terrific. A letter is only a report to someone who already likes you for reasons other than your brilliance. Take it easy.

Don't worry about form. It's not a term paper. When you come 13
to the end of one episode, just start a new paragraph. You can go from a few lines about the sad state of pro football to the fight with your mother to your fond memories of Mexico to your cat's urinary-tract infection to a few thoughts on personal indebtedness and on to the kitchen sink and what's in it. The more you write, the easier it gets, and when you have a True True Friend to write to, a *compadre*, a soul sibling, then it's like driving a car down a country road, you just get behind the keyboard and press on the gas.

Don't tear up the page and start over when you write a bad line— 14
try to write your way out of it. Make mistakes and plunge on. Let the letter cook along and let yourself be bold. Outrage, confusion, love—whatever is in your mind, let it find a way to the page. Writing is a means of discovery, always, and when you come to the end and write *Yours ever* or *Hugs and kisses*, you'll know something you didn't when you wrote *Dear Pal.*

Probably your friend will put your letter away, and it'll be read 15
again a few years from now—and it will improve with age. And forty years from now, your friend's grandkids will dig it out of the attic

and read it, a sweet and precious relic of the ancient eighties that gives them a sudden clear glimpse of you and her and the world we old-timers knew. You will then have created an object of art. Your simple lines about where you went, who you saw, what they said, will speak to those children and they will feel in their hearts the humanity of our times.

You can't pick up a phone and call the future and tell them about our times. You have to pick up a piece of paper. 16

QUESTIONS

Understanding

1. A letter is better, says Garrison Keillor, than a phone call. Why? For what specific purposes does he suggest you write a letter? Which one(s) can *only* be accomplished by writing?
2. According to Keillor, what's the hardest kind of letter to write? What advice does he give for avoiding this kind?
3. Except for a few "obligatory" (par. 6) kinds, a letter is a gift, says Keillor. What are the obligatory kinds? What happens if you don't write them?
4. If you don't know where to begin a letter, how does Keillor suggest you start after you've said "Dear You"?
5. When does a personal letter written between ordinary people become, in Keillor's view, "an object of art" (par. 15)?

Strategies and Structure

1. The speaker of "How to Write a Letter" presents himself as shy—why?
2. "How to Write a Letter" reads like one of the informal, personal letters it talks about. How does Keillor give his carefully wrought essay this just-dashed-off quality? What does his conception of the "True True Friend" (par. 13) to whom letters are written suggest about his conception of you, the recipient of Keillor's own "letter"? And about the relationship between the two of you, reader and writer?

3. Getting over the guilt of not writing one, says Keillor, is the "first step" (par. 6) in writing a letter. How many other steps does he give before getting to the salutation, or greeting? What are they?
4. Keillor tells you how to begin actually writing your letter in paragraph 10. In which of the paragraphs that follow does he deal more with the beginning and early stages of letter writing? With the "middle" stages? Why does he have so little to say about preparing for the ending?
5. Besides telling you what to do when you write a letter, Keillor also frequently tells you what not to do. Make a list, in order, of his Do's and Don't's.
6. The "episodes" that Keillor gives as examples in paragraph 13, including the cat's urinary-tract infection, don't seem to have much to do with each other. Is this lack of cohesion among them a flaw in his own writing? Why or why not? According to Keillor, who or what gives a letter its greatest coherence?
7. In which paragraphs of his essay does Keillor deal most explicitly with "audience"? How might the advice he gives here carry over to other kinds of writing?
8. Freewriting is the technique of finding something to say in writing by freely writing down what pops into your head as you are trying to think up something to write about. In which paragraph(s) does Keillor, in effect, advise you to follow this technique for getting started?

Words and Figures of Speech

1. The "Big Bopper" (par. 1) is an ALLUSION to fifties rock star Jape Richardson. To what is Keillor's cool persona alluding when he asks, "what's shakin', babes?" How is this opening paragraph of Keillor's essay anticipating the "precious relic" (par. 15) of the final paragraphs?
2. What is the effect of Keillor's rhyming *letter* with *better* in paragraph 1? Where else do you find similar mixes of humor and sentimentality in Keillor's essay?
3. In what sense is any piece of writing "handmade" (par. 2)?
4. The phrase "a giant rock star" (par. 5) could mean that the performer is a giant star or that he is a giant . . . what?
5. Why does Keillor contract "literary" into "lit'ry" (par. 10)?
6. How does the comic METAPHOR in the last sentence of paragraph 13 exemplify what Keillor has been saying about yoking ideas?

Comparing

1. As model explainers, how does Keillor's shy letter-writer compare with Nikki Giovanni's holiday reveler in the next essay in this chapter, "On Holidays and How to Make Them Work"? Which of them, would you say, gives the better advice? Why so?
2. How does Keillor's humor differ from Ann Hodgman's in "No Wonder They Call Me a Bitch" (Chapter 8)?
3. In what ways does the informal language of "How to Write a Letter" work like the "family talk" in Amy Tan's "Mother Tongue" (Chapter 2)?

Discussion and Writing Topics

1. When does Keillor, would you say, give good advice about writing? Bad advice? Preposterous advice?
2. "Writing is a means of discovery" (par. 14), says Keillor. How might this be so? What does he mean by "discovery" in this sense?
3. If Keillor is right, why shouldn't you worry too much about grammar and other niceties of "form" in the early stages of writing a letter or anything else? In formal writing, when do such matters need to be considered more carefully?
4. When he compares writing a friend with phoning one, Keillor is not so much analyzing the difference between electronic and mechanical means of communication—you can write on a computer—as between writing (in any form) and speaking. What are some of the essential differences between these two modes of communication?
5. In the style of "How to Write a Letter," write a letter to Keillor thanking (or chiding) him for his "letter" to you.

Nikki Giovanni

On Holidays and How to Make Them Work

Yolande Cornelia Giovanni was born in Knoxville, Tennessee, the daughter of a probation officer and a social worker. She was educated at Fisk University, the University of Pennsylvania, and Columbia University. As a lecturer and professor of creative writing, Nikki Giovanni has taught, among other places, at Queens College, Rutgers University, The Ohio State University, the College of Mount St. Joseph, and Virginia Polytechnic Institute. Her many volumes of poetry include *Black Feeling, Black Talk* (1968), *Cotton Candy on a Rainy Day* (1978), and *Those Who Ride the Night Winds* (1983). "On Holidays and How to Make Them Work" is from a collection of Giovanni's prose writings entitled *Sacred Cows . . . and Other Edibles* (1988). In 1989, Giovanni was named "Woman of the Year" by the Lynchburg, Virginia, chapter of the NAACP, a title she has also been awarded by *Ebony Magazine.*

A proper holiday, coming from the medieval *holy day*, is supposed to be a time of reflection on great men, great deeds, great people. Things like that. Somehow in America this didn't quite catch on. Take Labor Day. On Labor Day you take the day off, then go to the Labor Day sales and spend your devalued money with a clerk who is working. And organized labor doesn't understand why it suffers declining membership? Pshaw. Who wants to join an organization that makes you work on the day it designates as a day off? Plus, no matter how hidden the agenda, who wants a day off if they make you march in a parade and listen to some politicians talk on and on about nothing. 1

Hey. I'm a laborer. I used to work in Walgreen's on Linn Street. 2
We were open every holiday and I, being among the junior people,

always "got" to work the time-and-a-half holidays. I hated those people who came in. Every fool in the Western world, and probably in this universe, knows that Christmas is December 25. Has been that way for over a thousand years, yet there they'd be, standing outside the door, cold, bleary-eyed, waiting for us to open so they could purchase a present. Memorial Day, which used to be Armistice Day until we got into this situation of continuous war, was the official start of summer. We would want to be out with our boyfriends barbecuing . . . or something, but there we were behind the counter waiting to see who forgot that in order to barbecue you need: (1) a grill, (2) charcoal, (3) charcoal starter. My heart goes out to the twenty-four-hour grocery people, who are probably selling meat!

But hey. It's the American way. The big Fourth of July sales probably reduced the number of fatal injuries as people spent the entire day sober in malls, fighting over markdowns. Minor cuts and bruises were way up, though, I'll bet. And forget the great nonholiday, Presidents' Day. The damned thing could at least have a real name. What does that mean—Presidents' Day? Mostly that we don't care enough to take the time to say to Washington and Lincoln: Well done. But for sure, as a Black American I've got to go for it. Martin Luther King, Jr.'s birthday has come up for the first time as a national holiday. If we are serious about celebrating it, Steinberg's will be our first indication: GHETTO BLASTERS 30% OFF! FREE TAPE OF "I HAVE A DREAM" WITH EVERY VCR PURCHASED AT THE ALL-NEW GIGANTIC MARTY'S BIRTHDAY SALE. Then Wendy's will, just maybe, for Black patrons (and their liberal sympathizers) Burn-A-Burger to celebrate the special day. Procter & Gamble will withhold Clorox for the day, respectfully requesting that those Black spots be examined for their liberating influence. But what we really want, where we can know we have succeeded, is that every Federated department store offers 50 percent off to every colored patron who can prove he or she is Black in recognition of the days when colored citizens who were Black were not accorded all the privileges of other shoppers. That will be a big help because everybody will want to be Black for a Day. Sun tanneries will make fortunes during the week preceding MLK Day. Wig salons will reap great benefits. Dentists will have to hire extra help to put that distinctive gap between the middle front teeth. MLK Day will be accepted. And isn't that the heart of the American dream? 3

I really love a good holiday—it takes the people off the streets 4 and puts them safely in the shopping malls. Now think about it. Aren't you proud to be with Uncle Sam?

QUESTIONS

Understanding

1. What is a "proper holiday" (par. 1) supposed to be, according to Nikki Giovanni? How does she think holidays are actually celebrated in America?
2. In Giovanni's opinion, what forces and values in American society have caused holidays to degenerate?
3. How would Giovanni (or rather, her persona) have us celebrate Martin Luther King, Jr., Day?
4. Besides making money, what does Nikki Giovanni conceive to be the "heart" (par. 4) of the American Dream?

Strategies and Structure

1. What is the difference between IRONY and sarcasm (see SATIRE in the Glossary)? Which would you say Nikki Giovanni is practicing here? Why do you say so?
2. "On Holidays and How to Make Them Work" is just four paragraphs in length, with one paragraph (par. 3) taking up half the essay. Should the author have broken up this long paragraph into two or three smaller ones? Why or why not?
3. "Hey" (par. 2) is not a sentence. Neither is "But Hey" (par. 3). Why (and how) does Giovanni use these fragments as, hey, major transitional elements in her prose?
4. "On Holidays and How to Make Them Work" is riddled with RHETORICAL QUESTIONS. Point out several, and speculate why the author might use this device so many times in such a short essay.
5. Among the great American holidays that Nikki Giovanni refers to is the Fourth of July. Her persona might even be said to deliver a sort of

mock Fourth of July speech. How so? Where and how does Giovanni employ the language, gestures, and themes of political oratory in her satire?

6. Paragraph 2 of "On Holidays and How to Make Them Work" includes a mini-essay in process analysis. What is the subject of this analysis, and where does Giovanni break it down into steps or components?
7. Where does Giovanni launch into the main "how-to-do-it" part of her essay? What is she analyzing or explaining here, and how seriously are we supposed to take her suggestions?

Words and Figures of Speech

1. Why do you think Nikki Giovanni begins her essay with a brief ETYMOLOGY of the word *holiday?*
2. *Pshaw* (par. 1) is not only colloquial (like *Hey*) but old-fashioned. What is the purpose of putting such quaint diction in the mouth of a speaker with such "radical" ideas?
3. Why does Giovanni put *got* (par. 2) in quotation marks?
4. "On Holidays and How to Make Them Work" is taken from a volume of Nikki Giovanni's essays entitled *Sacred Cows . . . and Other Edibles.* What is a "sacred cow," and how (and why) does Giovanni's essay on holidays commit the sacrilege of eating one?
5. Where did Uncle Sam (par. 4) get his name?

Comparing

1. How and where does the TONE of Nikki Giovanni's essay on the commercialization of American holidays resemble that of Russell Baker in "A Nice Place to Visit" (Chapter 6)?
2. How might "On Holidays and How to Make Them Work" be said to parody an appeal to emotion and ethics such as Lynn Woolsey's "Reinvent Welfare, Humanely" (Chapter 10)?
3. Compare and contrast Nikki Giovanni's essay on holidays with Barbara Ehrenreich's "Maintaining the Crime Supply" (Chapter 9) as exercises in intentional illogic and HYPERBOLE.

Discussion and Writing Topics

1. How accurate do you find Nikki Giovanni's assessment of why and how we celebrate holidays in America? Please explain your answer. What other motives and means, if any, would you cite?
2. What do you think of Giovanni's specific proposals (par. 3) for celebrating Martin Luther King, Jr., Day?

Philip Weiss

How to Get Out of a Locked Trunk

Philip Weiss, a contributing editor at *Harper's Magazine* and *Esquire*, lives in New York, where he is at work on a novel. At the time he wrote "How to Get Out of a Locked Trunk," Weiss was still a bachelor. "How to Get Out of a Locked Trunk" first appeared in *Harper's*.

On a hot Sunday last summer my friend Tony and I drove my rental car, a '91 Buick, from St. Paul to the small town of Waconia, Minnesota, forty miles southwest. We each had a project. Waconia is Tony's boyhood home, and his sister had recently given him a panoramic postcard of Lake Waconia as seen from a high point in the town early in the century. He wanted to duplicate the photograph's vantage point, then hang the two pictures together in his house in Frogtown. I was hoping to see Tony's father, Emmett, a retired mechanic, in order to settle a question that had been nagging me: Is it possible to get out of a locked car trunk? 1

We tried to call ahead to Emmett twice, but he wasn't home. Tony thought he was probably golfing but that there was a good chance he'd be back by the time we got there. So we set out. 2

I parked the Buick, which was a silver sedan with a red interior, by the graveyard near where Tony thought the picture had been taken. He took his picture and I wandered among the headstones, reading the epitaphs. One of them was chillingly anti-individualist. It said, "Not to do my will, but thine." 3

Trunk lockings had been on my mind for a few weeks. It seemed to me that the fear of being locked in a car trunk had a particular hold on the American imagination. Trunk lockings occur in many movies and books—from *Goodfellas* to *Thelma and Louise* to *Hum-* 4 *boldt's Gift*. And while the highbrow national newspapers generally shy away from trunk lockings, the attention they receive in local papers suggests a widespread anxiety surrounding the subject. In an afternoon at the New York Public Library I found numerous stories about trunk lockings. A Los Angeles man is discovered, bloodshot, banging the trunk of his white Eldorado following a night and a day trapped inside; he says his captors went on joyrides and picked up women. A forty-eight-year-old Houston doctor is forced into her trunk at a bank ATM and then the car is abandoned, parked near the Astrodome. A New Orleans woman tells police she gave birth in a trunk while being abducted to Texas. Tests undermine her story, the police drop the investigation. But so what if it's a fantasy? That only shows the idea's hold on us.

5 Every culture comes up with tests of a person's ability to get out of a sticky situation. The English plant mazes. Tropical resorts market those straw finger-grabbers that tighten their grip the harder you pull on them, and Viennese intellectuals gave us the concept of childhood sexuality—figure it out, or remain neurotic for life.

6 At least you could puzzle your way out of those predicaments. When they slam the trunk, though, you're helpless unless someone finds you. You would think that such a common worry should have a ready fix, and that the secret of getting out of a locked trunk is something we should all know about.

7 I phoned experts but they were very discouraging.

8 "You cannot get out. If you got a pair of pliers and bat's eyes, yes. But you have to have a lot of knowledge of the lock," said James Foote at Automotive Locksmiths in New York City.

9 Jim Frens, whom I reached at the technical section of *Car and Driver* in Detroit, told me the magazine had not dealt with this question. But he echoed the opinion of experts elsewhere when he said that the best hope for escape would be to try and kick out the panel between the trunk and the backseat. That angle didn't seem worth pursuing. What if your enemies were in the car, crumpling beer cans and laughing at your fate? It didn't make sense to join them.

10 The people who deal with rules on auto design were uncomfortable with my scenarios. Debra Barclay of the Center for Auto Safety, an organization founded by Ralph Nader, had certainly heard of cases, but she was not aware of any regulations on the matter. "Now, if there was a defect involved—" she said, her voice trailing off,

implying that trunk locking was all phobia. This must be one of the few issues on which she and the auto industry agree. Ann Carlson of the Motor Vehicle Manufacturers Association became alarmed at the thought that I was going to play up a non-problem: "In reality this very rarely happens. As you say, in the movies it's a wonderful plot device," she said. "But in reality apparently this is not that frequent an occurrence. So they have not designed that feature into vehicles in a specific way."

When we got to Emmett's one-story house it was full of people. Tony's sister, Carol, was on the floor with her two small children. Her husband, Charlie, had one eye on the golf tournament on TV, and Emmett was at the kitchen counter, trimming fat from meat for lunch. I have known Emmett for fifteen years. He looked better than ever. In his retirement he had sharply changed his diet and lost a lot of weight. He had on shorts. His legs were tanned and muscular. As always, his manner was humorous, if opaque. 11

Tony told his family my news: I was getting married in three weeks. Charlie wanted to know where my fiancée was. Back East, getting everything ready. A big-time hatter was fitting her for a new hat. 12

Emmett sat on the couch, watching me. "Do you want my advice?" 13

"Sure." 14

He just grinned. A gold tooth glinted. Carol and Charlie pressed him to yield his wisdom. 15

Finally he said, "Once you get to be thirty, you make your own mistakes." 16

He got out several cans of beer, and then I brought up what was on my mind. 17

Emmett nodded and took off his glasses, then cleaned them and put them back on. 18

We went out to his car, a Mercury Grand Marquis, and Emmett opened the trunk. His golf clubs were sitting on top of the spare tire in a green golf bag. Next to them was a toolbox and what he called his "burglar tools," a set of elbowed rods with red plastic handles he used to open door locks when people locked their keys inside. 19

Tony and Charlie stood watching. Charlie is a banker in Minneapolis. He enjoys gizmos and is extremely practical. I would describe 20 him as unflappable. That's a word I always wanted to apply to myself, but my fiancée had recently informed me that I am high-strung. Though that surprised me, I didn't quarrel with her.

For a while we studied the latch assembly. The lock closed in 21
much the same way that a lobster might clamp on to a pencil. The claw portion, the jaws of the lock, was mounted inside the trunk lid. When you shut the lid, the jaws locked on to the bend of a U-shaped piece of metal mounted on the body of the car. Emmett said my best bet would be to unscrew the bolts. That way the U-shaped piece would come loose and the lock's jaws would swing up with it still in their grasp.

"But you'd need a wrench," he said. 22

It was already getting too technical. Emmett had an air of endless 23
patience, but I felt defeated. I could only imagine bloodied fingers, cracked teeth. I had hoped for a simple trick.

Charlie stepped forward. He reached out and squeezed the lock's 24
jaws. They clicked shut in the air, bound together by heavy springs. Charlie now prodded the upper part of the left-hand jaw, the thicker part. With a rough flick of his thumb, he was able to force the jaws to snap open. Great.

Unfortunately, the jaws were mounted behind a steel plate the 25
size of your palm in such a way that while they were accessible to us, standing outside the car, had we been inside the trunk the plate would be in our way, blocking the jaws.

This time Emmett saw the way out. He fingered a hole in the 26
plate. It was no bigger than the tip of your little finger. But the hole was close enough to the latch itself that it might be possible to angle something through the hole from inside the trunk and nudge the jaws apart. We tried with one of my keys. The lock jumped open.

It was time for a full-dress test. Emmett swung the clubs out of 27
the trunk, and I set my can of Schmidt's on the rear bumper and climbed in. Everyone gathered around, and Emmett lowered the trunk on me, then pressed it shut with his meaty hands. Total darkness. I couldn't hear the people outside. I thought I was going to panic. But the big trunk felt comfortable. I was pressed against a sort of black carpet that softened the angles against my back.

I could almost stretch out in the trunk, and it seemed to me I 28
could make them sweat if I took my time. Even Emmett, that sphinx, would give way to curiosity. Once I was out he'd ask how it had

been and I'd just grin. There were some things you could only learn by doing.

It took a while to find the hole. I slipped the key in and angled it to one side. The trunk gasped open. 29

Emmett motioned the others away, then levered me out with his big right forearm. Though I'd only been inside for a minute, I was disoriented—as much as anything because someone had moved my beer while I was gone, setting it down on the cement floor of the garage. It was just a little thing, but I could not be entirely sure I had gotten my own beer back. 30

Charlie was now raring to try other cars. We examined the latch on his Toyota, which was entirely shielded to the trunk occupant (i.e., no hole in the plate), and on the neighbor's Honda (ditto). But a 1991 Dodge Dynasty was doable. The trunk was tight, but its lock had a feature one of the mechanics I'd phoned described as a "tail-piece": a finger-like extension of the lock mechanism itself that stuck out a half inch into the trunk cavity; simply by twisting the tailpiece I could free the lock. I was even faster on a 1984 Subaru that had a little lever device on the latch. 31

We went out to my rental on Oak Street. The Skylark was in direct sun and the trunk was hot to the touch, but when we got it open we could see that its latch plate had a perfect hole, a square in which the edge of the lock's jaw appeared like a face in a window. 32

The trunk was shallow and hot. Emmett had to push my knees down before he could close the lid. This one was a little suffocating. I imagined being trapped for hours, and even before he had got it closed I regretted the decision with a slightly nauseous feeling. I thought of Edgar Allan Poe's live burials, and then about something my fiancée had said more than a year and a half before. I had been on her case to get married. She was divorced, and at every opportunity I would reissue my proposal—even during a commercial. She'd interrupted one of these chirps to tell me, in a cold, throaty voice, that she had no intention of ever going through another divorce: "This time, it's death out." I'd carried those words around like a lump of wet clay. 33

As it happened, the Skylark trunk was the easiest of all. The hole was right where it was supposed to be. The trunk popped open, and I felt great satisfaction that we'd been able to figure out a rule that seemed to apply about 60 percent of the time. If we publicized our success, it might get the attention it deserved. All trunks would be 34 fitted with such a hole. Kids would learn about it in school. The grip of the fear would relax. Before long a successful trunk-locking scene would date a movie like a fedora dates one today.

When I got back East I was caught up in wedding preparations. I live in New York, and the wedding was to take place in Philadelphia. We set up camp there with five days to go. A friend had lent my fiancée her BMW, and we drove it south with all our things. I unloaded the car in my parents' driveway. The last thing I pulled out of the trunk was my fiancée's hat in its heavy cardboard shipping box. She'd warned me I was not allowed to look. The lid was free but I didn't open it. I was willing to be surprised. 35

When the trunk was empty it occurred to me I might hop in and give it a try. First I looked over the mechanism. The jaws of the BMW's lock were shielded, but there seemed to be some kind of cable coming off it that you might be able to manipulate so as to cause the lock to open. The same cable that allowed the driver to open the trunk remotely . . . 36

I fingered it for a moment or two but decided I didn't need to test out the theory. 37

QUESTIONS

Understanding

1. How do the experts, especially in the auto industry, respond to Philip Weiss's suggestion that locked trunks are a serious, unexamined safety hazard?
2. What rate of escape, by percentage, does Weiss estimate victims of trunk lockings would achieve if his findings were properly publicized?
3. Of the cars he tests, which one alarms Philip Weiss the most yet turns out to be the easiest to get out of? Why is he so alarmed, then? Why is he so anxious to find "a simple trick" (par. 23) that will fit all instances?
4. So, according to Weiss, how *do* you get out of a locked trunk? How, according to his fiancée, do you get out of a marriage?
5. Why doesn't the author of "How to Get Out of a Locked Trunk" sneak a peak at his fiancée's new hat, since the lid is not locked and the box

would be so easy to open? Incidentally, how does he know that the lid is "free" (par. 35)?

6. Why doesn't Weiss test his theory about pulling the cable to open the trunk of the borrowed BMW, as if he were manipulating the mechanism remotely?
7. Why does Philip Weiss say, "There were some things you could only learn by doing" (par. 28)?

Strategies and Structure

1. "How to Get Out of a Locked Trunk" is divided into three parts—paragraphs 1–10, 11–34, and 35–37. Why does the author break up the flow of his prose at just these points? Why three sections instead of four or six?
2. In which section of his essay does Weiss most fully analyze the process of getting out of a locked car trunk? How clear and precise do you find his explanation?
3. What is Weiss's purpose in citing several "experts" in paragraphs 7–10? What is Emmett's role in the big experiment?
4. Why do you think the last section of Weiss's essay is the shortest? How effectively, in your opinion, does it bring the essay to a satisfying conclusion? Would the author have done just as well to leave it off? Why or why not?
5. "It's a wonderful plot device," Weiss quotes one expert as saying (par. 10). Is she right? How well plotted do you find the many NARRATIVE aspects of Weiss's essay? In particular, how and how well does he integrate the parts that explain the mechanics of getting out of a locked trunk (exposition, process analysis) with the parts that tell a story (narration)?
6. "How to Get Out of a Locked Trunk" would be right at home among the personal narratives in Chapter 1 of this collection, but it could just as easily fit into Chapter 7 (Essays That Use Metaphor and Analogy). What ANALOGY, largely unstated, is Philip Weiss developing here? When did you first see the connection?

Words and Figures of Speech

1. Why is Weiss reading tombstones (par. 3) as his "unflappable" (par. 20) friend looks at the natural panorama around him? How does the inscrip-

tion he singles out—"Not to do my will, but thine"—foreshadow what's to come, especially the ending, where the author decides not to look at the hat?

2. What is the purpose of Weiss's ALLUSION to Sigmund Freud and company ("Viennese intellectuals," par. 5)? For example, why does his persona fixate upon closed trunks, the tools and mechanics by which the jaws of a lock can be sprung open, and his fiancée's new hat?
3. Who writes "scenarios" (par. 10) and for what?
4. A "phobia" (par. 10) is an irrational fear. What is Weiss (or his persona) so afraid of here, and how irrational would you consider his fears to be?
5. The lock on the trunk of Emmett's Mercury Grand Marquis, says Weiss (par. 21), "closed in much the same way that a lobster might clamp on to a pencil." As a description of how a trunk lock works, how clear do you find this one? Where else (and how effectively) in his essay does Weiss use analogies like this to simplify his explanations—and to complicate what he is not directly explaining to us?
6. Why does Weiss call Emmett a "sphinx" (par. 28)? How does the younger man's "grin" recall paragraph 15? What is the significance of Emmett's cleaning his glasses in paragraph 18?
7. What does "just a little thing" like his concern for his beer (par. 30) tell us about Weiss's persona?
8. What are the implications of "reissue" and "chirp" (par. 33)?
9. Why does Weiss compare his future wife's succinct words about the binding nature of marriage ("death out") to "a lump of wet clay" (par. 33)? Why does he allude to Poe in the same breath?
10. He is "*willing* to be surprised" (par. 35, italics added), says Weiss's persona when he chooses not to look in the hat box. How has he changed?

Comparing

1. How does Philip Weiss's TONE of voice compare with Nikki Giovanni's in the preceding essay in this chapter?
2. Compare and contrast Weiss's treatment of marriage and divorce with Ann Raver's in "Pulling Up Roots" (Chapter 7).
3. Ann Hodgman ("No Wonder They Call Me a Bitch," Chapter 8) never tells us why she is eating dog food. How does Weiss's essay compare with hers in this matter of withholding essential information?

Discussion and Writing Topics

1. Would a "Freudian" reading of "How to Get Out of a Locked Trunk" be justified, in your opinion, even if Philip Weiss did not directly refer to "Viennese intellectuals" (par. 5)? Why or why not?
2. "Every culture," Weiss writes (par. 5), "comes up with tests of a person's ability to get out of a sticky situation." How well do you think Weiss proves this thesis? What specific examples would you use?
3. Are you or anyone else in your class aware of a case of phobic behavior? Analyze and describe the case, particularly in its visible manifestations.

Nikki Giovanni

"Writing," says Nikki Giovanni, "is like any other profession—break dancing, ninth grade, doctor of philosophy—it's what I do to justify the air I breathe, the food I ingest, the time I take up on earth." 1

How does she do it? "It's always a bit intimidating to try to tell how I write, since I, like most writers, I think, am not at all sure that I do what I do in the way that I think I do it." 2

One way that Giovanni (at least) *thinks* she writes is by reading. "I loved my profession well before I joined it," she says. "I have always been a lover of books and the ideas they contain. Sometimes I think it is easy for we who write to forget that that is only half the process; someone must read." Someone who would write must also, in Giovanni's view, listen to the music of words, not just to the ideas they signify. "I come from a long line of storytellers," she once told an interviewer. "I don't think I conceptualized, as I was sitting listening to stories, that I could use this or that line. I do think I appreciated the quality and the rhythm of the telling . . . and I know when I started to write that I wanted to retain that—I didn't want to become the kind of writer that was stilted or that used language in ways that could not be spoken. I try to use a very natural rhythm; I want my writing to sound like I talk." 3

Another way that Giovanni thinks she writes is simply by beginning—in a familiar place set aside for the purpose: "Every time I sit 4 down with my typewriter I am beginning to write. The 'beginning' cannot be told until I know the ending. I am, however, a writer very much grounded in my sense of place. I need my own coffee cup, my own chair, but most especially my own typewriter. I had a steam pipe burst in my apartment and my typewriter was uncovered and thereby ruined by the steam. I had had that typewriter since college. It was almost a year before I would even begin to touch this one. I think, by the way, that every intended writer should learn to type. . . . Thinking on a typewriter is different from thinking on a yellow pad. The sooner you can think on a keyboard, the less room you have for procrastination. And all writers are great procrastinators!" (The only people who are worse procrastinators than writers, she says, are "politicians.")

A teacher of writing as well as a practicing writer, Giovanni has a special "affection" for her students. She also feels "an obligation and a responsibility, and they know that I do. I think it's mutual." When asked if she has learned anything about writing from her students Giovanni responds that teaching "directly enriches my life." Many writers, she feels, "spend too much time alone," listening only to themselves and their own thoughts. Teaching, she says, "puts you in the position of listening to somebody else." 5

Is she pleased or disappointed with what she has achieved as a writer? "I am very proud of my work," Giovanni frankly admits. "I think that I have grown; I feel that my work has grown a lot. What I've always wanted to do is something different, and I think each book has made a change. I hope that the next book continues that. Like all writers, I guess, I keep looking for the heart." 6

Writing Topics for Chapter Three
Essays That Analyze a Process

Write an essay analyzing one of the following processes or giving directions for one of the following operations:

1. How to play chess
2. How to change a tire
3. How to install an electric circuit in a house
4. How to make wine, beer, or mead

5. How to milk a cow
6. How to keep bees
7. How to thread and operate a sewing machine
8. How to make butter
9. How a piano works
10. How a solar heating system works
11. How to conserve energy in a house
12. How to record a television show on a VCR
13. How to install software on a computer
14. How to make a good (or bad) impression on your boyfriend's or girlfriend's parents
15. How to excel in school
16. How to take and develop photographs
17. How iron ore is made into steel
18. How a fuel injection system works
19. How an internal combustion engine works
20. How to sail a boat
21. How to buy a used car
22. How to buy a horse or other livestock
23. How to buy stocks, bonds, or other securities
24. How to save money
25. How to get rich

Four

Essays That Analyze Cause and Effect

PROCESS ANALYSIS[1] (Chapter 3) is concerned with sequence in time and space. Sequence is one kind of relationship among objects and events; another is causation. When we confuse the two, we are reasoning as Mark Twain's hero does in *Adventures of Huckleberry Finn*. Alone in the woods one night, Huck sees an evil omen:

> Pretty soon a spider went crawling up my shoulder, and I flipped it off and it lit in the candle; and before I could budge it was all shriveled up. I didn't need anybody to tell me that that was an awful bad sign and would fetch me some bad luck, so I was scared and most shook the clothes off of me. I got up and turned around in my tracks three times and crossed my breast every time; and then I tied up a little lock of my hair to keep witches away. But I hadn't no confidence.

Huck is right to be scared; all sorts of misadventures are going to befall him and Jim in Mark Twain's masterpiece. But Huck commits the blunder of thinking that because the misadventures follow the burning of the spider, they were necessarily caused by it: he confuses mere sequence with causation. This mistake in logic is commonly known as the *post hoc, ergo propter hoc* fallacy—Latin for "after this, therefore because of this."

[1] Terms printed in small capitals are defined in the Glossary.

Huck Finn does not realize that two conditions have to be met to prove causation:

> B cannot have happened without A;
> Whenever A happens, B must happen.

The chemist who observes again and again that a flammable substance burns (B) only when combined with oxygen (A) and that it always burns when so combined, may infer that oxidation causes combustion. The chemist has discovered in oxygen the "immediate" cause of combustion. The flame necessary to set off the reaction and the chemist himself, who lights the match, are "ultimate" causes.

Often the ultimate causes of an event are more important than the immediate causes, especially when we are dealing with psychological and social rather than purely physical factors. Let us raise the following question about a college freshman: Why does Mary smoke? Depending upon whom we asked, we might get responses like these:

Mary:	"I smoke because I need something to do with my hands."
Mary's boyfriend:	"Mary smokes because she thinks it looks sophisticated."
Medical doctor:	"Because Mary has developed a physical addiction to tobacco."
Psychologist:	"Because of peer pressure."
Sociologist:	"Because 30 percent of all female Americans under 20 years of age now smoke. Mary is part of a trend."
Advertiser:	"Because she's come a long way, baby."

Each of these explanations tells only part of the story. For a full answer to our question about why Mary smokes, we must take all of these answers together. Together they form what is known as the "complex" cause of Mary's behavior.

Most essays in CAUSE AND EFFECT that you will be asked to read or to write will examine the complex cause of an event or phenomenon. There are two reasons for addressing all the contributing causes. The first is to avoid over-simplification. Interesting questions are usually complex, and complex questions probably have complex answers. The second reason is to anticipate objections that might be raised against your argument.

Often a clever writer will run through several causes to show that he or she knows the ground before making a special case for one or two. When a clergyman asked journalist Lincoln Steffens to name the ultimate cause of corruption in city government, Steffens replied with the following analysis:

> Most people, you know, say it was Adam. But Adam, you remember, he said that it was Eve, the woman; she did it. And Eve said no, no, it wasn't she; it was the serpent. And that's where you clergy have stuck ever since. You blame the serpent, Satan. Now I come and I am trying to show you that it was, it is, the apple.

Steffens was giving an original answer to the old question of original sin. Our fallen state, he said, is due not to innate depravity but to economic conditions.

When explaining causes, be as specific as you can without oversimplifying. When explaining effects, be even more specific. Here is your chance to display the telling fact or colorful detail that can save your essay from the ho-hum response. Consider this explanation of the effects of smoking written by England's King James I (of the King James Bible). His *Counter-Blaste to Tobacco* (1604) found smoking to be

> A custom lothsome to the eye, hatefull to the Nose, harmefull to the braine, dangerous to the Lungs, and in the blacke stinking fume thereof, neerest resembling the horrible Stigian smoke of the pit that is bottomelesse.

In a more recent essay on the evils of tobacco, Erik Eckholm strikes a grimmer note. "But the most potentially tragic victims of cigarettes," he writes, "are the infants of mothers who smoke. They are more likely than the babies of nonsmoking mothers to be born underweight and thus to encounter death or disease at birth or during the initial months of life."

In singling out the effects of smoking upon unwitting infants, Eckholm has chosen an example that might be just powerful enough to convince some smokers to quit. Your examples need not be so grim, but they must be specific to be powerful. And they must be selected with the interests of your audience in mind. Eckholm is addressing the young women who are smoking more today than ever before. When writing for a middle-aged audience, he points out that smoking causes cancer and heart disease at a rate 70 percent higher among pack-a-day men and women than among nonsmokers.

Your audience must be taken into account because writing a cause and effect analysis is much like constructing a persuasive argument. It is a form of reasoning that carries the reader step by step through a "proof." Your analysis may be instructive, amusing, or startling; but first it must be logical.

Mary Talbot

The Potato: How It Shaped the World

Mary Talbot's title identifies both the apparently trivial cause and the momentous effect she traces from it in this history of a staple of the Western diet. Talbot's chronicle appeared in a special issue of *Newsweek* devoted to the settlement of the New World. Talbot is a staff writer for that magazine.

It was the start of a beautiful friendship. Juan de Castellanos, a conquistador charting the wilds of Colombia, came upon a deserted Indian village in whose houses he found "maize, beans and truffles." In fact, the "truffles" were potatoes which, the explorer noted, were "good of flavor, a gift very acceptable to Indians and a dainty dish even for Spaniards." This union—potatoes and Europeans—would change the course of world history as much as any gold or silver pilfered from the Incan Empire. 1

The true daintiness of the potato would not be discovered until a later age. At the outset, Europeans treated it as a food for the masses. Potatoes were loaded aboard Spanish treasure ships as a cheap food for sailors bringing home the booty of the New World. They reached England and Germany courtesy of Sir Francis Drake, who apparently picked up a batch during a stop in Colombia in 1556, where he was seeking to stake out part of the New World for Elizabeth I. 2

It wasn't so much the potato's taste that appealed to the European elite; they imagined it was an aphrodisiac. "Let the sky rain potatoes!" cried Shakespeare's Falstaff in a moment of passion. Europe's peasants were more cautious: before they came to subsist on the potato, they mistrusted it, even thought it might be poisonous. In 1619 potatoes were banned in Burgundy because "too frequent use of them caused the leprosy." Even starving Prussians refused to 3 touch them when, in 1774, Frederick the Great sent a wagonload of potatoes to Kolberg to relieve famine.

Over time, however, necessity and familiarity dulled the peas- 4
antry's bias. "One and a half acres, planted with potatoes, would provide enough food, with the addition of a bit of milk, to keep a family hearty for a year," wrote Alfred Crosby in "The Columbian Exchange." In Ireland, the potato was not ruined when battle raged over the ground in which it grew, and it could remain safely hidden in the earth throughout the winter, even when a peasant's home and stores were raided or set afire by English soldiers. Because potatoes are ideally suited to northern climates, Catherine the Great launched a pro-potato campaign as an antidote to famine in 18th-century Russia. Vodka soon followed, and the potato thus became indelibly fixed in the Russian diet. (The instant popularity of vodka should be no surprise; one of the Russian drinks it replaced was fermented grapes with a hunk of meat thrown in for flavor.)

But it was in Ireland that the potato made its greatest mark. "It 5
was not exceptional for an Irishman to consume 10 pounds of potatoes a day and very little else," wrote Crosby. On this diet, the Irish population nearly tripled between 1754 and 1846. But depending on the potato was precarious; when the potato blight hit Europe in 1845 the consequences were devastating. In Ireland, as food historian Reay Tannahill describes it, "the potato famine meant more than food scarcity. It meant no seed potatoes from which to grow next year's crop. It meant that the pig or cow which would normally have been sold to pay the rent had to be slaughtered, because there was nothing to fatten it on." No cow for the rent could mean eviction, and hunger was soon compounded by scurvy, failing eyesight, even dementia, from vitamin deficiency. Nearly a million Irish men and women died as a result of the blight. Another million immigrated to the United States. They were, in a way, the New World's harvest from those first potato exports 300 years earlier.

QUESTIONS

Understanding

1. How many centuries does Talbot cover in her survey of potato history? When did Juan de Castellanos (par. 1) first come upon "truffles" in the New World?
2. Besides its nutritional value, why has the potato fared so well in Europe and Russia despite its slow start?
3. What did the New World receive in return for its gift of potatoes?
4. Besides destroying a food staple, why else was the potato blight of 1845 (par. 5) so devastating?

Strategies and Structure

1. Talbot's title falls into two parts. Which deals with "causes" and which with "effects"?
2. On which (causes or effects) does Talbot spend more time? Explain your answer.
3. Time is indeed an organizing principle in "The Potato." Point out all the references to time you can find, such as "until a later age" (par. 2). How consistently do they follow chronological order?
4. Another organizing principle here is geography. Where does Talbot refer to specific places? How does she link them?
5. Most of Talbot's paragraphs begin with a sentence that announces the "topic" of the discussion to follow. Which paragraph begins, instead, by telling you what it is not going to talk about?
6. How does the first sentence in "The Potato" anticipate the last?

Words and Figures of Speech

1. What is the "friendship" to which Talbot refers in her first sentence? Which word, later in the paragraph, tells you for sure?
2. By what word in the first sentence of paragraph 2 does Talbot link this paragraph to the one before it?
3. How effective do you find the ALLUSION to Shakespeare in paragraph 3?

4. "Harvest" (par. 5) is a METAPHOR. What is being compared to what? How about "friendship" (par. 1)? Is this a literal or a metaphoric comparison? Please explain.

Comparing

1. What aspects of the potato does Talbot not cover that Diane Ackerman ("Anosmia," Chapter 5) might dwell on if she were writing about potatoes?
2. How and why might Johnson C. Montgomery ("The Island of Plenty," Chapter 9) disagree with what Mary Talbot says about America's bountiful "harvest" (par. 5) from the potato trade?

Discussion and Writing Topics

1. Talbot does not say that the conquistadors "discovered" the potato. Should she have? Why or why not?
2. How does the history of the potato, as recounted by Talbot, illustrate the dangers of a one-crop economy?
3. What other crops or products can you think of that may be said to have "shaped the world"? Tell the history of one of them.

Jared Diamond

WHO KILLED EASTER ISLAND?

Jared Diamond is a professor of physiology in the School of Medicine at the University of California, Los Angeles, and is a MacArthur Fellows. His research focuses on biological membranes, ecology, and evolutionary biology, especially of bird faunas of New Guinea and other southwest Pacific islands. He is the author of over three hundred articles and books and a contributing editor of *Discover Magazine,* where "Who Killed Easter Island?" (editor's title) first appeared.

Among vanished civilizations, the former Polynesian society on 1
Easter Island remains unsurpassed in mystery and isolation.

The mystery stems especially from the island's gigantic stone stat- 2
ues and its impoverished landscape.

David Steadman, a paleontologist, has been working with a num- 3
ber of other researchers who are carrying out the first systematic excavations on Easter intended to identify the animals and plants that once lived there.

Their work is contributing to a new interpretation of the island's 4
history that makes it a tale not only of wonder but of warning as well.

Easter Island, with an area of only sixty-four square miles, is the 5
world's most isolated scrap of habitable land.

It lies in the Pacific Ocean more than 2,000 miles west of the 6
nearest continent (South America), 1,400 miles from even the nearest habitable island (Pitcairn).

Its subtropical location helps give it a rather mild climate, while 7
its volcanic origins make its soil fertile. In theory, this combination of blessings should have made Easter a miniature paradise.

The island derives its name from its "discovery" by the Dutch 8
explorer Jacob Roggeveen, on Easter (April 5) in 1722.

Roggeveen's first impression was not of a paradise but of a waste- 9
land: "We originally, from a further distance, have considered the said Easter Island as sandy. The reason for that is this, that we counted as sand the withered grass, hay or other scorched and burnt vegetation, because its wasted appearance could give no other impression than of a singular poverty and barrenness."

Roggeveen wrote that the Easter Islanders who greeted his ships 10
did so by swimming or paddling leaky canoes that were "bad and frail."

The canoes, only ten feet long, held at most two people, and only 11
three or four canoes were observed on the entire island.

With such flimsy craft, these people could never have colonized 12
Easter from even the nearest island, nor could they have traveled far offshore to fish. The islanders Roggeveen met were totally isolated, unaware that other people existed.

Easter Island's most famous feature is its huge stone statues, more 13
than 200 of which once stood on massive stone platforms lining the coast.

At least 700 more, in all stages of completion, were abandoned in 14
quarries or on ancient roads between the quarries and the coast.

Most of the erected statues were carved in a single quarry and 15
then somehow transported as far as six miles—despite heights as great as thirty-three feet and weights up to eighty-two tons. The abandoned statues, meanwhile, were as much as sixty-five feet tall and weighed up to 270 tons.

The stone platforms were equally gigantic: up to 500 feet long 16
and ten feet tall, with facing slabs weighing up to ten tons.

How did these people transport the giant statues for miles, even 17
before erecting them?

To deepen the mystery, the statues were still standing in 1770, 18
but by 1864 all had been pulled down by the islanders themselves.

Why then did they carve them in the first place? And why did 19
they stop?

Most importantly, what happened to those settlers? 20

The fanciful theories of the past must give way to evidence gath- 21
ered by hardworking practitioners in three fields: archaeology, pollen analysis and paleontology.

The earliest radiocarbon dates associated with human activities on 22
Easter Island are around 400 to 700, in reasonable agreement with the approximate settlement date of 400 estimated by linguists.

The period of statue construction peaked around 1200 to 1500, with few if any statues erected thereafter. 23

Densities of archaeological sites suggest a large population—an estimate of 7,000 people is widely quoted by archaeologists, but other estimates range up to 20,000. 24

Archaeologists also have enlisted surviving islanders in experiments aimed at figuring out how the statues might have been carved and erected. 25

Twenty people, using only stone chisels, could have carved even the largest completed statue within a year. 26

Given enough timber and fiber for making ropes, teams of at most a few hundred people could have loaded the statues onto wooden sleds, dragged them over lubricated wooden tracks or rollers and used logs as levers to maneuver them into a standing position. 27

Rope could have been made from the fiber of a small native tree, related to the linden, called the hauhau. 28

However, that tree is now extremely scarce on Easter, and hauling one statue would have required hundreds of yards of rope. Did Easter's now barren landscape once support the necessary trees? 29

That question can be answered by the technique of pollen analysis, which involves boring out a column of sediment from a swamp or pond. The absolute age of each layer of sediment can be dated by radiocarbon methods. 30

Then begins the hard work: examining tens of thousands of pollen grains under a microscope, counting them and identifying the plant species that produced each one. 31

Scientists John Flenley, now at Massey University in New Zealand, and Sarah King of the University of Hull in England performed the analysis and were rewarded by the striking new picture that emerged of Easter's prehistoric landscape. 32

For at least 30,000 years before human arrival and during the early years of Polynesian settlement, Easter was a subtropical forest. Woody bushes towered over shrubs, herbs, ferns and grasses. 33

What did the first settlers of Easter Island eat when they were not glutting themselves on the local equivalent of maple syrup? 34

Recent excavations by David Steadman, of the New York State Museum at Albany, have yielded a picture of Easter's original animal world. 35

Less than a quarter of the bones in Easter Island's early garbage 36 heaps (from the period 900 to 1300) belonged to fish; instead, nearly one-third of all bones came from porpoises.

On Easter, porpoises would have been the largest animal avail- 37
able. The porpoise species identified at Easter—the common dolphin—weighs up to 165 pounds. It generally lives out at sea, so it could not have been hunted by line fishing or spear fishing from shore.

Instead, it must have been harpooned far offshore, in big seawor- 38
thy canoes built from the extinct palm tree.

In addition to porpoise meat, Steadman found the early Polyne- 39
sian settlers were feasting on sea birds and land birds.

Bird stew would have been seasoned with meat from large num- 40
bers of rats, which the Polynesian colonists inadvertently brought with them.

Porpoises, seabirds, land birds and rats did not complete the list 41
of meat sources formerly available on Easter. A few bones hint at the possibility of breeding seal colonies as well.

All these delicacies were cooked in ovens fired by wood from the 42
island's forests.

Such evidence lets us imagine the island onto which Easter's first 43
Polynesian colonists stepped ashore some 1,600 years ago, after a long canoe voyage from eastern Polynesia. They found themselves in a pristine paradise.

What then happened to it? 44

The pollen grains and the bones yield a grim answer. Pollen 45
records show that destruction of Easter's forests was well under way by the year 800, just a few centuries after the start of human settlement.

Then charcoal from wood fires came to fill the sediment cores, 46
while pollen of palms and other trees and woody shrubs decreased or disappeared, and pollen of the grasses that replaced the forest became more abundant.

The fifteenth century marked the end not only for Easter's palm 47
but for the forest itself. Its doom had been approaching as people cleared land to plant gardens; as they felled trees to build canoes, to transport and erect statues, and to burn; as rats devoured seeds; and probably as the native birds died out that had pollinated the trees' flowers and dispersed their fruit.

The overall picture is among the most extreme examples of forest 48
destruction anywhere in the world.

The destruction of the island's animals was as extreme as that 49
of the forest: Without exception, every species of native land bird became extinct.

Even shellfish were over-exploited. Porpoise bones disappeared 50
abruptly from garbage heaps around 1500. No one could harpoon porpoises anymore, since the trees used for constructing the big sea-going canoes no longer existed.

The colonies of more than half of the seabird species breeding on 51
Easter or on its offshore islets were wiped out.

In place of these meat supplies, the Easter Islanders intensified 52
their production of chickens.

They also turned to the largest remaining meat source available: 53
humans, whose bones became common in late Easter Island garbage heaps. Oral traditions of the islanders are rife with cannibalism.

Intensified chicken production and cannibalism replaced only 54
part of all those lost foods. Preserved statuettes with sunken cheeks and visible ribs suggest that people were starving.

By around 1700, the population began to crash toward between 55
one-quarter and one-tenth of its former number. People took to living in caves for protection against their enemies.

By 1864 the last statue had been thrown down and desecrated. 56

By now the meaning of Easter Island for us should be chillingly 57
obvious. Easter Island is Earth writ small.

Today, again, a rising population confronts shrinking resources. 58
We too have no emigration valve, because all human societies are linked by international transport, and we can no more escape into space than the Easter Islanders could flee into the ocean.

If we continue to follow our present course, we shall have 59
exhausted the world's major fisheries, tropical rain forests, fossil fuels and much of our soil by the time my sons reach my current age.

Every day newspapers report details of famished countries where 60
soldiers have appropriated the wealth or where central government is yielding to local gangs of thugs.

With the risk of nuclear war receding, the threat of our ending 61
with a bang no longer has a chance of galvanizing us to halt our course. Our risk now is of winding down, slowly, in a whimper.

The Easter Islanders had no books and no histories of other 62 doomed societies. Unlike the Easter Islanders, we have histories of the past—information that can save us.

My main hope for my sons' generation is that we may now choose to learn from the fates of societies such as Easter's. 63

QUESTIONS

Understanding

1. Who "discovered" and named Easter Island? What was life on the island like then?
2. What is unique about the geographical location of Easter Island?
3. How did the inhabitants of Easter Island transport and erect the giant stone heads that once dotted their shore, some of them coming from as far as six miles away?
4. What did the Easter Islanders eat at the height of their culture? When did that culture decline? What did they eat then?
5. What three modern fields of study, according to Jared Diamond, have most helped investigators to piece together the lost history of Easter Island and its people? What did each field contribute to the investigation?

Strategies and Structure

1. What was the primary cause of the decline of Easter Island? What were the secondary causes? Where does Diamond set forth the various causes, and what proportion of his essay, approximately, does he devote to each?
2. As an essay in cause and effect, does "Who Killed Easter Island?" start mostly with causes or mostly with effects? Where (in what single-sentence paragraph) does the author shift emphasis from one to the other? Why do you think he chose this sequence, and not the other way around, for delving into the mysteries of a lost culture?
3. How (and how early) in his essay does Diamond alert (or warn) the reader that this may be a cautionary tale as well as one of scientific exploration and discovery?

4. "Who Killed Easter Island?" is an essay in cause and effect, but it also advances an argument that has implications far beyond the bounds of a tiny, isolated island in the Pacific Ocean. Where does the author shift from mostly explaining to mostly persuading? To what conclusion does this line of reasoning lead? Where is that conclusion stated most directly?
5. In which single sentence does Diamond sum up the major premise upon which his greater logical argument depends? How persuasively do you think he makes his case from there?
6. This essay was originally printed in newspaper columns, where the many short paragraphs of "Who Killed Easter Island?" perhaps didn't seem so short. How do they strike your eye in book form? If you were the author and were asked to reparagraph this essay for book publication, where would you draw the paragraphs?
7. The author of "Who Killed Easter Island?" never speculates about why the islanders carved their mammoth stone statues, or why the carving ceased, or why existing statues were pulled down. Does leaving these mysteries in place increase or decrease his credibility in your opinion? Please explain.
8. For 58 paragraphs, Jared Diamond maintains a degree of "scientific" distance from his subject; then, in paragraph 59, he drops into the first-person singular ("my sons"). Do you think such an abrupt change in grammatical person is warranted, and why do you think Diamond made it at this particular point in his essay?

Words and Figures of Speech

1. In "The Waste Land" (1922) and other poems, T. S. Eliot depicted the whole of modern culture as a physical and spiritual desert. Where can you detect echoes of Eliot's poetry in Diamond's prose? How appropriate do you find these ALLUSIONS, and why do you think Diamond invokes a poet here instead of another scientist?
2. The root meanings of *archaeology* and *paleontology* (par. 21) are the same. What are they, and how do the modern meanings of these terms differ from each other?
3. Why do you think Diamond casts his verbs in the subjunctive mood in instances such as the following: "might have been carved" (par. 25), "could have loaded" (par. 27), "could have been made" (28)?
4. What are the implications of "desecrated" (par. 56) as opposed, say to "destroyed" or "demolished"?

5. Point out the alliteration in paragraph 4; why do you think Diamond uses a "poetic" device here, and why does he refer to the revisionist history of Easter Island as a "tale"?
6. Why (and how accurately) do you think Diamond poses the question of human survival as a "choice" (par. 63)?
7. "Easter Island," says Diamond (par. 57), "is Earth writ small": why the archaic, almost biblical language?
8. How apt do you find Diamond's ANALOGY between the ocean and outer space (par. 58)?

Comparing

1. Compare and contrast "Who Killed Easter Island?" with Alan M. Dershowitz's "Shouting 'Fire!' " (Chapter 7) as arguments by analogy. In which essay is the analogy "closer" (and, therefore, more logical) in your opinion?
2. How does Diamond's example of rope, made from the hauhau tree of Easter Island in better days, resemble Mary Talbot's example of the potato (preceding essay in this chapter)?
3. Compare Diamond's application of the methods and findings of paleontology with Isaac Asimov's in "What Do You Call a Platypus?" (Chapter 2).

Discussion and Writing Topics

1. Why didn't the Eastern Islanders simply emigrate when their resources dwindled? Is Diamond right to say that the ecology and culture of the entire globe are similarly threatened now? Why or why not?
2. According to Diamond, what resource do we have that the Easter Islanders didn't? As a "main hope" (par. 63) for human survival, how much confidence does it inspire in you? Why?
3. The findings of good science can always be corroborated by independent research. With several others in your class, form a research party and (assuming you can't make it to the South Pacific) assign each member to look into a different aspect of Easter Island's history in the library or on the Internet. You may want to consult some of the authorities Diamond mentions, but there are many others (and other fields of study, such as linguistics) that he does not cite. What "tale" does your joint research tell? Does it corroborate or contradict Diamond's?

James Seilsopour

I Forgot the Words to the National Anthem

Born in California in 1962, James Seilsopour is an American citizen whose father is Iranian. After spending most of his early life in Teheran, he returned to the United States with his family during the Iranian revolution of 1979. Seilsopour entered high school in Norco, California, the scene of the political discrimination he describes in "I Forgot the Words to the National Anthem." He graduated in 1982 and entered Riverside City College, where his English teacher, W. F. Hunt, urged him to submit this essay to a national competition in student writing. It was selected for publication in *Student Writers at Work* (1984). The author discusses the task of composing and revising his prizewinning essay at the end of this chapter.

The bumper sticker read, "Piss on Iran." 1

To me, a fourteen-year-old living in Teheran, the Iranian revolution was nothing more than an inconvenience. Although the riots were just around the corner, although the tanks lined the streets, although a stray bullet went through my sister's bedroom window, I was upset because I could not ride at the Royal Stable as often as I used to. In the summer of 1979 my family—father, mother, brothers, sister, aunt, and two cousins—were forced into exile. We came to Norco, California. 2

In Iran, I was an American citizen and considered myself an American, even though my father was Iranian. I loved baseball and apple pie and knew the words to the "Star-Spangled Banner." That summer before high school, I was like any other kid my age; I listened to rock 'n' roll, liked fast cars, and thought Farrah Fawcett was a fox. Excited about going to high school, I was looking forward to football games and school dances. But I learned that it was not meant 3 to be. I was not like other kids, and it was a long, painful road I traveled as I found this out.

The American embassy in Iran was seized the fall I started high 4
school. I did not realize my life would be affected until I read that bumper sticker in the high school parking lot which read, "Piss on Iran." At that moment I knew there would be no football games or school dances. For me, Norco High consisted of the goat ropers, the dopers, the jocks, the brains, and one quiet Iranian.

I was sitting in my photography class after the hostages were 5
taken. The photography teacher was fond of showing travel films. On this particular day, he decided to show a film about Iran, knowing full well that my father was Iranian and that I grew up in Iran. During the movie, this teacher encouraged the students to make comments. Around the room, I could hear "Drop the bomb" and "Deport the mothers." Those words hurt. I felt dirty, guilty. However, I managed to laugh and assure the students I realized they were just joking. I went home that afternoon and cried. I have long since forgiven those students, but I have not and can never forgive that teacher. Paranoia set in. From then on, every whisper was about me: "You see that lousy son of a bitch? He's Iranian." When I was not looking, I could feel their pointing fingers in my back like arrows. Because I was absent one day, the next day I brought a note to the attendance office. The secretary read the note, then looked at me. "So you're Jim Seilsopour?" I couldn't answer. As I walked away, I thought I heard her whisper to her coworker, "You see that lousy son of a bitch? He's Iranian." I missed thirty-five days of school that year.

My problems were small compared to those of my parents. In 6
Teheran, my mother had been a lady of society. We had a palatial house and a maid. Belonging to the women's club, she collected clothes for the poor and arranged Christmas parties for the young American kids. She and my father dined with high government officials. But back in the States, when my father could not find a job, she had to work at a fast-food restaurant. She was the proverbial pillar of strength. My mother worked seventy hours a week for two years. I never heard her complain. I could see the toll the entire situation was taking on her. One day my mother and I went grocery shopping at Stater Brothers Market. After an hour of carefully picking our food, we proceeded to the cashier. The cashier was friendly and began a conversation with my mother. They spoke briefly of the weather as my mother wrote the check. The cashier looked at the

check and casually asked, "What kind of name is that?" My mother said, "Italian." We exchanged glances for just a second. I could see the pain in her eyes. She offered no excuses; I asked for none.

Because of my father's birthplace, he was unable to obtain a job. 7
A naturalized American citizen with a master's degree in aircraft maintenance engineering from the Northrop Institute of Technology, he had never been out of work in his life. My father had worked for Bell Helicopter International, Flying Tigers, and McDonnell Douglas. Suddenly, a man who literally was at the top of his field was unemployable. There is one incident that haunts me even today. My mother had gone to work, and all the kids had gone to school except me. I was in the bathroom washing my face. The door was open, and I could see my father's reflection in the mirror. For no particular reason I watched him. He was glancing at a newspaper. He carefully folded the paper and set it aside. For several long moments he stared blankly into space. With a resigned sigh, he got up, went into the kitchen, and began doing the dishes. On that day, I know I watched a part of my father die.

My father did get a job. However, he was forced to leave the 8
country. He is a quality control inspector for Saudi Arabian Airlines in Jeddah, Saudi Arabia. My mother works only forty hours a week now. My family has survived, financially and emotionally. I am not bitter, but the memories are. I have not recovered totally; I can never do that.

And no, I have never been to a high school football game or 9
dance. The strike really turned me off to baseball. I have been on a diet for the last year, so I don't eat apple pie much anymore. And I have forgotten the words to the national anthem.

QUESTIONS

Understanding

1. How did James Seilsopour expect to be treated when he moved with his family to California during the Iranian revolution of 1979? What incident first made him realize how wrong he had been?

2. Ostracized by his teachers and classmates at Norco High, the author sums up in a single word in paragraph 5 the immediate effect of their discrimination upon him. What is it?
3. Seilsopour has forgiven the students who taunted him in high school. With whom does he still refuse, however, to let bygones be bygones? Why?
4. Seilsopour's experience at an American high school has not left him bitter, he says; but what lasting effect *has* it had?
5. His own mistreatment is only one reason for the author's regret in "I Forgot the Words to the National Anthem." To what other causes in the past does he also assign his present painful memories?

Strategies and Structure

1. James Seilsopour tells in paragraph 5 how life in America affected *him*. By what two specific incidents does he convey the cumulative effect of their American experience upon each of his parents?
2. The author classifies students at Norco High into "the goat ropers, the dopers, the jocks, the brains, and one quiet Iranian" (par. 4). What purpose does this brief CLASSIFICATION serve in an essay otherwise devoted to cause and effect?
3. Any political statement about the nation's treatment of immigrants remains implicit in Seilsopour's essay. Should he have made it more explicit, as in the persuasive arguments of Chapters 9 and 10? Or do you find his letting the effects of discrimination speak for themselves to be just as persuasive in this case? Explain your answer.
4. Seilsopour can say "I felt dirty, guilty" because he is revealing his own feelings in paragraph 5. How does he elsewhere tell us about his parents' feelings without violating the limited, first-person POINT OF VIEW he has already set up?
5. In paragraph 2 Seilsopour stacks up three clauses beginning with "although." Why? Whose insensitivity to danger signs is he imitating?
6. Most of the time, Seilsopour is writing about the temporary effects of their American experience upon himself and his family. What seems to be his intention in the last two paragraphs of the essay?

Words and Figures of Speech

1. Is the profanity in Seilsopour's essay justified? Why or why not? To whom is he always careful to attribute it?

2. Do you find Seilsopour's use of the CLICHÉ "pillar of strength" (par. 6) to describe his mother's stoicism to be more or less effective than his references to baseball and apple pie? Explain your answer.
3. Why would you suppose Seilsopour chose the national anthem to "forget" rather than some other song?
4. What is surprising about the use of the word *inconvenience* in paragraph 2? Of *exile* in the same paragraph?

Comparing

1. Both James Seilsopour and Eric A. Watts ("The Color of Success," Chapter 2) write as nonconformists; compare and contrast the causes of their dissent.
2. Compare and contrast "I Forgot the Words to the National Anthem" with Mary Mebane's "The Back of the Bus" (Chapter 1) as personal accounts of discrimination.

Discussion and Writing Topics

1. Judging from the specific acts he mentions, how seriously, in your view, were James Seilsopour and his family discriminated against? Is his essay, therefore, reasonable in its criticism, too forgiving, or unfairly condemning?
2. Have you ever been the victim of political, racial, sexual, or any other form of discrimination? Write a personal account of the experiences that emphasizes the *effects* it had upon you and your family.
3. Have you ever committed or condoned an act of discrimination? Write about the occasion in a personal essay that makes the causes of your behavior understandable without justifying or approving it.

Henry Louis Gates, Jr.

A Giant Step

Born in Keyser, West Virginia, Henry Louis Gates, Jr. was educated at Yale *(summa cum laude)* and Clare College, Cambridge (Ph.D., 1979). When he wrote "A Giant Step" for the *New York Times Magazine,* he was teaching at Duke University. Now W. E. B. Du Bois Professor of the Humanities at Harvard, he is the author or editor of many works on black literature and in literary criticism, including *Figures in Black* (1987), *The Signifying Monkey: Towards a Theory of Afro-American Literary Criticism* (1988), and *The Norton Anthology of African American Literature* (1997). *The Future of the Race* (with Cornel West) appeared in 1996.

What's this?" the hospital janitor said to me as he stumbled over my right shoe. 1

"My shoes," I said. 2

"That's not a shoe, brother," he replied, holding it to the light. "That's a brick." 3

It *did* look like a brick, sort of. 4

"Well, we can throw these in the trash now," he said. 5

"I guess so." 6

We had been together since 1975, those shoes and I. They were orthopedic shoes built around molds of my feet, and they had a 2¼-inch lift. I had mixed feelings about them. On the one hand, they had given me a more or less even gait for the first time in 10 years. On the other hand, they had marked me as a "handicapped person," complete with cane and special license plates. I went through a pair a year, but it was always the same shoe, black, wide, weighing about four pounds. 7

It all started 26 years ago in Piedmont, W. Va., a backwoods town of 2,000 people. While playing a game of touch football at a Method- 8 ist summer camp, I incurred a hairline fracture. Thing is, I didn't know it yet. I was 14 and had finally lost the chubbiness of my youth. I was just learning tennis and beginning to date, and who knew where that might lead?

Not too far. A few weeks later, I was returning to school from lunch when, out of the blue, the ball-and-socket joint of my hip sheared apart. It was instant agony, and from that time on nothing in my life would be quite the same. 9

I propped myself against the brick wall of the schoolhouse, where the school delinquent found me. He was black as slate, twice my size, mean as the day was long and beat up kids just because he could. But the look on my face told him something was seriously wrong, and—bless him—he stayed by my side for the two hours it took to get me into a taxi. 10

"It's a torn ligament in your knee," the surgeon said. (One of the signs of what I had—a "slipped epithysis"—is intense knee pain, I later learned.) So he scheduled me for a walking cast. 11

I was wheeled into surgery and placed on the operating table. As the doctor wrapped my leg with wet plaster strips, he asked about my schoolwork. 12

"Boy," he said, "I understand you want to be a doctor." 13

I said, "Yessir." Where I came from, you always said "sir" to white people, unless you were trying to make a statement. 14

Had I taken a lot of science courses? 15

"Yessir. I enjoy science." 16

"Are you good at it?" 17

"Yessir, I believe so." 18

"Tell me, who was the father of sterilization?" 19

"Oh, that's easy, Joseph Lister." 20

Then he asked who discovered penicillin. 21

Alexander Fleming. 22

And what about DNA? 23

Watson and Crick. 24

The interview went on like this, and I thought my answers might get me a pat on the head. Actually, they just confirmed the diagnosis he'd come to. 25

He stood me on my feet and insisted that I walked. When I tried, the joint ripped apart and I fell on the floor. It hurt like nothing I'd ever known. 26

The doctor shook his head. "Pauline," he said to my mother, his 27 voice kindly but amused, "there's not a thing wrong with that child. The problem's psychosomatic. Your son's an overachiever."

Back then, the term didn't mean what it usually means today. In Appalachia, in 1964, "overachiever" designated a sort of pathology: the overstraining of your natural capacity. A colored kid who thought he could be a doctor—just for instance—was headed for a breakdown. 28

What made the pain abate was my mother's reaction. I'd never, ever heard her talk back to a white person before. And doctors, well, their words were scripture. 29

Not this time. Pauline Gates stared at him for a moment. "Get his clothes, pack his bags—we're going to the University Medical Center," which was 60 miles away. 30

Not great news: the one thing I knew was that they only moved you to the University Medical Center when you were going to die. I had three operations that year. I gave my tennis racket to the delinquent, which he probably used to club little kids with. So I wasn't going to make it to Wimbledon. But at least I wasn't going to die, though sometimes I wanted to. Following the last operation, which fitted me for a metal ball, I was confined to bed, flat on my back, immobilized by a complex system of weights and pulleys. It was six weeks of bondage—and bedpans. I spent my time reading James Baldwin, learning to play chess and quarreling daily with my mother, who had rented a small room—which we could ill afford—in a motel just down the hill from the hospital. 31

I think we both came to realize that our quarreling was a sort of ritual. We'd argue about everything—what time of day it was—but the arguments kept me from thinking about that traction system. 32

I limped through the next decade—through Yale and Cambridge . . . as far away from Piedmont as I could get. But I couldn't escape the pain, which increased as the joint calcified and began to fuse over the next 15 years. My leg grew shorter, as the muscles atrophied and the ball of the ball-and-socket joint migrated into my pelvis. Aspirin, then Motrin, heating pads and massages, became my traveling companions. 33

Most frustrating was passing store windows full of fine shoes. I used to dream about walking into one of those stores and buying a pair of shoes. "Give me two pairs, one black, one cordovan," I'd say. "Wrap 'em up." No six-week wait as with the orthotics in which I was confined. These would be real shoes. Not bricks. 34

In the meantime, hip-joint technology progressed dramatically. 35

But no surgeon wanted to operate on me until I was significantly older, or until the pain was so great that surgery was unavoidable. After all, a new hip would last only for 15 years, and I'd already lost too much bone. It wasn't a procedure they were sure they'd be able to repeat.

This year, my 40th, the doctors decided the time had come. 36

I increased my life insurance and made the plunge. 37

The nights before my operations are the longest nights of my life—but never long enough. Jerking awake, grabbing for my watch, I experience a delicious sense of relief as I discover that only a minute or two have passed. You never want 6 A.M. to come. 38

And then the door swings open. "Good morning, Mr. Gates," the nurse says. "It's time." 39

The last thing I remember, just vaguely, was wondering where amnesiac minutes go in one's consciousness, wondering if I experienced the pain and sounds, then forgot them, or if these were somehow blocked out, dividing the self on the operating table from the conscious self in the recovery room. I didn't like that idea very much. I was about to protest when I blinked. 40

"It's over, Mr. Gates," says a voice. But how could it be over? I had merely *blinked*. "You talked to us several times," the surgeon had told me, and that was the scariest part of all. 41

Twenty-four hours later, they get me out of bed and help me into a "walker." As they stand me on my feet, my wife bursts into tears. "Your foot is touching the ground!" I am afraid to look, but it is true: the surgeon has lengthened my leg with that gleaming titanium and chrome-cobalt alloy ball-and-socket-joint. 42

"You'll need new shoes," the surgeon says. "Get a pair of Dock-Sides; they have a secure grip. You'll need a 3/4-inch lift in the heel, which can be as discreet as you want." 43

I can't help thinking about those window displays of shoes, those elegant shoes that, suddenly, I will be able to wear. Dock-Sides and sneakers, boots and loafers, sandals and brogues. I feel, at last, a furtive sympathy for Imelda Marcos, the queen of soles. 44

The next day, I walk over to the trash can, and take a long look at the brick. I don't want to seem ungracious or unappreciative. We have walked long miles together. I feel disloyal, as if I am abandoning an old friend. I take a second look. 45

Maybe I'll have them bronzed. 46

QUESTIONS

Understanding

1. Why did the surgeons want to put off Gates's hip surgery as long as possible?
2. How, according to Gates, has the meaning of the term "overachiever" (par. 27) changed since 1964, at least as it was defined where he grew up?
3. What is a "psychosomatic" problem (par. 27)?
4. What is a "slipped epithysis" (par. 11)? Why does the local doctor diagnose Gates's as a "torn ligament" in his knee?

Strategies and Structure

1. Why does Gates begin with a conversation between himself and the hospital janitor? Why not, say, one with his wife?
2. How much time elapses between when the "bricks" go in the trash can (par. 5) and when Gates thinks of having them bronzed (par. 46)? How does Gates take us outside this time period in paragraph 7 and following?
3. How does Gates *prevent* his essay from turning into a speech about breeding success through adversity?
4. When he wrote this essay, Gates was a chaired professor of English. How does the bedridden boy (par. 31) anticipate the distinguished academic?
5. Gates glances at the boy's future in paragraph 33, when he mentions Yale and Cambridge. How does he play down the "overachiever's" accomplishments even here? Suppose he had played them up?
6. As Gates presents her, what is Pauline Gates's part in setting her son's feet on the pathway to becoming the adult who writes about her? What role does the first doctor play (par. 27)?
7. In most of paragraph 9, Gates is telling about what happened to him as a teenager. In which sentence, however, does he give us the direct cue to read such events as part of a causal sequence?
8. Is Gates talking about direct or indirect causes here? Please explain.

Words and Figures of Speech

1. How might Gates's tennis racket (par. 31) be said to serve as an emblem of his early days? What about the METAPHORIC value of his orthopedic shoes?
2. What kind of shoes, besides baby shoes, do people sometimes bronze?
3. Besides the physical ones, what other big step(s) does Gates's title imply?
4. Surgeons these days often use the term "procedure" (par. 35) in place of the more familiar "operation." Why?
5. What does *overachiever* mean in your lexicon? How might you argue that the word is a contradiction in terms?

Comparing

1. As an essay about success, how does "A Giant Step" compare with Eric A. Watts's "The Color of Success" in Chapter 2?
2. How and to what extent might Gates's essay be said to resemble Lee K. Abbott's personal narrative, "The True Story of Why I Do What I Do" (Chapter 1)? Please explain.

Discussion and Writing Topics

1. How resentful toward the doctor who called him an overachiever does Gates sound here? Should he have presented himself as any more or less indignant? Please explain.
2. "Where I came from," says Gates, "you always said 'sir' to white people, unless you were trying to make a statement" (par.14). To what extent, if any, do you think "A Giant Step" makes an ethnic or racial "statement"? How about a "personal" one?

James Seilsopour

James Seilsopour's "I Forgot the Words to the National Anthem" is an example of dealing with pain by writing about it. When the author returned with his family to the United States during the Iranian revolution of 1979, he expected to be what he had been in Teheran: an American citizen who "loved baseball and apple pie and knew the words to the 'Star-Spangled Banner.' " He was "excited" about entering high school and "looking forward to football games and school dances." Unprepared for the anti-Iranian sentiment in this country, Seilsopour was stunned by the treatment he received at Norco High, California. 1

After Seilsopour entered Riverside City College in 1982, he felt the need "to talk about that part of my life." He planned to deal with it by writing poetry but turned to the essay form to meet a course assignment. ("I had fallen behind in my English class," he explains, "and needed a paper to turn in.") Seilsopour's teacher encouraged him to write as if for publication and guided him through several revisions. Revising the essay was almost as "painful" as the experience it describes—"like cutting yourself with a hot blade." 2

The author survived and his essay improved with such excisions as the one he made at the end of paragraph 7. In his first draft, Seilsopour ended the paragraph with the line, "To this day we have never spoken of that incident." The sentence specifies no particular 3 feeling, but it makes the mistake Annie Dillard identifies in the introduction to this book. It stops evoking and starts to *describe* emotion.

Another revision in Seilsopour's essay is harder to justify. Seilso- 4
pour's teacher recommended the finished essay for a prize in a national competition of student writers. It was selected and eventually published, along with the other prize essays. As he submitted it, Seilsopour's final, typed version located what is now the first paragraph in a different place. In the typescript, the line about the bumper sticker is centered a few lines above the rest, as a sort of epigraph. The author apparently intended for the body of his essay to begin with what is now paragraph 2.

Epigraphs are fine for books but out of place in most short pieces; 5
so when Seilsopour's typed version was prepared for the printer, the raised line was dropped down to become the opening paragraph. This "solution," however, raises a problem of its own, for Seilsopour encountered the bumper sticker after he moved to America, yet his essay proper begins with his experience in Iran. Since the obscene bumper sticker is mentioned again in paragraph 4, would it not have been better to omit the first reference altogether? The blemish hardly disfigures a fine essay, but you might consider how to fix it.

Writing to cope with painful experience can be good therapy. As 6
the considered revisions in Seilsopour's essay attest, however, good writing holds the writer's experience at sufficient distance to consider the reader's needs, too. The real problem he had to work out during the writing process, says Seilsopour, "was toning the paper down from an angry commentary to a straightforward personal essay." When it was chosen to be published, Seilsopour was happy that the story of his personal trial "will finally get told." His main task as a writer, however, was not to rail about the pain his experience caused him but to make the reader feel its effects: "When people read my essay, I want them to imagine themselves in my place for just a moment—then never think about it again."

Writing Topics for Chapter Four
Essays That Analyze Cause and Effect

Write an essay analyzing the probable causes or effects (or both) of one of the following:

1. Global warming
2. Deforestation
3. Urban blight
4. Drug or alcohol abuse
5. Heart disease, sickle cell anemia, or AIDS
6. Divorce within the first year or two of marriage
7. Loss of religious faith
8. Loss of self-esteem
9. Racial discrimination or ethnic jokes and slurs
10. Success in college
11. Student cheating
12. Sibling rivalry
13. The Civil War or other historical event
14. Invention of the assembly-line system
15. Dropping out of high school or college
16. A sudden shift in status: from high school senior (or working mother) to college freshman, for example

17 - add something

Five

ESSAYS THAT DEFINE

To make a basic DEFINITION,[1] put whatever you are defining into a class and then list the characteristics that distinguish it from all other members of that class. The Greek philosopher Plato, for example, defined man by putting him in the class "biped." Then Plato thought of a quality that sets man off from other two-legged creatures. "Man," he said, "is a *featherless* biped."

When the rival philosopher Diogenes heard this definition, he brought a plucked chicken into the lecture room and observed, "Here is Plato's man." Plato responded by adding that man is a featherless biped "having broad nails." The general principle that Plato was obeying holds for the basic definitions you will write. If at first you choose qualities that do not sufficiently distinguish your subject from others in the same class, refine those attributes until they do.

You can tell when a basic definition is essentially complete by testing whether it is true if reversed. "Man is a biped" proves to be an incomplete definition when we turn it around, for it is not true that "all bipeds are men." Likewise, we know that the final version of Plato's definition is sound because it is truly reversible. All featherless bipeds having broad nails (instead of claws) are indeed humans.

When it can be reversed, a basic definition is complete enough to

[1] Terms printed in small capitals are defined in the Glossary.

be accurate; but it still may be scanty or undeveloped. One way of developing a basic definition is by listing qualities or attributes of a thing beyond those needed merely to identify it. Food expert Raymond Sokolov defines the Florida tomato, for example, as a vegetable that is "mass-produced, artificially ripened, mechanically picked, long-hauled" (all qualities or attributes)."It has no taste and it won't go splat" (more qualities, though negative ones). Sokolov advises that we grow our own tomatoes if we want them to be "antique-style, squishable, blotchy, tart, and sometimes green-dappled."

Another common strategy of basic definition is to define the whole by naming its parts. "Ketchup is long-haul tomatoes combined with sugar, vinegar, salt, onion powder, and 'natural' flavoring." Or you might define a word by tracing its origins: "The English *ketchup* (or *catsup*) comes from the Malay word kechap, derived in turn from the Chinese word meaning 'fish brine.' " This word history may seem to take us far from the tomatoes at the base of America's favorite sauce, but it suggests where ketchup originally got its salty taste. Such word histories (or ETYMOLOGIES) can be found in parentheses or brackets before many of the definitions in your dictionary.

Yet another way of developing a basic definition is to give synonyms for the word or concept being defined. A botanist might well tell us that the tomato is a plant used as a vegetable. But if pushed, he would add that the tomato is actually a "berry," or "fleshy fruit," akin to the "hesperidium" and the "pepo." His botanical definition would then proceed to explain what these closely related terms have in common, as well as the shades of difference among them. You can find synonyms for the word you are defining in any good desk dictionary or dictionary of synonyms. (The etymologies usually come at the beginning of a dictionary entry; the "synonymies," or lists of synonyms, at the end.)

The definitions we have discussed so far are short and limited to defining a basic word or phrase. When the strategy of an entire essay is to define something, the author produces what is called an extended definition. Extended definitions seek first and last to explain the nature or meaning of a thing, but they often use many of the other strategies of exposition. An extended definition of the detective story, for example, might divide it into types according to the kind of detective involved: the hard-boiled cop, the bumbling private eye, the clever priest. This would be an example of supporting a definition by CLASSIFICATION.

If we distinguished the detective story from the mystery story or the thriller, we might go on to define it by COMPARISON AND CONTRAST with similar forms. If we noted that Edgar Allan Poe invented the detective story and we gave the history of great detectives from Poe's Dupin to Sherlock Holmes to Columbo, we might draw upon NARRATIVE. Or if we speculated that the detective story came into being because Poe wanted to discover a walk of life in which the scientific mind blended with the poetic mind, we would be analyzing CAUSE AND EFFECT.

There is no set formula for writing an extended definition, but here are some questions to keep in mind when working one up: What is the essential nature or purpose of the thing you are defining? What are its qualities? How does it work? How is it different from others like it? Why do we need to know about it? In answering these questions, be as specific as you can. Vivid details make definitions interesting, and interest (after accuracy) is the best test of a good definition. Plato's definition of man surprises us into attention by reducing a lofty concept to the homely term "featherless." The poet Emily Dickinson does the same when she defines Hope as "the thing with feathers." It is the vivid specific detail that startles us here, as Woody Allen well knows when he reduces Dickinson's definition to absurdly specific terms: "The thing with feathers has turned out to be my nephew. I must take him to a specialist in Zurich."

Cindy Schneider

A Name Is Just a Name?

A nurse by profession, Cindy Schneider was a returning student at Kent State University when she wrote "A Name Is Just a Name?" which appears for the first time in print here. Schneider's essay is a personal narrative with a twist, but it is also about the nature of names and how they define us to other people.

My life has been guided by two philosophies, helping and caring for others, and judging people by their own actions—not taking the words of others. I always wanted to be a nurse and thought these philosophies complimented the profession. With this in mind, I was not prepared for the following incident. 1

In the early 1970s, I was working afternoon shift in the CCU. A gentleman in his early fifties had been admitted after having a heart attack. He had had more complications than the usual MI (myocardial infarction, or heart attack) patient. He was temporarily on a respirator and had been given more sedation than the usual patient. As expected, his family and the staff were very anxious about him. After hearing the report, I did the routine tasks of documenting the monitor patterns of each patient and preparing medications. At that time, all the patterns appeared stable. I hadn't worked in CCU very long, and the technical abilities of all the machinery still impressed me. On the regular floors, a nurse had to look at a patient to see what was wrong; in here, a machine told you what was happening to the patient on the inside too. The aide and I proceeded into the gentleman's room to change his position, check his vital signs, and straighten the linen. 2

All employees wore name tags that consisted of their title, first initial, last name, and position. Patients did not call staff by their first names. In fact, the staff did not address each other by their first names while on duty. 3

As we entered the room, I introduced myself and started to 4
explain what we were going to do. He looked only at my name tag. In a matter of seconds, the man's eyes opened very wide, his body stiffened, perspiration formed on his forehead, his breathing was harder, and his monitor showed an increase in his heart rate to the point of setting off the high-limit alarm at the desk. (Each monitor had a high and low limit set to alarm when that limit was reached.) The other nurse immediately came to help. Since the man was on the respirator and could not talk to us, we assumed that he must be experiencing pain. He watched me as I drew up some medication for pain. He was very restless, and it took all three of us to hold his arm while I gave the medication through the intravenous. It seemed to take a long time for him to return to his base rate on the monitor. I tried to touch his arm for reassurance, but he moved away. Finally, he appeared to be sleeping.

The man's pattern stayed stable through the family's visit. While 5
his wife was with him, he tried very hard to talk to her from around the respirator. At the desk, I told her about his condition, including the episode of pain.

When I came back to the unit after dinner, I discovered that the 6
man's physician was in the hospital for a meeting and had stopped in to check on his patients. The respirator had been removed. The patient was progressing favorably, breathing on his own, and his monitor was stable. He was again sleeping, and the evening became routine.

A few hours later, the aide and I again went into his room to rub 7
his back and help him get comfortable. I called his name; he opened his eyes, saw my name tag, and shouted forcefully, "Get out of my room!" I was as stunned as if I had been hit with a paralyzing gun. Patients in here usually didn't have the energy to shout like that. What did I do wrong? The aide stared at me, and the other nurse working came into the room to see what was happening. The patient was again showing signs of agitation, and his monitor pattern was changing. The nurse ordered me out of the room and attended to the patient, who didn't offer any conversation other than, "I don't want her near me again!" I was shaking, stunned, hurt, and confused. What did the nurse and aide think of me? Did the other patients hear? Would the head nurse ask me to leave the unit? My mind was jumping to all kinds of conclusions: being fired, being humiliated throughout the hospital, and even being sued by the

patient and family. But what did I do? While still stunned, the physician again stopped in the unit after his meeting to check on his patient. The other nurse took him aside to tell him what had happened. I was still glued to the same spot.

This physician was the head of the cardiac unit. He was a very fair and positive person. He knew everyone who worked in the unit; surely he would know that I would never do anything to hurt someone, and surely he would listen to my account of the events. He just looked seriously at me and went into the patient's room, pulling the sliding glass door shut behind him. Watching them talk, I felt like I was tied to a post awaiting the firing squad. I felt sick all over. 8

The conversation finally finished and the physician stood up, shook the patient's hand, and walked out of the room toward me. Even though it was only a few steps, it seemed as if it took an eternity for him to reach me. The eyes of the other staff members were on me; it seemed as though everything was in suspended animation. Finally, he reached me, put his arm around my shoulders, and said, "Your name tag. He spent some horrifying times in a concentration camp. 'Schneider' is just too German for him to handle now." 9

I felt physically drained. I wanted to run in there and explain to him that I would never hurt him, but I stayed away throughout his hospitalization. What must he have been thinking, seeing my name tag, unable to talk, watching me draw up medication, thinking that I was poisoning him. Instead of helping him, I was "killing" him. 10

Throughout my nursing career, I have had a few other patients who have witnessed those accounts of history. For these patients, I approach cautiously, name tag off, and introduce myself as "Cindy." 11

QUESTIONS

Understanding

1. Cindy Schneider writes that her life has been guided by "two philosophies" (par. 1). What are they? Why, then, was she especially "stunned" (par. 7) when the cardiac patient ordered her out of his hospital room?
2. How long had nurse Schneider worked in the Cardiac Care Unit when this central event of her NARRATIVE occurred? Why is the timing significant?

3. Why does Schneider force herself (par. 10) to accept the sick man's point of view, even though she felt wrongly accused by him?
4. Why does the author of "A Name Is Just a Name?" now introduce herself to some patients as just "Cindy"?

Strategies and Structure

1. Why do you think Cindy Schneider punctuates the title of her essay with a question mark?
2. Which sentence (or sentences) in paragraph 1 prepare readers to expect a narrative? Why does Schneider refer to "the *words* of others" (italics added) in that same introductory paragraph?
3. Why does Schneider pay so much attention (par. 3) to the form of her name tag and to the forms of address used by the staff and patients in her hospital? Where (and how) does the idea of a name as more than a tag come up again in her essay?
4. "I called his name," Schneider says of the distraught heart patient (par. 7); but she doesn't tell us what it is. Should she have? Why or why not?
5. What is the role of the physician in Schneider's narrative? Why doesn't he speak until paragraph 9, and then only a few brief words?
6. Besides telling a story, Cindy Schneider is also making a point about how names define us. What is it, exactly, and where does she extend her argument to words in general?
7. How and how well, in your opinion, does the central incident of Schneider's narrative illustrate what she has to say about the power of words over deeds or, rather, intentions?

Words and Figures of Speech

1. What is the IRONY of Schneider's observation that, in the impressive CCU, "a machine told you what was happening to the patient on the inside too" (par. 2)?
2. How would you fix the modifier problem in the following sentence: "While still stunned, the physician again stopped in the unit after his meeting to check on his patient" (par. 7)?
3. If you were Schneider's classmate and she asked you to comment on her essay, what would you say about the following phrases: "glued to

the same spot" (par. 7); "awaiting the firing squad" (par. 8); "took an eternity" (par. 9)?

4. Is "accounts" (par. 11) the word you would use here? What alternatives, if any, would you suggest? Why, given her keen perceptions about the shaping power of language, might the author of "A Name Is Just a Name?" equate historical events with *accounts* of those events?
5. What are the connotations of *witnessed* (par. 11)? What sort of "witness" does Cindy Schnieder prove herself to be in this essay? Please explain your answer.

Comparing

1. How do Cindy Schneider's observations reinforce what Isaac Asimov has to say ("What Do You Call a Platypus?" Chapter 2) about the power of names as defining devices?
2. Besides the fact that they are both nurses, how else does the speaker of "A Name Is Just a Name?" resemble the speaker of "No Rainbows, No Roses" (Chapter 8)? Consider, especially, what Beverly Dipo calls the "observational method."

Discussion and Writing Topics

1. Nurses and doctors are trained to be good observers; why might they also make good *recorders* of what they observe?
2. How could "A Name Is Just a Name?" be read as an account of maturation?
3. Do you have any "what's-in-a-name" stories to share with your classmates? How would you lead up to (or down from) your equivalent of the moment Cindy Schneider realizes what's "wrong" with her name in the eyes of the person she is trying to help?

Ellen Goodman

The Maidenform Woman Administers Shock Treatment

A columnist for the *Boston Globe,* Ellen Goodman writes about national but also "private" affairs of home, marriage and the family, school, and work. Her syndicated column, carried in over two hundred newspapers throughout the country, was awarded the 1980 Pulitzer Prize for Commentary. A graduate of Radcliffe College and former Nieman Fellow at Harvard, Goodman is the author of *Turning Points* (1979), a study of people whose lives have been changed by the feminist movement. Her essays are collected in *Close to Home* (1979), *At Large* (1981), and *Making Sense* (1989). In this one, Goodman looks at Madison Avenue's definition of "the new woman." She explains how she wrote it and other columns in "Writers on the Writing Process."

It's not that I'd never seen her before. 1

Years ago, she was photographed outside of her apartment building, dressed in a fur coat and bra and panties. Since then she's been found in similar attire in theater and hotel lobbies. Usually, of course, you get used to this sort of thing if you live in a city long enough. 2

But it was a shock to see her in a hospital room. There she was, hair tied back primly, medical chart in her left hand, pen in her right hand, long white jacket over her shoulders, exposing her lacy magenta bra and panties. 3

Was it possible? Why, yes! Stop the presses! The Maidenform Woman Had Become a Doctor! According to the caption under this photograph, she was "making the rounds in her elegant Delectables." 4

At some point when I wasn't looking, everybody's favorite exhibi- 5
tionist must have actually gone to medical school. I suppose that I had underestimated her intelligence—this happens so often with attractive women. I always thought she was a candidate for a cold, not a medical degree. I can only imagine the difficulties she had getting accepted, what with her portfolio and all.

By now any number of magazines are featuring her personal suc- 6
cess story. On their pages, the Maidenform woman is willingly displaying her new bedside manner in living color. Poised, concerned, even prim, young Dr. Maidenform is photographed looking down compassionately at her bedridden patient. We don't know exactly what the patient thinks of all this. Fortunately for her, his leg is in traction and he can't move. The other doctors in the ad seem quite unconcerned about her outfit. Dr. Maidenform seems to have made it in a world that is entirely non-sexist. They aren't even glancing in the direction of her non-air-brushed belly button!

Quite frankly, I must admit that the Maidenform Woman cured 7
me of a disease. She cured me of creeping complacency.

Until I saw her, I had become virtually numb to the advertising 8
image of that handy creature, "The New Woman." We are now out of the era of housewife-as-airhead. We've even come a long way from the year of coming a long way, baby.

We are plunging into the "successful woman as sex object" syn- 9
drome. The more real women break out of the mold, the more advertisers force them back in. We are now told that, for all the talk, the New Woman is just the Total Woman in updated gear.

Under the careful dress-for-success suit of an MBA is a woman 10
buying Office Legs for sex appeal. Around the briefcase of a lawyer is a hand shining with high-color nail gloss. Take away the lab coat, the stethoscope and syringe, and the doctor is just another set of "elegant delectables." The point in all this isn't especially subtle. As Jean Kilbourne, who has long studied media images of women, said, "It's out of the question that they would ever show a male doctor like that. She is aloof but available. Underneath she is still a sex object." Kilbourne's favorite entry in this category is a perfume ad that shows the successful woman mixing business with, uh, pleasure. In the first frame we see the busy executive at a business lunch with three men. In the second frame, we see her under the covers with one.

Advertisers have a big investment in this new-old image. I'm not 11 talking about the professional woman market. There are hardly enough women doctors to keep the magenta lace factory in business. But there are now an increasing number of women who see professionals as glamorous and want to identify with them.

The advertisers are betting that these women want, as the Maidenform ad puts it, "just what the doctor ordered." So the doctor is ordered to strip, literally, her professional cover. She is revealed in the flesh, to be—yes, indeed—just another woman insecure about her femininity, just another woman in search of sex appeal, just another woman who needs "silky satin tricot with antique lace scalloping." 12

Pretty soon, I suppose, she will need it in the Senate, in the Supreme Court, even in the Oval Office. The Maidenform Woman. You never know where she'll turn up. 13

QUESTIONS

Understanding

1. According to Ellen Goodman, how do the Maidenform (and other) advertisements in the media define "The New Woman" (par. 8)?
2. What's wrong with Madison Avenue's definition as Goodman sees it?
3. If Goodman is right, to whom are the advertisers appealing (or hoping to appeal) with their redefinition of the "modern" woman? Why does she think doctors and other professional women are *not* their main audience?
4. *The Total Woman* (1973), by Marabel Morgan, advised the reader to explore her sensuality by, for example, greeting her husband at the door in plastic wrap and cowboy boots. Why does Goodman identify the Maidenform Woman as merely the Total Woman "in updated gear" (par. 9)?
5. To whom does the Maidenform Woman in the hospital administer a "shock"? Why is this jolt therapeutic?

Strategies and Structure

1. Without Goodman's title, we would not know until paragraph 4 that the woman she introduces here is an "image" rather than a real person.

How does this deliberate confusion help prepare us for what Goodman is about to argue concerning the effects of advertising?

2. Why does Goodman end paragraph 6 with an exclamation point? What has "shocked" her into *hyperbole?*
3. Why does Goodman quote media specialist Jean Kilbourne in paragraph 10? Why does she then paraphrase what Kilbourne says about perfume ads instead of quoting her directly?
4. "You never know where she'll turn up" (par. 13), of course, is the last line from the Maidenform ads that Goodman is satirizing. Where do Goodman's other closing lines about the Senate and the Supreme Court come from?
5. Though she finds scant virtue in it, Goodman doesn't expect the advertising business to change; who then is her audience here? Whom might she actually hope to convince? Of what?
6. How would you describe Goodman's TONE throughout her "attack" on the advertising industry? Should she have been more harshly critical? Why or why not?

Words and Figures of Speech

1. Why does Goodman repeat the word *delectables* (pars. 4, 10)? What kind of "portfolio" is she referring to in paragraph 5?
2. Goodman presents herself as "numb" (par. 8) to the treatment of women in advertisements. How does this condition call for the "shock treatments" administered by Dr. Maidenform? How does her numbness show the effect of such image making upon a real "professional woman" (par. 11)?
3. When a writer says, "quite frankly" or "let's be frank," it can imply that the writer sometimes isn't. Should Goodman have found some other transitional phrase at the beginning of paragraph 7? Why or why not?
4. In the Maidenform commercials, a set of underwear is made to stand for the woman who wears it (the part for the whole). How does Goodman overturn this FIGURE OF SPEECH in her essay and thus make an object back into a woman?

Comparing

1. How do the "lacy magenta bra and panties" (par. 3) of Goodman's essay resemble the "windbreaker and porkpie hat" in paragraph 39 of Mary

Mebane's "The Back of the Bus" (Chapter 1)? Or Henry Louis Gates, Jr.'s old shoes in "A Giant Step" (Chapter 4)?

2. In her final paragraph, Goodman speculates that the Maidenform Woman might turn up any day now in Congress. Is Congresswoman Lynn Woolsey ("Reinvent Welfare, Humanely," Chapter 10) what Madison Avenue had in mind? Why or why not?
3. Roger Verhulst ("Being Prepared in Suburbia," Chapter 10) holds that reason cannot sway emotion. How might Goodman be shown to disagree in "The Maidenform Woman Administers Shock Treatment"?

Discussion and Writing Topics

1. How would you define the "new" woman or man? Sketch her/his portrait in a brief (not briefs) essay.
2. The image of women in advertising, says media expert Marshall McLuhan, is that of a "mechanical bride," an object with interchangeable parts, like a robot. How and how well do the Maidenform commercials (and other advertisements cited by Ellen Goodman) bear out this theory?
3. "It's out of the question that they would ever show a male doctor like that," says one authority in Goodman's essay (par. 10). Do you agree? How *are* men presented in underwear ads? What do these ads assume about the people to whom they are pitched?
4. Is sex in advertising necessarily sexist? Whatever your opinion, back it up with at least one main example (from television, newspapers, popular magazines) and several minor ones (as Goodman does).

Diane Ackerman

ANOSMIA

Diane Ackerman's life as a sensualist began in Waukegan, Illinois, where her father owned a restaurant. "I try to give myself passionately, totally, to whatever I'm observing," says Ackerman, yet she cannot keep "science" out of her observations. As a result, Ackerman (a semi-finalist in the Journalist-in-Space Project) has become a poet of natural history. Now a staff writer for the *New Yorker,* she holds M.F.A. and Ph.D. degrees from Cornell and has taught writing at a number of colleges and universities, including Ohio University and Columbia. "Anosmia" is a complete section from Ackerman's *A Natural History of the Senses* (1990). Her *Natural History of Love* was published in 1994.

One rainy night in 1976, a thirty-three-year-old mathematician went out for an after-dinner stroll. Everyone considered him not just a gourmet but a wunderkind, because he had the ability to taste a dish and tell you all its ingredients with shocking precision. One writer described it as a kind of "perfect pitch." As he stepped into the street, a slow-moving van ran into him and he hit his head on the pavement when he fell. The day after he got out of the hospital, he discovered to his horror that his sense of smell was gone. 1

Because his taste buds still worked, he could detect foods that were salty, bitter, sour, and sweet, but he had lost all of the heady succulence of life. Seven years later, still unable to smell and deeply depressed, he sued the driver of the van and won. It was understood, first, that his life had become irreparably impoverished and, second, that without a sense of smell his life was endangered. In those seven years, he had failed to detect the smell of smoke when his apartment building was on fire; he had been poisoned by food whose putrefaction he couldn't smell; he could not smell gas leaks. Worst of all, perhaps, he had lost the ability of scents and odors to provide him 2 with heart-stopping memories and associations. "I feel empty, in a sort of limbo," he told a reporter. There was not even a commonly known name for his nightmare. Those without hearing are labeled "deaf," those without sight "blind," but what is the word for someone without smell? What could be more distressing than to be sorely afflicted by an absence without a name? "Anosmia" is what scientists call it, a simple Latin/Greek combination: "without" + "smell." But no casual term—like "smumb," for instance—exists to give one a sense of community or near-normalcy.

The "My Turn" column in *Newsweek* of March 21, 1988, by Judith R. Birnberg, contains a deeply moving lament about her sudden loss of smell. All she can distinguish is the texture and temperature of food. "I am handicapped: one of 2 million Americans who suffer from anosmia, an inability to smell or taste (the two senses are physiologically related). . . . We so take for granted the rich aroma of coffee and the sweet flavor of oranges that when we lose these senses, it is almost as if we have forgotten how to breathe." Just before Ms. Birnberg's sense of smell disappeared, she had spent a year sneezing. The cause? Some unknown allergy. "The anosmia began without warning. . . . During the past three years there have been brief periods—minutes, even hours—when I suddenly became aware of odors and knew that this meant that I could also taste. What to eat first? A bite of banana once made me cry. On a few occasions a remission came at dinner time, and my husband and I would dash to our favorite restaurant. On two or three occasions I savored every miraculous mouthful through an entire meal. But most times my taste would be gone by the time we parked the car." Although there are centers for treating smell and taste dysfunction (of which Monell is probably the best known), little can be done about anosmia. "I have had a CAT scan, blood tests, sinus cultures, allergy tests, allergy shots, long-term zinc therapy, weekly sinus irrigations, a biopsy, cortisone injections into my nose and four different types of sinus surgery. My case has been presented to hospital medical committees. . . . I have been through the medical mill. The consensus: anosmia caused by allergy and infection. There can be other causes. Some people are born this way. Or the olfactory nerve is severed as a result of concussion. Anosmia can also be the result of aging, a brain tumor or exposure to toxic chemicals. Whatever the cause, we are all at risk in detecting fires, gas leaks and spoiled food." Finally, she took a risky step and allowed a doctor to give her prednisone, an anti- 3 inflammatory steroid, in an effort to shrink the swelling near olfactory nerves. "By the second day, I had a brief sense of smell when I inhaled deeply. . . . The fourth day I ate a salad at lunch, and I suddenly realized that I could taste everything. It was like the moment in 'The Wizard of Oz' when the world is transformed from black and white to Technicolor. I savored the salad: one garbanzo bean, a shred of cabbage, a sunflower seed. On the fifth day I sobbed—less from the experience of smelling and tasting than from believing the craziness was over."

At breakfast the next day, she caught her husband's scent and "fell on him in tears of joy and started sniffing him, unable to stop. His was a comfortable familiar essence that had been lost for so long and was now rediscovered. I had always thought I would sacrifice smell to taste if I had to choose between the two, but I suddenly realized how much I had missed. We take it for granted and are unaware that *everything* smells: people, the air, my house, my skin. . . . Now I inhaled all odors, good and bad, as if drunk." Sadly, her pleasures lasted only a few months. When she began reducing the dosage of prednisone, as she had to for safety's sake (prednisone causes bloating and can suppress the immune system, among other unpleasant side effects), her ability to smell waned once more. Two new operations followed. She's decided to go back on prednisone, and yearns for some magical day when her smell returns as mysteriously as it vanished. 4

Not everyone without a sense of smell suffers so acutely. Nor are all smell dysfunctions a matter of loss; the handicap can take strange forms. At Monell, scientists have treated numerous people who suffer from "persistent odors," who keep smelling a foul smell wherever they go. Some walk around with a constant bitter taste in their mouths. Some have a deformed or distorted sense of smell. Hand them a rose, and they smell garbage. Hand them a steak and they smell sulfur. Our sense of smell weakens as we get older, and it's at its peak in middle age. Alzheimer's patients often lose their sense of smell along with their memory (the two are tightly coupled); one day Scratch-and-Sniff tests may help in diagnosis of the disease. 5

Research done by Robert Henkin, from the Center for Sensory Disorders at Georgetown University, suggests that about a quarter of the people with smell disorders find that their sex drive disappears. What part does smell play in lovemaking? For women, especially, a large part. I am certain that, blindfolded, I could recognize by smell 6 any man I've ever known intimately. I once started to date a man who was smart, sophisticated, and attractive, but when I kissed him I was put off by a faint, cornlike smell that came from his cheek. Not cologne or soap: It was just his subtle, natural scent, and I was shocked to discover that it disturbed me viscerally. Although men seldom report such detailed responses to their partner's natural smell, women so often do that it's become a romantic cliché: When her lover is away, or her husband dies, an anguished woman goes to his closet and takes out a bathrobe or shirt, presses it to her face, and is overwhelmed by tenderness for him. Few men report similar habits, but it's not surprising that women should be more keenly attuned to smells. Females score higher than males in sensitivity to odors, regardless of age group. For a time scientists thought estrogen might be involved, since there was anecdotal evidence that pregnant women had a keener sense of smell, but as it turned out prepubescent girls were better sniffers than boys their age, and pregnant women were no more adept at smelling than other women. Women in general just have a stronger sense of smell. Perhaps it's a vestigial bonus from the dawn of our evolution, when we needed it in courtship, mating, or mothering; or it may be that women have traditionally spent more time around foods and children, ever on the sniff for anything out of order. Because females have often been responsible for initiating mating, smell has been their weapon, lure, and clue.

QUESTIONS

Understanding

1. Why, according to Ackerman, do people with "anosmia" also have trouble tasting food?
2. What other "sense" do anosmiacs often lose?
3. What are the most common causes of anosmia? And the cures?
4. Ackerman says that women, as a rule, have a keener sense of smell than men. Why does she think this is so?

Strategies and Structure

1. In which paragraph does Ackerman define anosmia most directly?
2. Basic definitions work by citing the distinguishing features, (lack of smell in this case) of the term being defined. How does Ackerman extend this basic definition?
3. If you had to put Ackerman's essay in another chapter in this book, would it be Chapter 2 (Classification and Division) or Chapter 4 (Cause and Effect)? Please explain your choice. How might you justify leaving it where it is?
4. Try breaking Ackerman's essay into stand-alone units. Which individual paragraphs could stand alone as mini-essays? Any two-paragraph units?
5. Besides her own experience, Ackerman cites two case histories of anosmia. Why must they, as written, come in the order in which she presents them? Why can't the mathematician's account come after Mrs. Birnberg's instead of before?
6. How does Ackerman's reference to research done at the Center for Sensory Disorders (par. 6) differ from her case-history approach elsewhere? Why might case histories be of more use to her here than statistical studies?

Words and Figures of Speech

1. How and where does Ackerman use the *etymology* (word history) of the term *anosmia* in her definition?
2. From what root words do you suppose *smumb* (par. 2) is concocted?
3. What is a "portmanteau" word (check your dictionary)? Who invented this term for invented terms?
4. Why does Ackerman find the clinical term for a chronic loss of smell to be slightly, well, distasteful?

Comparing

1. Compare how the author of "A View From the Bridge" (Chapter 8) conveys what the boy does not see with how Ackerman conveys what her "subjects" do not smell.

2. In "What Do You Call a Platypus?" (Chapter 2), the author uses the name of his subject to help classify and define it. Where and how does Ackerman do the same?

Discussion and Writing Topics

1. Can you think of any other informal names (like "smumb") for the condition Ackerman describes?
2. Do you know of a case history of anosmia that you might report in writing?
3. To what extent do you agree or disagree with Ackerman's explanation for why women are better at smelling than men?

Jane Smiley

Reflections on a Lettuce Wedge

Born in California and educated at Vassar College and the University of Iowa, Jane Smiley lists her politics as "Skeptical" and her religion as "Vehement agnostic." Since 1981 she has taught English at Iowa State University in Ames, a locale that bears an undisclosed relation to the setting of her best-selling novel *Moo* (1995). Smiley's other works of fiction, most of which deal with "families and their troubles," include *Barn Blind* (1980), *The Age of Grief* (1987), *The Greenlanders* (1988), *Ordinary Love and Good Will* (1989), and *A Thousand Acres* (1991). "Reflections on a Lettuce Wedge" is from *The Hungry Mind Review.*

1 Some years ago, I went to a dinner party where the ideal midwestern repast was presented in its most extreme manifestation: baked potatoes the size of shoes, slices of beefsteak tomatoes as red as stoplights and nearly as large, mammoth rings of nacreous onion. If there was a leafy green vegetable other than lettuce, its memory does not linger, nor was it meant to. The show revolved around the phenomenal slab of beef, lapping the edges of the plate, visibly juicy, dangerously sizzling, borne to the table like a potentate on a litter, casting all around it into shadow. When the philosophy professor who cooked the meal committed suicide only two weeks later, I was not actually surprised. His manner at the table was personable though a bit edgy—I wasn't perspicacious enough to divine what was coming through the scrim of conviviality—but the menu, I always thought, was despair incarnate—five simple and distinct tastes, served in chokingly large pieces, everything juxtaposed but not allowed to mingle; nothing hidden, all conspicuous, raw materials mistaken for cuisine.

I was raised and have lived most of my life in the Midwest. Very little about the Midwest surprises me. The people are friendly, generous, and honest. The divisions of social class are minimal. Tact is a universally cherished virtue. Function is valued over style, the inner self over appearance. Nevertheless, it still astounds me, after forty years, that there is no good bread between Chicago and San Francisco. 2

Diners in the heartland, in fact, have been known to go for the white meal—pork chops and mashed potatoes in cream gravy, with a little cauliflower on the side and a dish of vanilla ice cream for dessert. I prefer recipes that begin with a head or two of garlic and go on to call for a packed cup of coriander and some chili peppers. 3

I do not ascribe the sorry state of midwestern cuisine to the northern European heritage of many of its denizens. In Northern Europe I've eaten plenty of scrumptious chow, from sauerbraten to liver pâté, from rye bread to pickled herring, not to mention towering cream cakes flavored with mysterious tasting liqueurs. If only you could get *that* in Galesburg, Illinois. Nor does the fault lie in scarcity. I understand that French *boulangers* prefer hard wheat flour from our Midwest. Midwestern gardens abound with perfect tomatoes, peppers, broccoli, and sweet corn. The filet I get at my local supermarket compares with the best steaks at the best restaurants on either coast. 4

Quoting me back to myself, my daughter says, "De gustibus non est disputandum." Okay, let them eat instant mashed potatoes dished up with an ice cream scoop, machine-formed turkey breast injected with artificially flavored turkey juice, string beans the color of army fatigues, and a pie-shaped wedge of cranberry jelly still bearing the imprint of its No. 42 can. Let them go out and eat it at a restaurant. Let them pay ten or fifteen real dollars for the privilege of eating it. It's neurotic of me to think that this is any of my business. 5

But I'm here! I'm hungry! And there isn't anything else on the menu! Here comes the salad. Is it a few simple leaves of spinach and romaine, dressed with the plainest vinaigrette—wine vinegar, olive oil, Dijon mustard, a crushed garlic clove, salt, and pepper? No! It is a wedge of flavorless and nutrient-free iceberg lettuce floating in bright orange "French" dressing, and sporting a tomato wedge that's been held near the freezing point ever since its embarkation in California. The clearest flavor note we have here is the potent taste of the sugar in the dressing. I'm the angriest person in the restaurant; I'm 6 the only angry person in the restaurant. I consider this salad a spiritual assault. I ask for bread, and they give me, not a stone, but a white spongy thing called a "roll."

The spirit is inescapably connected to the body. The body, 7
through the senses, seeks connection to the world. When a connection is made that is pleasurable, the spirit lifts. When the connection is routine, mundane, careless, the spirit sinks. What American commerce has done to bread, tomatoes, salad, turkey, the tartly sublime and healthful cranberry, the fresh and crunchy pole bean is to make them routine, mundane, and careless, multicolored fodder for merely biologic hunger, the hunger that sets in after five or six hours and craves only calories, not connection, delight, or even savor. That commerce alters all it touches is a truism, but why, of all Americans, do midwesterners most widely and passively accept the damage? Why do midwesterners hold their tastebuds in lower esteem than everyone else in the whole world, even the notorious British? (Five British delicacies worth making the trip: Devonshire cream, toasted Cheshire cheese, cider, ginger cake, and, since the Act of Union, shortbread.)

My husband says it all has to do with religion—militant Protes- 8
tantism expressing itself as distaste for all the senses, including the least aggressive. Or perhaps the ubiquity of sugar, which serves as a pick-me-up through the light-deprived days of winter, has aborted the development of sharper, less easily learned preferences. In his more bitter moments, Garrison Keillor has commented that midwesterners are early taught the "Who do you think you are?" lesson—as in, "Who do you think you are to aspire to something more beautiful, more exotic, or more unusual than what is put before you?" The "Who do you think you are?" lesson is quickly internalized as the "Anything is good enough for me" attitude, an attitude that no one should ever bring to the table, considering the limitations placed on us all by appetite, physique, and the fact that no human life is long enough to sample more than a portion of the results of human imagination as it is applied to food.

Of course, I am told that there are those who care nothing for 9
what they eat, but can a whole region of eaters be so ascetic or, perhaps, such poor producers of endorphins?

I don't know what it is, myself. This is a diatribe, not a diagnosis. 10
But I do think that people tend to use the earth better if they take delight in its fruits. Eating is the one sensuous thing we do many

times a day, day after day, year after year. Eating is our oftenest repeated connection to our agricultural roots. It seems to me that there are two choices: We can continue to process our food, as through a machine, from field to table, and continue to content ourselves with mechanically opening our jaws and processing it through our alimentary canals, or we can sow the seed, harvest the fruits, bring care and interest to the preparation of meals, and take our daily reward in the pleasures of aroma, flavor, and visceral satisfaction. We can decide that what doesn't taste good cannot be good for us. We can resist having our appetites dulled in the name of the countless mouths one single American farmer and all his machinery, petrochemicals, and sacrificed topsoil are alleged to feed. The future begins at dinnertime. I hope mine contains a measure of very green, strong olive oil and a baguette of crusty, slightly sour, and perfectly fresh bread. A silky sauce with a flavor both rounded and tangy, enigmatic enough to deliberate over again and again. I hope my future contains ropes of garlic. And I hope it contains an Earth that is cherished, cared for, and abundant.

QUESTIONS

Understanding

1. Why do the meat-and-potatoes and the "white" (par. 3) meals served up in her first three paragraphs give Jane Smiley indigestion?
2. The Latin adage at the beginning of paragraph 5 is usually translated, "There is no disputing in matters of taste." What do you interpret these words to mean? How well does Smiley follow this ancient rule, which her daughter repeats back to her?
3. How does Smiley's husband explain midwestern taste? What possible causes does Smiley herself advance? How seriously do you think we are supposed to take these explanations?
4. What are "endorphins" (par. 9)?
5. Smiley is not exactly suggesting that the philosophy professor (par. 1) died because of the meal he served, rather she considers the food to be symptomatic. Of what?

6. Why do you think Smiley chose a wedge of iceberg lettuce rather than watery mashed potatoes, long-haul tomatoes, cauliflower shards, or even a lettuce *leaf* as her prime example?

Strategies and Structure

1. How would you describe Smiley's TONE throughout "Reflections on a Lettuce Wedge"? Do you find her reference to the philosophy professor's suicide, for example, appropriate to her subject, or in bad taste? Would it make any difference if it had been an English professor? Please explain.
2. Should anyone present her with a single loaf of good bread baked somewhere between Chicago and San Francisco, Smiley's final assertion in paragraph 2 would be disproved. How concerned does she seem to be about such niceties of logic? Why do you think so?
3. A "diatribe" (par. 10), from the Latin for "learned discourse," is a formal disquisition that so relentlessly hammers at its subject (such as a lettuce wedge) that the author comes across as obsessive and ill-tempered. How (and how well) does Jane Smiley counteract such onerous expectations? For example, what is the effect of the first six sentences in paragraph 2?
4. At the beginning of paragraph 7, Jane Smiley lays out the premises of the deductive argument (see Chapter 9) that threads throughout her essay. Which of these propositions is the widest assumption (or major premise) of her logical argument? What are the (largely) unstated conclusions of this line of reasoning?
5. As explained in Chapter 9, deductive arguments are only as strong as their premises. How sound do you find Smiley's premises, major and minor? Please explain.
6. What is the effect of the "let thems" in paragraph 5 of "Reflections on a Lettuce Wedge"? Where else in her essay does Smiley use a similarly formulaic device to link her statements?
7. Smiley's "Reflections" is a comic smorgasbord of traditional rhetorical forms: it is simultaneously a diatribe, a logical argument, an appeal to the senses, a display of wit, an oracular pronouncement. It is also, and perhaps foremost, an essay in definition. What particular quality of body, mind, and spirit—said to be sadly lacking in midwesterners—is Smiley defining here, and how does she herself define it?
8. Most of Smiley's examples are "negative" in the sense that they tell what her central subject is not. Where does she give more "positive" exam-

ples that actually specify the characteristics, or distinguishing features, of the thing (not a lettuce wedge) that she is defining?

Words and Figures of Speech

1. Look up the word *nacreous* (par. 1) in your dictionary. What's the joke here, and why does it work better with onions than with steak or potatoes?
2. One meaning of *scrim* (par. 1) is a gauzy curtain in a theater. What are the implications of this METAPHOR in the context of a dinner party where the host is suicidal?
3. Chances are, the potatoes cited in Smiley's first paragraph were not literally as big as shoes, an adult's anyway. Cite similar instances of HYPERBOLE in this paragraph and throughout her essay. Do these exaggerations enhance or diminish the author's credibility in your opinion? Please explain.
4. What are the connotations of "nutrient-free" (par. 6), "aborted" (par. 8), "internalized" (par. 8), and "sensuous" (par. 10)?
5. What are the implications of the word *reflections* in Smiley's title?
6. How do the metaphoric meals in Smiley's first three paragraphs contrast with her reflections, which flow seamlessly from economic explanations for the phenomenon she describes to religious, medical, and psychological ones?
7. How does your dictionary define *wit*? To what extent do you think Smiley's essay exemplifies the definition, especially the part about discovering connections among disparate objects and ideas? How is wit related to SATIRE?

Comparing

1. In his "more bitter moments" (par. 8), says Smiley, Garrison Keillor also ponders why the midwestern psyche likes the world to be flat. How would you describe Keillor's mood or tone in "How to Write a Letter" (Chapter 3)? How does it compare with Smiley's?
2. The eighteenth-century satirist Jonathan Swift was the master of the comic diatribe. How does his persona in "A Modest Proposal" (Essays for Further Reading) *contrast* with Smiley's in "Reflections on a Lettuce Wedge"?

3. Food is the vehicle in Smiley's essay, but the tenor points elsewhere. How does the play of Philip Weiss's wit in "How to Get Out of a Locked Trunk" (Chapter 3) resemble hers in this regard?

Discussion and Writing Topics

1. "I'm here! I'm hungry!" (par. 6). What kind of philosophical reasoning is this? (Note: Smiley's essay first appeared in *The Hungry Mind Review*.)
2. Do you think Smiley is too hard (or too soft) on midwesterners? Write a defense of iceberg lettuce (or similar symbolic vegetable) and the characteristic qualities of mind of those who consume it.
3. In collaboration with others in your class, compile a list of possible topics or propositions for a diatribe of your own. For example: "The future begins (does not begin) at dinnertime." Then choose one topic and, in consultation with several other classmates, compile a list of the arguments and examples you might use.
4. Or, alternatively, compose a paragraph or two of a diatribe that you then give to another member of your class, who makes his or her contribution and passes it on to the next collaborator.

Writers on the Writing Process

ELLEN GOODMAN

1 Asked if she revises much during the writing process, Ellen Goodman responds: "I rewrite, rewrite, rewrite." Her comments on her methods, however, are mainly about choosing a subject.

2 Most syndicated columnists, Goodman feels, write about "important" topics like politics. But for Goodman, politics is "basically a game men play like any other sport." "The Maidenform Woman Administers Shock Treatment" deals with the kinds of issues that Goodman considers actually "much more important" than the political "trivia" of the editorial page. Instead of politics and economics, Goodman's subjects are "the underlying values by which the country exists."

3 Goodman professes to a "lousy memory" for the history of her news stories and essays. "Alas, I have to write the next column rather than analyzing the old one," she confides. Goodman recalls one story she wrote before becoming a columnist, however, that may have nudged her toward editorial writing. It was on abortion, and it was written for *The Boston Globe*. The article, says Goodman, took a "radical" form for a news story. It was written more like an opinion piece than straight reportage. After interviewing a woman who had had an abortion, Goodman wrote her story "very much like a narrative and I didn't use one quote from her, which is very unusual. In a lot of papers, I wouldn't have been able to get that through."

When did she become a columnist? "I started writing a column about 1970 when the *Globe* first opened up its op-ed page [the one across from the editorial page] to inside columns [that is, columns written by the newspaper's own staff]. I wrote about six the first year and after that I was asked if I could do it once a week and I said yes." 4

Distinct from a feature writer, a columnist is responsible for discovering her or his own subjects. "With features stories," explains Goodman, "very often you wait until someone gives you the idea, and you're not putting yourself on the line all the time, either." It's different for the columnist and essayist. "You're totally self-starting, totally dependent on your own ideas, when you write a column." 5

Goodman used to write three columns per week; now she writes two. Still she is "constantly having to think and figure out what you think." Which is both the burden and the reward of her kind of work. "Why do I write? I like to," she asserts; "it helps me form my own thoughts. It's the only work I've done as an adult and it is, as Pete Hamill once said, the hardest work in the world that doesn't include heavy lifting." 6

Writing Topics for Chapter Five

Essays That Define

Write extended definitions of one or more of the following:

1. Photosynthesis or mitosis
2. Obscenity
3. A liberal education
4. Success
5. A happy marriage
6. A feminist
7. A true friend
8. Self-reliance
9. Inertia (physical or spiritual)
10. Non-Euclidian geometry

11. Calculus
12. The big-bang theory of creation
13. Your idea of the ideal society
14. Blues music
15. Tragedy, comedy, romance, novel, satire, or some other literary form

Six

Essays That Compare and Contrast

Before you begin an essay in COMPARISON AND CONTRAST,[1] it is a good idea to make a list of the qualities of the two objects or ideas to be compared. Suppose, for example, that our "objects" were all-time basketball greats Wilt ("The Stilt") Chamberlain and Bill Russell. Our lists might look like this:

CHAMBERLAIN	RUSSELL
7-feet-3-inches tall	6-feet-9-inches tall
good team	better team
fast	faster
style	discipline
loser (almost)	winner (almost)
Goliath	David

Each of these lists is an abbreviated DESCRIPTION of the player whose attributes it compiles. At this early stage, our comparison and contrast essay seems indistinguishable from descriptive writing. As soon as we bring our two lists together, however, the descriptive impulse yields to the impulse to explain. Consider the following

[1] Terms printed in small capitals are defined in the Glossary.

excerpt from an actual comparison of Chamberlain with Russell by sportswriter Jeremy Larner:

> Wilt's defenders could claim with justice that Russell played with a better team, but it was all too apparent that Boston was better partly because Russell played better with them. Russell has been above all a team player—a man of discipline, self-denial and killer instinct; in short, a *winner,* in the best American Calvinist tradition. Whereas Russell has been able somehow to squeeze out his last ounce of ability, Chamberlain's performances have been marked by a seeming nonchalance—as if, recognizing his Giantistic fate, he were more concerned with personal style than with winning. "I never want to set records. The only thing I strive for is perfection" Chamberlain has said. When Wilt goes into his routine, his body proclaims from tip to toe, it's not my fault, folks, honestly—and though I've got to lose, if you look close, you'll see I'm beautiful through and through!

Even though it describes the two men in some detail, this passage is EXPOSITION rather than description. Like most comparative writing, its comparisons are cast as statements or propositions: Russell is more efficient than Chamberlain; Chamberlain is concerned with style, while Russell plays to win. The controlling proposition of Larner's entire essay is that Chamberlain was a Goliath "typecast" by fans to lose to Russell the giant-killer; but Chamberlain broke the stereotype to become the greatest basketball player ever.

We can take a number of hints from Jeremy Larner about writing comparison and contrast essays. First, stick to two and only two subjects at a time. Second, choose subjects that invite comparison because they belong to the same general class: two athletes, two religions, two sororities, two mammals. You might point out many differences between a mattress and a steamboat, but no one is likely to be impressed by this exercise in the obvious. The third lesson is that you do not have to give equal weight to similarities and differences. Larner assumes the similarities between Chamberlain and Russell (both are towering champions), but he works carefully through the differences. An essay that compares a turtle to a tank, on the other hand, might concentrate upon the similarities of the two if it proposes that both belong to the class of moving things with armor.

Our example suggests, finally, that comparison and contrast essays proceed by alternation. From paragraph to paragraph, Larner dispenses his subject in "slices." His assertion that Russell is a team player is followed immediately by the counterassertion that Chamberlain plays to a private standard. Chamberlain's free throws are always uncertain; Russell's are accurate in the clutch. And so on, point by point. Another way of comparing and contrasting is in "chunks." Larner might have said all he had to say about Russell in several paragraphs and then followed up with all of his remarks on Chamberlain. Either method (or a combination of the two) is correct if it works. The aim is to set forth clear alternatives.

Debi Davis

Body Imperfect

Debi Davis wrote "Body Imperfect" for her freshman composition class at Wayne County Community College in Michigan. Before she went back to school, Davis was a folk singer, a dental assistant, a "plastic hippie" (her phrase) in San Francisco, a cabin builder in Alaska, and a teacher of equitation at stables in North Carolina and Indiana. When she is not taking classes, Davis teaches calligraphy and design at the Center for Creative Studies in Detroit and at Glen Oaks College, Centerville, Michigan. Davis is not sure how much longer she will be able to use her hands, however, because they are afflicted by the same vascular disease "of unknown etiology" that cost Davis her legs. Nominated by Marjorie Oliver, Davis's writing teacher, "Body Imperfect" won first place in the inaugural *Norton Textra Extra* contest for student writers sponsored by the publisher of this book. In "Writers on the Writing Process," Debi Davis explains how she pared her entry down to size.

When I became a double amputee at the age of 29, I was forced to shed many misconceptions I had unknowingly embraced regarding the importance of physical perfection. In the space of one hour I changed from an acceptably attractive female to an object of pity and fear. 1

I was not aware of this at first. I was too busy dealing with the physical pain and new limitations in mobility I now faced. Yet I was determined to succeed and proud of my progress on a daily basis. My contact with physicians, rehabilitation specialists, close friends and family only enhanced my perceptions of myself as a "winner." 2

My new status in society, however, was brought to my attention on my first excursion outside the hospital walls. Jubilant to be free of confinement, I rolled through the shopping mall in my wheelchair 3 with the inimitable confidence of a proud survivor, a war hero anticipating a ticker-tape reception. As I glanced around, I sensed that all eyes were upon me, yet no one dared to make eye contact. Their downcast glances made me realize that they did not see the triumph in my eyes, only my missing limbs.

I noticed that shoppers gave me a wide berth, walking far around 4
me as if I were contagious. Mothers held their children closer as I passed, and elderly women patted me on the head saying, "Bless you!" Men, who might normally wink and smile now looked away. Like bruised fruit on a produce stand, I existed, but was bypassed for a healthier looking specimen.

Children, in contrast, found my appearance clearly fascinating. 5
One small girl came up to me and stared with unabashed curiosity at my empty pantlegs. She knelt down and put her arm up one pantleg as far as she could reach, and finding nothing there, looked up at me with bewilderment. "Lady, where did your legs go?" she innocently inquired. I explained to her that my legs had been very sick, that they hadn't been strong and healthy like hers, and that my doctor removed my legs so that I could be healthy again. Tilting her head up she chirped, "But lady, did they go to 'Leg Heaven'?"

That incident made me think about how differently children and 6
adults react to the unknown. To a child, an odd appearance is an interesting curiosity and a learning experience while adults often view the unusual with fear and repulsion. I began to realize that prior to my disability I had been guilty of the same inappropriate reactions.

From observing children, I learned to reach out and reassure 7
adults of my humanness and to reaffirm the genuine worth of all human beings. To accentuate the wholeness of my mind and spirit, I smile warmly, coerce eye contact, and speak in a confident manner. By using a positive approach, I attempt to enlighten society that having a perfect body is not synonymous with quality of life.

QUESTIONS

Understanding

1. According to Davis, children react with curiosity to physical disabilities in other people, whereas adults react with "repulsion" (par. 6). What explanation, if any, does she give for the difference?
2. How does Davis behave in an effort to change the way people look at her?
3. What valuable lesson, according to Davis, do physically impaired people have to teach the physically unimpaired?

Strategies and Structure

1. Does Davis spend more time on points of similarity or points of contrast when she reports how people react to her disability? Please cite examples.
2. In paragraph 1, Davis speaks about shedding "misconceptions." Why, then, do you think she goes back (par. 2) to a time before her enlighting "excursion" (par. 3) from the hospital?
3. "Body Imperfect" has an argument to make: "that having a perfect body is not synonymous with quality of life" (par. 7). Where and how does Davis anticipate this conclusion in earlier paragraphs?
4. How would you describe the TONE throughout Davis's essay?
5. What difference does it make, would you say, that "Body Imperfect" is written in the first person *by* Debi Davis rather than in the third person *about* her?

Words and Figures of Speech

1. Comment on the IRONY of Davis's likening herself to a "war hero" (par. 3).
2. What are the connotations of *coerce* (par. 7)?
3. How effective do you find Davis's "bruised fruit" METAPHOR (par. 4)?

Comparing

1. As an essay in dealing with disappointment and loss, how does "Body Imperfect" compare with Kitty Burns Florey's "Ticky-tacky" (Chapter 7)?
2. Compare and contrast "Body Imperfect" with Naomi Shihab Nye's "Double Vision in a New Old World" (Chapter 8) as essays about the different ways in which children and adults view the world.

Discussion and Writing Topics

1. Do you agree with Davis's account of how children perceive physical imperfection in others? Why or why not?
2. What do you think of her attitude toward the adults she writes about?
3. Davis says she was twenty-nine years old when her legs were amputated. What bearing, if any, do you think age has upon the human ability to endure affliction?

Bruce Catton

Grant and Lee: A Study in Contrasts

A native of Michigan who attended Oberlin College, Bruce Catton was a former newspaper reporter, a one-time editor of *American Heritage,* and a noted historian of the Civil War. *A Stillness at Appomattox* (1953) won both the Pulitzer Prize and the National Book Award for history in 1954. It was not, said Catton, "the strategy or political meanings" that fascinated him but the "almost incomprehensible emotional experience which this war brought to our country." Among Catton's many other books are *This Hallowed Ground* (1956); *The Coming Fury* (1961); *The Army of the Potomac* (1962); *Terrible Swift Sword* (1963); *Never Call Retreat* (1965); *Grant Takes Command* (1969); and *Michigan: A Bicentennial History* (1976). "Grant and Lee: A Study in Contrasts" is reprinted from a collection of essays by distinguished historians. Catton died in 1979.

When Ulysses S. Grant and Robert E. Lee met in the parlor of a modest house at Appomattox Court House, Virginia, on April 9, 1865, to work out the terms for the surrender of Lee's Army of Northern Virginia, a great chapter in American life came to a close, and a great new chapter began. 1

These men were bringing the Civil War to its virtual finish. To be sure, other armies had yet to surrender, and for a few days the fugitive Confederate government would struggle desperately and vainly, trying to find some way to go on living now that its chief support was gone. But in effect it was all over when Grant and Lee signed the papers. And the little room where they wrote out the terms was the scene of one of the poignant, dramatic contrasts in American history. 2

They were two strong men, these oddly different generals, and they represented the strengths of two conflicting currents that, through them, had come into final collision. 3

Thesis

Back of Robert E. Lee was the notion that the old aristocratic concept might somehow survive and be dominant in American life. 4

Lee was tidewater Virginia, and in his background were family, culture, and tradition . . . the age of chivalry transplanted to a New World which was making its own legends and its own myths. He embodied a way of life that had come down through the age of knighthood and the English country squire. America was a land that was beginning all over again, dedicated to nothing much more complicated than the rather hazy belief that all men had equal rights and should have an equal chance in the world. In such a land Lee stood for the feeling that it was somehow of advantage to human society to have a pronounced inequality in the social structure. There should be a leisure class, backed by ownership of land; in turn, society itself should be keyed to the land as the chief source of wealth and influence. It would bring forth (according to this ideal) a class of men with a strong sense of obligation to the community; men who lived not to gain advantage for themselves, but to meet the solemn obligations which had been laid on them by the very fact that they were privileged. From them the country would get its leadership; to them it could look for the higher values—of thought, of conduct, of personal deportment—to give it strength and virtue. 5

Lee embodied the noblest elements of this aristocratic ideal. Through him, the landed nobility justified itself. For four years, the Southern states had fought a desperate war to uphold the ideals for which Lee stood. In the end, it almost seemed as if the Confederacy fought for Lee; as if he himself was the Confederacy . . . the best thing that the way of life for which the Confederacy stood could ever have to offer. He had passed into legend before Appomattox. Thousands of tired, underfed, poorly clothed Confederate soldiers, long since past the simple enthusiasm of the early days of the struggle, somehow considered Lee the symbol of everything for which they had been willing to die. But they could not quite put this feeling into words. If the Lost Cause, sanctified by so much heroism and so many deaths, had a living justification, its justification was General Lee. 6

Grant, the son of a tanner on the Western frontier, was everything Lee was not. He had come up the hard way and embodied nothing 7 in particular except the eternal toughness and sinewy fiber of the men who grew up beyond the mountains. He was one of a body of men who owed reverence and obeisance to no one, who were self-reliant to a fault, who cared hardly anything for the past but who had a sharp eye for the future.

These frontier men were the precise opposites of the tidewater aristocrats. Back of them, in the great surge that had taken people over the Alleghenies and into the opening Western country, there was a deep, implicit dissatisfaction with a past that had settled into grooves. They stood for democracy, not from any reasoned conclusion about the proper ordering of human society, but simply because they had grown up in the middle of democracy and knew how it worked. Their society might have privileges, but they would be privileges each man had won for himself. Forms and patterns meant nothing. No man was born to anything, except perhaps to a chance to show how far he could rise. Life was competition. 8

Yet along with this feeling had come a deep sense of belonging to a national community. The Westerner who developed a farm, opened a shop, or set up in business as a trader, could hope to prosper only as his own community prospered—and his community ran from the Atlantic to the Pacific and from Canada down to Mexico. If the land was settled, with towns and highways and accessible markets, he could better himself. He saw his fate in terms of the nation's own destiny. As its horizons expanded, so did his. He had, in other words, an acute dollars-and-cents stake in the continued growth and development of his country. 9

And that, perhaps, is where the contrast between Grant and Lee becomes most striking. The Virginia aristocrat, inevitably, saw himself in relation to his own region. He lived in a static society which could endure almost anything except change. Instinctively, his first loyalty would go to the locality in which that society existed. He would fight to the limit of endurance to defend it, because in defending it he was defending everything that gave his own life its deepest meaning. 10

The Westerner, on the other hand, would fight with an equal tenacity for the broader concept of society. He fought so because everything he lived by was tied to growth, expansion, and a constantly widening horizon. What he lived by would survive or fall with the nation itself. He could not possibly stand by unmoved in the face of an attempt to destroy the Union. He would combat it 11 with everything he had, because he could only see it as an effort to cut the ground out from under his feet.

So Grant and Lee were in complete contrast, representing two diametrically opposed elements in American life. Grant was the modern man emerging; beyond him, ready to come on the stage, was the great age of steel and machinery, of crowded cities and a restless burgeoning vitality. Lee might have ridden down from the old age of chivalry, lance in hand, silken banner fluttering over his head. Each man was the perfect champion of his cause, drawing both his strengths and his weaknesses from the people he led. 12

Yet it was not all contrast, after all. Different as they were—in background, in personality, in underlying aspiration—these two great soldiers had much in common. Under everything else, they were marvelous fighters. Furthermore, their fighting qualities were really very much alike. 13

Each man had, to begin with, the great virtue of utter tenacity and fidelity. Grant fought his way down the Mississippi Valley in spite of acute personal discouragement and profound military handicaps. Lee hung on in the trenches at Petersburg after hope itself had died. In each man there was an indomitable quality . . . the born fighter's refusal to give up as long as he can still remain on his feet and lift his two fists. 14

Daring and resourcefulness they had, too; the ability to think faster and move faster than the enemy. These were the qualities which gave Lee the dazzling campaigns of Second Manassas and Chancellorsville and won Vicksburg for Grant. 15

Lastly, and perhaps greatest of all, there was the ability, at the end, to turn quickly from war to peace once the fighting was over. Out of the way these two men behaved at Appomattox came the possibility of a peace of reconciliation. It was a possibility not wholly realized, in the years to come, but which did, in the end, help the two sections to become one nation again . . . after a war whose bitterness might have seemed to make such a reunion wholly impossible. No part of either man's life became him more than the part he played in this brief meeting in the McLean house at Appomattox. Their behavior there put all succeeding generations of Americans in their debt. Two great Americans, Grant and Lee—very different, yet under everything very much alike. Their encounter at Appomattox was one of the great moments of American history. 16

QUESTIONS

Understanding

1. Catton writes that generals Lee and Grant represented two conflicting currents (par. 3) of American culture. What were they? Describe the contrasting qualities and ideals that Catton associates with each man.
2. What qualities, according to Catton, did Grant and Lee have in common?
3. With Lee's surrender, says Catton, "a great new chapter" (par. 1) of American history began. He is referring, presumably, to the period of expansion between the Civil War and World War I, when industrialization really took hold in America. What characteristics of the new era does his description of Grant anticipate?
4. Catton does not describe, in any detail, how Grant and Lee behaved as they worked out the terms of peace at Appomattox; but what does he *imply* about the conduct of the two generals? Why was their conduct important to "all succeeding generations" (par. 16) of Americans?
5. Catton gives no specific reasons for the Confederacy's defeat. He says nothing, for example, about the Union's greater numbers or its superior communications system. What general explanation does he imply, however, when he associates Lee with a "static" society (par. 10) and Grant with a society of "restless burgeoning vitality" (par. 12)?

Strategies and Structure

1. Beginning with paragraph 3, Catton gets down to the particulars of his contrast between the two generals. Where does the contrast end? In which paragraph does he begin to list similarities between the two men?
2. Except for mentioning their strength, Catton says little about the unique physical appearance of either Grant or Lee. Is this a weakness in his essay or is there some justification for avoiding such details? Explain your answer.
3. Which sentence in paragraph 16 brings together the contrasts and the similarities of the preceding paragraphs? How does this final paragraph recall the opening paragraphs of the essay? Why might Catton end with an echo of his beginning?

4. Would you say that the historian's voice in this essay is primarily DESCRIPTIVE, NARRATIVE, or EXPOSITORY? Explain your answer.

Words and Figures of Speech

1. Catton describes the parlor where Grant and Lee met as the *scene* of a *dramatic* contrast (par. 2), and he says in paragraph 12 that the post–Civil War era was "ready to come on stage." Where do such METAPHORS come from, and what view of history do they suggest?
2. What is the Lost Cause of paragraph 6, and what does the phrase (in capital letters) CONNOTE?
3. Catton does not use the phrase *noblesse oblige*, but it could be applied to General Lee's beliefs as Catton defines them. What does the phrase mean?
4. What is the precise meaning of *obeisance* (par. 7), and why might Catton have chosen it instead of the more common *obedience* when describing General Grant?
5. Look up any of these words with which you are not on easy terms: *fugitive* (par. 2), *poignant* (2), *chivalry* (5), *sinewy* (7), *implicit* (8), *tenacity* (11), *diametrically* (12), *acute* (14), *profound* (14), and *indomitable* (14).

Comparing

1. Both Catton and Mary Talbot in "The Potato: How It Shaped the World" (Chapter 4) are writing about the past from vantage points in the present. How do they differ in their approaches to the past and in their roles as historians?
2. As a study in the clash of cultures, how does "Grant and Lee" compare with Naomi Shihab Nye's "Double Vision in a New Old World" (Chapter 8)?

Discussion and Writing Topics

1. Write an essay contrasting Thomas Jefferson and Alexander Hamilton (or John F. Kennedy and Richard Nixon) as men who represented the conflicting forces of their time.

2. "America," Catton writes, "was a land that was beginning all over again . . ." (par. 5). Discuss this idea as one way of formulating the "American dream."
3. Grant, we are told, saw the nation's "destiny" (par. 9) as coinciding with his own. What was the notion of "Manifest Destiny," and how did it help to shape American history?
4. Do you agree with Catton's assessment of General Lee as a man of the past and, therefore, a fitting emblem of the South? Why or why not?
5. Is history the story of forces acting through great personalities (as Catton assumes) or of great personalities who control forces? Or neither? Explain your answer.

Russell Baker

A Nice Place to Visit

For many years, Russell Baker lived and worked in New York City. To an insider's familiarity with the manners and folkways of that city, however, he brought the perspective of a relative late-comer who was born in Virginia in 1925 and lived in Baltimore and Washington, D.C., before moving to the Big Apple. Beginning in 1962, Baker contributed to the *New York Times* his nationally syndicated "Observer" column, known both for its keen eye upon American politics and for its attentive ear to the English language. Baker, who became the host of *Masterpiece Theatre* in 1993, is also the author of numerous books and collections of essays, including *Baker's Dozen* (1964), *The Rescue of Miss Yashell and Other Pipe Dreams* (1983), *Growing Up* (1983), *The Norton Book of Light Verse* (1986), *There's a Country in My Cellar* (1991), and *Russell Baker's Book of American Humor* (1994). He is the recipient of two Pulitzer Prizes. "A Nice Place to Visit" was collected in *So This Is Depravity* (1980). Baker here contrasts a mannerly Canadian neighbor, Toronto, with the American metropolis he loves to hate. In the final section of this chapter, the author, who now lives in Baltimore, explains how he wrote the column.

Having heard that Toronto was becoming one of the continent's noblest cities, we flew from New York to investigate. New Yorkers jealous of their city's reputation and concerned about challenges to its stature have little to worry about. 1

After three days in residence, our delegation noted an absence of hysteria that was almost intolerable and took to consuming large portions of black coffee to maintain our normal state of irritability. The local people to whom we complained in hopes of provoking comfortably nasty confrontations declined to become bellicose. They 2 would like to enjoy a gratifying big-city hysteria, they said, but believed it would seem ill-mannered in front of strangers.

Extensive field studies—our stay lasted four weeks—persuaded us that this failure reflects the survival in Toronto of an ancient pattern of social conduct called "courtesy." 3

"Courtesy" manifests itself in many quaint forms appalling to the New Yorker. Thus, for example, Yankee fans may be astonished to learn that at the Toronto baseball park it is considered bad form to heave rolls of toilet paper and beer cans at players on the field. 4

Official literature inside Toronto taxicabs includes a notification of the proper address to which riders may mail the authorities not only complaints but also compliments about the cabbie's behavior. 5

For a city that aspires to urban greatness, Toronto's entire taxi system has far to go. At present, it seems hopelessly bogged down in civilization. One day a member of our delegation listening to a radio conversation between a short-tempered cabbie and the dispatcher distinctly heard the dispatcher say, "As Shakespeare said, if music be the food of love, play on, give me excess of it." 6

This delegate became so unnerved by hearing Shakespeare quoted by a cab dispatcher that he fled immediately back to New York to have his nerves abraded and his spine rearranged in a real big-city taxi. 7

What was particularly distressing as the stay continued was the absence of shrieking police and fire sirens at 3 A.M.—or any other hour, for that matter. We spoke to the city authorities about this. What kind of city was it, we asked, that expected its citizens to sleep all night and rise refreshed in the morning? Where was the incentive to awaken gummy-eyed and exhausted, ready to scream at the first person one saw in the morning? How could Toronto possibly hope to maintain a robust urban divorce rate? 8

Our criticism went unheeded, such is the torpor with which Toronto pursues true urbanity. The fact appears to be that Toronto has very little grasp of what is required of a great city. 9

Consider the garbage picture. It seems never to have occurred to anybody in Toronto that garbage exists to be heaved into the streets. One can drive for miles without seeing so much as a banana peel in the gutter or a discarded newspaper whirling in the wind. 10

Nor has Toronto learned about dogs. A check with the authorities confirmed that, yes, there are indeed dogs resident in Toronto, but 11 one would never realize it by walking the sidewalks. Our delegation was shocked by the presumption of a town's calling itself a city, much less a great city, when it obviously knows nothing of either garbage or dogs.

The subway, on which Toronto prides itself, was a laughable imitation of the real thing. The subway cars were not only spotlessly clean, but also fully illuminated. So were the stations. To New Yorkers, it was embarrassing, and we hadn't the heart to tell the subway authorities that they were light-years away from greatness. 12

We did, however, tell them about spray paints and how effectively a few hundred children equipped with spray-paint cans could at least give their subway the big-city look. 13

It seems doubtful they are ready to take such hints. There is a disturbing distaste for vandalism in Toronto which will make it hard for the city to enter wholeheartedly into the vigor of the late twentieth century. 14

A board fence surrounding a huge excavation for a new highrise building in the downtown district offers depressing evidence of Toronto's lack of big-city impulse. Embedded in the fence at intervals of about fifty feet are loudspeakers that play recorded music for passing pedestrians. 15

Not a single one of these loudspeakers has been mutilated. What's worse, not a single one has been stolen. 16

It was good to get back to the Big Apple. My coat pocket was bulging with candy wrappers from Toronto and—such is the lingering power of Toronto—it took me two or three hours back in New Yorker before it seemed natural again to toss them into the street. 17

QUESTIONS

Understanding

1. When Toronto authorities pay no attention to Baker's advice about the need for sirens at 3 A.M., he remarks how slowly the city "pursues true urbanity" (par. 9). What definition of "urbanity" is Baker humorously assuming here and throughout his comparison of New York and Toronto?

2. What are some of the main conditions in Toronto that seem particularly backward to a New Yorker? How might New Yorkers define the idea of "civilization" in which the Canadian city is "hopelessly bogged down" (par. 6)?
3. What specific living conditions does Baker attribute to New York by contrast with the appallingly genteel ways of life in Toronto?
4. When Baker returns home from Canada, it takes "two or three hours" (par. 17) before he can start throwing litter in the streets again. How "lingering," actually, is the influence of the Canadian city upon the true New Yorker?

Strategies and Structure

1. In comparing the two cities, Baker does not so much tell us what New York is like as what Toronto is *not* like. How, then, does he nevertheless get across a clear picture of life in the American city?
2. Baker's IRONY is especially thick in sentences such as this, "What kind of a city was it, we asked, that expected its citizens to sleep all night and rise refreshed in the morning" (par. 8)? Point out other examples in which his mock exasperation is particularly transparent. Do you find such irony an effective device? Why or why not?
3. Why does the author of this essay adopt the plural pronoun "we" instead of saying "I"? Is his reason solely that he went to Canada with several other people?
4. Why does Baker refer to his ramblings in Toronto as "extensive field studies" (par. 3)? What is the difference between an expedition and a trip, or visit?
5. Baker uses a number of highly formal constructions: "our delegation noted an absence" (par. 2), "local people . . . declined to become bellicose" (par. 2), " 'courtesy' manifests itself in many quaint forms" (par. 4). Why might Baker adopt such ponderous SYNTAX, given the role he assumes in this essay.
6. Point out grammatical constructions that show Baker knows how to write in a plainer style.
7. What is a parody? What sort of language and general point of view is Baker having fun with here?

Words and Figures of Speech

1. Baker's title is the first half of an observation that returning travelers often make about strange, impressive places. What is the other half? How does it apply to the case of a dyed-in-the-wool New Yorker?
2. Why does Baker put the word *courtesy* (pars. 3 and 4) in quotation marks?
3. How would you describe Baker's vocabulary most of the time in this essay? Which is more typical of his diction throughout: words like *gummy-eyed* (par. 8) or like *bellicose* (par. 2)? Why the preponderance of such words?
4. What are the CONNOTATIONS of *robust* (par. 8)? Has Baker failed to consider the implications of the word? What reason might he have for choosing it in the context of divorce rates?
5. "What's worse" (par. 16) is a good example of verbal irony, that is, words that say one thing and mean another. In Baker's opening paragraph, what phrase is to be taken equally ironically? What is Baker really saying in both cases?

Comparing

How does Baker's mock railing against the shortcomings of Toronto resemble Jane Smiley's "diatribe" (her word) against midwestern food in "Reflections on a Lettuce Wedge" (Chapter 5)?

Discussion and Writing Topics

1. What is your opinion of the true American urbanite's understanding of urbanity, as reported by Baker? Is Baker being fair to New York and New Yorkers?
2. Confirmed urban dwellers, especially those born and bred in New York City, have been called the country's greatest provincials. Do you agree? Why or why not?
3. Compare and contrast two cities or towns of your acquaintance by assuming the prejudices of one and revealing the "faults" of the other in the glaring light of those prejudices.

Gary Soto

LIKE MEXICANS

Born in Fresno, California, Gary Soto teaches Chicano studies and English Literature at the University of California at Berkeley. Like his award-winning poems, Soto's prose often celebrates his Mexican-American heritage and "a view of the universe that is both apocalyptic and regenerative." He is the author of, among other books, *Where Sparrows Work Hard* (1981), *Black Hair* (1985), *Living Up the Street* (1985), *A Summer Life* (1990), and *Canto Familiar* (1995). "Like Mexicans" is from a collection of reminiscences, *Small Faces* (1985).

My grandmother gave me bad advice and good advice when I was in my early teens. For the bad advice, she said that I should become a barber because they made good money and listened to the radio all day. "Honey, they don't work como burros," she would say every time I visited her. She made the sound of donkeys braying. "Like that, honey!" For the good advice, she said that I should marry a Mexican girl. "No Okies, hijo"—she would say—"Look, my son. He marry one and they fight every day about I don't know what and I don't know what." For her, everyone who wasn't Mexican, black, or Asian were Okies. The French were Okies, the Italians in suits were Okies. When I asked about Jews, whom I had read about, she asked for a picture. I rode home on my bicycle and returned with a calendar depicting the important races of the world. "Pues si, son Okies tambien!"[1] she said, nodding her head. She waved the calendar away and we went to the living room where she lectured me on the virtues of the Mexican girl: first, she could cook and, second, she acted like a woman, not a man, in her husband's home. She said she would tell me about a third when I got a little older. 1

[1] Well yes, they're Okies too.

I asked my mother about it—becoming a barber and marrying 2
Mexican. She was in the kitchen. Steam curled from a pot of boiling beans, the radio was on, looking as squat as a loaf of bread. "Well, if you want to be a barber—they say they make good money." She slapped a round steak with a knife, her glasses slipping down with each strike. She stopped and looked up. "If you find a good Mexican girl, marry her of course." She returned to slapping the meat and I went to the backyard where my brother and David King were sitting on the lawn feeling the inside of their cheeks.

"This is what girls feel like," my brother said, rubbing the inside 3
of his cheek. David put three fingers inside his mouth and scratched. I ignored them and climbed the back fence to see my best friend, Scott, a second-generation Okie. I called him and his mother pointed to the side of the house where his bedroom was a small aluminum trailer, the kind you gawk at when they're flipped over on the freeway, wheels spinning in the air. I went around to find Scott pitching horseshoes.

I picked up a set of rusty ones and joined him. While we played, 4
we talked about school and friends and record albums. The horseshoes scuffed up dirt, sometimes ringing the iron that threw out a meager shadow like a sundial. After three argued-over games, we pulled two oranges apiece from his tree and started down the alley still talking school and friends and record albums. We pulled more oranges from the alley and talked about who we would marry. "No offense, Scott," I said with an orange slice in my mouth, "but I would never marry an Okie." We walked in step, almost touching, with a sled of shadows dragging behind us. "No offense, Gary," Scott said, "but I would *never* marry a Mexican." I looked at him: a fang of orange slice showed from his munching mouth. I didn't think anything of it. He had his girl and I had mine. But our seventh-grade vision was the same: to marry, get jobs, buy cars and maybe a house if we had money left over.

We talked about our future lives until, to our surprise, we were 5
on the downtown mall, two miles from home. We bought a bag of popcorn at Penneys and sat on a bench near the fountain watching Mexican and Okie girls pass. "That one's mine," I pointed with my chin when a girl with eyebrows arched into black rainbows ambled by. "She's cute," Scott said about a girl with yellow hair and a mouthful of gum. We dreamed aloud, our chins busy pointing out girls. We agreed that we couldn't wait to become men and lift them onto our laps.

But the woman I married was not Mexican but Japanese. It was a surprise to me. For years, I went about wide-eyed in my search for the brown girl in a white dress at a dance. I searched the playground at the baseball diamond. When the girls raced for grounders, their hair bounced like something that couldn't be caught. When they sat together in the lunchroom, heads pressed together, I knew they were talking about us Mexican guys. I saw them and dreamed them. I threw my face into my pillow, making up sentences that were good as in the movies. 6

But when I was twenty, I fell in love with this other girl who worried my mother, who had my grandmother asking once again to see the calendar of the Important Races of the World. I told her I had thrown it away years before. I took a much-glanced-at snapshot from my wallet. We looked at it together, in silence. Then grandma reclined in her chair, lit a cigarette, and said, "Es pretty." She blew and asked with all her worry pushed up to her forehead: "Chinese?" 7

I was in love and there was no looking back. She was the one. I told my mother who was slapping hamburger into patties. "Well, sure if you want to marry her," she said. But the more I talked, the more concerned she became. Later I began to worry. Was it all a mistake? "Marry a Mexican girl," I heard my mother say in my mind. I heard it at breakfast. I heard it over math problems, between Western Civilization and cultural geography. But then one afternoon while I was hitchhiking home from school, it struck me like a baseball in the back: my mother wanted me to marry someone of my own social class—a poor girl. I considered my fiancee, Carolyn, and she didn't look poor, though I knew she came from a family of farm workers and pull-yourself-up-by-your-bootstraps ranchers. I asked my brother, who was marrying Mexican poor that fall, if I should marry a poor girl. He screamed "Yeah" above his terrible guitar playing in his bedroom. I considered my sister who had married Mexican. Cousins were dating Mexican. Uncles were remarrying poor women. I asked Scott, who was still my best friend, and he said, "She's too good for you, so you better not." 8

I worried about it until Carolyn took me home to meet her parents. We drove in her Plymouth until the houses gave way to farms and ranches and finally her house fifty feet from the highway. When we pulled into the drive, I panicked and begged Carolyn to make a U-turn and go back so we could talk about it over a soda. She pinched my cheek, calling me a "silly boy." I felt better, though, 9 when I got out of the car and saw the house: the chipped paint, a cracked window, boards for a walk to the back door. There were rusting cars near the barn. A tractor with a net of spiderwebs under a mulberry. A field. A bale of barbed wire like children's scribbling leaning against an empty chicken coop. Carolyn took my hand and pulled me to my future mother-in-law who was coming out to greet us.

We had lunch: sandwiches, potato chips, and iced tea. Carolyn and her mother talked mostly about neighbors and the congregation at the Japanese Methodist Church in West Fresno. Her father, who was in khaki work clothes, excused himself with a wave that was almost a salute and went outside. I heard a truck start, a dog bark, and then the truck rattle away. 10

Carolyn's mother offered another sandwich, but I declined with a shake of my head and a smile. I looked around when I could, when I was not saying over and over that I was a college student, hinting that I could take care of her daughter. I shifted my chair. I saw newspapers piled in corners, dusty cereal boxes and vinegar bottles in corners. The wallpaper was bubbled from rain that had come in from a bad roof. Dust. Dust lay on lamp shades and window sills. These people are just like Mexicans, I thought. Poor people. 11

Carolyn's mother asked me through Carolyn if I would like a *sushi*. A plate of black and white things were held in front of me. I took one, wide-eyed, and turned it over like a foreign coin. I was biting into one when I saw a kitten crawl up the window screen over the sink. I chewed and the kitten opened its mouth of terror as she crawled higher, wanting in to paw the leftovers from our plates. I looked at Carolyn who said that the cat was just showing off. I looked up in time to see it fall. It crawled up, then fell again. 12

We talked for an hour and had apple pie and coffee, slowly. Finally, we got up with Carolyn taking my hand. Slightly embarrassed, I tried to pull away but her grip held me. I let her have her way as she led me down the hallway with her mother right behind me. When I opened the door, I was startled by a kitten clinging to the screen door, its mouth screaming "cat food, dog biscuits, *sushi*. . . ." I opened the door and the kitten, still holding on, whined in the language of hungry animals. When I got into Carolyn's car, I looked back: the cat was still clinging. I asked Carolyn if it were possibly hungry, but she said the cat was being silly. She started the car, waved to her mother, and bounced us over the rain-poked drive, 13 patting my thigh for being her lover baby. Carolyn waved again. I looked back, waving, then gawking at a window screen where there were now three kittens clawing and screaming to get in. Like Mexicans, I thought. I remembered the Molinas and how the cats clung to their screens—cats they shot down with squirt guns. On the highway, I felt happy, pleased by it all. I patted Carolyn's thigh. Her people were like Mexicans, only different.

Questions

Understanding

1. How does Soto's grandmother define an "Okie" (par 1)? Why doesn't she want her grandson to marry one?
2. What does his friendship with Scott reveal about the boys' mutual prejudices?
3. What is Soto implying about ethnic stereotypes when he refers the second time (par. 7) to the calendar showing the Important Races of the World? Why does his grandmother ask for the calendar again?
4. Why does young Soto keep saying (par. 11) that he's a college student (and not at barber college, either)?
5. "It was a surprise to me," says Soto (par. 6) about marrying a girl of Japanese descent. Why didn't he marry as his grandmother advised?
6. Why does Soto still say that half the advice his grandmother gave him was good advice?

Strategies and Structure

1. Soto's comparison takes the form of a NARRATIVE but the events don't all happen in the same time period. Point to as many different ones as you can. In which paragraphs does the author make especially big leaps in time?
2. How would you describe the perspective of the speaker in, for example, paragraph 3? Who says, "I ignored them": the seventh-grade boy? the adult author? both of them? Please explain.

3. While telling the story of his childhood and youth, Soto is showing us what "Mexicans" are "like." What are some of the specific details by which he characterizes himself and his family?
4. We meet Carolyn's family in paragraph 10. How has Soto already prepared us to expect more similarities than differences between the two families? Cite specific details by which Soto shows you what her people are "like."
5. Why does "Like Mexicans" refer several times to kittens?
6. Why do you suppose Soto mentions Western Civilization and cultural geography (par. 8) rather than other subjects his younger self might have been taking in college?
7. Besides giving advice, Soto's grandmother and all the other adult women in "Like Mexicans" are engaged in the same activity. What is it? What's the implication of Soto's presenting them thus?

Words and Figures of Speech

1. Why does Soto describe the orange slice in Scott's mouth as a "fang" (par. 4)? Why does he have young Soto say, "I didn't think anything of it" (par. 4)?
2. Where does Soto's grandmother get her favorite ethnic slur? Why doesn't she call Okies "gringos"? What's the derivation of *this* ethnic slur?
3. Soto adds "only different" at the end of paragraph 13—as if it were an afterthought. How would his entire essay itself be different without this understatement?
4. How is Soto defining a "social class" (par. 8)? Is the term and its definition his or his younger self's? Please explain.
5. How apt do you find Soto's comparison of *sushi* to a foreign coin (par. 12)? Point out other SIMILES like this one in his essay.

Comparing

1. How does Soto's treatment of the generations compare with Joyce Maynard's in "Four Generations" (Chapter 1)? Does it matter that his main representative of the new generation is male rather than female?
2. Compare "Like Mexicans" and "I Forgot the Words to the National Anthem" (Chapter 4) as essays about adapting to new cultural environments.

Discussion and Writing Topics

1. When Soto mentions "Jews" to his grandmother, she calls for a calendar of the races. Is "Jewish" a racial or an ethnic category? What's the difference? How about "Christian"?
2. What's the difference between an ethnic group and a "social class" (par. 8)? Please explain.
3. How helpful for differentiating human beings does "Like Mexicans" seem to find such terms? What's your evidence?
4. Write an account of your younger self or selves that shows what you and your family were like without actually drawing invidious comparisons with other people (as Soto does not).

Debi Davis and Russell Baker

When Debi Davis was given the assignment to generalize, in writing, about a personal experience, she first did "a memory dump," a technique she recommends to other writers. Sitting at her computer, Davis says, she started back at kindergarten and came forward in time searching rapidly for "topics in my life. I just jotted down a few words to remind me of things, such as: *ants in my pants, red dress, leap frog, falling off horse.*" Pretty soon Davis had 75 or 80 ideas to write about. She then "wrote up" four of the most promising ones: "I did quick sketches, three or four paragraphs each, looking for cohesion and to get an idea of what I could do with each topic. I didn't worry about punctuation or spelling at first. I just wrote. Then I picked the one that seemed to have the most substance: my release from the hospital, going to the mall, people's first reactions to me."

Next, Davis tried to recall everything she could about the incident in a first draft. It ran to almost 3,000 words and concentrated mostly "on paragraph structure" as Davis worked her way, chronologically, through the details she was remembering. Davis did two more drafts. In the second, she "jockied the parts around," cutting as she went; in the third, she picked through "word by word, looking for ones that weren't strong enough." For example, Davis had originally written, "Happy to be free of confinement." In the final version of "Body Imperfect" this became "jubilant to be free" (par. 3). She added the phrase "proud survivor" (par. 3) to the image of herself as a war hero, and put "triumph" in her eyes. In place of the blank space ("like ______") that she had left in the first draft, Davis also added (in the second) her "favorite sentence" in the whole essay, the one in paragraph 4 about being "like bruised fruit on a produce stand." "I was very happy with that sentence," says Davis, who first thought of comparing herself to "an old car, an old horse, an oak tree" before hitting on the metaphor she wanted.

Between the first draft and the one she turned in, Davis pared her essay down to less than 2,000 words. When her teacher suggested that she enter it in the Norton contest (limit: 500 words), Davis "made an outline of each paragraph—so I could see what was essential. It was an extremely useful exercise, a challenge: to see how strong my core was and in how few words I could get across what my story was going to show about how society looks at disability."

"I could tell stories of agonizing complication about a hundred others you might have chosen," Russell Baker replies to inquiries about the composition of "A Nice Place to Visit": "but this particular one was simply a piece of cake." 1

Baker's ironic comparison of two major North American cities appeared after a layoff from writing his regular columns for the *New York Times*. He was working, Baker explains, as a writer on a musical bound for Broadway if it could get off the ground in Canada. "It was my first stay in Toronto. I was impressed." 2

The play failed, and Baker returned to New York with a deadline to meet the next day. Having grown "rusty" during his time off from writing columns, he hoped to ease into the old routine. "I knew a piece comparing Toronto and New York would be a snap. The slobbishness of New York is an old familiar subject. I had written about it in earlier columns and have written about it since. New Yorkers seem to take perverse pleasure in reading about it and even to be slightly proud of their ability to thrive in it. After four weeks in Toronto, which many consider the finest city in North America, it seemed very easy to have another stab at New York's swinishness by invoking the charms of Toronto." 3

The original typescript of "A Nice Place to Visit"—the essay was composed from scratch at the typewriter apparently—shows why the author remembers it as "a very easy piece to write." The original ran to five pages, triple-spaced to allow room for editing. On three 4 of those pages, Baker made only minor corrections in ballpoint pen: a practiced writer proofreading deftly, altering a verb tense here, inserting an adjective there, deleting stray marks from the typewriter. Only two pages (reproduced on pages 229–30) bear revisions that gave the author pause.

When he defined "courtesy" in paragraph 4, Baker originally referred to its "curious forms appalling to the New Yorker in their small town quaintness." Perhaps to clear up any possible ambiguity in "their"—Toronto's or New York's?—Baker changed "curious" to "quaint" and crossed out the last five words. In the next sentence (about Toronto baseball parks), he then had to insert "Yankee fans may be astonished to learn that. . . ." 5

The next paragraph (about Toronto taxicabs) went smoothly until Baker reached the part that now reads "mail the authorities not only complaints but also compliments upon the cabbie's behavior." First he tried "mail compliments to the hack licensing authorities." Then he went back and added "for the driver" after "compliments." Still dissatisfied, Baker crossed out the whole phrase and tried again before making the final emendations: "mail the hack licensing authorities not only complaints but also compliments upon the service." 6

After this brief editorial stall, all went smoothly until the ending (even more troublesome sometimes than the beginning of an essay). Baker launched it with: "It makes you proud to get back to the Big Apple." Then: "It's good to be back in the Big Apple where the worms are. . . ." And again: "It was good to get back to the Big Apple, and we listened ["worms" scratched out] happily to the cabbie's radio blaring 'I Love New York' and threw candy wrappers out the window" [amended to "pulled out the candy wrappers"]. On the fourth try, Baker sailed into the version that concludes the essay as we have it, and his false starts lie neatly inked out behind him. The title, he reports, was added after the entire piece was written and corrected. 7

Often his essays take much longer. Was he gratified by the speedy delivery of this one? "Too easy," says Baker. "Afterwards, I thought the irony was a bit ham-handed and the quality of the piece not much above what a slick college newspaper columnist could have done." 8

Spoken like the true author of *Growing Up*.

WRITING TOPICS FOR CHAPTER SIX
Essays That Compare and Contrast

Write a comparison contrast essay on one of the following topics:

1. Two different cities (for example, San Francisco and Washington, D.C.)
2. The same city at different times of day or in different seasons
3. Two World War II generals (for example, Patton and Eisenhower)
4. Two teachers you have admired
5. Two neighborhoods you have lived in
6. The haves and the have-nots in your hometown
7. Two of your classmates from different geographical regions
8. Two roommates you have had
9. A job versus a profession
10. Modern versus old-fashioned families (or marriages)
11. Two churches or synagogues in your hometown
12. Life in a democracy versus life under some other form of government
13. Two styles of playing football, baseball, tennis, or golf
14. The styles of two political (or social) leaders on your campus
15. The styles of two national politicians
16. The work of two painters, singers, musicians, or writers
17. Two newspaper columns or magazines that you read
18. Two comic strips

observer 22222222

Extensive field studies---our stay lasted four (number 4) weeks---persuaded us that this failure reflects the survival in Toronto of an ancient pattern of social conduct called "courtesy."

"Courtesy" manifests itself in many quaint forms appalling to the New Yorker. Thus, for example, YANKEE FANS MAY BE ASTONISHED TO LEARN THAT at the Toronto baseball park it is considered bad form to heave rolls of toilet paper and beer cans at players on the field.

Official literature inside Toronto taxicabs includes notification of the proper address to which riders may mail the authorities not only complaints but also compliments upon the CABBIE'S BEHAVIOR.

For a city that aspires to urban greatness, TORONTO'S entire taxi system has far to go. At present it seems hopelessly bogged down in civilization. One day a member of our delegation listening to a radio conversation between a short-tempered cabbie and the despatcher distinctly heard the dispatcher say, "As Shakespeare said, If music be the fruit of love, then give me excess of it."

more

Revising "A Nice Place to Visit": two pages from the typescript show the main changes that Russell Baker made as he compared two North American cities.

observer 555555555

It seems doubtful they are ready to take such hints. There is a disturbing distaste for vandalism in Toronto which will make it hard for the city to enter wholeheartedly into the vigor of the late Twentieth century.

A board fence surrounding a huge excavation for a new high-rise building in the downtown district offers depressing evidence of Toronto's lack of big-city impulse. Embedded in the fence at intervals of about 50 feet are loudspeakers that play recorded music for the pleasure of passing pedestrians.

Not a single one of these loudspeakers has been mutilated. What's worse, not a single one has been stolen.

It was good to get back to the Big Apple. My coat pocket was bulging with candy wrappers from Toronto and---such is the lingering power of Toronto---it took me two or three hours back in New York before it seemed natural again to toss them into the street.

Seven

Essays That Use Metaphor and Analogy

METAPHORS[1] and ANALOGIES are figures of speech or "turns" of language that use words symbolically rather than literally. The poet Carl Sandburg created a metaphor when he wrote, "The woman named Tomorrow / sits with a hairpin in her teeth / and takes her time. . . ." His friend and fellow poet, Robert Frost, was developing an analogy when he told Sandburg that writing poetry without regular meter and rhyme is like playing tennis with the net down. Metaphors and analogies (or "extended metaphors"), then, are comparisons that reveal an object, event, or quality by identifying it with another object, event, or quality (usually one more familiar than the first, as tennis is more familiar to most of us than the rules of poetry).

The kinds of comparisons that metaphors and analogies make, however, should not be confused with those discussed in the last chapter ("Essays That Compare and Contrast"). When Bruce Catton compared Grant and Lee, he was as much interested in one general as the other. COMPARISON AND CONTRAST essays may not attend equally to the similarities and differences between their subjects, but they usually give equal weight to the subjects themselves. Essays that use metaphor and analogy, on the other hand, have a primary sub-

[1] Terms printed in small capitals are defined in the Glossary.

ject, which the object of comparison is introduced to explain. When Ernest Hemingway declared, for example, that a fine English sentence has the clean grace of a matador's sweeping cape, he was talking about writing, not bullfighting.

One common use of such comparisons is to advance an ARGUMENT. If you were trying to convince a friend that the government should spend more money on the space program, you might argue that Americans have a pioneering spirit and that outer space is like the western frontier of a century ago; to advance across this new frontier is simply to fulfill our national destiny. Such a line of reasoning is an "argument by analogy." It assumes that, because two entities or ideas are alike in some ways, they are alike in other significant ways. An argument by analogy is the most vulnerable form of argument; it is only as strong as the analogy is close and complete. Your argument would collapse if your friend observed that spaceships are much more expensive than covered wagons and that the original frontier was conquered by exploiting the first Americans.

Another common function of analogies is to explain; the EXPOSITORY essays in the following pages are used for this purpose. "Pulling Up Roots" by Anne Raver, for example, tells us something about "the art of compromise" by comparing marriage to planting a garden. In finished essays, such analogies are primarily organizing devices; but when you are in the process of composing an essay, they may actually aid you in finding things to say.

Suppose you were getting ready to write an essay on the expansion of the universe, and you were puzzled by the problem of locating the center of expansion. From our galaxy, all the other galaxies seem to be rushing out and away; yet astrophysicists tell us that we would experience the same sense of being left behind if we visited any other galaxy in the universe. To write your essay, you must resolve this apparent contradiction.

Now, suppose you hit upon the analogy of the balloon. (Your subject is the universe, remember, not balloons; an analogy illuminates a primary subject, it does not replace it with another.) You might begin to think of the many galaxies of our expanding universe as spots of dark paint dotting the surface of the inflating balloon. As the rubber surface expands, every dot draws apart from every other dot. Whichever dot you single out will appear to be the "center" of a surface that has no fixed middle point. Having used this analogy to grasp your subject, you may then turn around and use it to explain your complicated ideas to the reader.

Keep the following pointers in mind when developing an essay by analogy. Although an analogy will not "hold" if it compares objects that are too disparate, avoid obvious, trivial, or tired comparisons: life to a brief parade, a face without a smile to a day without sunshine. Analogies often liken the unfamiliar and the complicated to the common and the simple, but an analogy may also compare its primary subject with something exotic in order to discover the unexpected in the familiar. And, finally, try to compare your primary subject with something that is interesting and original in its own right. You are not likely to impress your reader if you explain the idea of blind choice by analogy with a stab in the dark or a number drawn from a hat.

Anne Raver

Pulling Up Roots

After growing up on a farm in western Maryland, Anne Raver attended Oberlin College and Johns Hopkins University, where she received a master's degree in creative writing. She is the former garden columnist for New York *Newsday* and now writes about gardening for the *New York Times*. She lives in Brooklyn Heights, New York. "Pulling Up Roots" is from *Deep in the Green* (1995), a collection of essays that Roger Swain of PBS's *Victory Garden* has called "cosmic and microscopic," proving again and again "that earth is still a great place from which to view the heavens."

I didn't plant my snap peas this year. I'm moving to Long Island— to a warmer, sandier soil—and someone else will be tilling my old plot in Ipswich, Massachusetts. 1

It's a beautiful site for a garden, a fifty-foot square in the middle of a wild meadow. It basks in full sunlight on the top of a knoll overlooking the confluence of the Ipswich River and a saltwater creek. At low tide, I can lean on my shovel and watch the clam diggers and the great blue herons; at high tide, the more frivolous boaters, speeding down the channel like Toady and Rat. 2

Leaving a piece of land is not an easy departure. Each place holds so many experiences—successes and failures with plants, bugs and people—that a move can't help feeling like some kind of erasure. 3

My husband and I first hacked at the matted field with borrowed pickaxes, ripping up the sod with our hands and shaking the topsoil from every piece back into the little square we had bounded by twine. He, a suburban kid, thought a small plot was plenty; I, a farmer's daughter, wanted half the field—for squash, potatoes and corn. 4

Months before, we'd argued over the seed catalogs. Why couldn't 5

I be satisfied with a tidy little list, he grumbled. That was just like me, always wanting too much. Why couldn't I plant corn if I wanted, I complained. That was just like him, always trying to control me. You want to do everything *your way,* we both yelled, like furious adolescents.

Neither of us had learned the art of compromise, and as we went down the rows planting the beans and putting in the tomatoes, our boundaries solidified into rock walls, instead of blending in a comfortable combination of desires and tastes. When a pound of Burpee's Early Sunglow arrived in the mail—I'd willfully, secretly added it to the list—my husband turned on our big color TV and began rooting for the Red Sox. After all, maybe his favorite vegetation was the bright green outfield of Fenway Park. 6

The next April, I knelt in the cold damp earth, putting in as many peas as I wanted. My husband and I had given up on gardening together—and on each other. The first little green shoots comforted me, in their sturdy urgency to get on with life, but the irony of my huge plot, for just me, was a bitter one. Who was going to eat all those vegetables that would fill the hefty Sears freezer my father had bought for us? 7

I began to grow flowers that summer. I realized why my father puttered in his rose beds, his own heart opening up as the hybrid teas and grandifloras bloomed. And by the time other men ventured into my garden, I knew enough to hand them the packet of Kentucky Wonder seeds and say, with a nonchalant shrug, "Plant them however you want, that's part of the fun." Sure, I was gritting my teeth, but I wanted to eat those beans across from a warm body. 8

Yet that little seaside plot also gave me clarity, helped me to trust my instincts. I longed for rhubarb, raspberries and asparagus, but I couldn't bring myself to put in any of these perennials with any of my gardening guests. 9

Perhaps I needed to do it all my own way for a while. I'd grown up with a man who'd welcomed his children in the vegetable plot—as long as we set the tomatoes out with military precision. No wonder my own garden grew in crooked rows and irregular patches, a slightly sloppy riot of vegetables and flowers. A kind of happy manifestation of my mind, which is more circular than linear. 10

But last summer, some blight seemed to pass through my healthy plot. The soil wasn't the problem; it had grown rich with years of compost and my neighbor's cow manure. It wasn't ignorance; I knew 11 how to combat every bug and fungus. No, some malaise of my own had crept up to that seaside garden. When the Japanese beetles arrived, I failed to pick them off the bush beans in the evenings. I no longer stood patiently with the hose, letting my thirsty tomatoes drink their fill. Days would pass, and I'd stay away—playing with friends or reading wintry books inside the house—and when I did climb to the top of my little knoll, I'd find weeds choking my cucumbers, spider mites smothering my Brussels sprouts. It was no longer a happy experience to grow all this stuff alone. My little paradise had become a Garden of Neglect.

And so last fall, as I brought in the green tomatoes, and cut off the drooping heads of my Mammoth sunflowers, I knew that the spring would send me out into some new territory. I don't know what my new garden will be like. Some small suburban plot, set right against my neighbor's private hedge? Or a more private place, tucked behind the cottage on some wealthy old estate? 12

I'll miss the sea, and the herons, and the deer stepping delicately out into the meadow as the sun goes down. But I know that my next garden will put down longer, woodier roots. I find myself reading up on those asparagus beds. I'm studying the art of orchards. And I want my own grape arbor—to make enough wine for two. 13

Questions

Understanding

1. Why is Anne Raver pulling up roots and leaving Ipswich, Massachusetts, in this essay? Where is she going?
2. What differences of opinion do Raver and her (former) husband exhibit concerning the techniques of planting and gardening?
3. Even though Raver looks forward to starting a new life (and garden), why is leaving the old plot of land still "not an easy departure" (par. 3) for her?
4. Why does Raver invite new visitors to her garden to plant seeds "however you want" (par. 8)? Why does she also silently grit her teeth when doing so?
5. Why does Raver intend to grow grapes in her new garden?

Strategies and Structure

1. When (in which paragraph) did you first suspect that Raver is writing about more than gardening here? When did you figure it out for sure?
2. If pulling up roots is a metaphor for making a new start in life and love, what is the garden itself a metaphor for in Raver's essay?
3. When Raver says that "last summer, some blight seemed to pass through my healthy plot" (par. 11), is she referring to a disease of plants or to a strictly metaphorical "blight"? Please explain your answer.
4. What is the function of Raver's father as she presents him here? Where does Raver hint that her father was suffering from heart disease at the time she wrote this essay?
5. Insofar as it incorporates elements of NARRATIVE, does Raver's essay have a happy or a "mixed" ending? How does her mentioning the grape arbor in the final paragraph affect the TONE of the ending?

Words and Figures of Speech

1. She is moving, Raver inserts parenthetically, "to a warmer, sandier soil" (par. 1). How does this apparently literal remark in the first paragraph anticipate the "metaphoric" ending of her essay, particularly the reference to "longer, woodier roots" (par. 13)?
2. Who were Toady and Rat (par. 2)?
3. Why might a writer, of all people, describe leaving as an *erasure* (par. 3)?
4. "Our boundaries solidified into rock walls" (par. 6): how and how well does this metaphor fit the "garden" context of Raver's essay?
5. How do the Red Sox (par. 6) pertain to the conflict, or contest, Raver is describing?
6. "My husband and I had given up on gardening together—and on each other" (par. 7). What is the effect of this UNDERSTATEMENT (see FIGURES OF SPEECH in the glossary)?
7. What is the "bitter" IRONY to which Raver refers in paragraph 7?
8. Why does Raver just happen to note that the seeds she hands to visitors in her garden are "Kentucky Wonders" (par. 8)?
9. Why does Raver capitalize "Garden of Neglect" (par. 11)?

10. How do we know that the author of "Pulling Up Roots" has learned something (or at least is willing to) from her experience in the garden, particularly something about "the art of compromise" (par. 6)?

Comparing

1. Compare and contrast "Pulling Up Roots" with "How to Get Out of a Locked Trunk" (Chapter 3) as essays about learning to deal with personal relationships.
2. How does the Anne Raver of "Pulling Up Roots" compare with the "Maidenform" ideal described by Ellen Goodman in "The Maidenform Woman Administers Shock Treatment" (Chapter 5)?

Discussion and Writing Topics

1. Couples should never wallpaper (or tend a garden) together if they want to stay together. Please comment.
2. Have you ever had to pull up roots? Would a gardening metaphor serve you well to describe the experience, or would another metaphor be better? Which one? Why?

Judith Ortiz Cofer

More Room

A poet and novelist, Judith Ortiz Cofer was born in Puerto Rico, where she lived until 1955. In that year, her father, serving in the U.S. Navy, sent for his family, and they moved to Paterson, New Jersey. "More Room" is one of the essays from *Silent Dancing* (1990), which Cofer subtitled "A Partial Remembrance of a Puerto Rican Childhood." Her other works include *Terms of Survival* (1987), *The Line of the Sun* (1989), *The Latin Deli* (1993), and *Reaching for the Mainland and Selected New Poems* (1995).

My grandmother's house is like a chambered nautilus; it has many rooms, yet it is not a mansion. Its proportions are small and its design simple. It is a house that has grown organically, according to the needs of its inhabitants. To all of us in the family it is known as *la casa de Mamá*. It is the place of our origin; the stage for our memories and dreams of Island life. 1

I remember how in my childhood it sat on stilts; this was before it had a downstairs—it rested on its perch like a great blue bird—not a flying sort of bird, more like a nesting hen, but with spread wings. Grandfather had built it soon after their marriage. He was a painter and housebuilder by trade—a poet and meditative man by nature. As each of their eight children were born, new rooms were added. After a few years, the paint didn't exactly match, nor the materials, so that there was a chronology to it, like the rings of a tree, and Mamá could tell you the history of each room in her *casa*, and thus the geneology of the family along with it. 2

Her own room is the heart of the house. Though I have seen it recently—and both woman and room have diminished in size, changed by the new perspective of my eyes, now capable of looking over countertops and tall beds—it is not this picture I carry in my 3 memory of Mamá's *casa*. Instead, I see her room as a queen's chamber where a small woman loomed large, a throneroom with a massive four-poster bed in its center, which stood taller than a child's head. It was on this bed, where her own children had been born, that the smallest grandchildren were allowed to take naps in the afternoons; here too was where Mamá secluded herself to dispense private advice to her daughters, sitting on the edge of the bed, looking down at whoever sat on the rocker where generations of babies had been sung to sleep. To me she looked like a wise empress right out of the fairy tales I was addicted to reading.

Though the room was dominated by the mahogany four-poster, it also contained all of Mamá's symbols of power. On her dresser there were not cosmetics but jars filled with herbs: *yerba* we were all subjected to during childhood crises. She had a steaming cup for anyone who could not, or would not, get up to face life on any given day. If the acrid aftertaste of her cures for malingering did not get you out of bed, then it was time to call *el doctor*. 4

And there was the monstrous chifforobe she kept locked with a little golden key she did not hide. This was a test of her dominion over us; though my cousins and I wanted a look inside that massive wardrobe more than anything, we never reached for that little key lying on top of her Bible on the dresser. This was also where she placed her earrings and rosary when she took them off at night. God's word was her security system. This chifforobe was the place where I imagined she kept jewels, satin slippers, and elegant silk, sequined gowns of heartbreaking fineness. I lusted after those imaginary costumes. I had heard that Mamá had been a great beauty in her youth, and the belle of many balls. My cousins had ideas as to what she kept in that wooden vault: its secret could be money (Mamá did not hand cash to strangers, banks were out of the question, so there were stories that her mattress was stuffed with dollar bills, and that she buried coins in jars in her garden under rosebushes, or kept them in her inviolate chifforobe); there might be that legendary gun salvaged from the Spanish-American conflict over the Island. We went wild over suspected treasures that we made up simply because children have to fill locked trunks with something wonderful. 5

On the wall above the bed hung a heavy silver crucifix. Christ's agonized head hung directly over Mamá's pillow. I avoided looking at this weapon suspended over where her head would have lain; and 6 on the rare occasions when I was allowed to sleep on that bed, I scooted down to the safe middle of the mattress, where her body's impression took me in like mother's lap. Having taken care of the obligatory religious decoration with the crucifix, Mamá covered the other walls with objects sent to her over the years by her children in the States. *Los Nueva Yores* was represented by, among other things, a postcard of Niagara Falls from her son Hernán, postmarked, Buffalo, N.Y. In a conspicuous gold frame hung a large color photograph of her daughter Nena, her husband and their five children at the entrance to Disneyland in California. From us she had gotten a black lace fan. Father had brought it to her from a tour of duty with the Navy in Europe. (On Sundays she would remove it from its hook on the wall to fan herself at Sunday mass.) Each year more items were added as the family grew and dispersed, and every object in the room had a story attached to it, a *cuento*, which Mamá would bestow on anyone who received the privilege of a day alone with her. It was almost worth pretending to be sick, though the bitter herb purgatives of the body were a big price to pay for the spirit revivals of her storytelling.

Except for the times when a sick grandchild warranted the privilege, or when a heartbroken daughter came home in need of more than herbal teas, Mamá slept alone on her large bed. 7

In the family there is a story about how this came to be. 8

When one of the daughters, my mother or one of her sisters, tells the *cuento* of how Mamá came to own her nights, it is usually preceded by the qualification that Papá's exile from his wife's room was not a result of animosity between the couple. But the act had been Mamá's famous bloodless coup for her personal freedom. Papá was the benevolent dictator of her body and her life who had had to be banished from her bed so that Mamá could better serve her family. Before the telling, we had to agree that the old man—whom we all recognize in the family as an *alma de Dios,* a saintly, soft-spoken presence whose main pleasures in life, such as writing poetry and reading the Spanish large-type editions of *Reader's Digest,* always took place outside the vortex of Mamá's crowded realm, was not to blame. It was not his fault, after all, that every year or so he planted a baby-seed in Mamá's fertile body, keeping her from leading the active life she needed and desired. He loved her and the babies. He would compose odes and lyrics to celebrate births and anniversaries, 9 and hired musicians to accompany him in singing them to his family and friends at extravagant pig-roasts he threw yearly. Mamá and the oldest girls worked for days preparing the food. Papá sat for hours in his painter's shed, also his study and library, composing the songs. At these celebrations he was also known to give long speeches in praise of God, his fecund wife, and his beloved Island. As a middle child, my mother remembers these occasions as a time when the women sat in the kitchen and lamented their burdens while the men feasted out in the patio, their rumthickened voices rising in song and praise of each other, *compañeros* all.

It was after the birth of her eighth child, after she had lost three at birth or infancy, that Mamá made her decision. They say that Mamá had had a special way of letting her husband know that they were expecting, one that had begun when, at the beginning of their marriage, he had built her a house too confining for her taste. So, when she discovered her first pregnancy, she supposedly drew plans for another room, which he dutifully executed. Every time a child was due, she would demand, *More space, more space*. Papá acceded to her wishes, child after child, since he had learned early that Mamá's renowned temper was a thing that grew like a monster along with a new belly. In this way Mamá got the house that she wanted, but with each child she lost in health and energy. She had knowledge of her body and perceived that if she had any more children, her dreams and her plans would have to be permanently forgotten, because she would be a chronically ill woman, like Flora with her twelve children, asthma, no teeth; in bed more than on her feet. 10

And so after my youngest uncle was born, she asked Papá to build a large room at the back of the house. He did so in joyful anticipation. Mamá had asked him for special things this time: shelves on the walls, a private entrance. He thought that she meant this room to be a nursery where several children could sleep. He thought it was a wonderful idea. He painted it his favorite color—sky blue—and made large windows looking out over a green hill and the church spires beyond. But nothing happened. Mamá's belly did not grow, yet she seemed in a frenzy of activity over the house. Finally, an anxious Papá approached his wife to tell her that the new room was finished and ready to be occupied. And Mamá, they say, replied: "Good, it's for *you*." 11

And so it was that Mamá discovered the only means of birth con- 12 trol available to a Catholic woman of her time: sacrifice. She gave up the comfort of Papá's sexual love for something she deemed greater: the right to own and control her body, so that she might live to meet her grandchildren, me among them, so that she could give more of herself to the ones already there, so that she could be more than a channel for other lives, so that even now that time has robbed her of the elasticity of her body and of her amazing reservoir of energy, she can still emanate the calm joy that can only be achieved by living according to the dictates of one's own heart.

QUESTIONS

Understanding

1. Mamá's house is located in Puerto Rico, Papá's "beloved Island" (par. 9). Why was it built on stilts?
2. After comparing it to a seashell (par. 1), Judith Ortiz Cofer compares her grandmother's house to a bird (par. 2). Why does she take care to make it a "nesting" rather than a "flying" bird? Why does the bird nonetheless have "spread wings" (par. 2)?
3. "Her own room is the heart of the house" (par. 3). To what is Cofer now comparing her grandmother's house? Which of these ANALOGIES does she enlarge upon most fully in the rest of "More Room"?
4. Besides the new babies in the family, who needs the additional space promised in Cofer's title? Why?
5. Cofer remembers her grandmother as a "queen" (par. 3) in her throne chamber. What serves as her throne, and why is it so queenly? What is the "chifforobe" (par. 5) in that same chamber?

Strategies and Structure

1. "More Room" is the story (*"cuento,"* par. 9) of a story. Which paragraphs serve as prologue? Where does Cofer tell the story itself? Who has established the traditional way of telling it?
2. Why is the story of Mamá's room(s) always told with the qualification that Papá was "a saintly, soft-spoken presence" (par. 9)? Does Cofer her-

self follow this convention in retelling the story of his exile? Why or why not?

3. What is the function of the family home in Cofer's essay? Of her grandmother's room within it? Of the new, last-to-be-added room?
4. How are the walls of Mamá's room decorated? What does it say about her that the "obligatory" (par. 6) crucifix is the only religious object on her walls? How does the bible, with the golden key on top (par. 5), fit into this scene?
5. How does Cofer give us the sense of seeing her grandmother's wondrous room through the eyes of a child?
6. Why does Cofer mention Flora and her twelve children (par. 10) just before Mamá finally reveals the purpose of the new room to Papá?

Words and Figures of Speech

1. "Build thee more stately mansions, O my soul, / As the swift seasons roll!" So begins the final stanza of "The Chambered Nautilus" (1858) by Oliver Wendell Holmes. How does Cofer build upon this ALLUSION as she goes on to describe her grandmother's house.
2. Why does Cofer use "baby-seed" (par. 9) instead of "sperm," or some other grown-up word, to explain her grandmother's plight?
3. Her grandmother's house, says Cofer, is "the place of our origin" (par. 1). In what multiple senses might this phrase be read?
4. Why does Cofer mention that she was addicted to reading fairy tales as a child (par. 3)?
5. Of all the objects in Cofer's account of her grandmother's room, why is the bed such a focal point?
6. How does the locked chifforobe anticipate the new room to which Papá is to be exiled?

Comparing

1. Cofer paints a portrait of her grandmother by filling in the physical details of the background against which she is to be seen. How, by contrast, does Amy Tan in "Mother Tongue" (Chapter 2) supply the details of her mother's portrait?
2. How might Naomi Shihab Nye's "Double Vision in a New Old World" (Chapter 8) be said to invert the perspective of "More Room"?

3. How, to a child's eye, do the "symbols" of the grandmother's power in "More Room" resemble the ritual killing of the spider in Gordon Grice's "Caught in the Widow's Web" (Essays for Further Reading)?

Discussion and Writing Topics

1. Is "More Room" fair to Papá? Why or why not?
2. "More Room" develops an analogy between a house and the people in it. To what extent is that analogy also an ARGUMENT? How valid or invalid?
3. Write a description of a place (your room, your grandmother's house, a study or shop or office) that reveals the person who inhabits it. Instead of explaining what the place tells us about the person, spend most of your space describing physical details that characterize both of them.

Kitty Burns Florey

TICKY-TACKY

A baby boomer, Kitty Burns Florey lived the American dream for a time—or at least she recalls it as a trancelike state—in a cookie-cutter "Cape Cod" house in a 1950s suburban development in central New York. When her father died, young Florey returned to the city, where she still lives (in Brooklyn) and writes about "Thoughts of Home," the title of the *House Beautiful* series in which "Ticky-tacky" first appeared. (In July 1993 in this same series, Florey published an earlier thoughts-of-home essay entitled "On Feeling Small.") Her sixth novel, *Vigil for a Stranger,* was published in 1995.

I remember everything about that house. We bought it for $5,500, and the monthly payments were $66. Our phone number was 5851. There were thirteen steps up to the attic. A spirea bush grew at the southeast corner. The dog next door was named Skippy. I kept my colored drawing pencils in a little blue box my mother gave me that still held the scent of Bluegrass soap. The neighbors were the Fitzmaurices, the Macks, the Vincelettes (they were from France), the Perciantes (they were from Canada), the Worshels, the Sawyers. Wild strawberries grew in the vast woods out back. My father paid me a penny for every gypsy moth caterpillar I picked off the willow tree we planted. 1

After years of moving from apartment to apartment, my parents bought the house when I was nine, in a brand-new housing development north of our city in central New York State. The first time I saw the place it was a quarter-acre of red dirt on a street lined with other plots of dirt, plus a few half-built houses and a couple of raw-looking finished ones with newly fledged bright green lawns. The houses would all be identical four-room "Capes." In those days, the early 1950s, the unquestioned practice was to bulldoze the woods, 2 level everything, put up straight rows of houses, and replant. My parents chose our particular plot because a large maple tree had been inexplicably spared just outside what would be their bedroom window. When we put down the deposit the tree was just budding; it was blushed with scarlet when we moved in.

We watched the house go up. My father and I would drive out to the site as often as we could all that spring and summer. Dad became friendly with the builders as they framed out the house, and he got them to change a few things that we agreed made ours subtly superior to the others on the block: a bigger closet, some built-in shelves, a lowered window. My parents and I had long discussions over paint colors, poring over the bright sample chips and finally choosing dusty rose for my room, pale green for my parents' room, and for the kitchen a color scheme we found in a magazine, a kind of soft faded-denim blue with wrought-iron hinges and knobs on the cupboards. I remember the day we moved in—the joy of arranging my books and my collection of miniature china animals in my deeply pink bedroom, and the odd combination of familiarity and strangeness that permeated the house, with its old furniture and its smooth new walls and pristine floors. 3

Buying the house was the central event of my childhood. It was an expression of faith. My father was ill—he had a damaged heart, the legacy of rheumatic fever when he was a child and the house meant that we believed he would get better. 4

My parents were extraordinarily hopeful and adaptable people. They came from very different backgrounds. My father's father was one of the founders of a major soft drink company; he worked in New York City where he lived in a hotel all week, leaving my grandmother at home with their twelve children in a big white house with pillars. I remember their Steinway grand piano, the huge pastoral tapestry on the living room wall, my grandmother's mirrored vanity table bearing dozens of cut-glass bottles of perfumes with intriguing French names. My mother's father had been a streetcar conductor, and that grandmother preferred to live above a store on a busy street where she could keep an eye on what was happening. On my birthday she always tucked a dollar bill into a card; my other grandmother sent pieces of silver flatware in the pattern she chose for me when I was born. 5

Before I came along, my parents led a romantic and glamorous life. My father's illness had not yet surfaced, and he traveled all over 6 the East as a quality-control supervisor in the family business. I have photographs of my parents from those days: my mother with her elegant legs, shoulder pads, and a perm, my father with his wavy red-gold hair and natty suits. They rode the *Broadway Limited* between New York and Chicago, stayed in swanky hotels, danced to the big bands in nightclubs in a world that always sounds to me like something from a Scott Fitzgerald novel.

It ended when I was born, of course. My parents waited ten years for me: That's the way they always put it, as if I were a late train to a place they desperately wanted to go. In perfect contentment, they settled down and became parents. Then when my father returned from the war in the Pacific in 1945 his health began to deteriorate. We lived with his bad heart, his illnesses and hospitalizations, his difficulty holding a job because of chest pains, his shortness of breath, and the wrenching chronic cough that marks heart patients. But my mother worked (the only mother I knew who did), and her income plus the G.I. Bill enabled us to buy the house. 7

After we moved in, my life was transformed in large and small ways. I didn't change schools, but instead of walking there with Ann and Barbara I took the school bus with Donna and Roseanne. Instead of coming home for lunch to eat hot soup and listen to "As the World Turns" on the radio, I brought my lunch and ate it in the cafeteria. I made new friends in the neighborhood: Laura Mae, whose exotic mother drank beer and read *True Romances* all day, and Terry, the Canadian boy next door, who taught me to ice-skate backward, and Penny the teenager on the other side who paid me a dime to play "Unchained Melody" and "Love Is a Many-Splendored Thing" and "Minuet in G" on the piano in their living room with my back turned while she necked with her boyfriend on the sofa. 8

My city friends came out to see me regularly. With the woods behind the house, it was almost rural, and in those last years of childhood we spent Saturdays building tree houses, eating wild strawberries, blazing trails through the infinite acres of trees. In winter, we skated on the Perciantes' homemade backyard rink or wasted long hours absorbed in Sneak, a made-up card game my best friend and I were obsessed with. 9

I was an indulged only child; my parents were incredibly hospitable for people who must have been under enormous stress. My friends came and stayed overnight, singly and in groups. For breakfast, my father made us dozens of teeny-weeny pancakes the size of 10 coins. I had parties and cookouts, and we played croquet and badminton on the lawn. I don't recall my parents ever saying no to any of these plans. Incessant bangings of "Chopsticks" on the piano, preteen girls trying on my mother's makeup in the bathroom, the cat dressed up in doll's hats and booties: They took it all in stride, feeling that one of the delights of home ownership was the freedom to let a dozen noisy kids practice jitterbugging to "Hound Dog" late on a Friday night.

Everyone loved our house. I don't remember anyone ever remarking on its similarity to its neighbors. I'm not sure anyone really noticed it but me. I was fascinated by it, and I liked going into other people's houses to check out the similarities. The picture window, the door to the attic, the distinctive half-wall to the kitchen—even the thermostats were in precisely the same place, in the hallway just outside the kitchen. The houses formed a small version of the Levittowns that we saw in aerial photographs years later, lined up in creepy anonymity like squares on a game board. 11

But what intrigued me was that they were also immeasurably different, not only in details but in aura—that indefinable character a house assumes, a distillation of the quirks and tastes and pretensions and hang-ups and backgrounds of the people who live there. The Worshels' was a thrilling mess, the Perciantes' was awesome in its fresh tidiness, the Fitzmaurices' antiques-filled living room seemed strange and grand. My friend Terry's bedroom, exactly like mine, was simultaneously from another planet: It contained very little but a bed, a bureau, and a fabulous electric train set. Only in our house was the thermostat painted to blend with the walls, because only my father knew you could do that, or cared enough, or, I realize now, had the invalid's leisure for such niceties. 12

Because, eventually, my father could hardly work at all. My mother went to her office job and came home tired at 5:30. My father sat at the kitchen table all day, smoking and coughing and listening to the radio. When I returned from school, we would talk, often about improvements he wanted to make in the house. He drew plans for an attached garage with a workshop, and upstairs, in the half-attic, a bedroom for me with a cozy sloping ceiling. Sometimes we would cook dinner together, if he was feeling well enough. I remember his brutal cough, his red face, the endless Camels no one realized he shouldn't be smoking. For a while he managed to work at a night watchman job—four to midnight—and I was alone for a 13 couple of hours between his departure and my mother's arrival. I had my own key, the only kid I knew who did. I loved that after-school solitude: just me and the cat and a book. But I knew that it was one of the things that made my family radically different from my friends' families.

14 Then, of course, the day came that somehow, all through my childhood, I had known would come: My father didn't return home from one of his trips to the hospital. There was a wake, perhaps more horrible to me than any experience before or since: my father lying dead, as if carved from rock and then painted. I screamed when I saw him in his blue satin-lined coffin—and then realized that a dozen of my friends were sitting in chairs watching. I remember feeling simultaneously frantic with sorrow and deeply embarrassed. I was thirteen. At school I became known as "the girl who lost her father." My mother and I sold the house and moved into an apartment in the city.

15 The worst thing about moving away was that the cat disappeared on moving day, as if he couldn't bear to go, as if he loved prowling in the woods and catching chipmunks more than he loved his faithful family who had raised him from a kitten. I took the bus out there every Saturday morning for weeks afterward, calling him, searching the woods, asking the neighbors, but I never learned what happened to him. Losing him wasn't worse than losing my father, but it was something I could talk about, and cry over in public. His desertion almost broke my heart.

16 A few years ago I returned to the old neighborhood and drove down our street. There were no woods left. Our backyard adjoined another backyard, part of an immense quilt of streets and houses. The little trees I remember our neighbors planting were tall and noble. The weeping willow had become a monster, shading the whole yard, and the majestic old maple was still there, towering over all the other trees. But the odd thing was that the houses, after all these years, didn't look alike at all. They had been altered out of recognition, with a second story here, a front porch there, a sweeping curved driveway, an English garden, a multipaned bay where a picture window once stared out. Our house had acquired the garage my father always wanted and a big screened porch just visible in back. The Perciantes' house had a brick path and shutters and a woodshed; the Worshels' was hidden behind overgrown yews. Without the eye of memory, it was hard to see the ticky-tacky boxes.

People who moved in recently may not even have been aware that they lived in one of those awful fifties developments, the kind that inspired a protest song about bourgeois conformity.

I parked the car and walked around the neighborhood, remembering things I had no idea were still stored in my brain, like the blistering hot day we planted the hedge (gone now) alongside the driveway, and the exact look of the fifties-geometric drapes that used to hang in our living room. I remembered Laura Mae's dog, Bouncer, a beagle who once bit my Uncle Frank in the leg. I remembered lying on the Perciantes' floor watching *Sergeant Bilko* and laughing until I thought I was going to throw up. I remembered that the full moon used to shine directly in the window of my bedroom, and that I tried to stay awake until it moved beyond the curtain and disappeared. 17

It really wasn't much of a house. I don't suppose I'd want to live in it today, and I've certainly inhabited more beautiful and better-designed and more dramatically situated places in which I've been just as happy. But that house, with its particular mix of bliss and loss, is the place in my head where I go when I need to pull comfort from the past. It was a house utterly without distinction except for what it gave to my family: a place of our own, a maple tree, a vegetable garden, a kitchen painted blue, and a chance to be—at least for a while, and at least in some ways—just like everybody else. 18

QUESTIONS

Understanding

1. Where did Kitty Burns Florey's family live immediately after she was born? Approximately how old was she when they all moved to "the house"?
2. Besides where they came from, what else made Florey's family "different" from the others in her new neighborhood?
3. The look-alike houses of her childhood gave Florey the chance, she says, to be for a time "just like everybody else" (par. 18). Why might young Florey (and the adult writer who recalls her in this essay) consider this an advantage?

4. Why is young Florey so concerned in paragraph 15 with the loss of her cat? What else might she be trying to get back or hold on to when she returns from the city on Saturday mornings to look for her pet? How successful is her quest—in her past life or in her remembrance of things past?
5. As an adult, Florey recalls her childhood home as a place she can go "to pull comfort from the past" (par. 18). Where is that place located—or lodged?

Strategies and Structure

1. What is the principle of selection by which Florey selects the specific details that characterize her family's first house in paragraph 1 of "Ticky-tacky"? Why does she then describe her father's "background" in terms of "a big white house with pillars" (par. 5)? How does the contrast, in this same paragraph, between the grandmother who lives there and the grandmother who lives "above a store on a busy street" help to prepare us for what follows?
2. After she moved to the suburbs, says Florey, her life was "transformed in large and small ways" (par. 8). What specific examples does she give? Are they, in your opinion, mostly "large" or "small"? Or both? What do such details suggest about young Florey's powers of observation?
3. Florey says that her house in the suburbs was similar to its neighbors and, at the same time, "immeasurably different" (par. 12). By what particular details (especially in paragraphs 12 and 13) does she capture the similarities? By what particular details does she convey the differences? Are they mostly large or small or both?
4. The scale of her experience is permanently altered when young Florey's father dies in paragraph 14. By what small object (par. 12) does the recollecting author link the dual orders of reality—large and small, like and unlike, significant and insignificant—in her childhood consciousness?
5. Besides a father who couldn't work, Florey's family was distinguished from the others in her neighborhood by a mother who did. How and how well does the key in paragraph 13 signify this difference? Be sure to consider the function of keys in relation to the structure or cabinet they unlock.
6. In the mind of her younger self as Florey reconstructs it here, a house is analogous to the family who inhabits it. For the adult author who

recalls "things I had no idea were still stored in my brain" (par. 17), the house is also a metaphor for . . . what?

7. When photography first came into general use in America after the Civil War, Oliver Wendell Holmes described the camera as "a mirror with a memory." A mirror can only reflect an object; memory can reflect upon it. What's the difference? How well do you think Holmes's analogy applies to the photographs (pars. 6 and 11) described in Florey's essay?

Words and Figures of Speech

1. Where did "Levittowns" (par. 11) get their name? Where and approximately when was the first one built?
2. "Years later" (par. 11), when Florey looked at aerial photographs of America's first extensive, suburban housing developments, she found their anonymity "creepy," comparing the individual houses to identical "squares on a game board" (par. 11). The streets and houses of her old neighborhood, however, remind her of "an immense quilt" (par. 16). What differences do these two SIMILES connote?
3. In the "protest song" to which Florey refers (par. 16), the houses "are all made out of ticky-tack, and they're all in a row." How does the word (or double word) *ticky-tacky* itself suggest the "conformity" that some protest singers found "bourgeois" in the 1960s and that Florey, as a child, found comforting and reassuring?
4. How does the word *character* (par. 12) contribute to the analogy between house and family that Florey is drawing throughout her essay?
5. When her teachers and classmates refer to young Florey as "the girl who lost her father," are they identifying her more in terms of likeness (to others in her school) or difference? Please explain your answer.
6. When Florey returns to the old neighborhood, the willow tree in her yard has grown into a "monster" (par. 16). How (and why) does she offset the negative connotations of this word in the same paragraph?
7. A *transformation* ("my life was transformed," par. 8) is literally a change in shape. How does the description of the houses in paragraph 16 suggest both a literal and a figurative transformation in Florey's old neighborhood and in her life? Why do you think Florey brings up again, in closing, her father's plans for a garage and other additions to their old house?

Comparing

1. In "More Room," the preceding essay in this chapter, Judith Ortiz Cofer's grandfather is constantly making additions to her childhood home. How does Cofer's account of these alterations contrast with Florey's account of *her* father's "plans" to add more room to their house in the suburbs?
2. Kitty Burns Florey was an only child, and her family background may seem so different from Judith Ortiz Cofer's (in "More Room") as to elude comparison. However, the basic conceit (house = family) is the same in both these essays. What other similarities can you make out in these two accounts—and thus in the families (and houses) they describe?
3. How does Florey's account of family relationships, especially its depiction of intimacy and distance between parent and child, compare with Joyce Maynard's in "Four Generations" (Chapter 1)?

Topics for Discussion and Writing

1. Kitty Burns Florey returns to her old neighborhood in the suburbs and finds it "altered out of all recognition" (par. 16). How might the same be said of the suburbs in general between the years immediately following World War II, with their rows upon rows of inexpensive tract houses, and today?
2. The automobile is usually credited (or discredited) with making the suburbs possible in America. How and why might this be (or not be) the case? What do you make of the fact that before the 1920s most American middle-class, detached, single-family homes had front porches but no garages? (Carriage houses were for the wealthy.)
3. Florey notes that her first house, like so many others built in the 1950s, displayed a large "picture window" (par. 11). Picture windows, as a rule, do not open, and the houses that introduced them also introduced the patio in the back, which was both cheaper to build than a front porch and hidden from the street. What do these innovations in American residential architecture tell you about changes in the American family and its lifestyles?
4. Make an inventory of the house or apartment you associate most immediately with your childhood. What did your friends have in their places that seemed unusual or "different" to you then?

Alan M. Dershowitz

SHOUTING "FIRE!"

Alan M. Dershowitz is a professor of law at Harvard, and is in active practice as a criminal and civil liberties attorney. He writes a weekly syndicated column and has written many books on legal and social issues, including *Taking Liberties* (1989), *Chutzpah* (1991), *The Advocate's Devil* (1994), and *Reasonable Doubts: The O.J. Simpson Case and the Criminal Justice System* (1996). This essay originally appeared in the *Atlantic Monthly*.

When the Reverend Jerry Falwell learned that the Supreme Court had reversed his $200,000 judgment against *Hustler* magazine for the emotional distress that he had suffered from an outrageous parody, his response was typical of those who seek to censor speech: "Just as no person may scream 'Fire!' in a crowded theater when there is no fire, and find cover under the First Amendment, likewise, no sleazy merchant like Larry Flynt should be able to use the First Amendment as an excuse for maliciously and dishonestly attacking public figures, as he has so often done." 1

Justice Oliver Wendell Holmes's classic example of unprotected speech—falsely shouting "Fire!" in a crowded theater—has been invoked so often, by so many people, in such diverse contexts, that it has become part of our national folk language. It has even appeared—most appropriately—in the theater: in Tom Stoppard's play *Rosencrantz and Guildenstern Are Dead* a character shouts at the audience, "Fire!" He then quickly explains: "It's all right—I'm demonstrating the misuse of free speech." Shouting "Fire!" in the theater may well be the only jurisprudential analogy that has assumed the status of a folk argument. A prominent historian recently characterized it as "the most brilliantly persuasive expression that ever came from Holmes' pen." But in spite of its hallowed position in both the 2 jurisprudence of the First Amendment and the arsenal of political discourse, it is and was an inapt analogy, even in the context in which it was originally offered. It has lately become—despite, perhaps even because of, the frequency and promiscuousness of its invocation—little more than a caricature of logical argumentation.

The case that gave rise to the "Fire!"-in-a-crowded-theater anal- 3
ogy—*Schenck* v. *United States*—involved the prosecution of Charles Schenck, who was the general secretary of the Socialist Party in Philadelphia, and Elizabeth Baer, who was its recording secretary. In 1917 a jury found Schenck and Baer guilty of attempting to cause insubordination among soldiers who had been drafted to fight in the First World War. They and other party members had circulated leaflets urging draftees not to "submit to intimidation" by fighting in a war being conducted on behalf of "Wall Street's chosen few."

Schenck admitted, and the Court found, that the intent of the 4
pamphlets' "impassioned language" was to "influence" draftees to resist the draft. Interestingly, however, Justice Holmes noted that nothing in the pamphlet suggested that the draftees should use unlawful or violent means to oppose conscription: "In form at least [the pamphlet] confined itself to peaceful measures, such as a petition for the repeal of the act" and an exhortation to exercise "your right to assert your opposition to the draft." Many of its most impassioned words were quoted directly from the Constitution.

Justice Holmes acknowledged that "in many places and in ordi- 5
nary times the defendants, in saying all that was said in the circular, would have been within their constitutional rights." "But," he added, "the character of every act depends upon the circumstances in which it is done." And to illustrate that truism he went on to say,

> The most stringent protection of free speech would not protect a man in falsely shouting fire in a theater, and causing a panic. It does not even protect a man from an injunction against uttering words that may have all the effect of force.

Justice Holmes then upheld the convictions in the context of a 6
wartime draft, holding that the pamphlet created "a clear and present danger" of hindering the war effort while our soldiers were fighting for their lives and our liberty.

The example of shouting "Fire!" obviously bore little relationship 7
to the facts of the Schenck case. The Schenck pamphlet contained a

substantive political message. It urged its draftee readers to *think* about the message and then—if they so chose—to act on it in a lawful and nonviolent way. The man who shouts "Fire!" in a crowded theater is neither sending a political message nor inviting his listener to think about what he has said and decide what to do in a rational, calculated manner. On the contrary, the message is designed to force action *without* contemplation. The message "Fire!" is directed not to the mind and the conscience of the listener but, rather, to his adrenaline and his feet. It is a stimulus to immediate *action,* not thoughtful reflection. It is—as Justice Holmes recognized in his follow-up sentence—the functional equivalent of "uttering words that may have all the effect of force."

Indeed, in that respect the shout of "Fire!" is not even speech, in any meaningful sense of that term. It is a *clang* sound—the equivalent of setting off a nonverbal alarm. Had Justice Holmes been more honest about his example, he would have said that freedom of speech does not protect a kid who pulls a fire alarm in the absence of a fire. But that obviously would have been irrelevant to the case at hand. The proposition that pulling an alarm is not protected speech certainly leads to the conclusion that shouting the word *fire* is also not protected. But the core analogy is the nonverbal alarm, and the derivative example is the verbal shout. By cleverly substituting the derivative shout for the core alarm, Holmes made it possible to analogize one set of words to another—as he could not have done if he had begun with the self-evident proposition that setting off an alarm bell is not free speech. 8

The analogy is thus not only inapt but also insulting. Most Americans do not respond to political rhetoric with the same kind of automatic acceptance expected of schoolchildren responding to a fire drill. Not a single recipient of the Schenck pamphlet is known to have changed his mind after reading it. Indeed, one draftee, who appeared as a prosecution witness, was asked whether reading a pamphlet asserting that the draft law was unjust would make him "immediately decide that you must erase that law." Not surprisingly, he replied, "I do my own thinking." A theatergoer would probably not respond similarly if asked how he would react to a shout of "Fire!" 9

Another important reason why the analogy is inapt is that Holmes emphasizes the factual falsity of the shout "Fire!" The Schenck pam- 10 phlet, however, was not factually false. It contained political opinions and ideas about the causes of the war and about appropriate and lawful responses to the draft. As the Supreme Court recently reaffirmed (in *Falwell* v. *Hustler*), "The First Amendment recognizes no such thing as a 'false' idea." Nor does it recognize false opinions about the causes of or cures for war.

A closer analogy to the facts of the Schenck case might have been 11
provided by a person's standing outside a theater, offering the patrons a leaflet advising them that in his opinion the theater was structurally unsafe, and urging them not to enter but to complain to the building inspectors. That analogy, however, would not have served Holmes's argument for punishing Schenck. Holmes needed an analogy that would appear relevant to Schenck's political speech but that would invite the conclusion that censorship was appropriate.

Unsurprisingly, a war-weary nation—in the throes of a know- 12
nothing hysteria over immigrant anarchists and socialists—welcomed the comparison between what was regarded as a seditious political pamphlet and a malicious shout of "Fire!" Ironically, the "Fire!" analogy is nearly all that survives from the Schenck case; the ruling itself is almost certainly not good law. Pamphlets of the kind that resulted in Schenck's imprisonment have been circulated with impunity during subsequent wars.

Over the past several years I have assembled a collection of 13
instances—cases, speeches, arguments—in which proponents of censorship have maintained that the expression at issue is "just like" or "equivalent to" falsely shouting "Fire!" in a crowded theater and ought to be banned, "just as" shouting "Fire!" ought to be banned. The analogy is generally invoked, often with self-satisfaction, as an absolute argument-stopper. It does, after all, claim the high authority of the great Justice Oliver Wendell Holmes. I have rarely heard it invoked in a convincing, or even particularly relevant, way. But that, too, can claim lineage from the great Holmes.

Not unlike Falwell, with his silly comparison between shouting 14
"Fire!" and publishing an offensive parody, courts and commentators have frequently invoked "Fire!" as an analogy to expression that is not an automatic stimulus to panic. A state supreme court held that "Holmes' aphorism . . . applies with equal force to pornography"—in particular to the exhibition of the movie *Carmen Baby* in a drive-

in theater in close proximity to highways and homes. Another court analogized "picketing . . . in support of a secondary boycott" to shouting "Fire!" because in both instances "speech and conduct are brigaded." In the famous Skokie case one of the judges argued that allowing Nazis to march through a city where a large number of Holocaust survivors live "just might fall into the same category as one's 'right' to cry fire in a crowded theater."

15 Outside court the analogies become even more badly stretched. A spokesperson for the New Jersey Sports and Exposition Authority complained that newspaper reports to the effect that a large number of football players had contracted cancer after playing in the Meadowlands—a stadium atop a landfill—were the "journalistic equivalent of shouting fire in a crowded theater." An insect researcher acknowledged that his prediction that a certain amusement park might become roach-infested "may be tantamount to shouting fire in a crowded theater." The philosopher Sidney Hook, in a letter to the *New York Times* bemoaning a Supreme Court decision that required a plaintiff in a defamation action to prove that the offending statement was actually false, argued that the First Amendment does not give the press carte blanche to accuse innocent persons "any more than the First Amendment protects the right of someone falsely to shout fire in a crowded theater."

16 Some close analogies to shouting "Fire!" or setting off an alarm are, of course, available: calling in a false bomb threat; dialing 911 and falsely describing an emergency; making a loud, gunlike sound in the presence of the President; setting off a voice-activated sprinkler system by falsely shouting "Fire!" In one case in which the "Fire!" analogy was directly to the point, a creative defendant tried to get around it. The case involved a man who calmly advised an airline clerk that he was "only here to hijack the plane." He was charged, in effect, with shouting "Fire!" in a crowded theater, and his rejected defense—as quoted by the court—was as follows: "If we built fire-proof theaters and let people know about this, then the shouting of 'Fire!' would not cause panic."

17 Here are some more-distant but still related examples: the recent incident of the police slaying in which some members of an onlooking crowd urged a mentally ill vagrant who had taken an officer's gun to shoot the officer; the screaming of racial epithets during a tense confrontation; shouting down a speaker and preventing him from continuing his speech.

Analogies are, by their nature, matters of degree. Some are closer to the core example than others. But any attempt to analogize political ideas in a pamphlet, ugly parody in a magazine, offensive movies in a theater, controversial newspaper articles, or any of the other expressions and actions catalogued above to the very different act of shouting "Fire!" in a crowded theater is either self-deceptive or self-serving. 18

The government does, of course, have some arguably legitimate bases for suppressing speech which bear no relationship to shouting "Fire!" It may ban the publication of nuclear-weapon codes, of information about troop movements, and of the identity of undercover agents. It may criminalize extortion threats and conspiratorial agreements. These expressions may lead directly to serious harm, but the mechanisms of causation are very different from that at work when an alarm is sounded. One may also argue—less persuasively, in my view—against protecting certain forms of public obscenity and defamatory statements. Here, too, the mechanisms of causation are very different. None of these exceptions to the First Amendment's exhortation that the government "shall make no law . . . abridging the freedom of speech, or of the press" is anything like falsely shouting "Fire!" in a crowded theater; they all must be justified on other grounds. 19

A comedian once told his audience, during a stand-up routine, about the time he was standing around a fire with a crowd of people and got in trouble for yelling "Theater, theater!" That, I think, is about as clever and productive a use as anyone has ever made of Holmes's flawed analogy. 20

QUESTIONS

Understanding

1. Dershowitz refers to Justice Holmes's ANALOGY as a "classic example of unprotected speech" (par. 2). "Unprotected" by what or whom?
2. Why does Dershowitz consider Holmes's analogy to be "inapt" (par. 8)?
3. Why does he also find it "insulting" (par. 9)?

4. Under what conditions did Holmes put forth the analogy between falsely shouting fire in a theater and unprotected free speech?

Strategies and Structure

1. As originally printed in the *Atlantic Monthly,* Dershowitz's essay had white space after paragraphs 8 and 12, thus clearly dividing it into three parts. What are the unifying principles of the individual parts? How are the three main parts related?
2. An analogy says A is like B. An *argument* by analogy says that (because A is like B) what is true of A is also true of B. Is Holmes's analogy, as quoted here, a simple analogy or an argument by analogy? Please explain.
3. How about Dershowitz's attack on Holmes's analogy—what is his basic argument against it? Is his argument an argument by analogy? Why or why not?
4. Where does Dershowitz draw analogies of his own? How apt do you find them?
5. Arguments by analogy are only as strong as the analogy is close. Where does Dershowitz himself, in effect, state this principle?
6. How close is the analogy between a man falsely shouting fire in a theater and a man falsely shouting theater at a fire? Why, then, do you think Dershowitz ends with this one?

Words and Figures of Speech

1. In what sense, precisely, is Dershowitz using the word *inapt* throughout this essay?
2. "Shouting 'Fire!' " argues that shouting fire "is not even speech, in any meaningful sense of that term" (par. 8). What is it, according to Dershowitz?
3. How apt do you find his comparison of shouting fire to a "*clang* sound" (par. 8)?
4. Linguistically, what is the difference between "shouting fire in a theater" (the written or spoken phrase) and actually doing it?

Comparing

1. How does Dershowitz's use of analogies in "Shouting 'Fire!' " compare with how the authors of other essays in this chapter use them?
2. Compare and contrast "Shouting 'Fire!' " with Amy Tan's "Mother Tongue" (Chapter 2) as essays about language.
3. Considered as a piece of persuasive writing, is Dershowitz's essay more like those in Chapter 9 or in Chapter 10? Please explain your answer.

Discussion and Writing Topics

1. Who's right, Dershowitz or Holmes? Why so?
2. What do you think of Dershowitz's argument that shouting fire in a theater is not really speech?
3. What's the difference between a red light and the words, "Please stop when you see the red light"?
4. If freedom of speech is guaranteed by the Constitution, why is it ever possible to consider any words "unprotected"?

Judith Ortiz Cofer

Like many writers with other lives and duties, Judith Ortiz Cofer 1
has to steal time for her writing. The following answers to the editor's questions about the composition of "More Room," for example, were written in the evening "on an uncomfortable chair and strange table in a hotel room in a city where I was doing some readings."

Asked how she got the idea of writing about *"la casa de Mamá"*— 2
and how, in particular, she developed the connections between her grandmother and her grandmother's bedroom, the family and the house—Cofer replied: "The word *casa* as used by most Latino people I know is charged with great emotional connotations. I had used images of *casa* in poems and in my novel, *The Line of the Sun,* before I wrote the essays in *Silent Dancing* [which include "More Room"]. So 'More Room' had been in my head for years before I wrote it. The connection between Mamá and the house was always there for me, but of course, since writing is a process of self-discovery, many of the more subtle parallels were revealed to me as I wrote the piece, which I prefer to call creative nonfiction rather than essay. In creative nonfiction the writer may employ the elements of fiction to dramatize a story and to arrive at a poetic truth that I feel the constraints of formal essay writing may inhibit. I try not to revise history in my creative nonfiction, but I cannot claim to remember things such as exact dialogue or precisely the dimensions of a room, so I let my

goal be what Virginia Woolf called 'the moment of being' of the story, the reason it means something to me, enough that I need to write it. I wanted to write about Mamá's casa and how she made it an extension of herself."

Among the "subtle parallels" that came to Cofer as she wrote "More Room" were those between the physical objects in Mamá's room and their "symbolic" values. "Mamá's symbols of power," she says, "became symbols when I put them in my narrative. They were certainly not 'symbols' to the children who wanted to have them or who feared them. The writer assigns them to that category in retrospect—she can see from the future that they represented power." 3

See from the future? "Yes. As in 'More Room,' I use the frame tale to structure my autobiographical writing quite a bit because it is a back-to-the-future technique, with an adult voice leading the journey back and forth through time. My advice to young writers is to see their subject as an exploration of known territory. They may start out with a familiar topic, but in writing some mysteries may be clarified and others made more complex. The point of writing a personal essay is not (necessarily) solving but seeing. So they don't have to have answers ready to insert in the concluding paragraph. If they are honest, the sharing of the experience will be satisfying enough for both writer and reader." 4

Is the chifforobe an example of a familiar object both clarified and made more mysterious by the process of writing about it? And, incidentally, why is it "monstrous" and not just "big"? "The chifforobe was monstrous then," said Cofer, "because it loomed over tiny me and because it contained secrets. Yet the 'monstrous' usage may have come from my fairy/folktale-saturated brain. I still translate Puerto Rican folktales and bore my family and friends with *cuentos*." 5

What about rewriting? Does she do much of it, and how, specifically, did she revise "More Room"? "When I'm working on a project," says Cofer, "I revise every day what I did the day before. My goal, since I have little time for my writing" (see "5 A.M." in *The Latin Deli*) "is two pages a day." (Cofer "still gets up at 5 A.M. to work," she confides; "it's no longer just my family duties that interrupt, but the world.") She revises and revises "until the moment of publication and sometimes after publication. I don't know any serious writer who doesn't revise. Writing is mostly revision. I treated 'More Room' like a poem, trying for economy of language, preciseness of imagery, 6 rhythmic and varied sentences. I made it more compact. The image of the chambered nautilus came to me after I described the house's organically changing shape. The last paragraph was my one percent inspiration (if creation is 99 percent perspiration); it made me feel good to write it because it was right, it had closure, and it told me that I had finished."

Writing Topics for Chapter Seven
Essays That Use Metaphor and Analogy

1. Explain your inner self by analogy with a car, truck, motorcycle, boat, or other vehicle that you consider to be a means of self-expression.
2. Write an essay using the shrinking size of American automobiles as indexes to the country's economic condition.
3. Describe a house you have seen as an emblem of the people that you know or imagine to inhabit it.
4. Define several different kinds of human intelligence by associating each type with a game that exemplifies it.
5. Explain how to develop self-confidence by comparing the process of acquiring it to weaving a design, cultivating a garden, or building a fire.
6. Explain the kind of education your college or university offers by comparing it to a meal in a restaurant or cafeteria.
7. Describe a typical day in your life as if you were threading your way through a maze.
8. Compare the maneuvers and challenges of a political campaign to those of a board game (or a battlefield).
9. Recall formative events of your past life by associating them with objects in an attic or pictures in a photo album.
10. Explain the typical life cycle of a human being by likening it to that of an insect or animal.

Description

Eight

Essays That Appeal to the Senses

DESCRIPTION[1] is the mode of writing that appeals most directly to the senses either by telling us the qualities of a person, place, or thing or by showing them. For example, here are two descriptions of cemeteries. The first, from *Natural History* magazine, is written in the language of detached observation:

> An old and popular New England tradition for resident and visitor alike, is a relaxing walk through one of our historical cemeteries. . . .
>
> Haphazard rows of slate tablets give way in time to simple marble tablets bearing urn and willow motifs. The latter in turn lose popularity to marble gravestones of a variety of sizes and shapes and often arranged in groups or family plots. The heyday of ornate marble memorials lasted into the 1920s, when measured rows of uniformly sized granite blocks replaced them.

Compare this passage with novelist John Updike's far-from-detached description of the cemetery in the town where he lives:

> The stones are marble, modernly glossy and simple, though I suppose that time will eventually reveal them as another fashion, dated and quaint. Now, the sod is still raw, the sutures of turf are unhealed, the earth still humped, the wreaths scarcely withered. . . . I remember my grandfather's funeral, the

[1] Terms printed in small capitals are defined in the Glossary.

hurried cross of sand the minister drew on the coffin lid, the whine of the lowering straps, the lengthening, cleanly cut sides of clay, the thought of air, the lack of air forever in the close dark space lined with pink satin. . . .

Our first example relies heavily upon adjectives: "historical," "haphazard," "simple," "ornate," "measured," "uniformly sized." Except when they identify minerals—slate tablets, marble memorials—these adjectives tend to be ABSTRACT. Indeed, the movement of the entire passage is away from the particular. No single grave is described in detail. Even the "urn and willow motifs" adorn a number of tombs. The authors seem interested in the whole sweep of the cemetery from the haphazard rows of the oldest section to the ordered ranks of modern headstones in the newest. It is the arrangement, or shift in arrangement, that most concerns them.

Arrangement is an abstract concept, and we should remember that description is not limited to people or things that can be perceived directly by the physical senses. Description may also convey ideas: the proportions of a building, the style of a baseball player, the infinitude of space. Our first description of cemeteries, in fact, moves from the concrete to the abstract because it was written to support ideas. It is part of a sociological study of cemeteries as they reveal changing American attitudes toward death, family, and society. The authors take their "relaxing walk" not because they want to examine individual tombstones but because they want to generalize from a multitude of physical evidence. As reporters, they stand between us and the actual objects they tell about.

By contrast, the movement of the Updike passage is from the general to the particular. Starting where the other leaves off—with a field of glossy modern slabs—it focuses quickly upon the newly dug graves and then narrows even more sharply to a single grave kept fresh in the author's memory. This time the adjectives are CONCRETE: "raw," "unhealed," "humped," "withered," "hurried," "close," "dark." The nouns are concrete too: "sod" and "earth" give way to the "space" lined with satin. Death is no abstraction for Updike; it is the suffocating loss of personal life. Updike makes us experience the finality of death by recreating his own sensations of claustrophobia at his grandfather's funeral.

Different as they are, these two passages illustrate a single peculiarity of description as a mode: it seldom stands alone. As in our first example, "scientific" description shades easily into exposition.

As in our second, "evocative" description shades just as easily into narration. The authors of the first example describe the changes in a cemetery in order to explain (EXPOSITION) what those changes mean for American culture. After evoking his feelings about a past event, the author of the second example goes on in later lines to show what happened (NARRATION) when his reverie was interrupted by his son, who was learning to ride a bicycle in the peaceful cemetery. Which kind of description is better—telling or showing, scientific or evocative? Neither is inherently better or worse than the other. The kind of description that a writer chooses depends upon what he wants to do with it.

Updike's reference to the "sutures" of "unhealed" turf suggests how easily description also falls into METAPHOR, SIMILE, and ANALOGY. This is hardly surprising, for we often describe a thing in everyday speech by telling what it is like. A thump in your closet at night sounds like an owl hitting a haystack. A crowd stirs like a jellyfish. The seams of turf on new graves are like the stitches binding a human wound.

The ease with which description shifts into other MODES does not mean that a good description has no unity or order of its own, however. When writing description, keep in mind that every detail should contribute to a dominant impression, mood, or purpose. The dominant impression he wanted to convey when describing his grandfather's funeral, says Updike, was "the foreverness, the towering foreverness." Updike creates this impression by moving from the outside to the inside of the grave. Depending upon the object or place you are describing, you may want to move from the inside out, from left to right, top to bottom, or front to back. Whatever arrangement you choose, present the details of your description systematically; but do not call so much attention to your system of organization that it dominates the thing you are describing.

What impression, mood, or purpose is your description intended to serve? What specific objects can contribute to it? What do they look, feel, smell, taste, or sound like? Does your object or place suggest any natural order of presentation? These are the questions to ask when you begin a descriptive essay.

Cherokee Paul McDonald

A View from the Bridge

A fiction writer and journalist, Cherokee Paul McDonald lives in Fort Lauderdale. "A View from the Bridge," originally published in *Sunshine* magazine, shows McDonald's usual expert handling of fish and fishermen, both in and out of water. McDonald is the author of *Gulf Stream* (1988) and of *Blue Truth: Walking the Thin Blue Line* (1991), an account of "one cop's . . . life in the street."

I was coming up on the little bridge in the Rio Vista neighborhood of Fort Lauderdale, deepening my stride and my breathing to negotiate the slight incline without altering my pace. And then, as I neared the crest, I saw the kid. 1

He was a lumpy little guy with baggy shorts, a faded T-shirt and heavy sweat socks falling down over old sneakers. 2

Partially covering his shaggy blond hair was one of those blue baseball caps with gold braid on the bill and a sailfish patch sewn onto the peak. Covering his eyes and part of his face was a pair of those stupid-looking '50s-style wrap-around sunglasses. 3

He was fumbling with a beat-up rod and reel, and he had a little bait bucket by his feet. I puffed on by, glancing down into the empty bucket as I passed. 4

"Hey, mister! Would you help me, please?" 5

The shrill voice penetrated my jogger's concentration, and I was determined to ignore it. But for some reason, I stopped. 6

With my hands on my hips and the sweat dripping from my nose I asked, "What do you want, kid?" 7

"Would you please help me find my shrimp? It's my last one and I've been getting bites and I know I can catch a fish if I can just find that shrimp. He jumped outta my hand as I was getting him from the bucket." 8

Exasperated, I walked slowly back to the kid, and pointed. 9

"There's the damn shrimp by your left foot. You stopped me for 10
that?"

As I said it, the kid reached down and trapped the shrimp. 11

"Thanks a lot, mister," he said. 12

I watched as the kid dropped the baited hook down into the 13
canal. Then I turned to start back down the bridge.

That's when the kid let out a "Hey! Hey!" and the prettiest tarpon 14
I'd ever seen came almost six feet out of the water, twisting and turning as he fell through the air.

"I got one!" the kid yelled as the fish hit the water with a loud 15
splash and took off down the canal.

I watched the line being burned off the reel at an alarming rate. 16
The kid's left hand held the crank while the extended fingers felt for the drag setting.

"No, kid!" I shouted. "Leave the drag alone . . . just keep that 17
damn rod tip up!"

Then I glanced at the reel and saw there were just a few loops of 18
line left on the spool.

"Why don't you get yourself some decent equipment?" I said, but 19
before the kid could answer I saw the line go slack.

"Ohhh, I lost him," the kid said. I saw the flash of silver as the 20
fish turned.

"Crank, kid, crank! You didn't lose him. He's coming back toward 21
you. Bring in the slack!"

The kid cranked like mad, and a beautiful grin spread across his 22
face.

"He's heading in for the pilings," I said. "Keep him out of those 23
pilings!"

The kid played it perfectly. When the fish made its play for the 24
pilings, he kept just enough pressure on to force the fish out. When the water exploded and the silver missile hurled into the air, the kid kept the rod tip up and the line tight.

As the fish came to the surface and began a slow circle in the 25
middle of the canal, I said, "Whooee, is that a nice fish or what?"

The kid didn't say anything, so I said, "Okay, move to the edge of 26
the bridge and I'll climb down to the seawall and pull him out."

When I reached the seawall I pulled in the leader, leaving the fish 27
lying on its side in the water.

"How's that?" I said. 28

"Hey, mister, tell me what it looks like." 29

"Look down here and check him out," I said, "He's beautiful." 30

But then I looked up into those stupid-looking sunglasses and it 31
hit me. The kid was blind.

"Could you tell me what he looks like, mister?" he said again. 32

"Well, he's just under three, uh, he's about as long as one of your 33
arms," I said. "I'd guess he goes about 15, 20 pounds. He's mostly silver, but the silver is somehow made up of *all* the colors, if you know what I mean." I stopped. "Do you know what I mean by colors?"

The kid nodded. 34

"Okay. He has all these big scales, like armor all over his body. 35
They're silver too, and when he moves they sparkle. He has a strong body and a large powerful tail. He has big round eyes, bigger than a quarter, and a lower jaw that sticks out past the upper one and is very tough. His belly is almost white and his back is a gunmetal gray. When he jumped he came out of the water about six feet, and his scales caught the sun and flashed it all over the place."

By now the fish had righted itself, and I could see the bright-red 36
gills as the gill plates opened and closed. I explained this to the kid, and then said, more to myself, "He's a beauty."

"Can you get him off the hook?" the kid asked."I don't want to 37
kill him."

I watched as the tarpon began to slowly swim away, tired but 38
still alive.

By the time I got back up to the top of the bridge the kid had his 39
line secured and his bait bucket in one hand.

He grinned and said, "Just in time. My mom drops me off here, 40
and she'll be back to pick me up any minute."

He used the back of one hand to wipe his nose. 41

"Thanks for helping me catch that tarpon," he said, "and for help- 42
ing me to see it."

I looked at him, shook my head, and said, "No, my friend, thank 43
you for letting *me* see that fish."

I took off, but before I got far the kid yelled again. 44

"Hey, mister!" 45

I stopped. 46

"Someday I'm gonna catch a sailfish and a blue marlin and a giant 47
tuna and *all* those big sportfish!"

As I looked into those sunglasses I knew he probably would. I 48
wished I could be there when it happened.

QUESTIONS

Understanding

1. How would you describe the attitude of McDonald's jogger toward the "kid" before he realizes the boy is blind?
2. How much does the jogger seem to know about fish and fishing?
3. The "drag" (par. 17) on a fishing reel makes the line harder to pull off. Why does the jogger tell the boy to leave it alone?
4. Why does the jogger get even more annoyed when he sees (par. 18) that "there were just a few loops of line left on the spool"?
5. How does the jogger feel about the kid when they part?

Strategies and Structure

1. In this brief essay, McDonald has 48 paragraphs. Why so many?
2. The speaker in "A View from the Bridge" doesn't realize until almost two-thirds of the way through (par. 31) that the boy is blind. Why do you think McDonald keeps him in the dark so long?
3. Did you realize the boy was blind before the jogger did? In which paragraph? By what clues?
4. If we see the boy's blindness before "McDonald" (the jogger) does, *who* is showing us what he (the jogger) does not yet know?
5. In which paragraphs, especially, does McDonald's speaker serve as eyes for the boy (and us)?
6. "No, my friend," says the jogger (par. 43), "thank you for letting *me* see that fish." Who, then, is helping whom to see in this essay? Please explain.

Words and Figures of Speech

1. Why does McDonald's speaker switch units of measure in paragraph 33?
2. In what ways can the boy's cap (par. 3) be seen as a an example of *metonomy?* (See FIGURES OF SPEECH.)
3. Point out words and phrases in McDonald's essay—for example, *sparkle* (par. 35)—that refer directly to sights or acts of seeing.

4. In how many senses might we interpret the word *view* in McDonald's title? What are they?
5. Why does McDonald mention the kid's "stupid-looking" sunglasses in paragraph 3?
6. Besides its literal meaning, how else might we take the word *bridge?* Who or what is being "bridged" here?

Comparing

1. The way McDonald's kid deals with his physical handicap resembles the way Debi Davis deals with hers in "Body Imperfect" (Chapter 6). How's that?
2. As a case history about a person who has lost a physical sense, how does the kid's case compare with those in Diane Ackerman's "Anosmia" (Chapter 5)?
3. Compare and contrast McDonald's speaker with the speaker in Beverly Dipo's "No Rainbows, No Roses" (later in this chapter) as watchers or onlookers.

Discussion and Writing Topics

1. Should the kid have let the fish go?
2. McDonald's boy never says that he is blind. How would the essay be different if he did so at the start?
3. Have you ever seen a tarpon or any of the other sport fish that McDonald mentions? Describe your fish in writing for someone who has never seen one.
4. How might a cook or game warden (as opposed to a fisherman) describe a tarpon in writing? How would that description compare with your own?

Beverly Dipo

No Rainbows, No Roses

A nurse by profession, Beverly Dipo was also a student when she wrote "No Rainbows, No Roses" for a class assignment. As she recalls composing it in "Writers on the Writing Process," the essay went smoothly as soon as she stopped struggling to give it a formal introduction and let the "observational method" of her profession take over. "No Rainbows, No Roses" won a Bedford Prize.

I have never seen Mrs. Trane before, but I know by the report I received from the previous shift that tonight she will die. Making my rounds, I go from room to room, checking other patients first and saving Mrs. Trane for last, not to avoid her, but because she will require the most time to care for. Everyone else seems to be all right for the time being; they have had their medications, backrubs and are easily settled for the night. 1

At the door to 309, I pause, adjusting my eyes to the darkness. The only light in the room is coming from an infusion pump, which is flashing its red beacon as if in warning, and the dim hall light that barely confirms the room's furnishings and the shapeless form on the bed. As I stand there, the smell hits my nostrils, and I close my eyes as I remember the stench of rot and decay from past experience. In my mouth I taste the bitter bile churning in the pit of my stomach. I swallow uneasily and cross the room in the dark, reaching for the light switch above the sink, and as it silently illuminates the scene, I return to the bed to observe the patient with a detached, medical routineness. 2

Mrs. Trane lies motionless: the head seems unusually large on a skeleton frame, and except for a few fine wisps of gray hair around the ears, is bald from the chemotherapy that had offered brief hope; the skin is dark yellow and sags loosely around exaggerated long 3 bones that not even a gown and bedding can disguise; the right arm lies straight out at the side, taped cruelly to a board to secure the IV fluid its access; the left arm is across the sunken chest, which rises and falls in the uneven waves of Cheyne-Stokes respirations; a catheter hanging on the side of the bed is draining thick brown urine from the bladder, the source of the deathly smell.

I reach for the long, thin fingers that are lying on the chest. They 4
are ice cold, and I quickly move to the wrist and feel for the weak, thready pulse. Mrs. Trane's eyes flutter open as her head turns toward me slightly. As she tries to form a word on her dry, parched lips, I bend close to her and scarcely hear as she whispers, "Water." Taking a glass of water from the bedside table, I put my finger over the end of the straw and allow a few droplets of the cool moisture to slide into her mouth. She makes no attempt to swallow; there is just not enough strength. "More," the raspy voice says, and we repeat the procedure. This time she does manage to swallow and weakly says, "Thank you." I touch her gently in response. She is too weak for conversation, so without asking, I go about providing for her needs, explaining to her in hushed tones each move I make. Picking her up in my arms like a child, I turn her on her side. She is so very small and light. Carefully, I rub lotion into the yellow skin, which rolls freely over the bones, feeling perfectly the outline of each vertebrae in the back and the round smoothness of the ileac crest. Placing a pillow between her legs, I notice that these too are ice cold, and not until I run my hand up over her knees do I feel any of the life-giving warmth of blood coursing through fragile veins. I find myself in awe of the life force which continues despite such a state of decomposition.

When I am finished, I pull a chair up beside the bed to face her 5
and, taking her free hand between mine, again notice the long, thin fingers. Graceful. There is no jewelry; it would have fallen off long ago. I wonder briefly if she has any family, and then I see that there are neither bouquets of flowers, nor pretty plants on the shelves, no brightly crayon-colored posters of rainbows, nor boastful self-portraits from grandchildren on the walls. There is no hint in the room anywhere that this is a person who is loved. As though she has been reading my mind, Mrs. Trane answers my thoughts and quietly tells me, "I sent . . . my family . . . home . . . tonight . . . didn't want . . . them . . . to see. . . ." She cannot go on, but knowingly, I have understood what it is she has done. I lower my eyes, not knowing what to say, so I say nothing. Again she seems to sense my unease,

"You . . . stay. . . ." Time seems to have come to a standstill. In the total silence, I noticeably feel my own heartbeat quicken and hear my breathing as it begins to match hers, stride for uneven stride. Our eyes meet and somehow, together, we become aware that this is a special moment between us, a moment when two human beings are so close we feel as if our souls touch. Her long fingers curl easily around my hand and I nod my head slowly, smiling. Wordlessly, through yellowed eyes, I receive my thank you and her eyes slowly close.

Some unknown amount of time passes before her eyes open again, only this time there is no response in them, just a blank stare. Without warning, her breathing stops, and within a few moments, the faint pulse is also gone. One single tear flows from her left eye, across the cheekbone and down onto the pillow. I begin to cry quietly. There is a tug of emotion within me for this stranger who so quickly came into and went from my life. Her suffering is done, yet so is the life. Slowly, still holding her hand, I become aware that I do not mind this emotional tug of war, that in fact, it was a privilege she has allowed me, and I would do it again, gladly. Mrs. Trane spared her family an episode that perhaps they were not equipped to handle and instead shared it with me, knowing somehow that I would handle it and, indeed, needed it to grow, both privately and professionally. She had not wanted to have her family see her die, yet she did not want to die alone. No one should die alone, and I am glad I was there for her. 6

Two days later, I read Mrs. Trane's obituary in the paper. She had been a widow for five years, was the mother of seven, grandmother of eighteen, an active member of her church, a leader of volunteer organizations in her community, college-educated in music, a concert pianist, and a piano teacher for over thirty years. 7

Yes, they were long and graceful fingers. 8

QUESTIONS

Understanding

1. How long have the patient and nurse in Beverly Dipo's essay known each other?

2. What kind of rainbows does Beverly Dipo's title refer to?
3. Why are there no rainbows or roses in Mrs. Trane's hospital room on her last night?

Strategies and Structure

1. Beverly Dipo uses all five senses in her depiction of room 309. Point out examples of each one at work.
2. Which sense (or senses) dominate(s) in Dipo's essay? Since this is a hospital at night, the scene is unusually quiet. For what main purpose, therefore, does Dipo use her sense of hearing?
3. Besides attending to the dying woman's immediate needs, the nurse's avowed purpose in "No Rainbows, No Roses" is "to observe the patient with a detached, medical routineness" (par. 2). Where and how does Dipo also enable us, throughout this essay, to observe the observer?
4. How do we know already (in paragraph 2) that the nurse will not be totally "detached" in the sense of being impersonal or emotionless?
5. When and where does the nurse leave off her routine medical care of the dying woman to care for her in a more personal, even a spiritual way?
6. Comment on Dipo's handling of time in paragraph 5. How does the total silence contribute to it?
7. Why does Dipo prolong her account beyond the night of her patient's death? What important new information does the obituary add to her eye-witness account?

Words and Figures of Speech

1. How "detached" (par. 2) do you find words and phrases like "brief hope" and "cruelly" (par. 3)?
2. How many times does Dipo refer to Mrs. Trane's hands and fingers? What aspect of Mrs. Trane and her life does this METONOMY represent? (See FIGURES OF SPEECH.) Why are her hands the last we see of her?
3. At their closest point of contact, Dipo says, nurse and patient "feel as if our souls touch" (par. 5). What is the effect of referring to "souls" here after so many acts of perception by the physical senses? Is this literal or FIGURATIVE language?

Comparing

1. How do Dipo's physical preparations for a moment of spiritual insight resemble Annie Dillards's in "Transfiguration" (The Writing Process)? Consider, for example, their treatment of light and darkness.
2. Compare and contrast the attitudes toward the human body expressed in "No Rainbow, No Roses" and in Debi Davis's "Body Imperfect" (Chapter 6).
3. E. B. White slows time to a standstill in "Once More to the Lake" (Essays for Further Reading). How do his techniques for doing so compare with Dipo's?

Discussion and Writing Topics

1. The nurse in "No Rainbows, No Roses" we are told, "needed" the experience she describes in order to "grow" (par. 6). What do these words tell us about her standards of conduct, "both privately and professionally" (par. 6)? To what extent is this nurse acting within or beyond the call of duty?
2. How might Dipo's writing about Mrs. Trane's last night be considered part of the care she gave her?
3. Try to recall the physical details of a sickroom you have visited. Describe them in such a way as to show your reader both the sick person in the room and your feelings towards that person. Do not describe your emotions so much as their objects.

Ann Hodgman

No Wonder They Call Me a Bitch

Ann Hodgman is a food critic for *Eating Well.* For reasons soon to be apparent, however, this tasteless essay on flavor and nutrition did not appear in her food column, "Sweet and Sour," but in *Spy,* to which Hodgman is a contributing editor. Author of several books of humor, including *Tiny Tales of Terror,* she is at work on a series of children's books called *Lunchroom*—wonder what's on the menu?—a Nancy Drew mystery, and *My Babysitter Is a Vampire,* a book for middle-schoolers. Her *Beat That! Cookbook* appeared in 1995.

I've always wondered about dog food. Is a Gaines-burger really like a hamburger? Can you fry it? Does dog food "cheese" taste like real cheese? Does Gravy Train actually make gravy in the dog's bowl, or is that brown liquid just dissolved crumbs? And exactly what *are* by-products? 1

Having spent the better part of a week eating dog food, I'm sorry to say that I now know the answers to these questions. While my dachshund, Shortie, watched in agonies of yearning, I gagged my way through can after can of stinky, white-flecked mush and bag after bag of stinky, fat-drenched nuggets. And now I understand exactly why Shortie's breath is so bad. 2

Of course, Gaines-burgers are neither mush nor nuggets. They are, rather, a miracle of beauty and packaging—or at least that's what I thought when I was little. I used to beg my mother to get them for our dogs, but she always said they were too expensive. When I finally bought a box of cheese-flavored Gaines-burgers—after twenty years of longing—I felt deliciously wicked. 3

"Dogs love real beef," the back of the box proclaimed proudly. "That's why Gaines-burgers is the only beef burger for dogs with real 4 beef and no meat by-products!" The copy was accurate: meat by-products did not appear in the list of ingredients. Poultry by-products did, though—right there next to preserved animal fat.

One Purina spokesman told me that poultry by-products consist 5
of necks, intestines, undeveloped eggs and other "carcass remnants," but not feathers, heads, or feet. When I told him I'd been eating dog food, he said, "Oh, you're kidding! Oh, *no!*" (I came to share his alarm when, weeks later, a second Purina spokesman said that Gaines-burgers *do* contain poultry heads and feet—but *not* undeveloped eggs.)

Up close my Gaines-burger didn't much resemble chopped beef. 6
Rather, it looked—and felt—like a single long, extruded piece of redness that had been chopped into segments and formed into a patty. You could make one at home if you had a Play-Doh Fun Factory.

I turned on the skillet. While I waited for it to heat up I pulled 7
out a shred of cheese-colored material and palpated it. Again, like Play-Doh, it was quite malleable. I made a little cheese bird out of it; then I counted to three and ate the bird.

There was a horrifying rush of cheddar taste, followed immedi- 8
ately by the dull tang of soybean flour—the main ingredient in Gaines-burgers. Next I tried a piece of red extrusion. The main difference between the meat-flavored and cheese-flavored extrusions is one of texture. The "cheese" chews like fresh Play-Doh, whereas the "meat" chews like Play-Doh that's been sitting out on a rug for a couple of hours.

Frying only turned the Gaines-burger black. There was no melt- 9
ing, no sizzling, no warm meat smells. A cherished childhood illusion was gone. I flipped the patty into the sink, where it immediately began leaking rivulets of red dye.

As alarming as the Gaines-burgers were, their soy meal began to 10
seem like an old friend when the time came to try some *canned* dog foods. I decided to try the Cycle foods first. When I opened them, I thought about how rarely I use can openers these days, and I was suddenly visited by a long-forgotten sensation of can-opener distaste. *This* is the kind of unsavory place can openers spend their time when you're not watching! Every time you open a can of, say, Italian plum tomatoes, you infect them with invisible particles of by-product.

I had been expecting to see the usual homogeneous scrapple 11
inside, but each can of Cycle was packed with smooth, round, oily

nuggets. As if someone at Gaines had been tipped off that a human would be tasting the stuff, the four Cycles really were different from one another. Cycle-1, for puppies, is wet and soyish. Cycle-2, for adults, glistens nastily with fat, but it's passably edible—a lot like some canned Swedish meatballs I once got in a Care package at college. Cycle-3, the "lite" one, for fatties, had no specific flavor; it just tasted like dog food. But at least it didn't make me fat.

Cycle-4, for senior dogs, had the smallest nuggets. Maybe old 12
dogs can't open their mouths as wide. This kind was far sweeter than the other three Cycles—almost like baked beans. It was also the only one to contain "dried beef digest," a mysterious substance that the Purina spokesman defined as "enzymes" and my dictionary defined as "the products of digestion."

Next on the menu was a can of Kal Kan Pedigree with Chunky 13
Chicken. Chunky *chicken?* There were chunks in the can, certainly—big, purplish-brown chunks. I forked one chunk out (by now I was becoming more callous) and found that while it had no discernible chicken flavor, it wasn't bad except for its texture—like meat loaf with ground-up chicken bones.

In the world of canned dog food, a smooth consistency is a sign 14
of low quality—lots of cereal. A lumpy, frightening, bloody, stringy horror is a sign of high quality—lots of meat. Nowhere in the world of wet dog foods was this demonstrated better than in the fanciest I tried—Kal Kan's Pedigree Select Dinners. These came not in a can but in a tiny foil packet with a picture of an imperious Yorkie. When I pulled open the container, juice spurted all over my hand, and the first chunk I speared was trailing a long gray vein. I shrieked and went instead for a plain chunk, which I was able to swallow only after taking a break to read some suddenly fascinating office equipment catalogues. Once again, though, it tasted no more alarming than, say, canned hash.

Still, how pleasant it was to turn to *dry* dog food! Gravy Train was 15
the first I tried, and I'm happy to report that it really does make a "thick, rich, real beef gravy" when you mix it with water. Thick and rich, anyway. Except for a lingering rancid-fat flavor, the gravy wasn't beefy, but since it tasted primarily like tap water, it wasn't nauseating either.

My poor dachshund just gets plain old Purina Dog Chow, but 16
Purina also makes a dry food called Butcher's Blend that comes in Beef, Bacon & Chicken flavor. Here we see dog food's arcane semiot-

ics at its best: a red triangle with a *T* stamped into it is supposed to suggest beef; a tan curl, chicken; and a brown *S*, a piece of bacon. Only dogs understand these messages. But Butcher's Blend does have an endearing slogan: "Great Meaty Tastes—without bothering the Butcher!" *You know, I wanted to buy some meat, but I just couldn't bring myself to bother the butcher . . .*

Purina O.N.E. ("Optimum Nutritional Effectiveness") is targeted at people who are unlikely ever to worry about bothering a tradesperson. "We chose chicken as a primary ingredient in Purina O.N.E. for several reasonings," the long, long essay on the back of the bag announces. Chief among these reasonings, I'd guess, is the fact that chicken appeals to people who are—you know—*like us.* Although our dogs do nothing but spend eighteen-hour days alone in the apartment, we still want them to be *premium* dogs. We want them to cut down on red meat, too. We also want dog food that comes in a bag with an attractive design, a subtle typeface, and no kitschy pictures of slobbering golden retrievers. 17

Besides that, we want a list of the Nutritional Benefits of our dog food—and we get it on O.N.E. One thing I especially like about this list is its constant references to a dog's "hair coat," as in "Beef tallow is good for the dog's skin and hair coat." (On the other hand, beef tallow merely provides palatability, while the dried beef digest in Cycle provides palatability *enhancement.*) 18

I hate to say it, but O.N.E. was pretty palatable. Maybe that's because it has about 100 percent more fat than, say, Butcher's Blend. Or maybe I'd been duped by the packaging; that's been known to happen before. 19

As with people food, dog snacks taste much better than dog meals. They're better looking too. Take Milk-Bone Flavor Snacks. The loving-hands-at-home prose describing each flavor is colorful; the writers practically choke on their own exuberance. Of bacon they say, "It's so good, your dog will think it's hot off the frying pan." Of liver: "The only taste your dog wants more than liver—is even more liver!" Of poultry: "All those farm fresh flavors deliciously mixed in one biscuit. Your dog will bark with delight!" And of vegetable: "Gardens of taste! Specially blended to give your dog that vegetable flavor he wants—but can rarely get!" 20

Well, I may be a sucker, but advertising *this* emphatic just doesn't convince me. I lined up all seven flavors of Milk-Bone Flavor Snacks on the floor. Unless my dog's palate is a lot more sensitive than 21 mine—and considering that she steals dirty diapers out of the trash and eats them, I'm loath to think it is—she doesn't detect any more difference in the seven flavors than I did when I tried them.

I much preferred Bonz, the hard-baked, bone-shaped snack stuffed with simulated marrow. I liked the bone part, that is; it tasted almost exactly like the cornmeal it was made of. The mock marrow inside was a bit more problematic: in addition to looking like the sludge that collects in the treads of my running shoes, it was bursting with tiny hairs. 22

I'm sure you have a few dog food questions of your own. To save us time, I've answered them in advance. 23

Q. Are those little cans of Mighty Dog actually branded with the sizzling word BEEF, *the way they show in the commercials?* 24

A. You should know by now that that kind of thing never happens. 25

Q. Does chicken-flavored dog food taste like chicken-flavored cat food? 26

A. To my surprise, chicken cat food was actually a little better—more chickeny. It tasted like inferior canned pâté. 27

Q. Was there any dog food that you just couldn't bring yourself to try? 28

A. Alas, it was a can of Mighty Dog called Prime Entree with Bone Marrow. The meat was dark, dark brown, and it was surrounded by gelatin that was almost black. I knew I would die if I tasted it, so I put it outside for the raccoons. 29

QUESTIONS

Understanding

1. How does Hodgman know what Play-Doh chews like after it's been sitting on a rug for a couple of hours (par. 8), that is, as opposed to fresh Play-Doh?
2. What is the chief ingredient in Gaines-burgers? How well, according to Hodgman, do they fry up when heated like real burgers?
3. What is "can-opener-distaste" (par. 10)? What's so distasteful about it?
4. Who's right, do you suppose, the Purina spokesman who says (par. 5) that poultry by-products include undeveloped eggs but not chicken

heads or the one who says they contain heads but no eggs? What does your Purina spokesman say?

5. What childhood fantasy is Hodgman fulfilling by writing this essay? How does the reality compare with the fantasy?
6. *Q: Why are you asking these unsavory questions?* A: Somebody has to honor those who do basic research in a new field.

Strategies and Structure

1. A major shift in Hodgman's discourse is from canned dog food to dry. Where does the shift occur? Why does she find the change so "pleasant"? When does she shift again—to snacks?
2. Why doesn't Hodgman ever tell us her reasons for writing this essay? Should she have? Why or why not?
3. If Hodgman is right that "only dogs understand these messages" (par. 16), then how can the human packagers of dog food know when they are labeling their products correctly for the consumption of dog readers? How serious is this lapse in logic? Please comment.
4. Why do you think Hodgman shifts to a Question-and-Answer format at the end of her essay?

Words and Figures of Speech

1. Hodgman refers to "some suddenly fascinating office equipment catalogues" (par. 14) that divert her, momentarily, from Kal Kan's best. Is this IRONY?
2. How does your dictionary define "dried beef digest" (par. 12)? Where else does Hodgman use the technical language of the industry she is SATIRIZING?
3. Hodgman says an experimental Gaines-burger, when fryed and flipped into the sink, "began leaking rivulets of red dye" (par. 9). Is this scientific detachment or HYPERBOLE? Please explain.
4. At the opposite end of the track from intentional exaggeration stands UNDERSTATEMENT. In Hodgman's lucid analysis of the simulated marrow in Bonz, would "problematic" (par. 22) qualify as an example? Why or why not?

5. Hodgman says Kal Kan Pedigree with Chunky Chicken tasted "like meat loaf with ground-up chicken bones" (par. 13). Is this a SIMILE, or do you suppose the chicken could be literally chunky because of the bones? Or is Hodgman actually talking about meat loaf and only *likening* the Kal Kan to it? If so, do you think she should change her meat loaf recipe?

Comparing

1. How does the marketing of dog food, as Hodgman critiques it, compare with the selling of underwear as analyzed by Ellen Goodman in "The Maidenform Woman Administers Shock Treatment" (Chapter 5)? Discuss the slogans and other techniques they describe as examples of truth in advertising.
2. To what extent do you think Hodgman would benefit, professionally, if she contracted "Anosmia" (as diagnosed in Diane Ackerman's essay on the subject, Chapter 5)?
3. As an evocation of childhood memories and longings, how does Hodgman's essay compare with Judith Ortiz Cofer's "More Room" (Chapter 7)?

Discussion and Writing Topics

1. Conduct a program of research similar to Hodgman's, but in the field of cat food. Write up your findings in an unbiased fashion and show them to your mother or father.
2. Quote a spokesperson (or copywriter) for your pet's favorite brands of food and make them eat their words in your witty account of what's really in their products.
3. Analyze the arcane semiotics on your morning cereal box. What do they say about a culture that markets hundreds of varieties of the same breakfast food? Do not neglect the illustrations.
4. To what extent to you find Hodgman's title politically incorrect? Please explain what's wrong (or right) with it.

Naomi Shihab Nye

DOUBLE VISION IN A NEW OLD WORLD

Naomi Shihab Nye was born in St. Louis to a Palestinian father and an American mother of German descent. After moving to Jerusalem with her family, she attended a year of high school in what was then part of Jordan. The Shihab family returned to America and settled in San Antonio, where Nye now lives with her husband (a lawyer and photographer) and her son. Increasingly visible as a writer of essays, Nye is known for her collections of poetry, including *Hugging the Juke Box* (1982), *Red Suitcase* (1994), and *Words under the Words* (1995). "My poems and stories often begin," Nye says, "with the voices of our neighbors, mostly Mexican American, always inventive and surprising. I never get tired of mixtures."

Because my six-year-old son has never held the hands of his great-grandmother, tattooed seventy years ago by a gypsy who said she could turn hands into birds about to fly away, I want him to hold them. Before they fly, far, and the knowing of great-grandmothers is denied him forever. 1

My father, Aziz, travels with us to my grandmother's home in the Middle East, upon my urging, to make the generational ladder complete. Also, he comes to translate; my Arabic remains limited to the zone of "What's the story?" and "salt." Besides, it's good to have my father along for general moral support; to take a child into the turbulent West Bank involves a kind of courage I can't depend on alone. 2

On the airplane, my son, Madison, chatters peacefully, and sleeps. He's told his friends he can't come to their birthday parties this month because he "has to go to the Middle East." He says it as if he has business there, as if he knows where it is. 3

I know where we are when we drive the pristine, stony slopes toward Jerusalem. The air smells crisp and cool. I think of the term my old uncles used to favor when they would leave the house for a walk—they were going out to "smell the air." My father hasn't heard anyone say this for a long time now. Now they say they're going out to "measure the streets." 4

We sleep heavily in an old stone hotel with high arched windows in east Jerusalem, on the Arab side of town. Twenty-five years ago I went to high school here for one year, at an Armenian school tucked into the Armenian convent sector of the Old City. Worlds within worlds. My family lived north of Jerusalem, in an upstairs flat of a wide stone house with balconies and a spectacular, craggy view. Shepherds would stand in the fields around our house all day, leaning against their curved canes. Their sheep drifted hungrily about them, poking for slim spokes of green. I liked to imagine what shepherds thought about as the light shifted slowly on the stones. I liked to wonder what the history of this land would have been had it all been left to shepherds. 5

The next morning a hard rain pounds the streets. We will take a taxi to the town of Ramallah, through a rolling countryside dotted with white stone houses and small grocery stores called "Garden of Eden," then switch to another car to take us deeper into the West Bank to my grandmother's village. License plates bear heightened implications here. Only certain colored plates are allowed to go certain places. Palestinians have been under curfew so often during the last few years, meaning they can't be out of their houses or traveling on the roads, that one must find out daily whether passage is even possible. Evening curfews—after 5:30—have been in effect for many months now. We call an American consul friend to find out today's regulation and he tells us the roads are open but iffy—they could close any moment. 6

Our bags stuffed with the usual assortment of oddball gifts—Ben-Gay in a tube for my grandmother's aching wrists, long scarves stitched with shiny threads, packets for making instant hot cocoa—we travel north, crowded in a car. Blacked-out graffiti on every wall shouts a muffled story. 7

In Ramallah, we huddle under a dripping awning while my father looks for a taxi driver he recognizes. The name of my grandmother's village, spelled variously Sinjil and Singel, comes from St. Giles, who 8 is said to have drunk from a well there about 1,200 years ago. I notice how time immediately stretches its dimension in this part of the world. To say something happened hundreds or thousands of years ago near a certain spot feels reasonable, unlike America, where houses built in the 1920s are considered old. I have tried to give a sense of this to my son, for whom "the old days" were two years ago.

"You are going to meet Sitti, my grandma, who is probably the oldest person you have ever met. She is definitely more than ninety-five years old. Everyone says she is more than a hundred." 9

"Can she talk?" he asks. "Can she walk?" Reports fluctuate as to her well-being. Some days she is weak and other days she feels more vigorous than the sixty-three-year-old widowed aunt she lives with. 10

West of Ramallah, the staunch hills grow larger, more rolling. I keep pressing my son down in the taxi seat, suggesting he take a nap, which insults him. Really I'm just trying to keep his head lower than the windows. My father has lapsed into his solemn, West Bank personality. He stares silently out at terraces of dusky gray-green olive trees rising on either side. Sometimes I try to imagine what it's like for him—the youngest, beloved son—to come back here. His family lost their home in Jerusalem in 1948. My grandfather, who worked variously as a builder of roads and a neighborhood mediator, moved with his family up to this village where they'd had relatives for a long time. My grandmother bore ten children; three survived to adulthood. And then my father left. Forty years ago, he had a scholarship for university study in America. Since he'd never been there before, he asked to be sent "to the middle," and ended up in Kansas. That's where my American mother—art school graduate, liberal thinker, and working woman—met him. 11

He became a naturalized citizen in St. Louis, city of my birth, when I was five. "The old country" sent him thin, blue air-letters that always made him grow very quiet. After reading them, he would stare through the window at our American trees. Sometimes he talked about "home," meaning a place other than the one we shared. 12

As a child, I felt secret pleasure in belonging to a world I had never seen, where women wore long embroidered dresses and dinners crackled with pine nuts, sprigs of mint. In our house we ate hummus spread lavishly on little plates, drizzled with olive oil. My friends took small, curious bites. My father perfected his English while my mother memorized his recipes. On the school playground at recess, I'd squint and see my world as a far-off one, too. If those 13 distant relatives were with me, what would they make of monkey bars and Hula-Hoops? Having parents from two worlds gave me a kind of double vision.

The road to the village curves abruptly up onto the side of a hill between houses and almond trees. We pull to a stop at the oldest-looking stone house with a door painted in linked blue and pink squares, leading to a courtyard. Once I was here in the spring, and white almond blossoms floated around our heads like snow. A few old men stare curiously at our car. Everyone knows everyone else's business in a village like this—who received a letter, who hosted a guest. The two times I visited during the 1980s, people came to see us whom I'd never met before, proclaimed themselves relatives, and asked why I'd forgotten them all this time. 14

A female cousin runs out, insists on carrying my father's bags. We stumble through the arched doorway calling out greetings. I've forgotten to prepare my son for the double kisses, one on each cheek. My grandmother is seated inside the high, vaulted main room of her 200-year-old house, warming her hands over some white-hot coals in a charcoal brazier. It's always amazed me how cold it gets here. Most people picture the Middle East as a stretch of hot desert, but this is neither desert, flat, nor warm. Weeping, I fling my arms around her. We are hugging hard not only for now, but for all the days of six years since we saw each other last. My tears spring out of great relief: *She is still here.* 15

She gazes at Madison with a kind of intimate knowing. I've tucked his pictures into envelopes and sent them here. On my last visit she predicted, "You'll have a son, soon—wait and see." We've told him she talks a little like a Munchkin in *The Wizard of Oz*. Her voice curves and lilts, dipping deeply into the lower registers, then rising up into girlish giggles. Madison hugs her tenderly. He's lived with her picture, too. The cousins swoop around him, removing his coat, offering oranges to moisten our throats after the drive. "Oranges from Jericho," they say, meaning the sweetest ones in the world. I've eaten ten oranges in a day here before. 16

Madison is fascinated with the charcoal heater and immediately wants to find a stick to poke the whitened coals around. Everyone complies with his wishes. In a minute he has five sticks. My aunt, my female cousins, and my grandmother are dressed in their most beautiful long dresses, with their large white scarves draped snugly 17 around their heads. It makes sense in this chilly weather. Before I leave I'll have my Nepalese muffler wrapped around my head, too.

My father plunges into the usual litany of questions, greetings 18 from relatives in the States, special messages. "Everyone says hello, everyone misses you, everyone wishes they were here, too." I've carried an extra suitcase of gifts—pastel cardigans and shoes—from cousins transplanted to San Antonio. Before I forget, I urge a cousin to take the four-generation portrait I've been dreaming of—mother, son, mother, son—spanning a hundred years. We congregate around Sitti, who suddenly acts shy and won't lift her face. What might have been the best picture will have our heads cut off entirely.

Everyone wants to know what we'd like for lunch so someone can 19 run out to the little store and buy the ingredients. I love that immediacy here. As usual, they're disappointed when we request the most humble dishes: hummus, rice with eggplant, yogurt, bread, and cheese. It must seem dull to them. We never ask for meat or chicken, which they'd rather prepare to celebrate our coming. Madison says he'd like something *he* can cook on the fire. They bring him a wide pan and a giant spoon. They begin shelling almonds ("from their own trees," I whisper to him) and give him all the shells to cook.

My eyes rove around the room, noting how little has changed 20 between visits: familiar pictures of family members, slightly more mottled around the edges; the same couch and round of chairs; our own old beds from when we lived in Jerusalem, sagging a bit more toward the middles; thick comforters and cupboards of extra comforters along the walls; and on them also, prayer rugs with scenes of Mecca. My aunt will rise up regularly at prayer times when the amplified voice of the muezzin calls to her from the nearby village mosque, and bow down repeatedly in the corner of the room. I love how Arabs do that. It's such a dependable part of a day. Madison accepts it naturally. I love how five-year-olds accept things without finding them odd.

My grandmother's lemon tree—she speaks of it as if it were a 21 person—stands bare in the center of the patio, encased in January chill. About fifteen years ago, she started refusing to go anywhere, even to the doctor in Ramallah, because she needed to stay home to "take care of her tree." I point it out to Madison and she tells him, "Wait, it's dreaming of lemons right now."

Food is served on a big woven head-carried tray. Madison is too 22 excited to eat. He doesn't want to leave his invented kitchenette at the brazier, growing more elaborate by the moment. Now he's cooking peanuts he brought from the plane. He offers them, one by one, to each person. He revels in their enthusiasm. Even my grandmother with scarcely any teeth is eating peanuts. She pats his head each time he stands near enough. He keeps stroking her cheek and hand. I grab my camera to photograph their two hands together, the small, plump, smooth hand next to the graceful, tattooed one. Where will this scene be lodged in his memory?

Of course, as the excitement of arrival wears off, there are the usual small arguments. My grandmother wants my father to build a house here in the village and stay. It's her endless hope, the undertone of every conversation. Also she wants him to participate in a ritual he finds ridiculous: "sponsor a meal" for his older brother, who died two years ago, to be offered to any strangers who pass by. The only problem is that few strangers pass here. The effect isn't the same if the meal's eaten by friends. Besides, my father already did this on last year's visit, and it didn't work. No strangers appeared, and all the food sat around a whole day. My grandmother acts glum for ten minutes after he refuses. 23

Then Madison offers Sitti a wrapped chocolate kiss he's found in his backpack. She pops it into her mouth, shiny paper, tag, and all. He shouts, "No! Stop! She's eating the paper!" I can't tell if she did it to tease him or because she didn't see. They're laughing together, laughing hard in a land hungry for laughter. The most humble items evoke the most response—thick slipper-socks with non-skid patches on the bottom. I always wish I had brought ten times more gifts. 24

We blow up balloons from Madison's pocket. Now even a formal elderly cousin wearing a suit rises to punch the happy red, yellow, and blue planets skyward—and a little six-year-old, Muhammad, grinning in the cowboy hat we've just balanced on his head, pokes a tentative finger out. Beyond the window, a crowd of shaggy sheep scuttles past on the way home from pasture. They're followed by their faithful shepherd with his cane and we run outside to watch. I climb the stairs to the roof to look out over the exquisite patchwork of winter grays and greens—so many far-flung rolling hills and fields. These families have lived on them hundreds of years. One year an old man in this village introduced me to his garden practically by inches, naming every plant and every coming sprout. 25

I feel I grew up somehow in the seam between this old, rooted world and my American one. Whenever I come here, a deep ease 26 overtakes me, as if these simple images and colors, this scent of bubbling lentil and damp sheep wool and water on stone permeated my blood and bones from the beginning. What must it feel like for my father? What will it feel like for my son?

Soon my cousins speak their Arabic questions and comments directly to Madison, without waiting for translation. Madison seems to catch their meanings, but asks me, "If I'm part Arab, why can't I speak Arabic?" It's the question I've always asked, too. I wear it as regret, as shame. When I studied Arabic in school here, I never seemed to learn any words people would really want to *say*. Muhammad and Madison read a bilingual Arabic / English storybook together—Spot, the famous dog, with lift-up flaps and grinning animals. Animals, at least, speak every language. 27

Later we'll play peekaboo with giant rounds of flat bread to make my cousin's new baby smile. We'll tuck ourselves under the weighty woolen comforters that my aunt lifts out of the cupboard. Once I climbed to the top of the stack and made someone take a picture of me, in *Princess and the Pea* fashion. Madison startles me by asking my aunt if he can do the very same thing. 28

When we're almost asleep, we hear a loud boom in the distance that worries me, considering where we are and how many booms there have been through history both ancient and modern. I sit up in bed. My aunt sits up in her bed on the other side of the room. "What's that?" I ask. "It's airplanes," she says calmly. Sonic booms. Of course. 29

They've locked the giant lock in the door to their patio with a giant iron key. My grandmother sleeps in her bed in the next room, beside a kerosene lamp and an ancient comb. Round straw trays hang on the wall above her head. How many meals did they carry? 30

And a little boy sleeps soundly, troubled by nothing, in this new old world which belongs to him, too. 31

QUESTIONS

Understanding

1. Why does Naomi Shihab Nye return to the Middle East with such a sense of urgency in this essay? How long ago were her last trips?

2. What is the "double vision" of Nye's title, and how did she acquire it? How can she expect her readers, especially those who have no direct ties to the Middle East, to do so?
3. What is the "West Bank," and why do license plates bear "heightened implications" (par. 6) there?
4. Why does Nye want to keep her five-year-old son's head below the level of the car windows (par. 11)?
5. Madison Nye has been told that his grandmother talks like a Munchkin in *The Wizard of Oz;* what other indications like this can you find that Nye has been preparing her son for their journey for some time?
6. How and how well does Madison seem to adapt to the unfamiliar (to him) ways of life at his great-grandmother's house? What sort of "vision" does he exhibit there? For example, why is he so taken with the charcoal heater (par. 17)?

Strategies and Structure

1. Why do you think Naomi Shihab Nye begins her NARRATIVE with the tattoos on her grandmother's hands?
2. Why doesn't Nye come out and tell us more explicitly why a curfew (par. 6) is so often imposed upon Palestinians, or why she fears snipers, or why her father assumes "his solemn, West Bank personality" (par. 11)?
3. Like many narratives, Nye's takes the form of a journey. Why does she limit her account primarily to a single day, the day of her family's arrival at the village where her grandmother lives?
4. "The most humble items evoke the most response" (par. 24). How well might this statement be taken as a summary of the basic principle of selection in "Double Vision in a New Old World"?
5. As her title suggests, sight is the dominant sense in Nye's essay. Point out some of the many references to seeing and to objects seen. Where does she actually take out the camera? Where will these pictures, she hopes, be lodged in the future?
6. How many different POINTS OF VIEW does Nye envision in her essay? Which one does she stick to most of the time? How does the point of view shift slightly in the final scene of people sleeping?

Words and Figures of Speech

1. Nye compares the generations to a "ladder" (par. 2). What are the implications of this METAPHOR?
2. How do the different phrases for taking a walk, which Nye translates in paragraph 4, reflect larger changes in the "Old World" environment where her father grew up?
3. "Worlds within worlds" (par. 5). This is a sentence fragment. Should it have a verb? Why or why not?
4. The "implications" of Nye's license plate as she travels into the West Bank territory are "heightened" (par. 6), to say the least. What is the effect of this understatement (see FIGURES OF SPEECH)?
5. "Blacked-out graffiti on every wall shouts a muffled story" (par. 7). What is the paradox, or apparent contradiction, in these words? How characteristic is it for Nye to find a "story" in such images?
6. Why does Nye mention the almond trees that grow around her grandmother's house (par. 14)? Where do they come up again in her narrative?
7. Inside her grandmother's old stone house at last, says Nye, her eyes "rove" around the room. What does this choice of verb suggest about her as an observer or central intelligence in this narrative?
8. Nye's grandmother says her lemon tree is "dreaming" (par. 21) of lemons in winter. What does this image tell you about her? How does it anticipate the ending of Nye's story?
9. Why does Nye call the balloons in paragraph 25 "planets"—they're round, of course, but what else?
10. What is the function of the shepherds who glide so silently in and out of Nye's narrative? Where does she explicitly speculate about them?
11. What is the effect, in the closing paragraphs, of Nye's juxtaposing the sonic boom of the jets with the giant old lock that shuts them in for the night?

Comparing

1. Compare and contrast "Double Vision in a New Old World" with Kitty Burns Florey's "Ticky-tacky" (Chapter 7) as exercises in remembering or memorializing.

2. Joyce Maynard also tells the story of "Four Generations" in her essay by that title in Chapter 1. How does Maynard's account of the generational ladder differ from Nye's?

Discussion and Writing Topics

1. "Most people," says Naomi Shihab Nye, "picture the Middle East as a stretch of hot desert" (par. 15). To what extent do you think this statement is accurate? What is your picture of the Middle East? How eye-opening (or distorted), then, do you find Nye's?
2. In consultation with several of your classmates, put together a composite description of some aspect or region of the Middle East. Where there are incongruities or contradictions, try to incorporate them into your account.

Beverly Dipo

"I just sat down and typed up a rough draft," says Beverly Dipo about composing "No Rainbows, No Roses" as an assignment for a writing class. Then she "made some minor working changes, typed a second draft, and turned in that." 1

Did it all go so smoothly? Did no part of the writing process give her pause? "I was worried about its needing some sort of introduction," Dipo admits, and she tried to supply one: "like 'I'm a nurse and I work the night shift,' or something like that." When nurse Dipo talked this way, however, she sounded to herself "like Jack Webb," the television detective who always began, "Give me the facts, just the facts." So Dipo the author plunges into the facts and details of room 309 without *announcing* that she is going to give them to us. 2

This bothered one of Dipo's classmates who critiqued the second draft of her essay. This reader advised her to use more personal pronouns in paragraph 3. Again, Dipo resisted the urge to explain emotion, to give feelings before facts: "As a nurse I frequently observe *things*," she explains, "before I ever speak to a patient or get to know them as human beings. Right or wrong, it's the way we are trained." 3

Dipo's training as a nurse may have colored another aspect of the writing process for her, too. "I am a pretty organized person," she acknowledges, so her "first thoughts seem to organize themselves." 4

Hence the ease with which she wrote her first draft: "I sit down at the typewriter and start typing my thoughts on paper. . . . [S]entences fall into paragraphs for me."

Writing Topics for Chapter Eight
Essays That Appeal to the Senses

Describe one of the following:

1. The oldest person you know
2. Your dream house
3. The place you associate most closely with family vacations
4. A ghost town or dying neighborhood you have visited
5. A shipyard, dock, or harbor you have seen
6. The worst storm you can remember and its aftermath
7. A room in a hospital or rest home
8. An old-fashioned general store, hardware store, or drugstore
9. A carnival or fair
10. A building, street, or town that has given you a glimpse of foreign culture
11. A statue that seems out of place to you
12. A tropical garden
13. The waiting room of a bus or train station
14. The main reading room of a public library
15. An expensive sporting goods store
16. A factory or plant you have worked in or visited
17. A well-run farm
18. A junkyard

Persuasion and Argumentation

Nine

Essays That Appeal to Reason

PERSUASION[1] is the strategic use of language to move an audience to action or belief. In persuasive writing, readers can be moved in three ways: (1) by appealing to their reason; (2) by appealing to their emotions; and (3) by appealing to their sense of ethics (their standards of what constitutes proper behavior). The first of these, often called ARGUMENTATION, is discussed in this chapter; the other two will be taken up in Chapter 10.

Argumentation, as the term is used here, refers both to logical thinking and to the expression of that thought in such a way as to convince others to accept it. Argumentation, in other words, analyzes a subject or problem in order to induce belief. It may or may not go on to urge a course of action. Whether they induce action or belief or both, however, persuasive arguments appeal through logic to our capacity to reason. There are two basic kinds of logical reasoning: INDUCTION and DEDUCTION. When we deduce something, we reason from general premises to particular conclusions. When we reason by induction, we proceed the other way—from particulars to generalities.

In Edgar Allan Poe's "The Murders in the Rue Morgue," master detective Auguste Dupin is investigating two brutal killings. One vic-

[1]Terms printed in small capitals are defined in the Glossary.

tim has been jammed up a chimney further than the strength of a normal man could have shoved her; the other lies in the courtyard below. Dupin notices a lightning-rod extending from the courtyard past the victims' window, but it is too far for an escaping man to negotiate. Putting these and other particulars together, Dupin reasons inductively that the murderer is not a man but a giant ape. Yet how did the animal escape?—the two windows of the apartment are nailed shut and the doors are locked from the inside. Reasoning deductively now, Dupin begins with the premise that a "material" killer—not the supernatural agent the authorities half-suspect—must have "escaped materially." Thus the closed windows must have the power of closing themselves: Dupin examines one window and finds a hidden spring; but the nail fastening the window is still intact. Therefore, Dupin reasons, the ape "must have escaped through the other window" and "there must be found a difference between the nails." Dupin examines the nail in the second window and, sure enough, it is broken; outside, moveover, hangs a shutter on which the animal could have swung to the lightning-rod. Dupin advertises for the owner of a missing orangutang, and that very night, a sailor appears at his door.

Inductive reasoning, then, depends upon examples—like the minute clues that lead Poe's Dupin to suspect an orangutang—and in many cases the validity of an inductive argument increases as the sheer number of examples increases. We are more likely to believe that UFOs exist if they have been sighted by ten thousand witnesses than by one thousand. In a short essay we seldom have room for more than a few examples, however. (You will be surprised how often they are reduced to the "magic" number three.) So we must select the most telling and representative ones.

Deductive reasoning depends upon the "syllogism." Here is Aristotle's famous example of this basic pattern of logical thinking:

Major premise: All men are mortal.
Minor premise: Socrates is a man.
Conclusion: Therefore, Socrates is mortal.

If we grant Aristotle's major assumption that all men must die and his minor (or narrower) assumption that Socrates is a man, the conclusion follows inevitably that Socrates must die. (Since Socrates had died about fifteen years before Aristotle was born, Aristotle was reasonably confident that his example would not be seriously challenged.)

When a conclusion follows from the premises or (in inductive reasoning) from the examples, we say that the argument is "valid." An invalid argument is one that jumps to conclusions: the conclusion does not follow logically from the premises or examples. Inductive arguments (from particulars to generalizations) are often invalid because they use too few examples, because the examples are not representative, or because the examples depend upon faulty authorities or faulty comparisons of the sort the Duchess makes in Lewis Carroll's *Alice in Wonderland*. In your own reasoning, strive to think like Alice:

"Very true," said the Duchess: "flamingoes and mustard both bite. And the moral of that is—'Birds of a feather flock together.' "

"Only mustard isn't a bird," Alice remarked.

"Right, as usual," said the Duchess: "what a clear way you have of putting things!"

A deductive argument may be valid without being true, of course. Consider this valid argument by satirist Ambrose Bierce:

Major Premise: Sixty men can do a piece of work sixty times as quickly as one man.
Minor Premise: One man can dig a posthole in sixty seconds; therefore—
Conclusion: Sixty men can dig a posthole in one second.

As Bierce was aware, this argument is valid but untrue. It would get too crowded around that posthole for efficiency. The trouble here, and with all deductive arguments that are valid but untrue, is a faulty premise. Sixty men cannot do work sixty times as fast as one if they have no place to stand. We can see why Bierce's *Devil's Dictionary* defines the syllogism as a "logical formula consisting of a major and a minor assumption and an inconsequent." The syllogism provides a manner for thinking logically; but as Bierce's irony would warn us, it does not provide the *matter* of logical thought. We have to supply that ourselves.

In real-life persuasive arguments, we seldom use the formal syllogism. We are much more likely to assert, "If one man can dig a posthole in sixty seconds, sixty men can do it in one." Or: "You know he is an atheist because he doesn't go to church." We can meet such faulty arguments more effectively if we realize that they are abbreviated syllogisms with one premise left unsaid. Stated as a formal syllogism, our second example would look like this:

Major premise: All people who do not go to church are atheists.
Minor premise: He does not go to church.
Conclusion: Therefore, he is an atheist.

The implied premise here is the major premise: "All people who do not go to church are atheists." Usually the implied premise is the weak spot in your opponent's argument. If you can challenge it, your own position has won an excellent foothold.

Most extended debates in real life arise because the parties disagree over the truth or untruth of one or more primary assumptions. "The U.S. should stay out of South American affairs." "Inflation will drop sharply next year." "All women should work." Propositions like these cannot be assumed; they must be debated. But in your own persuasive writing, be sure of your logic first. If it can be shown that your conclusions do not follow from your premises, the debate will be over before the crucial issue of truth can be raised.

In a short essay, you should not depend rigidly upon logical forms, and you cannot hope to prove anything worth proving to an absolute certainty. But an argumentative essay does not have to prove, remember. It has only to convince. Be as convincing as you reasonably can by appealing to your audience's reason.

Thomas Jefferson

The Declaration of Independence

The third American president, Thomas Jefferson (1743–1826) was born in Virginia, attended William and Mary College, and practiced law for several years. He entered local politics in 1769, was elected to the Continental Congress, and drafted the Declaration of Independence in 1776. After serving as Virginia's governor during the Revolution, he became American minister to France and later Washington's secretary of state. His conflict with Alexander Hamilton contributed to the formation of separate political parties in America. Jefferson became vice-president of the United States in 1796 and president in 1801. During the first (and more successful) of his two terms, he engineered the Louisiana Purchase. Retiring to his estate, Monticello, in 1809, he died there on the fiftieth anniversary of American independence, July 4, 1826. Jefferson preferred the role of the philosopher to that of the politician, and the Declaration of Independence, which announced the thirteen colonies' break with England, was as much an essay on human rights as a political document. It is based upon the natural-rights theory of government, derived from eighteenth-century rationalism. The Declaration, written by Jefferson, was revised by Benjamin Franklin, John Adams, and the Continental Congress at large. The fifty-six colonial representatives signed it on August 2, 1776.

When in the course of human events, it becomes necessary for one people to dissolve the political bands which have connected them with another, and to assume among the Powers of the earth, the separate and equal station to which the Laws of Nature and of Nature's God entitle them, a decent respect to the opinions of man- 1 kind requires that they should declare the causes which impel them to the separation.

We hold these truths to be self-evident, that all men are created equal, that they are endowed by their Creator with certain unalienable rights, that among these are Life, Liberty and the pursuit of Happiness. That to secure these rights, Governments are instituted among Men, deriving their just powers from the consent of the governed. That whenever any Form of Government becomes destructive of these ends, it is the Right of the People to alter or to abolish it, and to institute new Government, laying its foundation on such principles and organizing its powers in such form, as to them shall seem most likely to effect their Safety and Happiness. Prudence, indeed, will dictate that Governments long established should not be changed for light and transient causes; and accordingly all experience hath shown, that mankind are more disposed to suffer, while evils are sufferable, than to right themselves by abolishing the forms to which they are accustomed. But when a long train of abuses and usurpations pursuing invariably the same Object evinces a design to reduce them under absolute Despotism, it is their right, it is their duty, to throw off such government, and to provide new Guards for their future security. Such has been the patient sufferance of these Colonies; and such is now the necessity which constrains them to alter their former Systems of Government. The history of the present King of Great Britain[1] is a history of repeated injuries and usurpations, all having in direct object the establishment of absolute Tyranny over these States. To prove this, let Facts be submitted to a candid world. 2

He has refused his Assent to Laws, the most wholesome and necessary for the public good. 3

He has forbidden his Governors to pass Laws of immediate and pressing importance, unless suspended in their operation till his Assent should be obtained; and when so suspended, he has utterly neglected to attend to them. 4

He has refused to pass other Laws for the accommodation of large districts of people, unless those people would relinquish the right of Representation in the Legislature, a right inestimable to them and formidable to tyrants only. 5

He has called together legislative bodies at places unusual, 6

[1]George III (ruled 1761–1820).

uncomfortable, and distant from the depository of their Public Records, for the sole purpose of fatiguing them into compliance with his measures.

He has dissolved Representative Houses repeatedly, for opposing 7
with manly firmness his invasions on the rights of the people.

He has refused for a long time, after such dissolutions, to cause 8
others to be elected; whereby the Legislative Powers, incapable of Annihilation, have returned to the People at large for their exercise; the State remaining in the mean time exposed to all the dangers of invasion from without, and convulsions within.

He has endeavoured to prevent the population of these States; for 9
that purpose obstructing the Laws of Naturalization of Foreigners; refusing to pass others to encourage their migration hither, and raising the conditions of new Appropriations of Lands.

He has obstructed the Administration of Justice, by refusing his 10
Assent to Laws for establishing Judiciary Powers.

He has made Judges dependent on his Will alone, for the tenure 11
of their offices, and the amount and payment of their salaries.

He has erected a multitude of New Offices, and sent hither 12
swarms of Officers to harass our People, and eat out their substance.

He has kept among us, in time of peace, Standing Armies without 13
the Consent of our Legislature.

He has affected to render the Military independent of and superior 14
to the Civil Power.

He has combined with others to subject us to jurisdictions foreign 15
to our constitution, and unacknowledged by our laws; giving us Assent to their acts of pretended Legislation:

For quartering large bodies of armed troops among us: 16

For protecting them, by a mock Trial, from Punishment for any 17
Murders which they should commit on the Inhabitants of these States:

For cutting off our Trade with all parts of the world: 18

For imposing Taxes on us without our Consent: 19

For depriving us in many cases, of the benefits of Trial by Jury: 20

For transporting us beyond the Seas to be tried for pretended 21
offenses:

For abolishing the free System of English Laws in a Neighbouring 22
Province, establishing therein an Arbitrary government, and enlarging its boundaries so as to render it at once an example and fit instrument for introducing the same absolute rule into these Colonies:

For taking away our Charters, abolishing our most valuable Laws, and altering fundamentally the Forms of our Governments: 23

For suspending our own Legislatures, and declaring themselves invested with Power to legislate for us in all cases whatsoever. 24

He has abdicated Government here, by declaring us out of his Protection and waging War against us. 25

He has plundered our seas, ravaged our Coasts, burnt our towns and destroyed the Lives of our people. 26

He is at this time transporting large Armies of foreign Mercenaries to complete the works of death, desolation and tyranny, already begun with circumstances of Cruelty & perfidy scarcely paralleled in the most barbarous ages, and totally unworthy the Head of a civilized nation. 27

He has constrained our fellow Citizens taken Captive on the high Seas to bear Arms against their Colony, to become the executioners of their friends and Brethren, or to fall themselves by their Hands. 28

He has excited domestic insurrections amongst us, and has endeavoured to bring on the inhabitants of our frontiers, the merciless Indian Savages, whose known rule of warfare, is an undistinguished destruction of all ages, sexes and conditions. 29

In every stage of these Oppressions We have Petitioned for Redress in the most humble terms: Our repeated petitions have been answered only by repeated injury. A Prince, whose character is thus marked by every act which may define a Tyrant, is unfit to be the ruler of a free People. 30

Nor have We been wanting in attention to our British brethren. We have warned them from time to time of attempts by their legislature to extend an unwarrantable jurisdiction over us. We have reminded them of the circumstances of our emigration and settlement here. We have appealed to their native justice and magnanimity and we have conjured them by the ties of our common kindred to disavow these usurpations, which would inevitably interrupt our connections and correspondence. They too have been deaf to the voice of justice and of consanguinity. We must, therefore acquiesce in the necessity, which denounces our Separation, and hold them, as we hold the rest of mankind, Enemies in War, in Peace Friends. 31

We, therefore,the Representatives of the United States of America, in General Congress, Assembled, appealing to the Supreme Judge of the world for the rectitude of our intentions, do, in the Name, and 32 by Authority of the good People of these Colonies, solemnly publish and declare, That these United Colonies are, and of Right ought to be Free and Independent States; that they are Absolved from all Allegiance to the British Crown, and that all political connection between them and the State of Great Britain, is and ought to be totally dissolved; and that as Free and Independent States, they have full power to levy War, conclude Peace, contract Alliances, establish Commerce, and to do all other Acts and Things which Independent States may of right do. And for the support of this Declaration, with a firm reliance on the protection of Divine Providence, we mutually pledge to each other our lives, our Fortunes and our sacred Honor.

QUESTIONS

Understanding

1. What is the purpose of government, according to Thomas Jefferson?
2. Where, in Jefferson's view, does a ruler get his authority?
3. "We hold these truths to be self-evident . . ." (par. 2). Another name for a self-evident "truth" granted at the beginning of an ARGUMENT is a *premise*. Briefly summarize the initial premises on which Jefferson's entire argument is built.
4. Which of Jefferson's premises is most crucial to his logic?
5. What is the ultimate conclusion of Jefferson's argument? Where is it stated?
6. Which of the many "injuries and usurpations" (par. 2) attributed by Jefferson to the British king seem most intolerable to you? Why?

Strategies and Structure

1. Jefferson gives the impression that the colonies are breaking away with extreme reluctance and only because of forces beyond any colonist's personal power to overlook them. How does he create this impression?
2. What is the function of paragraph 31, which seems to be a digression from Jefferson's main line of argument?

3. A *hypothesis* is a theory or supposition to be tested by further proof. What is the hypothesis, introduced in paragraph 2, that Jefferson's long list of "Facts" is adduced to test?
4. Where is Jefferson's hypothesis restated (indirectly) as an established conclusion? Is the process of arriving at this conclusion basically INDUCTION (from examples to generalizations) or DEDUCTION (from premises to particular conclusions)?
5. Jefferson's conclusion to this line of argument might be restated simply as, "King George is a tyrant." We can take this conclusion as the *minor premise* of the underlying argument of the entire Declaration. If the *major premise* is "Tyrannical governments may be abolished by the People," what is the *conclusion* of that underlying argument?
6. Which sentence in paragraph 2 states Jefferson's major premise in so many words?
7. Is this underlying argument of the Declaration basically inductive or deductive? Explain your answer.
8. The signers of the Declaration of Independence wanted to appear as men of right reason, and they approved the logical form that Jefferson gave that document. Many of the specific issues their reason addressed, however, were highly emotional. What traces of strong feelings can you detect in Jefferson's wording of individual charges against the king?
9. The eighteenth century is said to have admired and imitated "classical" balance and symmetry (as in the facade of Jefferson's Monticello). Does the form of the Declaration confirm or deny this observation? Explain your answer.

Words and Figures of Speech

1. Look up *unalienable* (or *inalienable*) in your dictionary. Considering that the Declaration was addressed, in part, to a "foreign" tyrant, why might Jefferson have chosen this adjective (par. 2) instead of, say, *natural, God-given,* or *fundamental?*
2. A *proposition* is a premise that is waiting to be approved. What single word signals us each time that Jefferson introduces a new proposition in his argument?
3. What is *consanguinity* (par. 31)? How may it be said to have a "voice"?
4. Look up *metonymy* under FIGURES OF SPEECH in the Glossary. What example of this figure can you find in paragraph 32?
5. For any of the following words you are not quite sure of, consult your dictionary: *transient* (par. 2), *usurpations* (2), *evinces* (2), *despotism* (2),

constrains (2), *candid* (2), *abdicated* (25), *perfidy* (27), *redress* (30), *magnanimity* (31), *conjured* (31), *acquiesce* (31), *rectitude* (32).

Comparing

Like the Declaration of Independence, Chief Seattle's "Reply" (Chapter 10) is addressed to a "superior" head of state. Unlike Jefferson's, however, Chief Seattle's nation was toppling instead of rising. How does this difference in circumstances change the way the two speakers address their adversaries?

Discussion and Writing Topics

1. Compose a reply to Jefferson's charges by King George in defense of his actions and policies toward the colonies.
2. Jefferson lists "the pursuit of Happiness" (par. 2) as one of our basic rights. Construct an argument urging that this promise was unwise, that happiness cannot be guaranteed, and, therefore, that Americans have been set up for inevitable disappointment by the founding fathers. Your argument will have to anticipate the objection that the Declaration protects the *pursuit* of happiness, not happiness itself.
3. Some "loyalists" remained true to England at the time of the American Revolution. How might they have justified their "patriotism"?

Johnson C. Montgomery

THE ISLAND OF PLENTY

Johnson C. Montgomery was a California attorney and an early member of the Zero Population Growth organization. Born in 1934, Montgomery attended Harvard University and the Stanford University Law School; he was admitted to the California bar in 1960. "The Island of Plenty," in his own words, is an "elitist" argument in favor of American social isolationism. Until we have enough food to feed ourselves, he says, we owe it to future generations not to share our material resources with other countries of the world.

The United States should remain an island of plenty in a sea of hunger. The future of mankind is at stake. We are not responsible for the rest of humanity. We should not accept responsibility for all humanity. We owe more to the hundreds of billions of *Homo futurans* than we do to the hungry millions—soon to be billions—of our own generations. 1

Ample food and resources exist to nourish man and all other creatures indefinitely into the future. This planet is indeed an Eden—to date our only Eden. Admittedly our Eden is plagued by pollution. Some of us have polluted the planet by reproducing too many of us. Too many people have made excessive demands on the long-range carrying capacity of our garden; and during the last 200 years there has been dramatic, ever-increasing destruction of the web of life on earth. If we try to save the starving millions today, we will simply destroy what's left of Eden. 2

The problem is not that there is too little food. The problem is there are too many people—many too many. It is not that the children should never have been born. It is simply that we have mindlessly tried to cram too many of us into too short a time span. Four billion humans are fine—but they should have been spread over several hundred years. 3

But the billions are already here. What should we do about them? 4
Should we send food, knowing that each child saved in Southeast Asia, India or Africa will probably live to reproduce and thereby bring more people into the world to live even more miserably? Should we eat the last tuna fish, the last ear of corn and utterly destroy the garden? That is what we have been doing for a long time and all the misguided efforts have merely increased the number who go to bed hungry each night. There have never been more miserable, deprived people in the world than there are right now.

It was obvious even in the late 1950s that the famine the world 5
now faces was coming unless people immediately began exercising responsibility for reducing population levels. It was also obvious that too many people contributed to the risk of nuclear war, global pestilence, illiteracy and even to many problems that are usually classified as purely economic. For example, unemployment is having too many people for the available jobs. Inflation is in part the result of too much demand from too many people. But in the 1950s, population control was taboo and those who warned of impending disasters received a cool reception.

By the time Zero Population Growth, Inc., was formed, those of 6
us who wanted to do something useful decided to concentrate our initial efforts on our own families and friends and then on the white American middle and upper classes. Our belief was that by setting an example, we could later insist that others pay attention to our proposals.

I think I was the first in the original ZPG group to have had a 7
vasectomy. Nancy and I had two children—each doing superbly well and each getting all the advantages of the best nutrition, education, attention, love and other resources available. I think Paul Ehrlich[1] (one child) was the next. Now don't ask me to cut my children back to the same number of calories that children from large families eat. In fact, don't ask me to cut my children back on anything. I won't do it without a fight; and in today's world, power is in knowledge, not numbers. Nancy and I made a conscious decision to limit the number of our children so each child could have a larger share of whatever we could make available. We intend to keep the best for them.

[1]Biology professor at Stanford, founder and past- president of Zero Population Growth.

The future of mankind is indeed with the children. But it is with the nourished, educated and loved children. It is not with the starving, uneducated and ignored. This is of course a highly elitist point of view. But that doesn't make the view incorrect. As a matter of fact, the lowest reproductive rate in the nation is that of one of the most elite groups in the world—black, female Ph.D.'s. They had to be smart and effective to make it. Having made it, they are smart enough not to wreck it with too many kids. 8

We in the United States have made great progress in lowering our birth rates. But now, because we have been responsible, it seems to some that we have a great surplus. There is, indeed, waste that should be eliminated, but there is not as much fat in our system as most people think. Yet we are being asked to share our resources with the hungry peoples of the world. But why should we share? The nations having the greatest needs are those that have been the least responsible in cutting down on births. Famine is one of nature's ways of telling profligate peoples that they have been irresponsible in their breeding habits. 9

Naturally, we would like to help; and if we could, perhaps we should. But we can't be of any use in the long run—particularly if we weaken ourselves. 10

Until we have at least a couple of years' supply of food and other resources on hand to take care of our own people and until those asking for handouts are doing at least as well as we are at reducing existing excessive population-growth rates, we should not give away our resources—not so much as one bushel of wheat. Certainly we should not participate in any programs that will increase the burden that mankind is already placing on the earth. We should not deplete our own soils to save those who will only die equally miserably a decade or so down the line—and in many cases only after reproducing more children who are inevitably doomed to live and die in misery. 11

We know the world is finite. There is only so much pie. We may be able to expand the pie, but at any point in time, the pie *is* finite. How big a piece each person gets depends in part on how many people there are. At least for the foreseeable future, the fewer of us there are, the more there will be for each. That is true on a family, community, state, national and global basis. 12

At the moment, the future of mankind seems to depend on our maintaining the island of plenty in a sea of deprivation. If everyone 13 shared equally, we would all be suffering from protein-deficiency brain damage—and that would probably be true even if we ate every last animal on earth.

As compassionate human beings, we grieve for the condition of mankind. But our grief must not interfere with our perception of reality and our planning for a better future for those who will come after us. Someone must protect the material and intellectual seed grain for the future. It seems to me that that someone is the U.S. We owe it to our children—and to their children's children's children's children. 14

These conclusions will be attacked, as they have been within Zero Population Growth, as simplistic and inhumane. But truth is often very simple and reality often inhumane. 15

QUESTIONS

Understanding

1. What is Montgomery's main proposition in this essay? In which two paragraphs is it stated most directly?
2. What other general propositions does he put forth in support of his main proposition?
3. In paragraph 4, what is the last sentence (about the number of miserable people in the world) intended to prove?
4. Montgomery warns us not to "ask me to cut my children back on anything" (par. 7). How is this position consistent with what he says about the planet's not having enough to go around?

Strategies and Structure

1. The logic of Montgomery's basic ARGUMENT can be represented by a syllogism. *Major premise:* To provide undamaged human stock for the future, some people must remain healthy. *Minor premise:* All will suffer if all share equally in the world's limited bounty. *Conclusion:* Some must not share what they have. How sound is this logic? Will you grant Montgomery's premises? Why or why not?

2. Montgomery's hard-headed realism would show us the "truth" (par. 15) of the human condition, but it would also move us to action. What would Montgomery have us do?
3. Logic is only part of Montgomery's persuasive arsenal. Which paragraphs in his essay appeal more to emotion and ethics than to logic?
4. Montgomery seems to be speaking from authority. Where does he get his authority, and how much weight should it carry?
5. Montgomery admits that his position is "elitist" (par. 8). How does he head off the charge that it is racist?
6. Is Montgomery's last paragraph necessary? Why or why not?
7. Are you persuaded by Montgomery's essay? Why or why not?

Words and Figures of Speech

1. How does the METAPHOR of the island contribute to Montgomery's argument? Is there any IRONY in his title?
2. For the sake of the future, says Montgomery, we must save some "material and intellectual seed grain" (par. 14). Explain this metaphor: What is being compared to what? Why is the metaphor appropriate?
3. How is Montgomery altering the traditional definition of Eden? Is he rejecting the traditional idea altogether? Explain your answer.
4. *Homo futurans* (par. 1), meaning "man of the future," is modeled after such scientific terms as *Homo erectus* ("upright man") and *Homo sapiens* ("thinking man"). Why might Montgomery choose to use the language of science at the beginning of his argument?
5. How does Montgomery's use of the word *mindlessly* (par. 3) fit in with his entire argument?
6. What is the meaning of *profligate* (par. 9)?

Comparing

1. By comparison with Debi Davis's "Body Imperfect," does "The Island of Plenty" seem more concerned with analyzing a social condition or with persuading the reader to act? Explain.
2. Opponents of Montgomery's argument might charge that he has written "a modest proposal." What would they mean by this? Would they be justified? (See Jonathan Swift's "A Modest Proposal" in Essays for Further Reading.)

Discussion and Writing Topics

1. Attack Montgomery's position on the grounds that he is confusing compassion with weakness.
2. Defend Montgomery's assertion that "there is not as much fat in our system as most people think" (par. 9).
3. Write your own "modest proposal" (for feeding the world, curing inflation, regulating human breeding habits, or some other "simple" task).

Kori Quintana

The Price of Power: Living in the Nuclear Age

A student at the University of New Mexico when she wrote "The Price of Power," Kori Quintana grew up in Utah, where she contracted Lupus at age seventeen. In this brief term paper, complete with citations, she records the moment she became aware of the high cancer rate among Mormons and other citizens of Utah, including her own family. Were their genes altered by the nuclear testing of the 1950s? Can the effects of nuclear radiation be inherited? Along with her personal reasons for such inquiries, Quintana presents her impersonal findings.

I became interested in the topic of genetic mutation last May after coming across an article in Time magazine entitled "Legacy of a Disaster." The article included photos and descriptions of animal deformities caused by the nuclear meltdown at Chernobyl. Having always been fascinated by biology and genetics, I was intrigued with the subject of environmentally induced changes in genetic structure. What I did not know when I began researching the connection between radioactivity and genetic damage was that I would find the probable cause of my own family's battle with cancer and other health problems. 1

Hailing from Utah, the state known for its Mormon population's healthy lifestyle, my family has been plagued with a number of seemingly unrelated health problems. My grandmother was recently diagnosed as having bone cancer. My mother has suffered from allergies and thyroid problems most of her life. When I was diagnosed at the age of 17 as having Lupus, an auto-immune disease with an unknown cause, I accepted it as being determined by fate. Assuming 2 that our family was just genetically predisposed to such ailments, I never considered any external causes, until now.

During my research on the effects of radiation on human genes, I 3
noticed that there were several references to studies of Mormons in Utah. My curiosity piqued, I studied on. Apparently, the atmospheric bomb tests of the 1950s over Nevada were performed only when winds were blowing away from Las Vegas toward Utah. Subsequent studies of residents of towns with high nuclear fallout showed that various illnesses, especially leukemia, had stricken people who had no family history of them. Of course, it is possible that the emergence of my family's illnesses following the bomb tests is purely coincidental; however, as the evidence against radiation unfolded before me, I became convinced that some sort of connection did exist. I also wondered if the cell damage sustained by people exposed to radiation could be passed on to future generations.

Once met by the public with wild enthusiasm for their potential 4
benefits to humanity, X-rays, radium, nuclear energy, and nuclear arms now generate fear and foreboding as their unforeseen side effects become known. While it is true that radiation occurs naturally from the sun and cosmic rays, these levels are minuscule when compared to the levels that humans are exposed to from fallout, nuclear accidents, medical treatments, consumer products and nuclear waste. Considering that nuclear power has only been available for the past 25 years, we have just begun to see the effects of widespread exposure to radiation.

According to Catherine Caufield, author of *Multiple Exposures:* 5
Chronicles of the Radiation Age, radiation sets off a "chain of physical, chemical, and biological changes that can result in serious illness, genetic defects, or death" (Caufield, 10). It is possible for radiation damage to be inherited by offspring because the beta and gamma rays affect the most basic elements of the human body, the genes. Radiation alters the electrical charge of the atoms and molecules that make up our cells. Within the cell lies the DNA, containing the genetic code that controls the function and reproduction of the cell. Genetic mutations, which are basically changes in the composition of the DNA, occur whenever a gene is chemically or structurally changed. When a radioactive particle collides with a cell, the cell usually dies. But when the damaged cell lives, it may function normally for a while until one day, maybe years later, it "goes berserk

and manufactures billions of identically damaged cells" (Caldicott, 40). Cancerous tumors are formed this way.

Although mutations do occur naturally in organisms over the course of many generations, research has shown that environmental factors—radiation and chemicals—increase the rates and types of mutations. A prime example of this is the enormous increase in animal deformations in areas surrounding the Chernobyl nuclear plant. Since the accident, 197 deformed calves (some with up to eight legs) and about 200 abnormal piglets have been born. The severity of these deformities is frightening, including animals with no eyes, deformed skulls, and distorted mouths (Toufexis, 70). There have also been indications that human babies have been born in the area with gross deformities, but due to the Soviets' strict control over such information, no evidence has been made public. The disaster was followed immediately by an overwhelming rise in human mortality, spanning several countries and continents. Residents of the area continue to experience dramatic rises in cases of thyroid disease, anemia, and cancer as well as a drop in immunity levels. 6

In *Secret Fallout,* Ernest Sternglass, a well known authority on radiation and health, claims that a human, "especially during the stage of early embryonic life, is hundreds or thousands of times more sensitive to radiation than anyone had ever suspected" (Sternglass, 17). Fetuses formed from a mutated egg or sperm cell usually spontaneously abort. This explains the unusually high miscarriage rate for areas surrounding nuclear plants. If the fetus survives pregnancy, Sternglass says that it may turn out to be a "sickly, deformed individual with a shortened life span" (Sternglass, 41). Down's Syndrome is caused by a chromosomal abnormality sometimes linked to radiation damage. According to genetic principles, if an affected person reproduces, one half of his or her children will inherit the deformities or illnesses. 7

In addition to contributing to a higher infant mortality rate and birth defects, the damage sustained by radiation manifests itself as a myriad of diseases including: leukemia; lymphoid, brain, liver and lung cancers; Hodgkin's disease, and central nervous system diseases (Gould, 184). Among Japan's bomb survivors, instances of stomach, ovary, breast, bowel, lung, bone and thyroid cancers doubled. In addition, some researchers have theorized that radiation may have created many new organisms that take advantage of weakened immune systems. In their new book, *Deadly Deceit,* Jay Gould and 8

Benjamin Goldman give an example of this hypothesis. In 1975, after huge releases of radiation from the nearby Millstone nuclear reactor, the town of Old Lyme experienced an outbreak of the previously rare disease now bearing its name, Lyme disease. The disease, which is carried by ticks, had been virtually unknown to humans for several generations. The authors suggest that radiation caused a sudden lethal change in the ticks, so that its bite became lethal to the victim. Gould and Goldman also link the recent emergence of AIDS to radiation by applying this hypothesis to the mutation of viruses.

Scientists and government officials have known for several years 9
that radiation causes the mutations I have described, which lead to illness, genetic damage, and death; yet, they continue to allow the unsuspecting public to be exposed to dangerous levels of radiation, and to have their food, water, and air contaminated by it. Ernest Sternglass made the comment that because of man's fascination with nuclear power, "it appears that we have unwittingly carried out an experiment with ourselves as guinea pigs on a worldwide scale" (Sternglass, 189). Millions of innocent people have paid the price of nuclear power through their suffering and untimely deaths. By inheriting genetic damage caused by radiation, the future generations of mankind may bear the burden as well. A multi-million dollar settlement was awarded to Utah residents who proved that their cancers were caused by radioactive fallout. Whether or not radiation is indeed responsible for my own illness may never be proven. Nevertheless, the image I once had of my grandparents' farm in Utah as an unspoiled, safe haven, untouched by the tainted hands of modern evils, has been forever changed in my mind. I must live with the knowledge that, because of atmospheric bomb tests performed before I was born, I am a prime candidate for developing some form of cancer in my lifetime, and if that happens, it won't be because of fate or the will of God, but because of man's unleasing a power he cannot control.

BIBLIOGRAPHY

Caldicott, Dr. Helen. "Radiation: Unsafe at Any Level." *Medical Hazards of Radiation Packet*. Boston: Autumn Press, 1978.

Congress of the United States. *Technologies for Detecting Heritable Mutagens in Human Beings*. Washington: GPO, 1986.

Gould, Jay M., and Benjamin Goldman. *Deadly Deceit Low-Level Radiation, High-Level Cover-Up*. New York: Four Walls Eight Windows, 1990.

Kotulak, Ronald, and Peter Gorner. "The Gene is out of the Bottle." *Chicago Tribune,* 8 April 1990: AI.

Science Policy Research Division, Congressional Research Service, Library of Congress. *Genetic Engineering, Human Genetics and Cell Biology: Evolution of Technological Issues* (Supplemental Report III). Washington: GPO, 1980.

Sternglass, Ernest. *Secret Fallout.* New York: McGraw Hill, 1981.

Toufexis, Anastasia. "Legacy of a Disaster." *Time,* 9 April 1990: 68–70.

World Health Organization. *Health Aspects of Human Rights.* Geneva: WHO, 1976.

QUESTIONS

Understanding

1. What is the nature of the medical condition that afflicts the author of this essay?
2. Why is it important to Quintana's argument that she grew up in Utah?
3. Is Quintana arguing that nuclear fallout from the fifties directly *caused* her and her family's diseases? Why or why not?
4. What, then, is the main point of her argument? State it as a direct assertion or conclusion.
5. Can cell damage due to radiation be inherited, Quintana asks (par. 3). What does she conclude on *this* issue?

Strategies and Structure

1. Why does Quintana cite other writers? Is she wise to do so? Why or why not?
2. How (and where) does Quintana personalize her appeal to reason?
3. How does the conclusion (par. 9) of "The Price of Power"—especially the references to the farm—recall the opening paragraphs?
4. Quintana's logical argument is also a study in cause and effect (Chapter 4). Which is subordinate to which: the logic or the causal analysis? Please explain.

5. If Quintana is not arguing direct causation in her case, why does she cite all those effects of nuclear radiation in other cases?
6. "X-rays, radium, nuclear energy, and nuclear arms," says Quintana par. 4), "now generate fear and foreboding as their unforeseen side effects become known." Is this an appeal to reason or to emotion or to both? Please explain.
7. Nuclear power plants emit far less radiation than nuclear accidents or unprotected nuclear waste. Yet Quintana lumps all three together (par. 4), implying "guilt by association." Is this practice fair or foul in argument? Please explain.

Words and Figures of Speech

1. Quintana uses the word *power* in at least two senses here. What are they, and where does she use them?
2. *Lupus* (par. 2) derives from the Latin for *wolf*: why this name for a disease that often causes disfiguring lesions of the skin?
3. Her grandparents' farm, says Quintana, once seemed to her "untouched by the tainted hands of modern evils" (par. 9). How does the language of this METAPHOR differ from the prevailing language of her discourse, for example in paragraph 6? Should Quintana have used more such FIGURES OF SPEECH? Why or why not?

Comparing

1. How does Quintana's attitude toward facts and figures compare with Roger Verhulst's in "Being Prepared in Suburbia" (Chapter 10)? Which is closer to your own attitude? Why?
2. On the matter of the federal government's responsibility for the prevention and treatment of disease, how does "The Price of Power" compare with "Good AIDS, Bad AIDS" (by Randy Shilts, Chapter 10)?

Discussion and Writing Topics

1. To what extent, would you say, should government be held liable for damages resulting from nuclear tests it conducted forty years ago?

2. Coal-burning power plants release far more radiation (radon) than properly functioning nuclear plants. What bearing, if any, does this fact have upon Quintana's argument?
3. What is a "class-action" suit and for what types of cases is one appropriate?

James Q. Wilson

Reasonable Search and Seizure

Professor of public policy at the University of California, Los Angeles, James Q. Wilson has been described by *Psychology Today* as a "leading neoconservative social theorist." With the publication of *Varieties of Police Behavior* (1968), *Thinking About Crime* (1975), and *Crime and Human Nature* (1985), however, he has become one of the best-known commentators on crime and the police in America. Professor Wilson's most recent book is *The Moral Sense* (1993). "Reasonable Search and Seizure" is the editor's title.

The President wants still tougher gun control legislation and thinks it will work. The public supports more gun control laws but suspects they won't work. The public is right. 1

Legal restraints on the lawful purchase of guns will have little effect on the illegal use of guns. There are some 200 million guns in private ownership, about one-third of them handguns. Only about 2 percent of the latter are employed to commit crimes. It would take a Draconian, and politically impossible, confiscation of legally purchased guns to make much of a difference in the number used by criminals. Moreover, only about one-sixth of the handguns used by serious criminals are purchased from a gun shop or pawnshop. Most of these handguns are stolen, borrowed or obtained through private purchases that wouldn't be affected by gun laws. 2

What is worse, any successful effort to shrink the stock of legally purchased guns (or of ammunition) would reduce the capacity of law-abiding people to defend themselves. Gun control advocates scoff at the importance of self-defense, but they are wrong to do so. Based on a household survey, Gary Kleck, a criminologist at Florida State University, has estimated that every year, guns are used—that 3 is, displayed or fired—for defensive purposes more than a million times, not counting their use by the police. If his estimate is correct, this means that the number of people who defend themselves with a gun exceeds the number of arrests for violent crimes and burglaries.

The available evidence supports the claim that self-defense is a legitimate form of deterrence. People who report to the National Crime Survey that they defended themselves with a weapon were less likely to lose property in a robbery or be injured in an assault than those who did not defend themselves. Statistics have shown that would-be burglars are threatened by gun-wielding victims about as many times a year as they are arrested (and much more often than they are sent to prison) and that the chances of a burglar being shot are about the same as his chances of going to jail. Criminals know these facts even if gun control advocates do not and so are less likely to burgle occupied homes in America than occupied ones in Europe, where the residents rarely have guns. 4

Some gun control advocates may concede these points but rejoin that the cost of self-defense is self-injury: Handgun owners are more likely to shoot themselves or their loved ones than a criminal. Not quite. Most gun accidents involve rifles and shotguns, not handguns. Moreover, the rate of fatal gun accidents has been declining while the level of gun ownership has been rising. There are fatal gun accidents just as there are fatal car accidents, but in fewer than 2 percent of the gun fatalities was the victim someone mistaken for an intruder. 5

Those who urge us to forbid or severely restrict the sale of guns ignore these facts. Worse, they adopt a position that is politically absurd. In effect, they say, "Your government, having failed to protect your person and your property from criminal assault, now intends to deprive you of the opportunity to protect yourself." 6

Opponents of gun control make a different mistake. The National Rifle Association and its allies tell us that "guns don't kill, people kill" and urge the Government to punish more severely people who use guns to commit crimes. Locking up criminals does protect society from future crimes, and the prospect of being locked up may deter criminals. But our experience with meting out tougher sentences is mixed. The tougher the prospective sentence the less likely it is to be imposed, or at least to be imposed swiftly. If the Legislature adds on time for crimes committed with a gun, prosecutors often bargain away the add-ons; even when they do not, the judges in many states are reluctant to impose add-ons. 7

Worse, the presence of a gun can contribute to the magnitude of 8
the crime even on the part of those who worry about serving a long prison sentence. Many criminals carry guns not to rob stores but to protect themselves from other armed criminals. Gang violence has become more threatening to bystanders as gang members have begun to arm themselves. People may commit crimes, but guns make some crimes worse. Guns often convert spontaneous outbursts of anger into fatal encounters. When some people carry them on the streets, others will want to carry them to protect themselves, and an urban arms race will be under way.

Our goal should not be the disarming of law-abiding citizens. It 9
should be to reduce the number of people who carry guns unlawfully, especially in places—on streets, in taverns—where the mere presence of a gun can increase the hazards we all face. The most effective way to reduce illegal gun-carrying is to encourage the police to take guns away from people who carry them without a permit. This means encouraging the police to make street frisks.

The Fourth Amendment to the Constitution bans "unreasonable 10
searches and seizures." In 1968 the Supreme Court decided *(Terry v. Ohio)* that a frisk—patting down a person's outer clothing—is proper if the officer has a "reasonable suspicion" that the person is armed and dangerous. If a pat-down reveals an object that might be a gun, the officer can enter the suspect's pocket to remove it. If the gun is being carried illegally, the suspect can be arrested.

The reasonable-suspicion test is much less stringent than the 11
probable-cause standard the police must meet in order to make an arrest. A reasonable suspicion, however, is more than just a hunch; it must be supported by specific facts. The courts have held, not always consistently, that these facts include someone acting in a way that leads an experienced officer to conclude criminal activity may be afoot; someone fleeing at the approach of an officer; a person who fits a drug courier profile; a motorist stopped for a traffic violation who has a suspicious bulge in his pocket; a suspect identified by a reliable informant as carrying a gun. The Supreme Court has also upheld frisking people on probation or parole.

Some police departments frisk a lot of people, but usually the 12
police frisk rather few, at least for the purpose of detecting illegal guns. In 1992 the police arrested about 240,000 people for illegally possessing or carrying a weapon. This is only about one-fourth as

many as were arrested for public drunkenness. The average police officer will make *no* weapons arrests and confiscate *no* guns during any given year. Mark Moore, a professor of public policy at Harvard University, found that most weapons arrests were made because a citizen complained, not because the police were out looking for guns.

It is easy to see why. Many cities suffer from a shortage of officers, 13
and even those with ample law-enforcement personnel worry about having their cases thrown out for constitutional reasons or being accused of police harassment. But the risk of violating the Constitution or engaging in actual, as opposed to perceived, harassment can be substantially reduced.

Each patrol officer can be given a list of people on probation or 14
parole who live on that officer's beat and be rewarded for making frequent stops to insure that they are not carrying guns. Officers can be trained to recognize the kinds of actions that the Court will accept as providing the "reasonable suspicion" necessary for a stop and frisk. Membership in a gang known for assaults and drug dealing could be made the basis, by statute or Court precedent, for gun frisks.

And modern science can be enlisted to help. Metal detectors at 15
airports have reduced the number of airplane bombings and skyjackings to nearly zero. But these detectors only work at very close range. What is needed is a device that will enable the police to detect the presence of a large lump of metal in someone's pocket from a distance of ten or fifteen feet. Receiving such a signal could supply the officer with reasonable grounds for a pat-down. Underemployed nuclear physicists and electronics engineers in the post-cold-war era surely have the talents for designing a better gun detector.

Even if we do all these things, there will still be complaints. Inno- 16
cent people will be stopped. Young black and Hispanic men will probably be stopped more often than older white Anglo males or women of any race. But if we are serious about reducing drive-by shootings, fatal gang wars and lethal quarrels in public places, we must get illegal guns off the street. We cannot do this by multiplying the forms one fills out at gun shops or by pretending that guns are not a problem until a criminal uses one.

QUESTIONS

Understanding

1. Why will "legal restraints on the lawful purchase of guns" (par. 2), in James Q. Wilson's opinion, "have little effect on the illegal use of guns"?
2. Why, according to Wilson, are advocates of gun control wrong to "scoff" (par. 3) at the self-defense argument advanced by gun proponents?
3. *Opponents* of gun control, such as the National Rifle Association, make a "different mistake" (par. 7), says Wilson. What's wrong, in his view, with the argument that "guns don't kill, people kill" (par. 7)?
4. "Our goal should not be the disarming of law-abiding citizens," contends Wilson. "It should be to reduce the number of people who carry guns unlawfully . . ." (par. 9). How does Professor Wilson propose to accomplish this "goal"?
5. How would Wilson reduce "the risk of violating the Constitution or engaging in . . . harassment" (par. 13) by police officers conducting searches for illegal guns?
6. How, according to Wilson, can the aid of modern science be enlisted in the "reasonable" search and seizure of illegal weapons before they are used to commit crimes?

Strategies and Structure

1. "Legal restraints on the lawful purchase of guns will have little effect on the illegal use of guns" (par. 2) is the conclusion of a DEDUCTIVE logical argument. On what premises, major and minor, stated and implied, does Wilson base this conclusion? Does it follow logically, in your opinion, from the premises? Please explain your answer.
2. "Self-defense is a legitimate form of deterrence" (par. 4) is the conclusion of an INDUCTIVE logical argument. On what evidence does Wilson base it; and, again, how logically do you think the conclusion follows from the proof cited? Why do you think so?
3. How does James Q. Wilson counter the argument "that the cost of self-defense is self-injury" (par. 5)? Would you say his rejoinder is mainly inductive or deductive? How reasonable do you find his reasoning this time? Why so?

4. What evidence (and how convincing do you find it) does Wilson offer in support of the following proposition: "People may commit crimes, but guns make some crimes worse" (par. 8)?
5. Why does Wilson cite the work of Mark Moore, a professor of public policy at Harvard, in paragraph 12? Where else (and why) does he appeal to the authority of experts in his essay?
6. Wilson defines "reasonable" grounds for the search and seizure of concealed weapons mainly by giving examples. What are some of them, and how reasonable would they be, do you think, in actual practice? Again, please explain your answer.

Words and Figures of Speech

1. What is the difference between the "reasonable-suspicion test" and the "probable-cause standard" (par. 11)?
2. "Reasonable" is a relative term. Who has the ultimate responsibility for determining whether an action is reasonable or unreasonable under the U.S. Constitution? Where and how does Wilson acknowledge this authority?
3. In legal terms, a proposition—"But if we are serious about reducing drive-by shootings, fatal gang wars and lethal quarrels in public places, we must get illegal guns off the street" (par. 16)—cannot be reasonable or unreasonable in and of itself; it must appear so to "a reasonable man or woman." Whether or not you agree with him, how well do you think the speaker in Wilson's essay creates the impression of a man who arrives at his conclusions through reason and logic? How does he do it, or why does he fail?
4. Justice, when PERSONIFIED as a woman in trailing robes, wears a blindfold because she is supposed to play no favorites. She also carries a pair of scales, in part because many judicial decisions are rendered "on balance"—that is, in a choice among rights, the positive benefits to society of upholding one are weighed against the negative effects of denying the other. When and where in particular does the "reasonable man" of Wilson's essay claim to make tough decisions "on balance"?
5. How is the author of "Reasonable Search and Seizure" defining "politically" in such phrases as "politically impossible" (par. 2) and "politically absurd" (par. 6)?
6. There are relatively few METAPHORS or other FIGURES OF SPEECH in James Q. Wilson's essay on gun control. Perhaps this is merely a matter of

writing style, but can you suggest any other reasons why the author of such a piece might avoid figurative language in general?

Comparing

1. Like James Q. Wilson, Alan M. Dershowitz also deals with a Constitutional issue in "Shouting 'Fire!' " (Chapter 7). How might the concept of "reasonableness" or "the reasonable man" be used to link two issues as distinct from each other, on the surface, as search and seizure and free speech?
2. Would you say "Reasonable Search and Seizure" is more or less personal and emotional than "The Declaration of Independence" (reprinted earlier in this chapter)? Please explain your answer. How would you account for the differences?
3. Compare and contrast "Reasonable Search and Seizure" with Kori Quintana's "The Price of Power" (the immediately preceding essay in this chapter) as exercises in reasoning "on balance."

Discussion and Writing Topics

1. "Criminals know these facts," says Wilson, "even if gun control advocates do not . . ." (par. 4). How important is this assertion to Professor Wilson's argument? What evidence does he cite to back it up? Should he have cited more evidence, or do you think this is an accurate statement on the face of it? Please explain your opinion.
2. Professor Wilson acknowledges that "innocent people will be stopped" (par. 16) if police are encouraged to frisk suspects for illegal guns more frequently than they do now. "Young black and Hispanic men will probably be stopped more often than older white Anglo males or women of any race" (par. 16), he says. Is this potential for discrimination a reasonable price to pay "to get illegal guns off the street" (par. 16) or is it an unreasonable social penalty? Debate this question with several of your classmates, make a list of the reasons on both sides of the issue, and then present the rest of the class with a decision, one way or the other, plus the reasons your group chose to "vote" as they do. If you must dissent from the group, explain the reasons for your minority opinion.
3. To what extent should your answer to the preceding question depend upon how confident you are that an increase in searches will, in fact,

lead to significantly more seizures of illegal guns, as Professor Wilson says they will? What if he is wrong? Should we try anyway? Why or why not? Here again, you may want to debate the issue with other members of your class before arriving at a tentative conclusion.

4. Examine the logic of the proposition that "guns don't kill, people kill" (par. 7).

Barbara Ehrenreich

Maintaining the Crime Supply

A feminist and co-chairperson of the Democratic Socialists of America, Barbara Ehrenreich is *The Snarling Citizen* (the title of the recent collection of her trenchant columns and essays from which "Maintaining the Crime Supply" is reprinted). Ehrenreich's wit—she offers her only son to anyone who will pay his college tuition—and biting social criticism have been directed, most notably, at the American health care "empire" and the "flight from commitment" that, she believes, has led to the "listlessness" of the 1990s. "I had given up hope of again finding someone who was literate, interesting, and constructive in an adequately mean way," writes John Kenneth Galbraith. "Then I encountered Barbara Ehrenreich. Very satisfying!"

It's impossible to address the problem of crime without beginning to worry about the law of supply and demand. Not that many people go around breaking that particular law, but you can be sure we'd get them if they did. Thanks to tough new legislation, we will soon have the most massive and splendid Punishment Industry on earth today: shiny new prisons for every state, harsh new sentences for every infringement, lethal injections more readily available than measles vaccine! Already the United States has a larger proportion of its population locked up than any other nation, South Africa included, so the only worry is—what if we run out of crime? 1

If punishment actually worked, a crime shortage would develop in no time at all. Would-be criminals would study the available sentences, do a careful cost-benefit analysis, and conclude that armed robbery or, say, aggravated assault just wasn't their cup of tea. Yes, 2 if deterrence worked, as our leaders seem to think it does, we would soon have a vast oversupply of electric chairs and unattractive, heavily walled, rural real estate.

And if crime frightens you, try to imagine a world without a crime. It would be unthinkable: Nothing on TV except *Sesame Street* and *Jeopardy* reruns. Chuck Norris reduced to panhandling. No execution tailgate parties, no Court Channel or *NYPD Blue*. Because—let us be honest about it—crime is our favorite entertainment spectacle, crime and punishment, that is. Think how many happy hours the average family spends watching the bad guys get perforated by bullets or menaced by Nazi-biker fiends in the pen. 3

This is nothing to be ashamed of. Historically, people have long demanded the pleasure of seeing others punished, and usually in live, nonfiction form. Executions were public as a matter of course, providing a festive occasion for the masses. Participatory punishment, in the form of lynchings and stonings, offered the average citizen a vivid, hands-on experience. In fact, historically speaking, the problem has been not to "stop crime" but to keep the local Punishment Industry supplied with victims. When the Romans ran out of criminals to feed to the lions, they scoured the world for edible prisoners of war. The Athenians used to designate some poor vagrant every year, drive him out of town, and subject him to a ritual stoning-to-death. 4

We think of ourselves as far more enlightened because our victims must be genuine criminals as certified by a court of law. The only exception is in the case of death-row inmates who turn out, at the very last moment, not to be guilty at all. In some cases the courts have ruled that they should fry anyway—because the facilities are ready and waiting and everyone is in the mood. 5

Other than that, we are restricted to criminals, as the word is generally defined, and the supply is by no means unlimited. One line of criminological reasoning, which might be called the "liberal" theory, holds that there is nothing wrong with our present approach to maintaining the crime supply. Just take a quarter of the child population, raise them in desperate poverty (with racial discrimination thrown in where applicable), and subject them to commercials, night and day, advising that life without one-hundred-dollar footwear is not worth living. As an added measure, make sure none of the available jobs pay more than about five dollars an hour, and 6 presto—little muggers are born, and in numbers sufficient to stock the Punishment Industry for years to come!

Conservatives naturally question the liberal theory. They point to 7
the occasional person who grows up poor and virtuous, or, alternatively, affluent and twisted. Deprivation and temptation are not enough, they say—a good supply of crime requires technology too. Hence the Republicans' understandable reluctance to get behind gun control. Why make it even marginally more difficult for a teenager to get his hands on a gun just as we are about to beef up the Punishment Industry with ultra-tough new legislation? As even the National Rifle Association is too modest to point out, there is no way we would lead the world in the business of crime and punishment if it were not for our wide-open supply of guns.

The other tried-and-true approach is to simply broaden the defi- 8
nition of crime. This is the function of drug prohibition. A few decades ago, a person who smoked marijuana was a degenerate rake or a dashing bohemian, depending on your point of view. Now he or she is a criminal, qualifying for years in the slammer. Some states have gone further, making possession of rolling papers an equally dastardly crime. Similarly the "crime" of graffiti writing could be broadened to include possession of a Magic Marker, or crossing state lines with intent to buy one. The possibilities are endless once you realize that there is no crime, no matter how seemingly minor, that cannot be federalized, subjected to mandatory minimum sentencing, or transformed into a capital offense.

But a growing number of experts, including many criminal 9
judges, assure us that there is nothing to worry about. No matter how fiercely Draconian it becomes, the Punishment Industry will never diminish the supply of crime. On the contrary, there is evidence that a few years in the pen serves to season a criminal and make him more productive at his work. So as long as we do nothing to disturb the marvelous synergy of poverty and temptation, guns on the street and gun-fun on the tube, the supply of crime will never fall below the widespread demand for punishment.

Or we could decide, all of us law-abiding citizens, to cut off crime 10
at the source, where poverty intersects with weaponry, and to satisfy the public appetite for cruelty with something other than the Punishment Industry. Bearbaiting has been proposed; also cockfighting and the public torment of stray dogs.

QUESTIONS

Understanding

1. What is the "law of supply and demand" (par. 1), and how, according to Barbara Ehrenreich's tongue-in-cheek analysis, does it apply to the "supply" of crime in America?
2. What is the "liberal" theory of crime production, according to Ehrenreich? How do the "conservatives" respond to these views?
3. If both conservatives and liberals are wrong about how to maintain the crime supply in America, what other alternative does Ehrenreich say we have?
4. One "industry" in particular, says Ehrenreich, would be hurt by a serious drop-off in either the supply of crime or the demand for it. What is that industry?
5. How likely is it, in Ehrenreich's view, that a serious crime shortage will actually develop in America? How can she be so confident?
6. Should the demand for crime and punishment inexplicably dry up in the American market, how would Ehrenreich satisfy "the public appetite for cruelty" (par. 10) that, she says, fuels "the Punishment Industry" (par. 10)?

Strategies and Structure

1. IRONY does not necessarily say the opposite of what it means. The point of Jonathan Swift's "A Modest Proposal" (Essays for Further Reading), remember, is not that we should not eat babies but that poverty inures a nation to the commercial exploitation of human commodities (to use the language of supply and demand). If Barbara Ehrenreich is not really saying that we should not fight crime because the American people have an insatiable appetite for it, what *is* she arguing?
2. Ehrenreich's basic strategy of mock argument in "Maintaining the Crime Supply" is to treat crime as if it were a commodity rather than a form of human behavior. Once you accept this proposition, how "logical" do you find the rest of her reasoning? What other evidence of conditional (or if-then) logic can you point to in Ehrenreich's essay?

3. "This is nothing to be ashamed of" (par. 4). Eschewing logic, Ehrenreich appeals to whom or what in support of this intentionally absurd proposition? What aspect of the appeal to ethics (next chapter) is she also parodying in this line of argument (and elsewhere)?
4. What is parody, anyway; and how does it relate to SATIRE?
5. Where and how does Ehrenreich insinuate what she thinks are really the root causes of so much crime in America? Is her own view, then, would you say, closer to the "liberal" or the "conservative" views as she mockingly defines them in paragraphs 6 and 7? Please explain.
6. Where does Ehrenreich actually make a "modest" (that is a seemingly practical but outlandishly callous) proposal for satisfying what she says is the American appetite for violence? How does she signal a logical shift here, and how does she relate that alternative conclusion to what has gone before?

Words and Figures of Speech

1. "So the only worry is—what if we run out of crime?" (par. 1): How does the choice of words in this clause alert us that Ehrenreich is being ironic here?
2. What are the possible meanings of *unthinkable* in paragraph 3 of "Maintaining the Crime Supply"? What other "double-edged" terms like this can you point to in Ehrenreich's prose? How do they support her irony?
3. How does the following sentence in Ehrenreich's arsenal illustrate what is sometimes called "guilt by association": "No execution tailgate parties, no Court Channel or *NYPD Blue*" (par. 3)?
4. Where does Ehrenreich capitalize on the language of pop economics? Cite two or three of the most shameless examples.
5. Why does Ehrenreich lapse into CLICHÉ ("tried-and-true") in paragraph 8? Why does she put "crime" (later in that same paragraph) in quotation marks?
6. Don't worry how "fiercely Draconian" the criminal justice system becomes, Ehrenreich reassures us, "it will never diminish the supply of crime" (par. 9). Who was Draco, and what was he known for in seventh-century (B.C.) Athens?
7. In scientific or biological terminology, what constitutes a "synergy" (par. 9)?

Comparing

1. How does the TONE of "Maintaining the Crime Supply" resemble that of Nikki Giovanni's "On Holidays and How to Make Them Work" (Chapter 3)?
2. In "A Modest Proposal" (Essays for Further Reading) Jonathan Swift uses logic to attack the use of logic as a sole guide to human conduct. How might Barbara Ehrenreich be said to do the same in "Maintaining the Crime Supply"? Some readers of Swift's ironic prose make the mistake of identifying the author with his persona. How (and how well) do you think Ehrenreich avoids this misdemeanor?
3. Do you think Barbara Ehrenreich would agree with James Q. Wilson's views as set forth in "Reasonable Search and Seizure" (the preceding essay in this chapter); or would Wilson, to Ehrenreich's mind, represent the very point of view she is satirizing in "Maintaining the Crime Supply"? Please explain your answer.

Discussion and Writing Topics

1. Do you agree or disagree with Barbara Ehrenreich's assertion that the penal system in America is ineffectual in deterring crime? What's your evidence?
2. What about Ehrenreich's suggestion (par. 8, especially) that some "crimes" should be decriminalized? Is this a separate issue from the punishment-deters-or-fails-to-deter debate? If so, is it right or wrong, logical or illogical, to link the two?
3. Write a modest proposal of your own for maintaining the current supply of crime (or poverty or cruelty or violence) in America.

Barbara Ehrenreich

As with most topics, Barbara Ehrenreich speaks with a fine irony on the subject of how she writes. "Most of the insights in the following essays," she says of *The Snarling Citizen* (from which "Maintaining the Crime Supply" is taken), were obtained in this way: "First comes the phone call or, most likely, just a message on the answering machine from the editor of one of our major media outlets. 'Barbara,' the voice says, or at least some similar-sounding name, 'I hope I have the right number because we need the Mood in America (or the Future of Life on Earth, or Whatever Happened to Our Way of Life?) by Thursday at the latest. And if I've got the wrong number, I'd appreciate knowing if there's someone else there who could do it instead.' Then, flattered and brimming with investigative zeal," she writes, "I rush to the den, wrestle the remote out of a loved one's hand, and settle down to work." 1

Why does the modern journalist (even in jest) turn to television rather than print or live people to place her remote squarely on the pulse of her times? It's because "the modern zeitgeist feeds on images," says Ehrenreich, "and it hardly matters to the zeitgeist whether the scenes it consumes are the result of actual real-world events or artful cinematic deception." Thus the "geist," bloated indifferently on images of corpses from real wars or Arnold Schwarzenegger reruns, "oozes from the TV and settles lumplike in the middle of 2 the den," where it sometimes attacks the dog. "If you were hoping maybe for a winged and helmeted figure of noble visage," says Ehrenreich of the spirit of the present age, "then you have been reading too much Hegel and not watching enough CNN."

Most people these days, however, Ehrenreich contends, do not read Hegel—or anything else. The reason that even a print journalist must turn to the images on TV for her material, she says, is that people no longer express their noble (or even just nice) ideas and emotions in writing. "Most people have figured out by now that print is the medium of intimidation, expropriation, and threat," as in the fine print on the back of a credit card statement. Or the typical writing of the times is simply incoherent and impenetrable, as in *The DOS Manual.* Opening her manual at random, Ehrenreich finds, for example, this: "The syntax for the PRINT command is PRINT / B:bufsize /D:device /M:maxtick /S:timeslice /U:busytick d:paths filename.ext /T/C/P . . . ." What does this mean? It means, says Ehrenreich, that "everywhere one looks, proofs of the futility of literacy fly into one's face." 3

Hence the alarming illiteracy rate in America. She herself has "almost given up on reading," Ehrenreich says, and turned to TV and other virtual images for her sustenance as a writer of prose. "It was a communication from the IRS that did me in, or possibly some incredible claim about unpaid parking tickets." The direct result of such bad writing is that intelligent people refuse to read. They have figured out that "when someone has something nice to say, they say it with pictures or flowers or strippers-by-wire." The problem, then, according to Ehrenreich, is not that people who can no longer read and write are "dumb." On the contrary: "The problem is that, in late-corporate-capitalist-bureaucratic society, there is not a whole lot one would willingly read. And most of the things that one really should read . . . are so relentlessly hostile to the human spirit that refusing to read may be the only dignified course of action. So mass illiteracy must be seen for what it is—a quiet, but determined, postmodern rebellion." 4

Writing Topics for Chapter Nine
Essays That Appeal to Reason

Write a logical argument defending one of the following propositions:

1. Buying a house, condominium, or trailer makes (does not make) better sense in the long run than renting one.
2. Grading standards are (are not) slipping in American colleges and universities.
3. College students are (are not) as bright now as they used to be.
4. College graduates get (do not get) better jobs than those who do not go to college.
5. Graduate or professional school is (is not) worth the expense these days.
6. Smoking is (is not) hazardous to your health.
7. America has (has not) developed into a "welfare state."
8. Farm-life is (is not) a dying institution in America.
9. Cities are (are not) dying in America.
10. The feminist movement has (has not) produced desirable results.
11. The "revolution" in sexual morality is (is not) a myth.
12. Religion is (is not) reviving in America.
13. Pollution is (is not) avoidable.
14. Our society has (has not) curtailed racism.

Ten

ESSAYS THAT APPEAL TO EMOTION AND ETHICS

PERSUASION,[1] we have said, is the strategic use of language to move an audience to action or belief. It works by appealing to our reason through logical ARGUMENT (the MODE OF PERSUASION discussed in Chapter 9). It also works by appealing to our emotions and to our sense of ethics.

The APPEAL TO EMOTION is nicely exemplified in "Being Prepared in Suburbia," the first essay in this chapter. Writing about gun-control legislation, Roger Verhulst deliberately sets aside reason and logic. He could produce statistics to show how many deaths will soon be caused by privately owned firearms, says Verhulst; but he finds "no point in citing those statistics again; they may prove something, but they're not likely to prompt any concrete action. There is nothing moving about statistics."

Here is the essence of the emotional appeal. It assumes, in Verhulst's words, that "what is needed to produce results is passion"; it aims at "the gut." Even if his own passion has cooled in the process of writing it down—and what passion can flare through several rewritings?—the author of an emotional appeal must kindle his original feelings in the reader. He cannot do this, however, simply by being emotional.

[1] Terms printed in small capitals are defined in the Glossary.

It is a fallacy to think that you can appeal to an emotion in your reader by imitating it: hysteria by being hysterical, anger by raging. Often the best measure is to appear calm, detached, thoroughly in control of your feelings—now. However intensely felt, your testimony must be orderly, or at least coherent. You may want to recreate the circumstances or perception that first excited in you the emotions that you want to excite in your readers; but here again your narrative must be controlled and directed toward its desired effect. Even your choice of individual words cannot be haphazard; you must pay close attention to their CONNOTATIONS. If you are addressing a labor union, for example, it will make a great difference whether you refer to the members as drones, workers, comrades, or just people.

The APPEAL TO ETHICS is an appeal to the reader's sense of how people ought to behave. This mode of persuasion convinces the reader that it is written by a person of good character whose judgment should be heeded. We are moved by the force of the speaker's personality.

Because the author's personality is so important in an appeal to ethics, great care must be taken to measure his or her tone of voice. TONE is an author's revealed attitude toward the material; it conveys his or her temper. A writer can be a decent human being and may have the reader's best interests at heart; but the reader may not trust the writer if the tone clashes with the message. Sincerity is the soul of the ethical appeal, and a writer must take pains to appear trustworthy as well as to be so.

To appear trustworthy, the writer must seem to be not only a person of good character and even temper but also a person who is well-informed. When noted attorney F. Lee Bailey tells us to "watch out for trial lawyers" because too many are competent only in the research library, we tend to believe him. Bailey's own expertise in the courtroom makes him an expert witness. The appeal of the expert witness, in fact, is one of the most common modern forms of the appeal to ethics. We are won over not by the moral uprightness of the expert but by his or her knowledge and intellectual integrity.

For study purposes, the appeals to emotion and to ethics have been separated here from the appeal to reason and from each other. (The first three essays in this chapter appeal to emotions; the last two appeal to ethics.) In practice you may want to combine all three modes of persuasion in the same essay (as Kori Quintana does in the previous chapter). The goal of persuasive writing is to bring others around to your way of thinking in a good cause. Any honest means to this end is sound RHETORIC.

Roger Verhulst

Being Prepared in Suburbia

Roger Verhulst lives with his wife and children in Grand Rapids, Michigan. Most of his professional writing is in advertising, though he also contributes essays to newspapers and magazines, including *Newsweek* (from which the following is reprinted). Verhulst has long believed in gun-control legislation, but "Being Prepared in Suburbia" testifies to a conversion of sorts. After acquiring a Crossman 760 because his Cub Scout den wanted target practice, Verhulst found owners of guns to have an irrational attachment to their weapons that, he says, is stronger than the rational arguments against owning deadly firearms. Analyzing the emotion it arouses, his essay argues that gun control is as dead as the victims of uncontrolled guns. How he came to this conclusion and how he wrote about it are examined in detail by Verhulst himself in "Writers on the Writing Process" at the end of this chapter.

Gun legislation is dead for another year. As a result, if statistics are any guide, there's every likelihood that a lot of people now living will also be dead before the year is over. 1

There's no point in citing those statistics again; they may prove something, but they're not likely to prompt any concrete action. There is nothing very moving about statistics. 2

What is needed to produce results is passion—and that's where the antigun-control lobby has it all over the rest of us. Those who favor stronger gun legislation—a solid majority of Americans—can't hold a candle to the lovers of guns when it comes to zeal. 3

I had a taste of that passion recently, and I begin to understand something of what it is that fosters in gun libbers such dedicated resolve. Thanks to a bunch of Cub Scouts and an absurd little crea- 4 ture that went bump in the night, I've begun to realize why cold, unemotional tabulations of gun deaths will never lead to effective gun control. It's because of what can happen to people—even sane, rational, firearm-hating people like me—when they get their hands on a genuine, authentic, real-life gun.

5 Until last fall, I had never owned any weapon more lethal than a water pistol. I opposed guns as esthetically repugnant, noisy, essentially churlish devices whose only practical purpose was to blast holes of various sizes in entities that would thereby be rendered less functional than they would otherwise have been. I didn't object merely to guns that killed people; I also objected to guns that killed animals, or shattered windows, or plinked away at discarded beer bottles. Whenever a gun was put to effective use, I insisted, something broke; and it seemed absurd to go through life breaking things.

6 With arguments such as these, bolstered by assorted threats, I tried to instill holey terror also in my sons. Initially, I imposed an absolute ban on even toy guns. When that didn't work—their determination to possess such toys exceeding by scores of decibels my determination to ban them—I tried substituting lectures on the merits of nonviolence and universal love. Nice try.

7 Then, last fall, I became co-leader of a Cub Scout den here in Grand Rapids, Mich., consisting of half a dozen 9-, 10- and 11-year-old boys. Sharing the leadership responsibilities with me was a kind and gentle man named Mickey Shea, who happens to be extremely fond of outdoor activities—including, of course, hunting.

8 It was in Mickey's basement, in full view of an imposing gun rack, that I yielded to the pressure of pleading Cubbers and agreed to add target shooting to our scheduled activities. (Though I should make it clear that it wasn't Mickey who forced, or even strongly urged, that agreement; it was rather a wish to be accepted by the boys—to be regarded as appropriately adult and masculine—that prompted my decision. I've no one to blame but myself.)

9 So, for the sake of my kids and under the auspices of the Boy Scouts of America, I bought a gun—a Crossman Power Master 760 BB Repeater pump gun, with bolt action, adjustable sight and a satisfying heft. It was capable of putting holes in all sorts of things.

10 A few nights later we got the Cubs together and spent an hour or two aiming and firing at targets taped to paper-filled cardboard cartons. After which I unloaded the gun and locked it in my study, intending to leave it there until future target shoots came along to

justify bringing it out again. But a roving opossum that took up residence in our garage for a few cold nights in January undermined my good intentions.

We were entertained, at first. We called the kids down to see our 11
visitor perched on the edge of the trash barrel; we recorded the event on film. We regarded the presence of authentic wild animals in our corner of suburbia as delightfully diverting.

Almost at once, however, the rat-faced prowler began to make 12
himself obnoxious. There was the midnight clatter of falling objects, and the morning-after disarray of strewn garbage. The possum, we decided, would have to go.

But he proved to be not only an unwelcome but also a recalcitrant 13
guest. It was cold outside, and rather than waddling willingly back through the open garage door he took refuge behind a pile of scrap lumber; my vigorous thrusts with a broomstick were parried by obstinacy, and an occasional grunt.

I was cold, too, by now; and tired; and becoming frustrated. Dras- 14
tic action was indicated; I poured a handful of BB's into the Crossman 760, pumped it up, pointed the barrel blindly into the woodpile and pulled the trigger.

Nothing happened. The opossum did not move. Shivering, I went 15
back inside the house, still holding my weapon. I sat down with a drink and a cigarette to warm up.

With little else to do, I put the gun to my shoulder and aimed it 16
idly at the clock above the fireplace; I aimed it at a light fixture across the room, pressing gently against the trigger; I aimed it at a row of glasses behind the bar, imagining the snap and shatter of breaking glass; I aimed it at my own reflection in the TV set, thinking how absurdly easy it would be to eliminate television from my life.

The more imaginary targets I selected, the stronger became the 17
urge to shoot—something, anything. The gun extended my potential range of influence to everyone within sight; I could alter the world around me without even moving from the couch, simply by pulling the trigger. Gun in hand, I was bravely prepared to defend myself against any intruder, man or beast. I felt omnipotent as Zeus,[1] with lightning bolts at my fingertips.

No wonder, I thought, that people become hooked on guns. This 18
is the feeling that explains their passion, their religious fervor, their

[1] Ruler of the Greek gods; lightning was his special weapon.

refusal to yield. It's rooted in the gut, not in the head. And in the recurrent struggle over gun legislation it is no wonder that their stamina exceeds mind.

I can understand that passion because I've felt it in my own gut. 19
I've felt the gun in my hand punch psychic holes in my intellectual convictions. And having felt all that, I do not have much hope that private ownership of deadly weapons will be at all regulated or controlled in the foreseeable future.

QUESTIONS

Understanding

1. According to Verhulst, what is the appeal of guns to those who own them? In which paragraph does he explain that appeal most explicitly?
2. Verhulst thinks that gun-control legislation is doomed. Why? What is his main reason?
3. Verhulst says that he yielded to the Scouts' demand for target practice because he wished "to be accepted by the boys—to be regarded as appropriately adult and masculine" (par. 8). How far does this motive go toward explaining why some men like guns? How "sane" is it?
4. Why do you think Verhulst takes pains to point out that he came into contact with guns through the Cub Scouts?
5. In paragraph 19, Verhulst says that his gun opened "psychic holes" in his resolve. Which earlier paragraphs of his essay does this statement hark back to? How? With what unexpected twist has Verhulst's original theory about guns been confirmed?
6. Why is Verhulst's subject especially suited to an appeal to emotion?

Strategies and Structure

1. Verhulst writes as a "convert," an opponent of free guns who has come reluctantly to understand the appeal of firearms. Would his prediction about the failure of gun control be more or less convincing if he were speaking as a long-time gun enthusiast? Explain your answer.
2. By telling the story of the author's conversion, this essay uses NARRATION to help achieve its persuasive purpose. Where does the narration

begin? Where does it end? How compelling do you find Verhulst's narrative? Why?

3. As a general rule, do you think narration is more likely to be found in an APPEAL TO REASON or an APPEAL TO EMOTION? Why?
4. What is the strategy of Verhulst's first and second paragraphs? How successful is it?
5. Verhulst says that his sons' demand for toy guns exceeded "by scores of decibels" (par. 6) his resistance. What is the TONE of this remark? Of "Nice try" in the same paragraph? Describe Verhulst's TONE throughout the essay.
6. Why does Verhulst make himself look foolish, even mean, in the encounter with the "possum"?
7. How do the length and rhythm of the single sentence in paragraph 16 capture the author's state of mind at that point in his essay?
8. Far from assuming that a writer stirs emotion simply by being emotional, Verhulst comes across as remarkably cool-headed. How does he create this impression?
9. Whom do you take to be Verhulst's audience? In which paragraph does he, in effect, define it? Why is his cool-headed approach a good one for this audience?
10. When do you think a writer is better advised to be emotional (not just to describe emotions and appeal to them in the reader)—when he is addressing an audience that essentially agrees with him or one that disagrees? Why?

Words and Figures of Speech

1. Why does Verhulst use the word *hooked* in paragraph 18? What are the CONNOTATIONS of the term?
2. "Holey terror" (par. 6) and "delightfully diverting" (par. 11) represent two different LEVELS OF DICTION. Define the two levels and point out other examples of each. Why do you think Verhulst mixes the two?
3. *Psychic* (par. 19) has two basic meanings. What are they? Which one is intended here?
4. Look up the following words in your dictionary: *churlish* (par. 5), *decibels* (6), *auspices* (9), *obnoxious* (12), *recalcitrant* (13), *obstinacy* (13), *frustrated* (14), *omnipotent* (17), *fervor* (18).

Comparing

1. Compare and contrast "Being Prepared in Suburbia" with Johnson C. Montgomery's "The Island of Plenty" (Chapter 9) as representative examples of two different MODES OF PERSUASION: the appeal to reason and the appeal to emotion, respectively.
2. Both Verhulst and James Q. Wilson ("Reasonable Search and Seizure," Chapter 9) argue that legislation aimed at gun control does not work. Whose appeal—the one to emotion, the other to reason—do you find more convincing—and why? What's wrong, in your opinion (if anything), with both of their positions on this complicated issue?

Discussion and Writing Topics

1. Write a persuasive essay in favor of gun-control legislation that appeals to emotion and that argues that guns are "esthetically repugnant, noisy, essentially churlish devices" (par. 5).
2. Construct a persuasive rational argument *against* gun-control legislation—the sort of argument, though on the opposite side, that Verhulst declines to make at the start of his essay.
3. If Verhulst's experience is at all typical, under what circumstances do our irrational impulses come forth? Are they any less real for being irrational? Why or why not?

Lynn Woolsey

REINVENT WELFARE, HUMANELY

A former welfare mother with three small children, Lynn Woolsey speaks in this essay as a Democratic congresswoman from California. A member of the House Committee on Education and Labor, she offers, in "Reinvent Welfare, Humanely," a brief point-by-point program for reforming the welfare system.

It's time to end welfare as I knew it. 1

Twenty-five years ago I was a single, working mother, unable to provide for my three children, ages one, three, and five. I know what it is like to lie awake at night and worry about not having any health insurance. I know how hard it is to find good child care—I had thirteen different baby-sitters in one year. I know what it is like to choose between paying the rent and buying new shoes. 2

Like so many American families, we turned to Aid to Families with Dependent Children. 3

As the only former welfare mother ever to serve in Congress, I know firsthand the merits and faults of our welfare system. And I know we must create a fair and just system that would provide families with the tools they need to get off welfare and become self-sufficient. 4

Sadly, the ideas that seem to be gaining ground these days are misguided or worse. Proposals like that of the social scientist Charles Murray—which would abolish everything from food stamps to subsidized housing—would starve families only to feed alarmist myths about welfare. Such brutal proposals would have devastated my family. The denial of essential services would rip the safety net from under families in temporary need and burn the ladder to self-sufficiency for those trapped in long-term poverty. 5

Time limits on welfare benefits, the centerpiece of both Demo- 6
cratic and Republican proposals, would be just as damaging to families. While the purpose—to move individuals off welfare and into the workforce—is laudable, a rigid approach is unworkable. The recent proposal by Gov. William F. Weld of Massachusetts, to cut off benefits after sixty days for all able-bodied recipients who did not accept full-time community service jobs at less than the minimum wage, is a case in point: curtailing benefits without first reducing the need for assistance hurts children, who account for 70 percent of welfare recipients; perpetuates the cycle of poverty, and may force families to live on the streets.

My own vision of a just and fair welfare system is based on experi- 7
ence, not theory. Here is what it would do:

- Establish Federal job-training programs that would insure self-sufficiency.
- Overhaul our child-support system by stiffening enforcement and guaranteeing that all families receive a minimum level of payment.
- Abolish financial penalties against two-parent families.
- Encourage welfare recipients to work by allowing them to keep more of their earnings and benefits.
- Provide a full range of support services like child care, health care and counseling, as well as qualified case management.
- Build partnerships of labor, business, and government to create jobs that pay a living wage.

Make no mistake: welfare reform will cost money in the short 8
term. But it will reap long-term results. The Clinton Administration wants a welfare plan that doesn't increase the deficit. I want a plan that works. We must craft a plan that both respects the budget and achieves our common goal for financial independence for all American families.

This debate is about what we value as a nation. I turned to welfare 9
so I could take care of my children. Now we must fix the welfare system to make sure all of our children are given the care they need.

QUESTIONS

Understanding

1. Why does Lynn Woolsey think "it's time to end welfare" (par. 1) as she knew it? What aspects of the old system, in particular, does she have in mind?
2. What would be the effect, in Woolsey's view, of ending *all* forms of welfare, as some opponents of the old system have advocated?
3. Who, according to Woolsey, accounts for 70 percent of the recipients of welfare benefits in America?
4. What are the major points of Woolsey's own program of welfare reform?

Strategies and Structure

1. Lynn Woolsey's main reason for why readers should accept her vision of the welfare system is in effect, "I've been there, and I know." Where specifically does she claim this special kind of knowledge, and how effective do your find that appeal? Why do you say so?
2. What (largely unstated) argument about welfare is Lynn Woolsey also advancing, merely by identifying herself both as a former welfare recipient and as a member of Congress?
3. How and where does Woolsey insinuate that most theorists of welfare and reform are less qualified than she to suggest constructive alternatives to the present system of welfare rules and restrictions?
4. Why do you think that Woolsey, as a strategy of argument, presents herself as a welfare *mother* rather than just a recipient of welfare benefits? How effective do you find this strategy in establishing her authority and credibility?
5. Woolsey advances her own proposals for welfare reform in paragraph 7. Why do you suppose she presents them in the form of a list, replete with "bullets"?

Words and Figures of Speech

1. Examine the metaphors in the following sentence and explore the overriding comparison or analogy being drawn: "The denial of essential services would rip the safety net from under families in temporary need and burn the ladder to self-sufficiency for those trapped in long-term poverty" (par. 5).
2. Where else in this same paragraph does Lynn Woolsey use highly charged, even incendiary, diction? How appropriate (or inappropriate) do you find such language in the context of a political program? Please explain why you think so.
3. Identify the grammatical mood (indicative, interrogative, imperative, subjunctive) of the following: "Make no mistake" (par. 8). Why do you think Woolsey switches from the mood (which is what?) that prevails elsewhere in her essay?
4. What are the implications of "unworkable" (par. 6), and "experience," "theory," "vision," "penalties," and "partnerships" (par. 7)? What are the implications of the word *humanely* in Woolsey's title?
5. "Reap" (par. 8) is something of a "dead" metaphor; what are its agricultural and biblical roots?

Comparing

1. How does Woolsey's claim to a special knowledge resemble Kori Quintana's in "The Price of Power: Living in the Nuclear Age" (Chapter 9)? How well, in your opinion, does each woman make her case for a special hearing?
2. Is Woolsey manipulating the English language to dubious political ends, as George Orwell describes in "Politics and the English Language" (Essays for Further Reading)? Why or why not?

Discussion and Writing Topics

1. Why do we need (or not need) a system of social and economic "welfare" in this country? How well, in your opinion and that of your classmates, does the present system work? Draft a "manifesto" explaining why you think so.

2. In partnership with others in your class, examine the specific proposals that constitute Lynn Woolsey's plan for welfare reform. Which items on her list would you delete or alter? What, specifically, would you add?
3. How much credibility do you think Lynn Woolsey's claim to being "the only former welfare mother ever to serve in Congress" (par. 4) should give her in the current debate in Washington and elsewhere over welfare reform? Why?

Randy Shilts

Good AIDS, Bad AIDS

Randy Shilts was a national correspondent for *The San Francisco Chronicle* and the author of *The Mayor of Castro Street,* a biography of politician Harvey Milk that chronicles the rise of gay political power in California. In 1988 the American Society of Authors and Journalists named Shilts "Outstanding Author" of the year for *And the Band Played On: Politics, People, and the AIDS Epidemic.* Like "Good AIDS, Bad AIDS" (which appeared in the *New York Times*), that book documented the spread of AIDS "without a concentrated government response" to combat it. Shilts's *Conduct Unbecoming: Lesbians and Gays in the U.S. Military* (1993) was completed in a hospital bed. Randy Shilts died in 1994 of AIDS.

Anyone who has a heart can sympathize with the Bergalis family over the death of their daughter, Kimberly, on Sunday. Like so many other victims of AIDS, she died too young. 1

No AIDS sufferer in the U.S. dominated the AIDS debate this year the way Kimberly Bergalis did. But the story of Ms. Bergalis and her family largely became a tale of anger. 2

The Bergalises are angry that their daughter was infected with the horrible virus. I understand that. I'm angry, too, that I've had to watch half of my friends waste away and die miserable deaths from the disease. What has made the Bergalises' anger different is that it has been so poorly informed. 3

They have been angry at the late Dr. David J. Acer, the Florida dentist they believe infected their daughter while she was being treated. They have been angry at politicians who they think have not moved quickly enough on the issue of H.I.V.-infected health care workers. That's where their anger ends. I wish they would understand that there are far greater villains in the AIDS epidemic. 4

One reason Kimberly Bergalis died is that we don't have better 5 treatments for the disease. This is because for the better part of a decade the Government did as little as it could possibly get away with to fight the epidemic, either in research or prevention. As President, Ronald Reagan found it difficult even to utter the word AIDS. President Bush has shown only slightly more concern.

What is also troubling about the anger of the Bergalises is that 6 they do not seem to acknowledge the suffering of others. When their daughter spoke before Congress in October to lobby for legislation that would require testing of health care workers for the virus that causes AIDS, she mentioned how unfair it was that she had to suffer from AIDS even though she "didn't do anything wrong." With those words, she seemed to be separating those who don't deserve AIDS from those who do. These were troubling words.

Gay men express their love differently from the majority, it's true, 7 but those who contracted AIDS didn't do anything "wrong." People who were infected by H.I.V. from dirty needles usually committed the "wrong" of being black or Hispanic in a society that offers them largely despair and poverty. Their plight is no less tragic than Ms. Bergalis's.

AIDS has spread without a concerted Government response 8 because so many Americans believe that only people who have done something "wrong" get the disease. Ms. Bergalis and many others might be alive now if those fighting AIDS did not also have to fight this prejudice. It's appalling that AIDS is considered serious only when it strikes a heterosexual young woman or a star basketball player.

In their anger and pain, the Bergalises focused national attention 9 on the one aspect of the epidemic that affected them—the apparent transfer of H.I.V. from a health care worker.

Yes, it is tragic that their daughter died from AIDS. But there are 10 one million other H.I.V.-infected Americans. Only five of them are thought to have contracted the virus from health care workers. Meanwhile, hundreds of thousands have contracted the disease sexually or through intravenous drug use. It is thousands of times more tragic that the U.S. lacks adequate programs in these arenas even today.

The lesson from the sad story of Kimberly Bergalis is that we will 11 not fight AIDS by fighting one another. The answer will come only when Americans extend to all people dying of AIDS the same compassion that she received.

QUESTIONS

Understanding

1. How is "bad" AIDS defined in Randy Shilts's essay? Who does he say has defined it?
2. What, then, is "good" AIDS?
3. Why, according to Shilts, is Kimberly Bergalis's family angry?
4. Should they be, in his opinion? Why or why not?
5. Why is Shilts himself angry? At whom or what in particular?

Strategies and Structure

1. Even as he divides AIDS into types, Randy Shilts is making an argument here. What "lesson" (par. 11) or conclusions would he have us draw from the sad case of Kimberly Bergalis?
2. How and where does Shilts show sympathy for Bergalis and her family? Why is he so careful to do so even when he is arguing *against* Bergalis's position?
3. Is Shilts himself really accepting the classification system he purports to adopt here? In which paragraph does he actually "use" it? Please explain your answer.
4. How does Shilts, simply by making a moral distinction between kinds of AIDS, make the argument against all such distinctions?

Words and Figures of Speech

1. "AIDS" is an acronym for "Acquired Immune Deficiency Syndrome." Why doesn't Randy Shilts tell us this?
2. Explain the IRONY of Shilts's title.
3. Shilts mentions "villains" (par. 4) of the AIDS epidemic and says that Kimberly Bergalis's death is "tragic" (par. 10). To what kind of writing do such terms refer? How appropriate do you find the ANALOGY?
4. *Good, bad, wrong* (par. 7), *right*—what do these words have in common? How appropriate do you find them in a discussion of disease?

Comparing

1. "Good AIDS, Bad AIDS" is an appeal for compassionate understanding. So is Chief Seattle's "Reply to the U.S. Government" (later in the chapter). How do the two essays *differ* in this regard?
2. In "Body Imperfect" (Chapter 6), Debi Davis contrasts the way adults often respond to other people's illness or injury and the way children respond. Which response would Shilts consider more appropriate for all AIDS victims?
3. As essays about terminal illness, how does Shilts's compare with Beverley Dipo's "No Rainbows, No Roses" (Chapter 8)?

Discussion and Writing Topics

1. Do you think either Shilts or the Bergalises are making false distinctions? Please explain.
2. How accurate do you find Shilts when he says (par. 8) "many Americans believe that only people who have done something 'wrong' " get AIDS? Why do you say so?

Anna Quindlen

THE WAR ON DRINKS

Until she left journalism in 1994 to make a "full-time commitment" to fiction, Anna Quindlen wrote a twice-weekly column for the *New York Times* entitled "Public & Private," the mix that has always marked her way of "taking things personally for a living." (Her greatest terror, says Quindlen, is that someday her young children will read her constant references to them and say, "Mom, how could you do this?") Oldest of five in an Irish Catholic family, Quindlen lost her own mother at age nineteen. "When I see a mother and daughter having lunch in a restaurant," she can now say, "I no longer want to murder them. I just stare a little longer than is polite." Quindlen's columns are collected in *Living Out Loud* (1988). Since then, she has written two novels, *Object Lessons* (1991) and *One True Thing* (1994), and won a Pulitzer Prize for commentary (1992).

When she was in fourth grade the girl wrote, "What do you think it does to somebody to live with a lot of pressure?" Starting at age 8 she had been cashing the public assistance check each month, buying money orders, paying the bills and doing the grocery shopping. One little brother she walked to school; the other she dressed and fed before leaving him at home. 1

Their mother drank. 2

"The pressure she was talking about wasn't even the pressure of running an entire household," said Virginia Connelly, who oversees substance abuse services in schools in New York City. "She didn't know there was anything strange about that. The pressure she was talking about was the pressure of leaving her younger brother at home." 3

Surgeon General Antonia Novello has opened fire on the alcohol industry, complaining that too much beer and wine advertising is aimed at young people. Her predecessor, C. Everett Koop, did the 4 same in 1988, and you can see how radically things have changed: Spuds MacKenzie is out and the Swedish bikini team is in. There's a move afoot to have warning labels on ads for beer, wine and liquor, much like the ones on cigarettes. Dr. Novello didn't mention that; she said she would be taking a meeting with the big guys in the liquor industry. That's not enough.

There's no doubt that beer ads, with their cool beaches, cool women and cool parties, are designed to make you feel you're cool if you drink, milking a concern that peaks in most human beings somewhat shy of the legal drinking age. And those sneaky little wine coolers are designed to look like something healthy and fruit-juicy; kids will tell you they're sort of like alcohol, but not really. This has joined "it's only beer" as a great kid drinking myth. 5

(I've got a press release here from an organization called the Beer Drinkers of America that notes that "many of the Founding Fathers were private brewers" and goes on to rail against "special interests" that would interfere with the right to a cold one. Isn't it amazing how much time people have on their hands?) 6

But Dr. Novello should take note of what many counselors discover: that the drinking problem that damages kids most is the one that belongs to their parents. The father who gets drunk and violent, the mother who drinks when she's depressed, the parents whose personality shifts with the movements of the sun and the bottle. The enormous family secret. 7

"An Elephant in the Living Room" is the title of one book for kids whose parents drink. "When I was about ten years old, I started to realize that my dad had a drinking problem," it begins. "Sometimes he drank too much. Then he would talk loudly and make jokes that weren't funny. He would say unkind things to my mom in front of the neighbors and my friends. I felt embarrassed." 8

That's the voice of an adult who has perspective on her past. This is the voice of a 12-year-old at a school in the kind of neighborhood where we talk, talk, talk about crack though the abuse of alcohol is much more widespread. She is talking about her father, who drinks: "I hate him. He should just stay in his room like a big dog." This would make a good commercial—the moment when your own kid thinks of you as an animal. 9

The folks who sell alcohol will say most people use it responsibly, but the fact remains that many people die in car accidents because of it, many wind up in the hospital because of it, and many families 10 are destroyed because of it. Dr. Novello is right to excoriate the commercials; it is not just that they make drinking seem cool, but that they make it seem inevitable, as though parties would not take place, Christmas never come, success be elusive without a bottle. It's got to be confusing to see vodka as the stuff of which family gatherings are made and then watch your mother pass out in the living room.

This is the drug that has been handed down from generation to generation, that most kids learn to use and abuse at home. I'd love to see warning labels, about fetal alcohol syndrome and liver damage and addiction. But it's time for a change, not just in the ads, but in the atmosphere that assumes a substance is innocuous because it's not illegal. For most of our children, the most powerful advertisement for alcohol may be sitting at the kitchen table. Or sleeping it off in the bedroom. 11

QUESTIONS

Understanding

1. Besides the alcohol and advertising industries, who else does Anna Quindlen think the Surgeon General, and other opponents of alcohol abuse, should declare "war" upon?
2. Why does Quindlen think the domestic front in the war on alcohol is even more important than the industrial ones that Dr. Novello has targeted?
3. Besides making it seem "cool" (par. 5) to drink alcohol, what other, more lasting impression do advertisers seek to give the consumer, according to Quindlen?
4. Just because a drug such as alcohol is legal, Quindlen is arguing, does not mean that we can assume what about it?
5. Why is the parent at the kitchen table a "powerful advertisement" *for* drinking alcohol, in Quindlen's view, even though that same parent may soon be "sleeping it off in the bedroom" (par. 11)?

Strategies and Structure

1. Though "many" (par. 10) people die or get hurt because of alcohol and though "many" families are destroyed by it, "most people use it responsibly" (par. 10). Therefore, most people are not harmed by the use of alcohol. Is this a valid argument? How sound are its premises? What does Quindlen seem to think? From what premises (or assumptions) does she appear to be arguing?
2. Should Quindlen have cited more statistics and case histories in addition to those of the sister under "pressure" (par. 1) and the daughter who "hates" (par. 9) her father? Please explain why you think she needs more evidence, or why you think her evidence is sufficient as stated.
3. Quindlen begins her essay with a contrast of voices and perspectives. How is it achieved?
4. Should paragraph 2 of Quindlen's essay be longer? Why or why not? Why does she put the whole of paragraph 6 in parentheses?
5. Why do you think Quindlen immediately follows the voice of the adult narrator of *An Elephant in the Living Room* (par. 8) with that of the twelve-year-old who calls her father a "dog" (par. 9)?
6. What is the effect, throughout her essay, of Quindlen's interweaving among these dissenting voices the words of the pro-alcohol lobby? Whose voice is represented by the warnings on printed labels? How does Quindlen insinuate that such warnings may come too late?

Words and Figures of Speech

1. How does the military METAPHOR of Quindlen's title carry over into the rest of her appeal? What does it imply about her assessment of the measures necessary to curb alcohol abuse?
2. Why does Quindlen launch her own campaign with the definition of a word (*pressure,* pars. 1 and 2)?
3. "Isn't it amazing," Quindlen asks (par. 6), "how much time some people have on their hands?" Why do you think she uses this RHETORICAL QUESTION to counter the argument she is citing here—instead of advancing a logical argument of her own against it?
4. Comparing a parent who drinks too much to an elephant (par. 8) suggests the enormity of the problem. What are the implications of comparing such a parent to a "dog" (par. 9)?

5. Why might Quindlen use the word *excoriate* (par. 10) instead of, say, *criticize* or *disagree with?* How reasonable does she presume the "arguments" of the alcohol industry to be? Point to other words and phrases (for example: "from generation to generation," par. 11) that call more for an emotional response than for strictly rational debate.

Comparing

1. "There is nothing very moving about statistics," says Roger Verhulst earlier in this chapter ("On Being Prepared in Suburbia," par. 2). How far does Anna Quindlen's attack on alcohol abuse seem to follow this principle?
2. As studies of parental influence, compare and contrast "The War on Drinks" with Lee K. Abbott's "The True Story of Why I Do What I Do" (Chapter 1).

Discussion and Writing Topics

1. Is Quindlen right to declare "war" on drinking, or is she overstating her case? What ammunition would you bring to the battle? On which side?
2. Should Quindlen's appeal to emotion be more attentive to the reasons parents drink? Why or why not?
3. Most advertising funded by the alcohol industry, Quindlen charges, appeals to childish emotion rather than adult reason. Do the commercials you've seen have more redeeming social value than Quindlen thinks, or do they all hover at the intellectual and emotional level of Spuds MacKenzie and the Swedish bikini team?

Chief Seattle

Reply to the U.S. Government

Chief Seattle (c. 1786–1866) was the leader of the Dwamish, Suquamish, and allied Native American tribes living in the region of the city that now bears his name. He welcomed white settlers from the time of their first arrival and loyally resisted uprisings against them. He later converted to Roman Catholicism and began holding morning and evening services among the tribe. He was not pleased when the village of Seattle, Washington, took his name because he believed that his spirit would be disturbed in the afterlife each time his name was spoken by mortals. Toward the end of his life, Seattle exacted compensation for his broken sleep by seeking gifts among citizens of the region. The "Reply" printed here purports to be Chief Seattle's response to the U.S. government's offer to buy two million acres of Indian land. The offer was made in 1854 through Governor Isaac Stevens of the Washington Territory. For his formal answer, spoken in the Dwamish language, Seattle gathered the tribe around him and placed his hand on Governor Stevens's head. He stood a foot taller than the governor, and his voice could be heard for half a mile. Henry A. Smith claimed to "translate" the speech, but his earliest published version (on which this one is based) did not appear until 1887 and bears little resemblance to Chief Seattle's two short speeches as preserved among the documents accompanying the Port Elliott Treaty, which Chief Seattle signed with the government on January 22, 1855. Perhaps Smith based his version upon "extensive notes" from his diary of the event.

Yonder sky that has wept tears of compassion upon my people 1
for centuries untold, and which to us appears changeless and eternal,
may change. Today is fair. Tomorrow may be overcast with clouds.

My words are like the stars that never change. Whatever Seattle says the great chief at Washington can rely upon with as much certainty as he can upon the return of the sun or the seasons. The White Chief says that Big Chief at Washington sends us greetings of friendship and goodwill. That is kind of him for we know he has little need of our friendship in return. His people are many. They are like the grass that covers vast prairies. My people are few. They resemble the scattering trees of a storm-swept plain. The great, and—I presume—good, White Chief sends us word that he wishes to buy our lands but is willing to allow us enough to live comfortably. This indeed appears just, even generous, for the Red Man no longer has rights that he need respect, and the offer may be wise also, as we are no longer in need of an extensive country. . . . I will not dwell on, nor mourn over, our untimely decay, nor reproach our paleface brothers with hastening it, as we too may have been somewhat to blame.

Youth is impulsive. When our young men grow angry at some 2
real or imaginary wrong, and disfigure their faces with black paint, it denotes that their hearts are black, and then they are often cruel and relentless, and our old men and old women are unable to restrain them. Thus it has ever been. Thus it was when the white men first began to push our forefathers further westward. But let us hope that the hostilities between us may never return. We would have everything to lose and nothing to gain. Revenge by young men is considered gain, even at the cost of their own lives, but old men who stay at home in times of war, and mothers who have sons to lose, know better.

Our good father at Washington—for I presume he is now our 3
father as well as yours, since King George[1] has moved his boundaries further north—our great good father, I say, sends us word that if we do as he desires he will protect us. His brave warriors will be to us a bristling wall of strength, and his wonderful ships of war will fill our harbors so that our ancient enemies far to the northward—the Hydas and Tsimpsians—will cease to frighten our women, children, and old men. Then in reality will he be our father and we his children. But can that ever be? Your God is not our God! Your God loves your people and hates mine. He folds his strong and protecting arms lovingly about the paleface and leads him by the hand as a father leads his infant son—but He has forsaken His red children—if they

[1] George IV, king of England from 1820 to 1830.

really are his. Our God, the Great Spirit, seems also to have forsaken us. Your God makes your people wax strong every day. Soon they will fill the land. Our people are ebbing away like a rapidly receding tide that will never return. The white man's God cannot love our people or He would protect them. They seem to be orphans who can look nowhere for help. How then can we be brothers? How can your God become our God and renew our prosperity and awaken in us dreams of returning greatness? If we have a common heavenly father He must be partial—for He came to his paleface children. We never saw Him. He gave you laws but He had no word for His red children whose teeming multitudes once filled this vast continent as stars fill the firmament. No; we are two distinct races with separate origins and separate destinies. There is little in common between us.

To us the ashes of our ancestors are sacred and their resting place is hallowed ground. You wander far from the graves of your ancestors and seemingly without regret. Your religion was written upon tables of stone by the iron finger of your God so that you could not forget. The Red Man could never comprehend nor remember it. Our religion is the traditions of our ancestors—the dreams of our old men, given them in solemn hours of night by the Great Spirit; and the visions of our sachems; and it is written in the hearts of our people. 4

Your dead cease to love you and the land of their nativity as soon as they pass the portals of the tomb and wander way beyond the stars. They are soon forgotten and never return. Our dead never forget the beautiful world that gave them being. 5

Day and night cannot dwell together. The Red man has ever fled the approach of the White Man, as the morning mist flees before the morning sun. However, your proposition seems fair and I think that my people will accept it and will retire to the reservation you offer them. Then we will dwell apart in peace, for the words of the Great White Chief seem to be the words of nature speaking to my people out of dense darkness. 6

It matters little where we pass the remnant of our days. They will not be many. A few more moons; a few more winters—and not one of the descendants of the mighty hosts that once moved over this broad land or lived in happy homes, protected by the Great Spirit, will remain to mourn over the graves of a people once more powerful and hopeful than yours. But why should I mourn at the untimely fate of my people? Tribe follows tribe, and nation follows nation, like 7 the waves of the sea. It is the order of nature, and regret is useless. Your time of decay may be distant, but it will surely come, for even the White Man whose God walked and talked with him as friend with friend, cannot be exempt from the common destiny. We may be brothers after all. We will see.

We will ponder your proposition, and when we decide we will let 8
you know. But should we accept it, I here and now make this condition that we will not be denied the privilege without molestation of visiting at any time the tombs of our ancestors, friends and children. Every part of this soil is sacred in the estimation of my people. Every hillside, every valley, every plain and grove, has been hallowed by some sad or happy event in days long vanished. . . . The very dust upon which you now stand responds more lovingly to their footsteps than to yours, because it is rich with the blood of our ancestors and our bare feet are conscious of the sympathetic touch. . . . Even the little children who lived here and rejoiced here for a brief season will love these somber solitudes and at eventide they greet shadowy returning spirits. And when the last Red Man shall have perished, and the memory of my tribe shall have become a myth among the White Men, these shores will swarm with the invisible dead of my tribe, and when your children's children think themselves alone in the field, the store, the shop, upon the highway, or in the silence of the pathless woods, they will not be alone. . . . At night when the streets of your cities and villages are silent and you think them deserted, they will throng with the returning hosts that once filled and still love this beautiful land. The White Man will never be alone.

Let him be just and deal kindly with my people, for the dead are 9
not powerless. Dead, did I say? There is no death, only a change of worlds.

QUESTIONS

Understanding

1. For what is Chief Seattle appealing to the White Man? What slightly veiled threat does he make in the last two paragraphs of his speech?
2. Describe the single condition that Chief Seattle puts upon his probable acceptance of the government's offer to buy the tribe's land. Why does

he make this condition? What does it show about the basis of his religion?

3. How does this belief help to explain why many Native Americans moved onto the reservation only with the greatest reluctance?
4. The last paragraph of Chief Seattle's speech sounds at first like a Christian denial of death and affirmation of heavenly life, but what does he mean by "a change of worlds" (par. 9)? What other differences does Chief Seattle mention between his religion and Christianity?
5. Why does the Dwamish chief doubt that the White Man and the Red Man will ever be brothers? In what grim sense may they prove "brothers after all" (par. 7)?
6. Why, according to Chief Seattle, did the young men of his tribe paint their faces and go to war? What was their motive, and what was the meaning of their war-paint?
7. Chief Seattle refuses to mourn the "untimely fate" (par. 7) of his people or to grant the eternal supremacy of his conquerors. Why? Explain the pervasive theme of his speech.

Strategies and Structure

1. Does Chief Seattle appear trustworthy to you? Why or why not?
2. How does he attempt to establish his authority and trustworthiness in paragraph 1? What equivalent devices might you find in a modern speech?
3. What personal qualities do you attribute to Chief Seattle after reading his entire speech? Point out specific statements and phrases that help to characterize him.
4. How does paragraph 2 show Chief Seattle's wisdom?
5. What distinction is Chief Seattle making when he refers to the "great, and—I presume—good, White Chief" (par. 1)? How does his being anxious to draw this distinction help to qualify the chief as a person worthy to make an APPEAL TO ETHICS?
6. The Dwamish chief shows his respect for the Big Chief at Washington by thanking him for "his greetings of friendship and goodwill" (par. 1) and by addressing him as "our good father" (par. 3). How does he also show that he is not afraid of the Big Chief?
7. Seattle's voice is said to have rumbled like the iron engine of a train when he delivered his speech. How is this rumbling quality conveyed

in the sentence patterns of paragraphs 1 and 7? Why is an "iron" pace appropriate to Seattle's message?

8. Seattle begins his appeal by acknowledging the justice (even the generosity) and the power of the government, but he declines to make up his mind at once and ends by asserting that the Red Man retains a degree of power. Is the order significant here? How would Seattle's speech have been changed if the order had been reversed?
9. When arguing at a disadvantage (against a popular opinion, for example), should you admit that disadvantage early on, mention it in closing, or not acknowledge it at all? Explain your answer.
10. Chief Seattle's ethical appeal also makes use of the APPEAL TO EMOTION. Discuss where and how the two work together. What emotion or emotions does his oration speak to?

Words and Figures of Speech

1. The White Man, we are told, is like "the grass that covers vast prairies" (par. 1), and the Indian is like "scattering trees" (par. 1) or the "receding tide" (par. 3), though once he was like the "stars" (par. 3). How do these natural METAPHORS fit in with Chief Seattle's general references to decay and to the cycle of the seasons?
2. What are the implications of the metaphor, "Day and night cannot dwell together" (par. 6)?
3. In what sense is the translator using the word *sympathetic* when he reports Seattle as saying that "our bare feet are conscious of the sympathetic touch" (par. 8)?
4. What analogy does Chief Seattle draw when he describes the role of the ideal leader or chief in paragraph 3?

Comparing

1. A representative of the old, dying order, Seattle resembles General Lee as Bruce Catton portrays him in "Grant and Lee: A Study in Contrasts" (Chapter 6). Pursue the parallel between the two men and the cultures they represent.
2. How and how well does Gordon Grice's analysis of natural magic and superstition ("Caught in the Widow's Web," Essays for Further Reading) comport with the beliefs of the Dwamish tribe as revealed by Chief Seattle?

3. Compare and contrast Seattle's view of nature with Annie Dillard's in "Transfiguration" (The Writing Process).

Discussion and Writing Topics

1. Speaking on behalf of the government, compose an appropriate reply to Chief Seattle's speech.
2. Write a persuasive ethical appeal in which you contend that it is not possible to restore all their lands to the Native Americans but that some reparation for past injustices is due them.
3. Judging from Chief Seattle's speech, why do you think Indian literature is full of natural metaphors?

Writers on the Writing Process

ROGER VERHULST

[EDITOR'S NOTE: The questions to which Roger Verhulst refers in the following notes on the composition of "On Being Prepared in Suburbia" were written inquiries from the editor about the process of writing the gun control essay and about his writing methods in general.]

Let me take on your questions and see what happens. 1

Where did the idea come from? I suppose it came first from the opossum, which innocently served as a peg to hang my sermon on. My feelings against guns were already well formed, and the events of that cold night were just about as I described them. So when I sat back to reflect that I had actually picked up a weapon to use aggressively on a living thing, the thesis of the article was staring me in the face. 2

Therefore, I can't say that I set out to write an antigun essay, and then, while looking for a peg, remembered this incident. It was the other way around. At the same time, I look at many experiences—things I see, read, hear, argue about, trip over, feel, fantasize, remember—as potential sources for writing. Most of them never get written about, but it has become a habit for me to reflect upon experience in an embryonic, prewriting fashion, so that I formulate ideas and conclusions in my head the way that I *intend*, later, to put them on paper. And occasionally do. In other words, I try to be receptive to pretexts for writing, so that when one stumbles into my life I can recognize it. 3

How did I *develop* the idea for the gun control essay? Very slowly. I had a rough notion of where I wanted to go, but little clear sense of how to get there. Since I was aiming for the "My Turn" section of 4

Newsweek, I had to write from a first-person point of view. Besides, how I felt was pretty central to my thesis.

5 Yet I didn't want to sound abjectly confessional, or grandly narcissistic. So I kept trying to take out stuff about me and my kids and my neighbors and my preferences in music. Then I had to put some of this back in order to explain, for example, why I had the gun in the first place. The analysis itself tended to get even more out of hand than the personal details. It had to be trimmed and refined and some of it dropped altogether.

6 Which spills into your question about revising. Yes, I revised. At one point I had a pile of drafts and fragments about an inch thick on the floor. I wish I could write briskly and beautifully and never have to touch a word more than once, but that almost never happens to me. I am never entirely sure, while I'm working on it, just what feel or tone a finished article is going to have. So I can't tell along the way whether the words I'm using at the moment are going to fit. Once a piece is roughed out, the process becomes a little easier, but even then I do a lot of reworking.

7 For what it may be worth to your students, I console myself for having been denied the gift of inspiration by telling myself that this time-consuming process of reworking and refining distinguishes the professional writer from the nonprofessional. If everything that first tumbled from the ends of my fingertips were the best I could do, I would starve as a writer. I like to think that I have learned enough about writing to recognize a problem when I see it, and to know a little how to fix it.

8 About the title. I didn't start with it. In fact, it was the last thing done. I wanted to arouse a little curiosity up front and also to give a clue to what followed. The "Being Prepared" of course plays off the boy scout motto, but I hoped it would serve as a snide commentary on what I regard as the foolish notion that guns are viable instruments of defense for average citizens. "Suburbia," I guess, was meant to sharpen the same point—who needs guns out here?

9 Problems? More with the beginning—which I'm still not crazy about, because it lunges rather gracelessly into the argument—than with the ending. By the time I got there, the ending had established itself pretty well in my mind. The basic problem was to discover for my self precisely what I wanted to say, and then to say it effectively in the space I had (1,200 words).

10 But of course that's always the problem. And the only way I know

to solve it is to write a while longer before giving up for the night. I try different words, different beginnings. It's an arduous process and it doesn't always work. But nothing else, including Scotch, works any better.

As for struggles with specific words and phrases: I remember having some doubts about the "holely terror" pun and then deciding, what-the-hell, leave it. That was self-indulgent, but I figured I was entitled. I had worked hard. 11

Would I make any changes now? Yes, in fact. One line has always bothered me—after I saw it in print, of course. It's the first line of paragraph 13: "But he proved to be not only an unwelcome but also a recalcitrant guest." Those "buts" are one too many; they are intrusive. Maybe it would be better to say, "He proved, however, to be . . ." I suppose I could find other flaws, but this article has been good to me, and I rather like it as it is. 12

Why do I write? For a number of reasons, not all of them known to me. Not least, I write because it's all I know how to do for which I can get paid. (Almost all the writing I do that earns any money is advertising copy.) 13

Also, writing satisfied some urges: to save the world, to touch other people, to tinker with words for the sheer fun (and the challenge) of it, to indulge myself. I'm not sure why else. But I can't imagine not writing. 14

Let me add just a couple of other notes that may be of interest to beginners. The response to the article when it appeared in *Newsweek* ran about 100-to-3 *against*—not only against the article, but against me. So the big ego trip of having it published in a national magazine quickly gave way to self-pity. There were now another 100 (at least) people in the world who didn't like me. Don't write because you want to be loved. 15

This piece was the first I sent to *Newsweek*. It has not been the last, but it remains the only one accepted. So, second, don't learn to write in the expectation that you'll be able to coast then. It doesn't get easy—at least not for me. 16

Finally, I'm not always sure why I make the decisions I do when I'm writing. I may use a particular word, for example, not because it is the best of all possible words for the immediate purpose but because it is the best word I know, or can think of. Or because I happen to like that word. 17

If a decision I make during the writing process seems to work, I 18 go with it. If not, I grope about for another. If all else fails, I yell at my kids.

WRITING TOPICS FOR CHAPTER TEN
Essays That Appeal to Emotion and Ethics

Write an emotional or ethical appeal on one of the following subjects:

1. Marriage is (is not) a wretched institution.
2. Doctors are (are not) technicians rather than healers.
3. Lawyers are (are not) a dishonest breed.
4. College athletics should (should not) be abolished.
5. ROTC should (should not) be abolished on college campuses.
6. Universities should (should not) allow radicals to speak in their facilities.
7. Teachers should (should not) pass judgment on their students' work.
8. Public schools are (are not) more responsive to the whole person than are private schools.
9. Most college requirements are (are not) worthwhile.
10. Seeking psychiatric help is (is not) a sign of weakness.
11. The drug laws should (should not) be tightened up.
12. Exercise: Analyze the appeal of several newspaper or magazine advertisements. For what audience are they intended? How do they attract that audience? What unstated assumptions do they make?

Essays for Further Reading: Combining the Modes

The essays in this chapter are longer and more complicated than most of the others in this collection. None is easily restricted to a single (or even a dominant) "mode" or form of writing. For example, Virginia Woolf's classic, "The Death of the Moth," describes its subject in detail and so might be placed in Chapter 8 (where it actually appeared in earlier editions of the *Sampler*). But it is a personal narrative as well (Chapter 1). And because the moth comes to represent "a pure bead" of life, it is also an essay in metaphor and analogy (Chapter 7). Does such plurality mean that these categories are meaningless?

Consider an analogy. According to Isaac Asimov ("What Do You Call a Platypus?," Chapter 2), the duck-billed platypus has some of the physical aspects of mammals (hair, milk glands), of reptiles (the peculiar nerve channel joining jaw to brain), and of birds (eggs, no teeth). Admittedly, a platypus is a living organism, whereas an essay must be laboriously constructed. Does its diversity of features mean, however, that the platypus does not exist?

Like the terms of any classification system (for example *Ornithorhynchus anatinus,* meaning "Bird-beak, duck-like"), the terms used for the kinds of writing discussed in this book are guides for interpreting specimens, not blueprints for producing them. Such categories as "exposition" and "persuasion"—and such subcategories as "definition," "comparison and contrast," "cause and effect"—are names for what people do in writing, not formulas for doing it. The study of anatomy—whether of a piece of writing or of a physical organism—is a species of reading. Thus the labels we attach to the parts (narrative, descriptive, argumentative) come after the fact, as the naming of the parts of a platypus (beak of bird, feet of duck) comes after the platypus.

Nobody expects you to build a full-scale essay (or a platypus) simply by looking at one. The specimens of writing in this chapter, especially, are far too complex to serve as models for you to imitate as a whole. Yet by reading them closely and by taking them apart, these essays may help you identify techniques of writing that you can use in assembling complex prose structures of your own.

As in physical anatomy, the most instructive question to keep in mind when you are reading a complicated piece of writing is not: is this a platypus (or other beast)? Nor even: what constitutes a platypus? It is rather the question of articulation. How do the parts of this beast (of whatever kind) fit together? By what connection(s) is a particular fin or wing or tail—especially if it looks at first like a useless spare part—joined to the main body of the essay?

No writer in English is better known for the things she leaves unstated than Virginia Woolf. Though Woolf tells us explicitly why the dancing moth fascinates her—it is an image of life reduced to its lowest terms, pure motion soon stilled—she does not finally explain, in so many words, why she is describing the other visible objects in her famous essay.

By restricting the moth's range to a single window pane, Woolf comments directly on the narrow compass of this tiny embodiment of the life force, both in space as well as time. "What remained for him but to fly to a third corner and then to a fourth?" Then she glances (as the uncomprehending moth cannot) beyond the window: "That was all he could do, inspite of the size of the downs, the width of the sky, the far-off smoke of the houses. . . ."

As you read, analyze, and interpret "The Death of the Moth," consider what "the rooks, the ploughmen, the horses, and even . . . the lean, bare-backed downs" (par. 2) have in common. Furthermore, ask yourself how they are connected, exactly, with the moth.

Obviously, all of the physical details in Woolf's essay are part of a description, and the scene they describe helps to form the setting for her little narrative about the death of the moth. Do description and narration here in any way contribute to an explanation or argument that Woolf might be making about life and living?

Like the moth, the birds and the fields and the earth itself (scored by the men and horses) are all part of nature. Woolf must be *defining* nature here as she describes the natural scene and her place in it. Evidently this is an essay about the "energy" (par. 2) that animates all the objects framed, inside and out, by the window of the writer, the person who is making the connections here.

The fields are "bare-backed" because it is autumn, the "lean" time of the year, when the remains of the harvest must be ploughed under to make way for the next growing season. So the condition of the fields in "mid-September" (par. 1) and the activities of the men and horses are just as much "annual festivities " (par. 1) as the cries of the black birds settling into winter. All describe seasons and cycles—like the little circuit of the moth. However grandly it may deck itself out, Woolf implies, even human life is little more, essentially, than instinctive movement.

(Editor's note: As I write, a moth actually appears inside my south-facing window and dances there for a while. I look outside. Instead of the sights and sounds of nature, I get heavy construction. From the campus building next door, a crew is removing asbestos that was installed about the time that Woolf's moth succumbed.)

Jonathan Swift

A Modest Proposal

The great satirist Jonathan Swift (1667–1745) was born in Dublin, Ireland, and educated at Trinity College, Dublin, where he was censured for breaking the rules of discipline and graduated only by "special grace." He was ordained an Anglican clergyman in 1694 and became Dean of St. Patrick's, Dublin, in 1713. His satires in prose and verse addressed three main issues: political relations between England and Ireland; Irish social questions; and matters of church doctrine. He is most famous for *The Battle of the Books* (1704); *A Tale of a Tub* (1704); and *Gulliver's Travels* (1726). His best-known essay was published in 1729 under the full title "A Modest Proposal for Preventing the Children of Poor People from Being a Burden to Their Parents or the Country." Assuming a mask, or persona, Swift poured into the essay his contempt for human materialism and for logic without compassion.

It is a melancholy object to those who walk through this great town[1] or travel in the country, when they see the streets, the roads, and cabin doors, crowded with beggars of the female sex, followed by three, four, or six children, all in rags and importuning every passenger for an alms. These mothers, instead of being able to work for their honest livelihood, are forced to employ all their time in strolling to beg sustenance for their helpless infants, who, as they grow up, either turn thieves for want of work, or leave their dear native country to fight for the Pretender in Spain, or sell themselves to the Barbadoes.[2] 1

I think it is agreed by all parties that this prodigious number of 2

[1] Dublin, capital city of Ireland.
[2] The pretender to the throne of England was James Stuart (1688–1766), son of the deposed James II. Barbados is an island in the West Indies.

children in the arms, or on the backs, or at the heels of their mothers, and frequently of their fathers, is in the present deplorable state of the kingdom a very great additional grievance; and therefore whoever could find out a fair, cheap, and easy method of making these children sound, useful members of the commonwealth would deserve so well of the public as to have his statue set up for a preserver of the nation.

But my intention is very far from being confined to provide only 3
for the children of professed beggars; it is of a much greater extent, and shall take in the whole number of infants at a certain age who are born of parents in effect as little able to support them as those who demand our charity in the streets.

As to my own part, having turned my thoughts for many years 4
upon this important subject, and maturely weighed the several schemes of other projectors,[3] I have always found them grossly mistaken in their computation. It is true, a child just dropped from its dam may be supported by her milk for a solar year, with little other nourishment; at most not above the value of two shillings,[4] which the mother may certainly get, or the value in scraps, by her lawful occupation of begging; and it is exactly at one year old that I propose to provide for them in such a manner as instead of being a charge upon their parents or the parish, or wanting food and raiment for the rest of their lives, they shall on the contrary contribute to the feeding, and partly to the clothing, of many thousands.

There is likewise another great advantage in my scheme, that it 5
will prevent those voluntary abortions, and that horrid practice of women murdering their bastard children, alas, too frequent among us, sacrificing the poor innocent babes, I doubt, more to avoid the expense than the shame, which would move tears and pity in the most savage and inhuman breast.

The number of souls in this kingdom being usually reckoned one 6
million and a half, of these I calculate there may be about two hundred thousand couple whose wives are breeders; from which number I subtract thirty thousand couples who are able to maintain their own children, although I apprehend there cannot be so many under the present distress of the kingdom; but this being granted, there

[3]Men whose heads were full of foolish schemes or projects.

[4]The British pound sterling was made up of twenty shillings; five shillings made a crown.

will remain an hundred and seventy thousand breeders. I again subtract fifty thousand for those women who miscarry, or whose children die by accident or disease within the year. There only remain an hundred and twenty thousand children of poor parents annually born. The question therefore is, how this number shall be reared and provided for, which, as I have already said, under the present situation of affairs, is utterly impossible by all the methods hitherto proposed. For we can neither employ them in handicraft or agriculture; we neither build houses (I mean in the country) nor cultivate land. They can very seldom pick up a livelihood by stealing till they arrive at six years old, except where they are of towardly parts;[5] although I confess they learn the rudiments much earlier, during which time they can however be looked upon only as probationers, as I have been informed by a principal gentleman in the county of Cavan, who protested to me that he never knew above one or two instances under the age of six, even in a part of the kingdom so renowned for the quickest proficiency in that art.

I am assured by our merchants that a boy or a girl before twelve 7
years old is no salable commodity; and even when they come to this age they will not yield above three pounds, or three pounds and half a crown at most on the Exchange; which cannot turn to account either to the parents or the kingdom, the charge of nutriment and rags having been at least four times that value.

I shall now therefore humbly propose my own thoughts, which I 8
hope will not be liable to the least objection.

I have been assured by a very knowing American of my acquain- 9
tance in London, that a young healthy child well nursed is at a year old a most delicious, nourishing, and wholesome food, whether stewed, roasted, baked, or boiled; and I make no doubt that it will equally serve in a fricassee or a ragout.

I do therefore humbly offer it to public consideration that of the 10
hundred and twenty thousand children, already computed, twenty thousand may be reserved for breed, whereof only one fourth part to be males, which is more than we allow to sheep, black cattle, or swine; and my reason is that these children are seldom the fruits of marriage, a circumstance not much regarded by our savages, therefore one male will be sufficient to serve four females. That the remaining hundred thousand may at a year old be offered in sale

[5] Having natural ability.

to the persons of quality and fortune through the kingdom, always advising the mother to let them suck plentifully in the last month, so as to render them plump and fat for a good table. A child will make two dishes at an entertainment for friends; and when the family dines alone, the fore or hind quarter will make a reasonable dish, and seasoned with a little pepper or salt will be very good boiled on the fourth day, especially in winter.

I have reckoned upon a medium that a child just born will weigh 11
twelve pounds, and in a solar year if tolerably nursed increaseth to twenty-eight pounds.

I grant this food will be somewhat dear, and therefore very proper 12
for landlords, who, as they have already devoured most of the parents, seem to have the best title to the children.

Infant's flesh will be in season throughout the year, but more 13
plentiful in March, and a little before and after. For we are told by a grave author, an eminent French physician,[6] that fish being a prolific diet, there are more children born in Roman Catholic countries about nine months after Lent than at any other season; therefore, reckoning a year after Lent, the markets will be more glutted than usual, because the number of popish infants is at least three to one in this kingdom; and therefore it will have one other collateral advantage, by lessening the number of Papists among us.

I have already computed the charge of nursing a beggar's child 14
(in which list I reckon all cottagers, laborers, and four fifths of the farmers) to be about two shillings per annum, rags included; and I believe no gentleman would repine to give ten shillings for the carcass of a good fat child, which, as I have said, will make four dishes of excellent nutritive meat, when he hath only some particular friend or his own family to dine with him. Thus the squire will learn to be a good landlord, and grow popular among the tenants; the mother will have eight shillings net profit, and be fit for work till she produces another child.

Those who are more thrifty (as I must confess the times require) 15
may flay the carcass; the skin of which artificially[7] dressed will make admirable gloves for ladies, and summer boots for fine gentlemen.

As to our city of Dublin, shambles[8] may be appointed for this 16

[6] François Rabelais (1494?–1553), French satirist.
[7] Skillfully, artfully.
[8] Slaughterhouses.

purpose in the most convenient parts of it, and butchers we may be assured will not be wanting; although I rather recommend buying the children alive, and dressing them hot from the knife as we do roasting pigs.

A very worthy person, a true lover of his country, and whose virtues I highly esteem, was lately pleased in discoursing on this matter to offer a refinement upon my scheme. He said that many gentlemen of this kingdom, having of late destroyed their deer, he conceived that the want of venison might be well supplied by the bodies of young lads and maidens, not exceeding fourteen years of age nor under twelve, so great a number of both sexes in every country being now ready to starve for want of work and service; and these to be disposed of by their parents, if alive, or otherwise by their nearest relations. But with due deference to so excellent a friend and so deserving a patriot, I cannot be altogether in his sentiments; for as to the males, my American acquaintance assured me from frequent experience that their flesh was generally tough and lean, like that of our schoolboys, by continual exercise, and their taste disagreeable; and to fatten them would not answer the charge. Then as to the females, it would, I think with humble submission, be a loss to the public, because they soon would become breeders themselves: and besides, it is not improbable that some scrupulous people might be apt to censure such a practice (although indeed very unjustly) as a little bordering upon cruelty; which, I confess, hath always been with me the strongest objection against any project, how well soever intended. 17

But in order to justify my friend, he confessed that this expedient was put into his head by the famous Psalmanazar,[9] a native of the island Formosa, who came from thence to London above twenty years ago, and in conversation told my friend that in his country when any young person happened to be put to death, the executioner sold the carcass to persons of quality as a prime dainty; and that in his time the body of a plump girl of fifteen, who was crucified for an attempt to poison the emperor, was sold to his Imperial Majesty's prime minister of state, and other great mandarins of the court, in joints from the gibbet, at four hundred crowns. Neither indeed can I deny that if the same use were made of several plump young 18

[9]George Psalmanazar (1679?–1763), a Frenchman, fooled English society for several years by masquerading as a pagan Formosan.

girls in this town, who without one single groat to their fortunes cannot stir abroad without a chair, and appear at the playhouse and assemblies in foreign fineries which they never will pay for, the kingdom would not be the worse.

Some persons of a desponding spirit are in great concern about that vast number of poor people who are aged, diseased, or maimed, and I have been desired to employ my thoughts what course may be taken to ease the nation of so grievous an encumbrance. But I am not in the least pain upon that matter, because it is very well known that they are every day dying and rotting by cold and famine, and filth and vermin, as fast as can be reasonably expected. And as to the younger laborers, they are now in almost as hopeful a condition. They cannot get work, and consequently pine away for want of nourishment to a degree that if at any time they are accidentally hired to common labor, they have not strength to perform it; and thus the country and themselves are happily delivered from the evils to come. 19

I have too long digressed, and therefore shall return to my subject. I think the advantages by the proposal which I have made are obvious and many, as well as of the highest importance. 20

For first, as I have already observed, it would greatly lessen the number of Papists, with whom we are yearly overrun, being the principal breeders of the nation as well as our most dangerous enemies; and who stay at home on purpose to deliver the kingdom to the Pretender, hoping to take their advantage by the absence of so many good Protestants, who have chosen rather to leave their country than stay at home and pay tithes against their conscience to an Episcopal curate.[1] 21

Secondly, the poorer tenants will have something valuable of their own, which by law may be made liable to distress, and help to pay their landlord's rent, their corn and cattle being already seized and money a thing unknown. 22

Thirdly, whereas the maintenance of an hundred thousand children, from two years old and upward, cannot be computed at less than ten shillings a piece per annum, the nation's stock will be thereby increased fifty thousand pounds per annum, besides the profit of a new dish introduced to the tables of all gentlemen of fortune in the kingdom who have any refinement in taste. And the 23

[1] Swift blamed much of Ireland's poverty upon large landowners who avoided church tithes by living (and spending their money) abroad.

money will circulate among ourselves, the goods being entirely of our own growth and manufacture.

Fourthly, the constant breeders, besides the gain of eight shillings 24
sterling per annum by the sale of their children, will be rid of the charge of maintaining them after the first year.

Fifthly, this food would likewise bring great custom to taverns, 25
where the vintners will certainly be so prudent as to procure the best receipts for dressing it to perfection, and consequently have their houses frequented by all the fine gentlemen, who justly value themselves upon their knowledge in good eating; and a skillful cook, who understands how to oblige his guests, will contrive to make it as expensive as they please.

Sixthly, this would be a great inducement to marriage, which all 26
wise nations have either encouraged by rewards or enforced by laws and penalties. It would increase the care and tenderness of mothers toward their children, when they were sure of a settlement for life to the poor babes, provided in some sort by the public, to their annual profit instead of expense. We should see an honest emulation among the married women, which of them could bring the fattest child to the market. Men would become as fond of their wifes during the time of their pregnancy as they are now of their mares in foal, their cows in calf, or sows when they are ready to farrow; nor offer to beat or kick them (as is too frequent a practice) for fear of a miscarriage.

Many other advantages might be enumerated. For instance, the 27
addition of some thousand carcasses in our exportation of barreled beef, the propagation of swine's flesh, and improvement in the art of making good bacon, so much wanted among us by the great destruction of pigs, too frequent at our tables, which are no way comparable in taste or magnificence to a well-grown, fat, yearling child, which roasted whole will make a considerable figure at a lord mayor's feast or any other public entertainment. But this and many others I omit, being studious of brevity.

Supposing that one thousand families in this city would be con- 28
stant customers for infants' flesh, besides others who might have it at merry meetings, particularly weddings and christenings, I compute that Dublin would take off annually about twenty thousand carcasses, and the rest of the kingdom (where probably they will be sold somewhat cheaper) the remaining eighty thousand.

I can think of no one objection that will possibly be raised against 29
this proposal, unless it should be urged that the number of people

will be thereby much lessened in the kingdom. This I freely own, and it was indeed one principal design in offering it to the world. I desire the reader will observe, that I calculate my remedy for this one individual kingdom of Ireland and for no other that ever was, is, or I think ever can be upon earth. Therefore let no man talk to me of other expedients[2]: of taxing our absentees at five shillings a pound: of using neither clothes nor household furniture except what is of our own growth and manufacture: of utterly rejecting the materials and instruments that promote foreign luxury: of curing the expensiveness of pride, vanity, idleness, and gaming in our women: of introducing a vein of parsimony, prudence, and temperance: of learning to love our country, in the want of which we differ even from Laplanders and the inhabitants of Topinamboo[3]: of quitting our animosities and factions, nor acting any longer like the Jews, who were murdering one another at the very moment their city[4] was taken: of being a little cautious not to sell our country and conscience for nothing: of teaching landlords to have at least one degree of mercy toward their tenants: lastly, of putting a spirit of honesty, industry, and skill into our shopkeepers; who, if a resolution could now be taken to buy only our native goods, would immediately unite to cheat and exact upon us in the price, the measure, and the goodness, nor could ever yet be brought to make one fair proposal of just dealing, though often and earnestly invited to it.

Therefore I repeat, let no man talk to me of these and the like 30
expedients, till he hath at least some glimpse of hope that there will ever be some hearty and sincere attempt to put them in practice.

But as to myself, having been wearied out for many years with 31
offering vain, idle, visionary thoughts, and at length utterly despairing of success, I fortunately fell upon this proposal, which, as it is wholly new, so it hath something solid and real, of no expense and little trouble, full in our own power, and whereby we can incur no danger in disobliging England. For this kind of commodity will not bear exportation, the flesh being of too tender a consistence to admit a long continuance in salt, although perhaps I could name a country[5] which would be glad to eat up our whole nation without it.

[2] The following are all measures that Swift himself proposed in various pamphlets.
[3] In Brazil.
[4] Jerusalem, sacked by the Romans in A.D. 70.
[5] England.

After all, I am not so violently bent upon my own opinion as to reject any offer proposed by wise men, which shall be found equally innocent, cheap, easy, and effectual. But before something of that kind shall be advanced in contradiction to my scheme, and offering a better, I desire the author or authors will be pleased maturely to consider two points. First, as things now stand, how they will be able to find food and raiment for an hundred thousand useless mouths and backs. And secondly, there being a round million of creatures in human figure throughout this kingdom, whose sole subsistence put into a common stock would leave them in debt two millions of pounds sterling, adding those who are beggars by profession to the bulk of farmers, cottagers, and laborers, with their wives and children who are beggars in effect; I desire those politicians who dislike my overture, and may perhaps be so bold to attempt an answer, that they will first ask the parents of these mortals whether they would not at this day think it a great happiness to have been sold for food at a year old in the manner I prescribe, and thereby have avoided such a perpetual scene of misfortunes as they have since gone through by the oppression of landlords, the impossibility of paying rent without money or trade, the want of common sustenance, with neither house nor clothes to cover them from the inclemencies of the weather, and the most inevitable prospect of entailing the like or greater miseries upon their breed forever. 32

I profess, in the sincerity of my heart, that I have not the least personal interest in endeavoring to promote this necessary work, having no other motive than the public good of my country, by advancing our trade, providing for infants, relieving the poor, and giving some pleasure to the rich. I have no children by which I can propose to get a single penny; the youngest being nine years old, and my wife past childbearing. 33

George Orwell

Politics and the English Language

Eric Arthur Blair (1903–1950, pseudonym George Orwell) was a British novelist and essayist born in Bengal, India. He was educated at Eton but, he said, "learned very little," returning to the East, where he served with the Indian Imperial Police in Burma from 1922 to 1927 and ruined his health. A dishwasher, a poor tutor, and an assistant in a London bookshop, Orwell finally began earning enough money from his writing to move to the country about 1935. He served briefly in the Spanish Civil War, was wounded, and afterwards settled in Hertfordshire, England, to raise hens and vegetables and write books. A brilliant political satirist, Orwell is best known for *Animal Farm* (1945) and *Nineteen Eighty-Four* (1949), an attack on political dictatorship. "Politics and the English Language" is perhaps the best essay in English on the social necessity of responsible writing.

Most people who bother with the matter at all would admit that the English language is in a bad way, but it is generally assumed that we cannot by conscious action do anything about it. Our civilization is decadent and our language—so the argument runs—must inevitably share in the general collapse. It follows that any struggle against the abuse of language is a sentimental archaism, like preferring candles to electric light or hansom cabs to aeroplanes. Underneath this lies the half-conscious belief that language is a natural growth and not an instrument which we shape for our own purposes. 1

Now, it is clear that the decline of a language must ultimately have political and economic causes: it is not due simply to the bad influence of this or that individual writer. But an effect can become a cause, reinforcing the original cause and producing the same effect in an intensified form, and so on indefinitely. A man may take to 2 drink because he feels himself to be a failure, and then fail all the more completely because he drinks. It is rather the same thing that is happening to the English language. It becomes ugly and inaccurate because our thoughts are foolish, but the slovenliness of our language makes it easier for us to have foolish thoughts. The point is that the process is reversible. Modern English, especially written English, is full of bad habits which spread by imitation and which can be avoided if one is willing to take the necessary trouble. If one gets rid of these habits one can think more clearly, and to think clearly is a necessary first step towards political regeneration: so that the fight against bad English is not frivolous and is not the exclusive concern of professional writers. I will come back to this presently, and I hope that by that time the meaning of what I have said here will have become clearer. Meanwhile, here are five specimens of the English language as it is now habitually written.

These five passages have not been picked out because they are 3
especially bad—I could have quoted far worse if I had chosen—but because they illustrate various of the mental vices from which we now suffer. They are a little below the average, but are fairly representative samples. I number them so that I can refer back to them when necessary:

1. I am not, indeed, sure whether it is not true to say that the Milton who once seemed not unlike a seventeenth-century Shelley had not become, out of an experience ever more bitter in each year, more alien [*sic*] to the founder of that Jesuit sect which nothing could induce him to tolerate.

Professor Harold Laski (Essay in *Freedom of Expression*)

2. Above all, we cannot play ducks and drakes with a native battery of idioms which prescribes such egregious collocations of vocables as the Basic *put up with* for *tolerate* or *put at a loss* for *bewilder*.

Professor Lancelot Hogben (*Interglossa*)

3. On the one side we have the free personality: by definition it is not neurotic, for it has neither conflict nor dream. Its desires, such as they are, are transparent, for they are just what institutional approval keeps in the forefront of consciousness; another institutional pattern would alter their number and intensity; there is little in them that is natural, irreducible, or culturally dangerous. But *on the other side,* the social bond itself is nothing but the mutual reflection of these self-secure integrities. Recall the definition of love. Is not this the very picture of a small academic? Where is there a place in this hall of mirrors for either personality or fraternity?

Essay on psychology in *Politics* (New York)

4. All the 'best people' from the gentlemen's clubs, and all the frantic fascist captains, united in common hatred of Socialism and bestial horror of the rising tide of the mass revolutionary movement, have turned to acts of provocation, to foul incendiarism, to medieval legends of poisoned wells, to legalize their own destruction of proletarian organizations, and rouse the agitated petty-bourgeoisie to chauvinistic fervour on behalf of the fight against the revolutionary way out of the crisis.

Communist pamphlet

5. If a new spirit is to be infused into this old country, there is one thorny and contentious reform which must be tackled, and that is the humanization and galvinization of the B.B.C. Timidity here will bespeak cancer and atrophy of the soul. The heart of Britain may be sound and of strong beat, for instance, but the British lion's roar at present is like that of Bottom in Shakespeare's *Midsummer Night's Dream*—as gentle as any sucking dove. A virile new Britain cannot continue indefinitely to be traduced in the eyes or rather ears, of the world by the effete languors of Langham Place, brazenly masquerading as 'standard English'. When the Voice of Britain is heard at nine o'clock, better far and infinitely less ludicrous to hear aitches honestly dropped than the present priggish, inflated, inhibited, school-ma'amish arch braying of blameless bashful mewing maidens!

Letter in *Tribune*

Each of these passages has faults of its own, but, quite apart from avoidable ugliness, two qualities are common to all of them. The first is staleness of imagery: the other is lack of precision. The writer either has a meaning and cannot express it, or he inadvertently says something else, or he is almost indifferent as to whether his words mean anything or not. This mixture of vagueness and sheer incompetence is the most marked characteristic of modern English prose, and especially of any kind of political writing. As soon as certain topics are raised, the concrete melts into the abstract and no one seems able to think of turns of speech that are not hackneyed: prose consists less and less of *words* chosen for the sake of their meaning, and more and more of *phrases* tacked together like the sections of a prefabricated hen-house. I list below, with notes and examples, various of the tricks by means of which the work of prose-construction is habitually dodged: 4

Dying Metaphors

A newly invented metaphor assists thought by evoking a visual image, while on the other hand a metaphor which is technically "dead" (e.g. *iron resolution*) has in effect reverted to being an ordinary 5 word and can generally be used without loss of vividness. But in between these two classes there is a huge dump of worn-out metaphors which have lost all evocative power and are merely used because they save people the trouble of inventing phrases for themselves. Examples are *Ring the changes on, take up the cudgels for, toe the line, ride roughshod over, stand shoulder to shoulder with, play into the hands of, no axe to grind, grist to the mill, fishing in troubled waters, on the order of the day, Achilles' heel, swan song, hotbed.* Many of these are used without knowledge of their meaning (what is a "rift", for instance?), and incompatible metaphors are frequently mixed, a sure sign that the writer is not interested in what he is saying. Some metaphors now current have been twisted out of their original meaning without those who use them even being aware of the fact. For example, *toe the line* is sometimes written *tow the line*. Another example is *the hammer and the anvil,* now always used with the implication that the anvil gets the worst of it. In real life it is always the anvil that breaks the hammer, never the other way about: a writer who stopped to think what he was saying would be aware of this, and would avoid perverting the original phrase.

Operators or Verbal False Limbs

These save the trouble of picking out appropriate verbs and nouns, and at the same time pad each sentence with extra syllables which give it an appearance of symmetry. Characteristic phrases are: *render inoperative, militate against, make contact with, be subjected to, give rise to, give grounds for, have the effect of, play a leading part (role) in, make itself felt, take effect, exhibit a tendency to, serve the purpose of, etc., etc.* The keynote is the elimination of simple verbs. Instead of being a single word, such as *break, stop, spoil, mend, kill,* a verb becomes a *phrase,* made up of a noun or adjective tacked on to some general-purposes verb such as *prove, serve, form, play, render*. In addition, the passive voice is wherever possible used in preference to the active, and noun constructions are used instead of gerunds (*by examination of* instead of *by examining*). The range of verbs is further cut down by means of the *-ize* and *de-* formation, and the banal statements are given an appearance of profundity by means of the *not un-* formation. Simple conjunctions and prepositions are replaced by such phrases as *with respect to, having regard to, the fact that, by dint of, in view of, in the interests of, on the hypothesis that;* and the ends of sentences are saved from anticlimax by such, resounding 6 commonplaces as *greatly to be desired, cannot be left out of account, a development to be expected in the near future, deserving of serious consideration, brought to a satisfactory conclusion,* and so on and so forth.

Pretentious Diction

Words like *phenomenon, element, individual* (as noun), *objective, categorical, effective, virtual, basic, primary, promote, constitute, exhibit, exploit, utilize, eliminate, liquidate,* are used to dress up simple statements and give an air of scientific impartiality to biased judgments. Adjectives like *epoch-making, epic, historic, unforgettable, triumphant, age-old, inevitable, inexorable, veritable,* are used to dignify the sordid processes of international politics, while writing that aims at glorifying war usually takes on an archaic colour, its characteristic words being: *realm, throne, chariot, mailed fist, trident, sword shield, buckler, banner, jackboot, clarion.* Foreign words and expressions such as *cul de sac, ancien régime, deus ex machina, mutatis mutandis, status quo, gleichschaltung, weltanschauung* are used to give an air of culture and elegance. Except for the useful abbreviations *i.e., e.g.,* and *etc.,* there is no real need for any of the hundreds of foreign phrases now current in English. Bad writers, and especially scientific, political and sociological writers, are nearly always haunted by the notion that Latin or Greek words are grander than Saxon ones, and unnecessary words like *expedite, ameliorate, predict, extraneous, deracinated, clandestine, subaqueous* and hundreds of others constantly gain ground from their Anglo-Saxon opposite numbers.[1] The jargon peculiar to Marxist writing (*hyena, hangman, cannibal, petty bourgeois, these gentry, lacquey, flunkey, mad dog, White Guard,* etc.) consists largely of words and phrases translated from Russian, German or French; but the normal way of coining a new word is to use a Latin or Greek root with the appropriate affix and, where necessary, the *-ize* formation. It is often easier to make up words of this kind (*deregionalize, impermissible, extramarital, nonfragmentatory* and so forth) than to think up 7

[1]An interesting illustration of this is the way in which the English flower names which were in use till very recently are being ousted by Greek ones, *snapdragon* becoming *antirrhinum, forget-me-not* becoming *myosotis,* etc. It is hard to see any practical reason for this change of fashion: it is probably due to an instinctive turning-away from the more homely word and a vague feeling that the Greek word is scientific [Orwell's note].

the English words that will cover one's meaning. The result, in general, is an increase in slovenliness and vagueness.

MEANINGLESS WORDS

In certain kinds of writing, particularly in art criticism and literary 8
criticism, it is normal to come across long passages which are almost completely lacking in meaning.[2] Words like *romantic, plastic, values, human, dead, sentimental, natural, vitality,* as used in art criticism, are strictly meaningless in the sense that they not only do not point to any discoverable object, but are hardly ever expected to do so by the reader. When one critic writes, "The outstanding feature of Mr. X's work is its living quality", while another writes, "The immediately striking thing about Mr. X's work is its peculiar deadness", the reader accepts this as a simple difference of opinion. If words like *black* and *white* were involved, instead of the jargon words *dead* and *living,* he would see at once that language was being used in an improper way. Many political words are similarly abused. The word *Fascism* has now no meaning except in so far as it signifies "something not desirable". The words *democracy, socialism, freedom, patriotic, realistic, justice,* have each of them several different meanings which cannot be reconciled with one another. In the case of a word like *democracy,* not only is there no agreed definition, but the attempt to make one is resisted from all sides. It is almost universally felt that when we call a country democratic we are praising it: consequently the defenders of every kind of régime claim that it is a democracy, and fear that they might have to stop using the word if it were tied down to any one meaning. Words of this kind are often used in a consciously dishonest way. That is, the person who uses them has his own private definition, but allows his hearer to think he means something quite different. Statements like *Marshal Pétain was a true patriot, The Soviet Press is the freest in the world, The Catholic Church is opposed to persecution,* are almost always made with intent to deceive. Other words used in variable meanings, in most cases more

[2]Example: "Comfort's catholicity of perception and image, strangely Whitmanesque in range, almost the exact opposite in aesthetic compulsion, continues to evoke that trembling atmospheric accumulative hinting at a cruel, an inexorably serene timelessness . . . Wrey Gardiner scores by aiming at simple bull's-eyes with precision. Only they are not so simple, and through this contented sadness runs more than the surface bittersweet of resignation" *(Poetry Quarterly)* [Orwell's note].

or less dishonestly, are: *class, totalitarian, science, progressive, reactionary, bourgeois, equality*.

Now that I have made this catalogue of swindles and perversions, let me give another example of the kind of writing that they lead to. This time it must of its nature be an imaginary one. I am going to translate a passage of good English into modern English of the worst sort. Here is a well-known verse from *Ecclesiastes*: 9

> I returned and saw under the sun, that the race is not to the swift, nor the battle to the strong, neither yet bread to the wise, nor yet riches to men of understanding, nor yet favour to men of skill; but time and chance happeneth to them all.

Here it is in modern English: 10

> Objective consideration of contemporary phenomena compels the conclusion that success or failure in competitive activities exhibits no tendency to be commensurate with innate capacity, but that a considerable element of the unpredictable must invariably be taken into account.

This is a parody, but not a very gross one. Exhibit (3), above, for 11 instance, contains several patches of the same kind of English. It will be seen that I have not made a full translation. The beginning and ending of the sentence follow the original meaning fairly closely, but in the middle the concrete illustrations—race, battle, bread—dissolve into the vague phrase "success or failure in competitive activities". This had to be so, because no modern writer of the kind I am discussing—no one capable of using phrases like "objective consideration of contemporary phenomena"—would ever tabulate his thoughts in that precise and detailed way. The whole tendency of modern prose is away from concreteness. Now analyse these two sentences a little more closely. The first contains forty-nine words but only sixty syllables, and all its words are those of everyday life. The second contains thirty-eight words of ninety syllables: eighteen of its words are from Latin roots, and one from Greek. The first sentence contains six vivid images, and only one phrase ("time and chance") that could be called vague. The second contains not a single fresh, arresting phrase, and in spite of its ninety syllables it gives only a shortened version of the meaning contained in the first. Yet without a doubt it is the second kind of sentence that is gaining ground in modern English. I do not want to exaggerate. This kind of writing is not yet universal, and outcrops of simplicity will occur here and there in the worst-written page. Still, if you or I were told to write a few lines on the uncertainty of human fortunes, we should probably come much nearer to my imaginary sentence than to the one from *Ecclesiastes*.

As I have tried to show, modern writing at its worst does not 12
consist in picking out words for the sake of their meaning and inventing images in order to make the meaning clearer. It consists in gumming together long strips of words which have already been set in order by someone else, and making the results presentable by sheer humbug. The attraction of this way of writing is that it is easy. It is easier—even quicker, once you have the habit—to say *In my opinion it is a not unjustifiable assumption that* than to say *I think*. If you use ready-made phrases, you not only don't have to hunt about for words; you also don't have to bother with the rhythms of your sentences, since these phrases are generally so arranged as to be more or less euphonious. When you are composing in a hurry—when you are dictating to a stenographer, for instance, or making a public speech—it is natural to fall into a pretentious, Latinized style. Tags like *a consideration which we should do well to bear in mind* or *a conclusion to which all of us would readily assent* will save many a sentence from coming down with a bump. By using stale metaphors, similes and idioms, you save much mental effort, at the cost of leaving your meaning vague, not only for your reader but for yourself. This is the significance of mixed metaphors. The sole aim of a metaphor is to call up a visual image. When these images clash—as in *The Fascist octopus has sung its swan song, the jack-boot is thrown into the melting pot*—it can be taken as certain that the writer is not seeing a mental image of the objects he is naming; in other words he is not really thinking. Look again at the examples I gave at the beginning of this essay. Professor Laski (1) uses five negatives in fifty-three words. One of these is superfluous, making nonsense of the whole passage, and in addition there is the slip *alien* for akin, making further nonsense, and several avoidable pieces of clumsiness which increase the general vagueness. Professor Hogben (2) plays ducks and drakes with a battery which is able to write prescriptions, and, while disapproving of the everyday phrase *put up with,* is unwilling to look egregious up in the dictionary and see what it means. (3), if one takes an uncharitable attitude towards it, is simply meaningless: probably one could work out its intended meaning by reading the whole of the

article in which it occurs. In (4), the writer knows more or less what he wants to say, but an accumulation of stale phrases chokes him like tea leaves blocking a sink. In (5), words and meaning have almost parted company. People who write in this manner usually have a general emotional meaning—they dislike one thing and want to express solidarity with another—but they are not interested in the detail of what they are saying. A scrupulous writer, in every sentence that he writes, will ask himself at least four questions, thus: What am I trying to say? What words will express it? What image or idiom will make it clearer? Is this image fresh enough to have an effect? And he will probably ask himself two more: Could I put it more shortly? Have I said anything that is avoidably ugly? But you are not obliged to go to all this trouble. You can shirk it by simply throwing your mind open and letting the ready-made phrases come crowding in. They will construct your sentences for you—even think your thoughts for you, to a certain extent—and at need they will perform the important service of partially concealing your meaning even from yourself. It is at this point that the special connection between politics and the debasement of language becomes clear.

In our time it is broadly true that political writing is bad writing. 13
Where it is not true, it will generally be found that the writer is some kind of rebel, expressing his private opinions and not a "party line". Orthodoxy, of whatever colour, seems to demand a lifeless, imitative style. The political dialects to be found in pamphlets, leading articles, manifestos, White Papers and the speeches of under-secretaries do, of course, vary from party to party, but they are all alike in that one almost never finds in them a fresh, vivid, home-made turn of speech. When one watches some tired hack on the platform mechanically repeating the familiar phrases—*bestial atrocities, iron heel, blood-stained tyranny, free peoples of the world, stand shoulder to shoulder*—one often has a curious feeling that one is not watching a live human being but some kind of dummy: a feeling which suddenly becomes stronger at moments when the light catches the speaker's spectacles and turns them into blank discs which seem to have no eyes behind them. And this is not altogether fanciful. A speaker who uses that kind of phraseology has gone some distance towards turning himself into a machine. The appropriate noises are coming out of his larynx, but his brain is not involved as it would be if he were choosing his words for himself. If the speech he is making is one that he is accustomed to make over and over again, he may be almost unconscious

of what he is saying, as one is when one utters the responses in church. And this reduced state of consciousness, if not indispensable, is at any rate favourable to political conformity.

In our time, political speech and writing are largely the defence of the indefensible. Things like the continuance of British rule in India, the Russian purges and deportations, the dropping of the atom bombs on Japan, can indeed be defended, but only by arguments which are too brutal for most people to face, and which do not square with the professed aims of political parties. Thus political language has to consist largely of euphemism, question-begging and sheer cloudy vagueness. Defenceless villages are bombarded from the air, the inhabitants driven out into the countryside, the cattle machine-gunned, the huts set on fire with incendiary bullets: this is called *pacification*. Millions of peasants are robbed of their farms and sent trudging along the roads with no more than they can carry: this is called *transfer of population* or *rectification of frontiers*. People are imprisoned for years without trial, or shot in the back of the neck or sent to die of scurvy in Arctic lumber camps: this is called *elimination of unreliable elements*. Such phraseology is needed if one wants to name things without calling up mental pictures of them. Consider for instance some comfortable English professor defending Russian totalitarianism. He cannot say outright, "I believe in killing off your opponents when you can get good results by doing so". Probably, therefore, he will say something like this: 14

"While freely conceding that the Soviet régime exhibits certain features which the humanitarian may be inclined to deplore, we must, I think, agree that a certain curtailment of the right to political opposition is an unavoidable concomitant of transitional periods, and that the rigours which the Russian people have been called upon to undergo have been amply justified in the sphere of concrete achievement." 15

The inflated style is itself a kind of euphemism. A mass of Latin words falls upon the facts like soft snow, blurring the outlines and covering up all the details. The great enemy of clear language is insincerity. When there is a gap between one's real and one's declared aims, one turns as it were instinctively to long words and exhausted idioms, like a cuttlefish squirting out ink. In our age there is no such thing as "keeping out of politics". All issues are political issues, and politics itself is a mass of lies, evasions, folly, hatred and schizophrenia. When the general atmosphere is bad, language must 16 suffer. I should expect to find—this is a guess which I have not sufficient knowledge to verify—that the German, Russian and Italian languages have all deteriorated in the last ten or fifteen years, as a result of dictatorship.

But if thought corrupts language, language can also corrupt thought. A bad usage can spread by tradition and imitation, even among people who should and do know better. The debased language that I have been discussing is in some ways very convenient. Phrases like *a not unjustifiable assumption, leaves much to be desired, would serve no good purpose, a consideration which we should do well to bear in mind,* are a continuous temptation, a packet of aspirins always at one's elbow. Look back through this essay, and for certain you will find that I have again and again committed the very faults I am protesting against. By this morning's post I have received a pamphlet dealing with conditions in Germany. The author tells me that he "felt impelled" to write it. I open it at random, and here is almost the first sentence that I see: "(The Allies) have an opportunity not only of achieving a radical transformation of Germany's social and political structure in such a way as to avoid a nationalistic reaction in Germany itself, but at the same time of laying the foundations of a co-operative and unified Europe." You see, he "feels impelled" to write—feels, presumably, that he has something new to say—and yet his words, like cavalry horses answering the bugle, group themselves automatically into the familiar dreary pattern. This invasion of one's mind by ready-made phrases *(lay the foundations, achieve a radical transformation)* can only be prevented if one is constantly on guard against them, and every such phrase anaesthetizes a portion of one's brain. 17

I said earlier that the decadence of our language is probably curable. Those who deny this would argue, if they produced an argument at all, that language merely reflects existing social conditions, and that we cannot influence its development by any direct tinkering with words and constructions. So far as the general tone or spirit of a language goes, this may be true, but it is not true in detail. Silly words and expressions have often disappeared, not through any evolutionary process but owing to the conscious action of a minority. Two recent examples were *explore every avenue* and *leave no stone unturned,* which were killed by the jeers of a few journalists. There is a long list of flyblown metaphors which could similarly be got rid 18 of if enough people would interest themselves in the job; and it should also be possible to laugh the not *un-* formation out of existence,[3] to reduce the amount of Latin and Greek in the average sentence, to drive out foreign phrases and strayed scientific words, and, in general, to make pretentiousness unfashionable. But all these are minor points. The defence of the English language implies more than this, and perhaps it is best to start by saying what it does not imply.

To begin with it has nothing to do with archaism, with the salvag- 19
ing of obsolete words and turns of speech, or with the setting up of a "standard English" which must never be departed from. On the contrary, it is especially concerned with the scrapping of every word or idiom which has outworn its usefulness. It has nothing to do with correct grammar and syntax, which are of no importance so long as one makes one's meaning clear, or with the avoidance of Americanisms, or with having what is called a "good prose style". On the other hand it is not concerned with fake simplicity and the attempt to make written English colloquial. Nor does it even imply in every case preferring the Saxon word to the Latin one, though it does imply using the fewest and shortest words that will cover one's meaning. What is above all needed is to let the meaning choose the word, and not the other way about. In prose, the worst thing one can do with words is to surrender to them. When you think of a concrete object, you think wordlessly, and then, if you want to describe the thing you have been visualizing you probably hunt about till you find the exact words that seem to fit. When you think of something abstract you are more inclined to use words from the start, and unless you make a conscious effort to prevent it, the existing dialect will come rushing in and do the job for you, at the expense of blurring or even changing your meaning. Probably it is better to put off using words as long as possible and get one's meaning as clear as one can through pictures or sensations. Afterwards one can choose—not simply accept—the phrases that will best cover the meaning, and then switch round and decide what impression one's words are likely to make on another person. This last effort of the mind cuts out all stale or mixed images, all prefabricated phrases, needless repetitions, and humbug and vagueness generally. But one

[3]One can cure oneself of the *not un-* formation by memorizing this sentence: *A not unblack dog was chasing a not unsmall rabbit across a not ungreen field* [Orwell's note].

can often be in doubt about the effect of a word or a phrase, and one needs rules that one can rely on when instinct fails. I think the following rules will cover most cases:

(i) Never use a metaphor, simile or other figure of speech which you are used to seeing in print.
(ii) Never use a long word where a short one will do.
(iii) If it is possible to cut a word out, always cut it out.
(iv) Never use the passive where you can use the active.
(v) Never use a foreign phrase, a scientific word or a jargon word if you can think of an everyday English equivalent.
(vi) Break any of these rules sooner than say anything outright barbarous.

These rules sound elementary, and so they are, but they demand a deep change of attitude in anyone who has grown used to writing in the style now fashionable. One could keep all of them and still write bad English, but one could not write the kind of stuff that I quoted in those five specimens at the beginning of this article.

I have not here been considering the literary use of language, but 20
merely language as an instrument for expressing and not for concealing or preventing thought. Stuart Chase and others have come near to claiming that all abstract words are meaningless, and have used this as a pretext for advocating a kind of political quietism. Since you don't know what Fascism is, how can you struggle against Fascism? One need not swallow such absurdities as this, but one ought to recognize that the present political chaos is connected with the decay of language, and that one can probably bring about some improvement by starting at the verbal end. If you simplify your English, you are freed from the worst follies of orthodoxy. You cannot speak any of the necessary dialects, and when you make a stupid remark its stupidity will be obvious, even to yourself. Political language—and with variations this is true of all political parties, from Conservatives to Anarchists—is designed to make lies sound truthful and murder respectable, and to give an appearance of solidity to pure wind. One cannot change this all in a moment, but one can at least change one's own habits, and from time to time one can even, if one jeers loudly enough, send some worn-out and useless phrase—some *jackboot, Achilles' heel, hotbed, melting pot, acid test, veritable inferno* or other lump of verbal refuse—into the dustbin where it belongs.

E. B. White

ONCE MORE TO THE LAKE

Elwyn Brooks White, the dean of American essayists, a storyteller and a poet, was born in Mount Vernon, New York, in 1899. After studying at Cornell University, he joined the staff of the *New Yorker* in 1926. A gifted reporter of urban life, White was to find the city too "seductive," and he gradually spent more and more time on his farm in Maine, where he moved more or less permanently in 1957. Widely praised for his prose style, White wrote a regular column, "One Man's Meat," for *Harper's* and editorials for the *New Yorker*. He also published numerous books, including *Charlotte's Web* (1952, for children); *The Second Tree from the Corner* (1954); *The Elements of Style* (1959, an enlargement of William Strunk's handbook for writers); *The Points of My Compass* (1967); and *The Letters of E. B. White* (1976). "Once More to the Lake," a narrative about the generations, is reprinted from *Essays of E. B. White* (1977); written in August 1941, it originally appeared in *Harper's* and later in *One Man's Meat* (1942). Shortly before his death in 1985 White recalled the process of writing this American classic in a letter to the editor, reproduced at the end of this chapter.

One summer, along about 1904, my father rented a camp on a lake in Maine and took us all there for the month of August. We all got ringworm from some kittens and had to rub Pond's Extract on our arms and legs night and morning, and my father rolled over in a canoe with all his clothes on; but outside of that the vacation was a success and from then on none of us ever thought there was any place in the world like that lake in Maine. We returned summer after summer—always on August 1 for one month. I have since become a salt-water man, but sometimes in summer there are days when the restlessness of the tides and the fearful cold of the sea water and the incessant wind that blows across the afternoon and into the evening 1 make me wish for the placidity of a lake in the woods. A few weeks ago this feeling got so strong I bought myself a couple of bass hooks and a spinner and returned to the lake where we used to go, for a week's fishing and to revisit old haunts.

I took along my son, who had never had any fresh water up his nose and who had seen lily pads only from train windows. On the journey over to the lake I began to wonder what it would be like. I wondered how the time would have marred this unique, this holy spot—the coves and streams, the hills that the sun set behind, the camps and the paths behind the camps. I was sure that the tarred road would have found it out, and I wondered in what other ways it would be desolated. It is strange how much you can remember about places like that once you allow your mind to return into the grooves that lead back. You remember one thing, and that suddenly reminds you of another thing. I guess I remembered clearest of all the early mornings, when the lake was cool and motionless, remembered how the bedroom smelled of the lumber it was made of and of the wet woods whose scent entered through the screen. The partitions in the camp were thin and did not extend clear to the top of the rooms, and as I was always the first up I would dress softly so as not to wake the others, and sneak out into the sweet outdoors and start out in the canoe, keeping close along the shore in the long shadows of the pines. I remembered being very careful never to rub my paddle against the gunwale for fear of disturbing the stillness of the cathedral. 2

The lake had never been what you would call a wild lake. There were cottages sprinkled around the shores, and it was in farming country although the shores of the lake were quite heavily wooded. Some of the cottages were owned by nearby farmers, and you would live at the shore and eat your meals at the farmhouse. That's what our family did. But although it wasn't wild, it was a fairly large and undisturbed lake and there were places in it that, to a child at least, seemed infinitely remote and primeval. 3

I was right about the tar: it led to within half a mile of the shore. But when I got back there, with my boy, and we settled into a camp near a farmhouse and into the kind of summertime I had known, I could tell that it was going to be pretty much the same as it had been before—I knew it, lying in bed the first morning, smelling the bedroom and hearing the boy sneak quietly out and go off along the shore in a boat. I began to sustain the illusion that he was I, and 4 therefore, by simple transposition, that I was my father. This sensation persisted, kept cropping up all the time we were there. It was not an entirely new feeling, but in this setting, it grew much stronger. I seemed to be living a dual existence. I would be in the middle of some simple act, I would be picking up a bait box or laying down a table fork, or I would be saying something, and suddenly it would be not I but my father who was saying the words or making the gesture. It gave me a creepy sensation.

We went fishing the first morning. I felt the same damp moss covering the worms in the bait can, and saw the dragonfly alight on the tip of my rod as it hovered a few inches from the surface of the water. It was the arrival of this fly that convinced me beyond any doubt that everything was as it always had been, that the years were a mirage and that there had been no years. The small waves were the same, chucking the rowboat under the chin as we fished at anchor, and the boat was the same boat, the same color green and the ribs broken in the same places, and under the floorboards the same freshwater leavings and débris—the dead helgramite, the wisps of moss, the rusty discarded fishhook, the dried blood from yesterday's catch. We stared silently at the tips of our rods, at the dragonflies that came and went. I lowered the tip of mine into the water, tentatively, pensively dislodging the fly, which darted two feet away, poised, darted two feet back, and came to rest again a little farther up the rod. There had been no years between the ducking of this dragonfly and the other one—the one that was part of memory. I looked at the boy, who was silently watching his fly, and it was my hands that held his rod, my eyes watching. I felt dizzy and didn't know which rod I was at the end of. 5

We caught two bass, hauling them in briskly as though they were mackerel, pulling them over the side of the boat in a businesslike manner without any landing net, and stunning them with a blow on the back of the head. When we got back for a swim before lunch, the lake was exactly where we had left it, the same number of inches from the dock, and there was only the merest suggestion of a breeze. This seemed an utterly enchanted sea, this lake you could leave to its own devices for a few hours and come back to, and find that it had not stirred, this constant and trustworthy body of water. In the shallows, the dark, water-soaked sticks and twigs, smooth and old, were undulating in clusters on the bottom against the clean ribbed sand, and the track of the mussel was plain. A school of minnows 6 swam by, each minnow with its small individual shadow, doubling the attendance, so clear and sharp in the sunlight. Some of the other campers were in swimming, along the shore, one of them with a cake of soap, and the water felt thin and clear and unsubstantial. Over the years there had been this person with the cake of soap, this cultist, and here he was. There had been no years.

Up to the farmhouse to dinner through the teeming, dusty field, 7 the road under our sneakers was only a two-track road. The middle track was missing, the one with the marks of the hooves and the splotches of dried, flaky manure. There had always been three tracks to choose from in choosing which track to walk in; now the choice was narrowed down to two. For a moment I missed terribly the middle alternative. But the way led past the tennis court, and something about the way it lay there in the sun reassured me; the tape had loosened along the backline, the alleys were green with plantains and other weeds, and the net (installed in June and removed in September) sagged in the dry noon, and the whole place steamed with midday heat and hunger and emptiness. There was a choice of pie for dessert, and one was blueberry and one was apple, and the waitresses were the same country girls, there having been no passage of time, only the illusion of it as in a dropped curtain—the waitresses were still fifteen; their hair had been washed, that was the only difference—they had been to the movies and seen the pretty girls with the clean hair.

Summertime, oh, summertime, pattern of life indelible, the fade- 8 proof lake, the woods unshatterable, the pasture with the sweetfern and the juniper forever and ever, summer without end; this was the background, and the life along the shore was the design, the cottages with their innocent and tranquil design, their tiny docks with the flagpole and the American flag floating against the white clouds in the blue sky, the little paths over the roots of the trees leading from camp to camp and the paths leading back to the outhouses and the can of lime for sprinkling, and at the souvenir counters at the store the miniature birch-bark canoes and the postcards that showed things looking a little better than they looked. This was the American family at play, escaping the city heat, wondering whether the newcomers in the camp at the head of the cove were "common" or "nice," wondering whether it was true that the people who drove up for Sunday dinner at the farmhouse were turned away because there wasn't enough chicken.

It seemed to me, as I kept remembering all this, that those times and those summers had been infinitely precious and worth saving. There had been jollity and peace and goodness. The arriving (at the beginning of August) had been so big a business in itself, at the railway station the farm wagon drawn up, the first smell of the pine-laden air, the first glimpse of the smiling farmer, and the great importance of the trunks and your father's enormous authority in such matters, and the feel of the wagon under you for the long ten-mile haul, and at the top of the last long hill catching the first view of the lake after eleven months of not seeing this cherished body of water. The shouts and cries of the other campers when they saw you, and the trunks to be unpacked, to give up their rich burden. (Arriving was less exciting nowadays, when you sneaked up in your car and parked it under a tree near the camp and took out the bags and in five minutes it was all over, no fuss, no loud wonderful fuss about trunks.) 9

Peace and goodness and jollity. The only thing that was wrong now, really, was the sound of the place, an unfamiliar nervous sound of the outboard motors. This was the note that jarred, the one thing that would sometimes break the illusion and set the years moving. In those other summertimes all motors were inboard; and when they were at a little distance, the noise they made was a sedative, an ingredient of summer sleep. They were one-cylinder and two-cylinder engines, and some were make-and-break and some were jump-spark, but they all made a sleepy sound across the lake. The one-lungers throbbed and fluttered, and the twin-cylinder ones purred and purred, and that was a quiet sound, too. But now the campers all had outboards. In the daytime, in the hot mornings, these motors made a petulant, irritable sound; at night, in the still evening when the afterglow lit the water, they whined about one's ears like mosquitoes. My boy loved our rented outboard, and his great desire was to achieve single-handed mastery over it, and authority, and he soon learned the trick of choking it a little (but not too much), and the adjustment of the needle valve. Watching him I would remember the things you could do with the old one-cylinder engine with the heavy flywheel, how you could have it eating out of your hand if you got really close to it spiritually. Motorboats in those days didn't have clutches, and you would make a landing by shutting off the motor at the proper time and coasting in with a dead rudder. But there was a way of reversing them, if you learned the trick, by cutting the 10 switch and putting it on again exactly on the final dying revolution of the flywheel, so that it would kick back against compression and begin reversing. Approaching a dock in a strong following breeze, it was difficult to slow up sufficiently by the ordinary coasting method, and if a boy felt he had complete mastery over his motor, he was tempted to keep it running beyond its time and then reverse it a few feet from the dock. It took a cool nerve, because if you threw the switch a twentieth of a second too soon you would catch the flywheel when it still had speed enough to go up past center, and the boat would leap ahead, charging bull-fashion at the dock.

We had a good week at the camp. The bass were biting well and 11
the sun shone endlessly, day after day. We would be tired at night and lie down in the accumulated heat of the little bedrooms after the long hot day and the breeze would stir almost imperceptibly outside and the smell of the swamp drift in through the rusty screens. Sleep would come easily and in the morning the red squirrel would be on the roof, tapping out his gay routine. I kept remembering everything, lying in bed in the mornings—the small steamboat that had a long rounded stern like the lip of a Ubangi, and how quietly she ran on the moonlight sails, when the older boys played their mandolins and the girls sang and we ate doughnuts dipped in sugar, and how sweet the music was on the water in the shining night, and what it had felt like to think about girls then. After breakfast we would go up to the store and the things were in the same place—the minnows in a bottle, the plugs and spinners disarranged and pawed over by the youngsters from the boys' camp, the Fig Newtons and the Beeman's gum. Outside, the road was tarred and cars stood in front of the store. Inside, all was just as it had always been, except there was more Coca-Cola and not so much Moxie[1] and root beer and birch beer and sarsaparilla. We would walk out with the bottle of pop apiece and sometimes the pop would backfire up our noses and hurt. We explored the streams, quietly, where the turtles slid off logs and dug their way into the soft bottom; and we lay on the town wharf and fed worms to the tame bass. Everywhere we went I had trouble making out which was I, the one walking at my side, the one walking in my pants.

One afternoon while we were there at that lake a thunderstorm 12
came up. It was like the revival of an old melodrama that I had seen

[1] Brand name of an old-fashioned soft drink.

long ago with childish awe. The second-act climax of the drama of the electrical disturbance over a lake in America has not changed in any important respect. This was the big scene, still the big scene. The whole thing was so familiar, the first feeling of oppression and heat and a general air around camp of not wanting to go very far away. In midafternoon (it was all the same) a curious darkening of the sky, and a lull in everything that had made life tick; and then the way the boats suddenly swung the other way at their moorings with the coming of a breeze out of the new quarter, and the premonitory rumble. Then the kettle drum, then the snare, then the bass drum and cymbals, then crackling light against the dark, and the gods grinning and licking their chops in the hills. Afterward the calm, the rain steadily rustling in the calm lake, the return of light and hope and spirits, and the campers running out in joy and relief to go swimming in the rain, their bright cries perpetuating the deathless joke about how they were getting simply drenched, and the children screaming with delight at the new sensation of bathing in the rain, and the joke about getting drenched linking the generations in a strong indestructible chain. And the comedian who waded in carrying an umbrella.

When the others went swimming, my son said he was going in, 13
too. He pulled his dripping trunks from the line where they had hung all through the shower and wrung them out. Languidly, and with no thought of going in, I watched him, his hard little body, skinny and bare, saw him wince slightly as he pulled up around his vitals the small, soggy, icy garment. As he buckled the swollen belt, suddenly my groin felt the chill of death.

Virginia Woolf

THE DEATH OF THE MOTH

Virginia Woolf (1882–1941), the distinguished novelist, was the daughter of Leslie Stephen, a Victorian literary critic. She became the center of the "Bloomsbury Group" of writers and artists that flourished in London from about 1907 to 1930. Terrified by the return of her recurring mental depression, she drowned herself in the river Ouse near her home at Rodmell, England. *The Voyage Out* (1915), *Mrs. Dalloway* (1925), *To the Lighthouse* (1927), *Orlando* (1928), and *The Waves* (1931) are among the works with which she helped to alter the course of the English novel. Today she is recognized as a psychological novelist especially gifted at exploring the minds of her female characters. "The Death of the Moth" is the title essay of a collection published soon after her suicide; it describes "a tiny bead of pure life."

Moths that fly by day are not properly to be called moths; they do not excite that pleasant sense of dark autumn nights and ivy-blossom which the commonest yellow underwing asleep in the shadow of the curtain never fails to rouse in us. They are hybrid creatures, neither gay like butterflies nor sombre like their own species. Nevertheless the present specimen, with his narrow hay-coloured wings, fringed with a tassel of the same colour, seemed to be content with life. It was a pleasant morning, mid-September, mild, benignant, yet with a keener breath than that of the summer months. The plough was already scoring the field opposite the window, and where the share had been, the earth was pressed flat and gleamed with moisture. Such vigour came rolling in from the fields and the down beyond that it was difficult to keep the eyes strictly turned upon the book. The rooks too were keeping one of their annual 1 festivities; soaring round the tree-tops until it looked as if a vast net with thousands of black knots in it has been cast up into the air; which, after a few moments sank slowly down upon the trees until every twig seemed to have a knot at the end of it. Then, suddenly, the net would be thrown into the air again in a wider circle this time, with the utmost clamour and vociferation, as though to be thrown into the air and settle slowly down upon the tree-tops were a tremendously exciting experience.

The same energy which inspired the rooks, the ploughmen, the 2
horses, and even, it seemed, the lean bare-backed downs, sent the moth fluttering from side to side of his square of the window-pane. One could not help watching him. One was, indeed, conscious of a queer feeling of pity for him. The possibilities of pleasure seemed that morning so enormous and so various that to have only a moth's part in life, and a day moth's at that, appeared a hard fate, and his zest in enjoying his meagre opportunities to the full, pathetic. He flew vigorously to one corner of his compartment, and, after waiting there a second, flew across to the other. What remained for him but to fly to a third corner and then to a fourth? That was all he could do, in spite of the size of the downs, the width of the sky, the far-off smoke of houses, and the romantic voice, now and then, of a steamer out at sea. What he could do he did. Watching him, it seemed as if a fiber, very thin but pure, of the enormous energy of the world had been thrust into his frail and diminutive body. As often as he crossed the pane, I could fancy that a thread of vital light became visible. He was little or nothing but life.

Yet, because he was so small, and so simple a form of the energy 3
that was rolling in at the open window and driving its way through so many narrow and intricate corridors in my own brain and in those of other human beings, there was something marvelous as well as pathetic about him. It was as if someone had taken a tiny bead of pure life and decking it as lightly as possible with down and feathers, had set it dancing and zigzagging to show us the true nature of life. Thus displayed one could not get over the strangeness of it. One is apt to forget all about life, seeing it humped and bossed and garnished and cumbered so that it has to move with the greatest circumspection and dignity. Again, the thought of all that life might have been had he been born in any other shape caused one to view his simple activities with a kind of pity.

After a time, tired by his dancing apparently, he settled on the window ledge in the sun, and the queer spectacle being at an end, I forgot about him. Then, looking up, my eye was caught by him. He was trying to resume his dancing, but seemed either so stiff or so awkward that he could only flutter to the bottom of the window-pane; and when he tried to fly across it he failed. Being intent on other matters I watched these futile attempts for a time without thinking, unconsciously waiting for him to resume his flight, as one waits for a machine, that has stopped momentarily, to start again without considering the reason for its failure. After perhaps a seventh attempt he slipped from the wooden ledge and fell, fluttering his wings, on to his back on the window-sill. The helplessness of his attitude roused me. It flashed upon me that he was in difficulties; he could no longer raise himself; his legs struggled vainly. But, as I stretched out a pencil, meaning to help him to right himself, it came over me that the failure and awkwardness were the approach of death. I laid the pencil down again. 4

The legs agitated themselves once more. I looked as if for the enemy against which he struggled. I looked out of doors. What had happened there? Presumably it was midday, and work in the fields had stopped. Stillness and quiet had replaced the previous animation. The birds had taken themselves off to feed in the brooks. The horses stood still. Yet the power was there all the same, massed outside indifferent, impersonal, not attending to anything in particular. Somehow it was opposed to the little hay-coloured moth. It was useless to try to do anything. One could only watch the extraordinary efforts made by those tiny legs against an oncoming doom which could, had it chosen, have submerged an entire city, not merely a city, but masses of human beings; nothing, I knew, had any chance against death. Nevertheless after a pause of exhaustion the legs fluttered again. It was superb this last protest, and so frantic that he succeeded at last in righting himself. One's sympathies, of course, were all on the side of life. Also, when there was nobody to care or to know, this gigantic effort on the part of an insignificant little moth, against a power of such magnitude, to retain what no one else valued or desired to keep, moved one strangely. Again, somehow, one saw life, a pure bead. I lifted the pencil again, useless though I knew it to be. But even as I did so, the unmistakable tokens of death showed themselves. The body relaxed, and instantly grew stiff. The struggle was over. The insignificant little creature now knew death. As I 5 looked at the dead moth, this minute wayside triumph of so great a force over so mean an antagonist filled me with wonder. Just as life had been strange a few minutes before, so death was now as strange. The moth having righted himself now lay most decently and uncomplainingly composed. O yes, he seemed to say, death is stronger than I am.

Joan Didion

On Keeping a Notebook

Novelist Joan Didion, author of *Play It As It Lays* (1970), *A Book of Common Prayer* (1977), *Democracy* (1984), *Miami* (1987), *After Henry* (1992), and *The Last Thing He Wanted* (1996), is one of America's leading essayists. In *Slouching Towards Bethlehem* (1968) and *The White Album* (1979), Didion probes our national life from the American family to the American freeway, recording its impressions upon her own jangled nerves. Didion is a native of California—she was born in Sacramento in 1934 and attended the University of California at Berkeley. "On Keeping a Notebook" first appeared in *Slouching Towards Bethlehem.*

" 'That woman Estelle,' " the note reads, " 'is partly the reason why George Sharp and I are separated today.' *Dirty crepe-de-Chine wrapper, hotel bar, Wilmington RR, 9:45 a.m. August Monday morning.*" 1

Since the note is in my notebook, it presumably has some meaning to me. I study it for a long while. At first I have only the most general notion of what I was doing on an August Monday morning in the bar of the hotel across from the Pennsylvania Railroad station in Wilmington, Delaware (waiting for a train? missing one? 1960? 1961? why Wilmington?), but I do remember being there. The woman in the dirty crepe-de-Chine wrapper had come down from her room for a beer, and the bartender had heard before the reason why George Sharp and she were separated today. "Sure," he said, and went on mopping the floor. "You told me." At the other end of the bar is a girl. She is talking, pointedly, not to the man beside her but to a cat lying in the triangle of sunlight cast through the open door. She is wearing a plaid silk dress from Peck & Peck, and the hem is coming down. 2

Here is what it is: the girl has been on the Eastern Shore, and now 3 she is going back to the city, leaving the man beside her, and all she can see ahead are the viscous summer sidewalks and the 3 a.m. long-distance calls that will make her lie awake and then sleep drugged through all the steaming mornings left in August (1960? 1961?). Because she must go directly from the train to lunch in New York, she wishes that she had a safety pin for the hem of the plaid silk dress, and she also wishes that she could forget about the hem and the lunch and stay in the cool bar that smells of disinfectant and malt and make friends with the woman in the crepe-de-Chine wrapper. She is afflicted by a little self-pity, and she wants to compare Estelles. That is what that was all about.

Why did I write it down? In order to remember, of course, but exactly what was it I wanted to remember? How much of it actually happened? Did any of it? Why do I keep a notebook at all? It is easy to deceive oneself on all those scores. The impulse to write things down is a peculiarly compulsive one, inexplicable to those who do not share it, useful only accidentally, only secondarily, in the way that any compulsion tries to justify itself. I suppose that it begins or does not begin in the cradle. Although I have felt compelled to write things down since I was five years old, I doubt that my daughter ever will, for she is a singularly blessed and accepting child, delighted with life exactly as life presents itself to her, unafraid to go to sleep and unafraid to wake up. Keepers of private notebooks are a different breed altogether, lonely and resistant rearrangers of things, anxious malcontents, children afflicted apparently at birth with some presentiment of loss. 4

My first notebook was a Big Five tablet, given to me by my mother with the sensible suggestion that I stop whining and learn to amuse myself by writing down my thoughts. She returned the tablet to me a few years ago; the first entry is an account of a woman who believed herself to be freezing to death in the Arctic night, only to find, when day broke, that she had stumbled onto the Sahara Desert, where she would die of the heat before lunch. I have no idea what turn of a five-year-old's mind could have prompted so insistently "ironic" and exotic a story, but it does reveal a certain predilection for the extreme which has dogged me into adult life; perhaps if I were analytically inclined I would find it a truer story than any I might have told about Donald Johnson's birthday party or the day my cousin Brenda put Kitty Litter in the aquarium. 5

So the point of my keeping a notebook has never been, nor is it now, to have an accurate factual record of what I have been doing or thinking. That would be a different impulse entirely, an instinct for reality which I sometimes envy but do not possess. At no point have I ever been able successfully to keep a diary; my approach to daily life ranges from the grossly negligent to the merely absent, and on those few occasions when I have tried dutifully to record a day's events, boredom has so overcome me that the results are mysterious at best. What is this business about "shopping, typing piece, dinner with E, depressed"? Shopping for what? Typing what piece? Who is E? Was this "E" depressed, or was I depressed? Who cares? 6

In fact I have abandoned altogether that kind of pointless entry; instead I tell what some would call lies. "That's simply not true," the members of my family frequently tell me when they come up against my memory of a shared event. "The party was not for you, the spider was *not* a black widow, *it wasn't that way at all.*" Very likely they are right, for not only have I always had trouble distinguishing between what happened and what merely might have happened, but I remain unconvinced that the distinction, for my purposes, matters. The cracked crab that I recall having for lunch the day my father came home from Detroit in 1945 must certainly be embroidery, worked into the day's pattern to lend verisimilitude; I was ten years old and would not now remember the cracked crab. The day's events did not turn on cracked crab. And yet it is precisely that fictitious crab that makes me see the afternoon all over again, a home movie run all too often, the father bearing gifts, the child weeping, an exercise in family love and guilt. Or that is what it was to me. Similarly, perhaps it never did snow that August in Vermont; perhaps there never were flurries in the night wind, and maybe no one else felt the ground hardening and summer already dead even as we pretended to bask in it, but that was how it felt to me, and it might as well have snowed, could have snowed, did snow. 7

How it felt to me: that is getting closer to the truth about a notebook. I sometimes delude myself about why I keep a notebook, imagine that some thrifty virtue derives from preserving everything observed. See enough and write it down, I tell myself, and then some morning when the world seems drained of wonder, some day when I am only going through the motions of doing what I am supposed to do, which is write—on that bankrupt morning I will simply open my notebook and there it will all be, a forgotten account with accu- 8 mulated interest, paid passage back to the world out there: dialogue overheard in hotels and elevators and at the hatcheck counter in Pavillon (one middle-aged man shows his hat check to another and says, "That's my old football number"); impressions of Bettina Aptheker and Benjamin Sonnenberg and Teddy ("Mr. Acapulco") Stauffer; careful *aperçus* about tennis bums and failed fashion models and Greek shipping heiresses, one of whom taught me a significant lesson (a lesson I could have learned from F. Scott Fitzgerald, but perhaps we all must meet the very rich for ourselves) by asking, when I arrived to interview her in her orchid-filled sitting room on the second day of a paralyzing New York blizzard, whether it was snowing outside.

I imagine, in other words, that the notebook is about other peo- 9
ple. But of course it is not. I have no real business with what one stranger said to another at the hat-check counter in Pavillon; in fact I suspect that the line "That's my old football number" touched not my own imagination at all, but merely some memory of something once read, probably "The Eighty-Yard Run." Nor is my concern with a woman in a dirty crepe-de-Chine wrapper in a Wilmington bar. My stake is always, of course, in the unmentioned girl in the plaid silk dress. *Remember what it was to be me:* that is always the point.

It is a difficult point to admit. We are brought up in the ethic that 10
others, any others, all others, are by definition more interesting than ourselves; taught to be diffident, just this side of self-effacing. ("You're the least important person in the room and don't forget it," Jessica Mitford's governess would hiss in her ear on the advent of any social occasion; I copied that into my notebook because it is only recently that I have been able to enter a room without hearing some such phrase in my inner ear.) Only the very young and the very old may recount their dreams at breakfast, dwell upon self, interrupt with memories of beach picnics and favorite Liberty lawn dresses and the rainbow trout in a creek near Colorado Springs. The rest of us are expected, rightly, to affect absorption in other people's favorite dresses, other people's trout.

And so we do. But our notebooks give us away, for however duti- 11
fully we record what we see around us, the common denominator of all we see is always, transparently, shamelessly, the implacable "I." We are not talking here about the kind of notebook that is patently for public consumption, a structural conceit for binding together a

series of graceful *pensées;*[1] we are talking about something private, about bits of the mind's string too short to use, an indiscriminate and erratic assemblage with meaning only for its maker.

And sometimes even the maker has difficulty with the meaning. There does not seem to be, for example, any point in my knowing for the rest of my life that, during 1964, 720 tons of soot fell on every square mile of New York City, yet there it is in my notebook, labeled "FACT." Nor do I really need to remember that Ambrose Bierce liked to spell Leland Stanford's[2] name "£eland $tanford" or that "smart women almost always wear black in Cuba," a fashion hint without much potential for practical application. And does not the relevance of these notes seem marginal at best?: 12

In the basement museum of the Inyo County Courthouse in Independence, California, sign pinned to a mandarin coat: "This MANDARIN COAT was often worn by Mrs. Minnie S. Brooks when giving lectures on her TEAPOT COLLECTION."

Redhead getting out of car in front of Beverly Wilshire Hotel, chinchilla stole, Vuitton bags with tags reading:

MRS LOU FOX
HOTEL SAHARA
VEGAS

Well, perhaps not entirely marginal. As a matter of fact, Mrs. Minnie S. Brooks and her MANDARIN COAT pull me back into my own childhood, for although I never knew Mrs. Brooks and did not visit Inyo County until I was thirty, I grew up in just such a world, in houses cluttered with Indian relics and bits of gold ore and ambergris and the souvenirs my Aunt Mercy Farnsworth brought back from the Orient. It is a long way from that world to Mrs. Lou Fox's world, where we all live now, and is it not just as well to remember that? Might not Mrs. Minnie S. Brooks help me to remember what I am? Might not Mrs. Lou Fox help me to remember what I am not? 13

But sometimes the point is harder to discern. What exactly did I have in mind when I noted down that it cost the father of someone I know $650 a month to light the place on the Hudson in which he 14

[1] Thoughts, reflections.

[2] A nineteenth-century American millionaire.

lived before the Crash?[3] What use was I planning to make of this line by Jimmy Hoffa: "I may have my faults, but being wrong ain't one of them"? And although I think it interesting to know where the girls who travel with the Syndicate have their hair done when they find themselves on the West Coast, will I ever make suitable use of it? Might I not be better off just passing it on to John O'Hara? What is a recipe for sauerkraut doing in my notebook? What kind of magpie keeps this notebook? *"He was born the night the Titanic went down."* That seems a nice enough line, and I even recall who said it, but is it not really a better line in life than it could ever be in fiction?

15 But of course that is exactly it: not that I should ever use the line, but that I should remember the woman who said it and the afternoon I heard it. We were on her terrace by the sea, and we were finishing the wine left from lunch, trying to get what sun there was, a California winter sun. The woman whose husband was born the night the *Titanic* went down wanted to rent her house, wanted to go back to her children in Paris. I remember wishing that I could afford the house, which cost $1,000 a month. "Someday you will," she said lazily. "Someday it all comes." There in the sun on her terrace it seemed easy to believe in someday, but later I had a low-grade afternoon hangover and ran over a black snake on the way to the supermarket and was flooded with inexplicable fear when I heard the checkout clerk explaining to the man ahead of me why she was finally divorcing her husband. "He left me no choice," she said over and over as she punched the register. "He has a little seven-month-old baby by her, he left me no choice." I would like to believe that my dread then was for the human condition, but of course it was for me, because I wanted a baby and did not then have one and because I wanted to own the house that cost $1,000 a month to rent and because I had a hangover.

16 It all comes back. Perhaps it is difficult to see the value in having one's self back in that kind of mood, but I do see it; I think we are well advised to keep on nodding terms with the people we used to be whether we find them attractive company or not. Otherwise they turn up unannounced and surprise us, come hammering on the mind's door at 4 a.m. of a bad night and demand to know who deserted them, who betrayed them, who is going to make amends. We forget all too soon the things we thought we could never forget.

[3] The stock market crash of 1929.

We forget the loves and the betrayals alike, forget what we whispered and what we screamed, forget who we were. I have already lost touch with a couple of people I used to be; one of them, a seventeen-year-old, presents little threat, although it would be of some interest to me to know again what it feels like to sit on a river levee drinking vodka-and-orange-juice and listening to Les Paul and Mary Ford and their echoes sing "How High the Moon" on the car radio. (You see I still have the scenes, but I no longer perceive myself among those present, no longer could even improvise the dialogue.) The other one, a twenty-three-year-old, bothers me more. She was always a good deal of trouble, and I suspect she will reappear when I least want to see her, skirts too long, shy to the point of aggravation, always the injured party, full of recriminations and little hurts and stories I do not want to hear again, at once saddening me and angering me with her vulnerability and ignorance, an apparition all the more insistent for being so long banished.

It is a good idea, then, to keep in touch, and I suppose that keeping in touch is what notebooks are all about. And we are all on our own when it comes to keeping those lines open to ourselves: your notebook will never help me, nor mine you. *"So what's new in the whiskey business?"* What could that possibly mean to you? To me it means a blonde in a Pucci bathing suit sitting with a couple of fat men by the pool at the Beverly Hills Hotel. Another man approaches, and they all regard one another in silence for a while. "So what's new in the whiskey business?" one of the fat men finally says by way of welcome, and the blonde stands up, arches one foot and dips it in the pool, looking all the while at the cabaña where Baby Pignatari is talking on the telephone. That is all there is to that, except that several years later I saw the blonde coming out of Saks Fifth Avenue in New York with her California complexion and a voluminous mink coat. In the harsh wind that day she looked old and irrevocably tired to me, and even the skins in the mink coat were not worked the way they were doing them that year, not the way she would have wanted them done, and there is the point of the story. For a while after that I did not like to look in the mirror, and my eyes would skim the newspapers and pick out only the deaths, the cancer victims, the premature coronaries, the suicides, and I stopped riding the Lexington Avenue IRT[4] because I noticed for the first time that all the 17

[4] A New York City subway line; one of its stops is the Grand Central railway terminal.

strangers I had seen for years—the man with the seeing-eye dog, the spinster who read the classified pages every day, the fat girl who always got off with me at Grand Central—looked older than they once had.

It all comes back. Even that recipe for sauerkraut: even that brings it back. I was on Fire Island when I first made that sauerkraut, and it was raining, and we drank a lot of bourbon and ate the sauerkraut and went to bed at ten, and I listened to the rain and the Atlantic and felt safe. I made the sauerkraut again last night and it did not make me feel any safer, but that is, as they say, another story. 18

Louise Erdrich

Skunk Dreams

A poet and novelist, author of *The Beet Queen* (1986), *The Bingo Palace* (1994), *The Blue Jay's Dance* (1995), and *Tales of Burning Love* (1996), Louise Erdrich, who is part Chippewa, grew up in Wahpeton, North Dakota, near a Sioux reservation. "Skunk Dreams," originally published in the *Georgia Review,* begins with her adventures as a fourteen-year-old camper and veers off into the realm of dream landscapes and out-of-self experience.

When I was fourteen, I slept alone on a North Dakota football field under the cold stars on an early spring night. May is unpredictable in the Red River Valley, and I happened to hit a night when frost formed in the grass. A skunk trailed a plume of steam across the forty-yard line near moonrise. I tucked the top of my sleeping bag over my head and was just dozing off when the skunk walked onto me with simple authority. 1

Its ripe odor must have dissipated in the frozen earth of its winter-long hibernation, because it didn't smell all that bad, or perhaps it was just that I took shallow breaths in numb surprise. I felt him—her, whatever—pause on the side of my hip and turn around twice before evidently deciding I was a good place to sleep. At the back of my knees, on the quilting of my sleeping bag, it trod out a spot for itself and then, with a serene little groan, curled up and lay perfectly still. That made two of us. I was wildly awake, trying to forget the sharpness and number of skunk teeth, trying not to think of the high percentage of skunks with rabies, or the reason that on camping trips my father always kept a hatchet underneath his pillow. 2

Inside the bag, I felt as if I might smother. Carefully, making only the slightest of rustles, I drew the bag away from my face and took a deep breath of the night air, enriched with skunk, but clear and 3 watery and cold. It wasn't so bad, and the skunk didn't stir at all, so I watched the moon—caught that night in an envelope of silk, a mist—pass over my sleeping field of teenage guts and glory. The grass in spring that has lain beneath the snow harbors a sere dust both old and fresh. I smelled that newness beneath the rank tone of my bag-mate—the stiff fragrance of damp earth and the thick pungency of newly manured fields a mile or two away—along with my sleeping bag's smell, slightly mildewed, forever smoky. The skunk settled even closer and began to breathe rapidly; its feet jerked a little like a dog's. I sank against the earth, and fell asleep too.

Of what easily tipped cans, what molten sludge, what dogs in yards on chains, what leftover macaroni casseroles, what cellar holes, crawl spaces, burrows taken from meek woodchucks, of what miracles of garbage did my skunk dream? Or did it, since we can't be sure, dream the plot of *Moby-Dick,* how to properly age parmesan, or how to restore the brick-walled, tumbledown creamery that was its home? We don't know about the dreams of any other biota, and even much about our own. If dreams are an actual dimension, as some assert, then the usual rules of life by which we abide do not apply. In that place, skunks may certainly dream themselves into the vests of stockbrokers. Perhaps that night the skunk and I dreamed each other's thoughts or are still dreaming them. To paraphrase the problem of the Chinese sage, I may be a woman who has dreamed herself a skunk, or a skunk still dreaming that she is a woman. 4

In a book called *Death and Consciousness,* David H. Lund—who wants very much to believe in life after death—describes human dream-life as a possible model for a disembodied existence: 5

> Many of one's dreams are such that they involve the activities of an apparently embodied person whom one takes to be oneself as long as one dreams. . . . Whatever is the source of the imagery . . . apparently has the capacity to bring about images of a human body and to impart the feeling that the body is mine. It is, of course, just an image body, but it serves as a perfectly good body for the dream experience. I regard it as mine, I act on the dream environment by means of it, and it constitutes the center of the perceptual world of my dream.

Over the years I have acquired and reshuffled my beliefs and doubts about whether we live on after death—in any shape or form, that is, besides the molecular level at which I am to be absorbed by 6 the taproots of cemetery elms or pines and the tangled mats of fearfully poisoned, too-green lawn grass. I want something of the self on whom I have worked so hard to survive the loss of the body (which, incidentally, the self has done a fairly decent job of looking after, excepting spells of too much cabernet and a few idiotic years of rolling my own cigarettes out of Virginia Blond tobacco). I am put out with the marvelous discoveries of the intricate biochemical configuration of our brains, though I realize that the processes themselves are quite miraculous. I understand that I should be self-proud, content to gee-whiz at the fact that I am the world's only mechanism that can admire itself. I should be grateful that life is here today, though gone tomorrow, but I can't help it. I want more.

Skunks don't mind each other's vile perfume. Obviously, they find each other more than tolerable. And even I, who have been in the presence of a direct skunk hit, wouldn't classify their weapon as mere smell. It is more on the order of a reality-enhancing experience. It's not so pleasant as standing in a grove of old-growth red cedars, or on a lyrical moonshed plain, or watching trout rise to the shadow of your hand on the placid surface of an Alpine lake. When the skunk lets go, you're surrounded by skunk presence: inhabited, owned, involved with something you can only describe as powerfully *there*. 7

I woke at dawn, stunned into that sprayed state of being. The dog that had approached me was rolling in the grass, half-addled, sprayed too. The skunk was gone. I abandoned my sleeping bag and started home. Up Eighth Street, past the tiny blue and pink houses, past my grade school, past all the addresses where I had baby-sat, I walked in my own strange wind. The streets were wide and empty; I met no one—not a dog, not a squirrel, not even an early robin. Perhaps they had all scattered before me, blocks away. I had gone out to sleep on the football field because I was afflicted with a sadness I had to dramatize. Mood swings had begun, hormones, feverish and brutal. They were nothing to me now. My emotions had seemed vast, dark, and sickeningly private. But they were minor, mere wisps, compared to skunk. 8

I have found that my best dreams come to me in cheap motels. One such dream about an especially haunting place occurred in a rattling room in Valley City, North Dakota. There, in the home of the 9

Winter Show, in the old Rudolph Hotel, I was to spend a weeklong residency as a poet-in-the-schools. I was supporting myself, at the time, by teaching poetry to children, convicts, rehabilitation patients, high-school hoods, and recovering alcoholics. What a marvelous job it was, and what opportunities I had to dream, since I paid my own lodging and lived low, sometimes taking rooms for less than ten dollars a night in motels that had already been closed by local health departments.

The images that assailed me in Valley City came about because the bedspread was so thin and worn—a mere brown tissuey curtain—that I had to sleep beneath my faux fur Salvation Army coat, wearing all of my clothing, even a scarf. Cold often brings on the most spectacular of my dreams, as if my brain has been incited to fevered activity. On that particular frigid night, the cold somehow seemed to snap boundaries, shift my time continuum, and perhaps even allow me to visit my own life in a future moment. After waking once, transferring the contents of my entire suitcase onto my person, and shivering to sleep again, I dreamed of a vast, dark, fenced place. The fencing was chain-link in places, chicken wire, sagging X wire, barbed wire on top, jerry-built with tipped-out poles and uncertain corners nailed to log posts and growing trees. And yet it was quite impermeable and solid, as time-tested, broken-looking things so often are. 10

Behind it, trees ran for miles—large trees, grown trees, big pines the likes of which do not exist on the Great Plains. In my dream I walked up to the fence, looked within, and saw tawny, humpbacked elk move among the great trunks and slashing green arms. Suave, imponderable, magnificently dumb, they lurched and floated through the dim-complexioned air. One turned, however, before they all vanished, and from either side of that flimsy-looking barrier there passed between us a look, a communion, a long and measureless regard that left me, on waking, with a sensation of penetrating sorrow. 11

I didn't think about my dream for many years, until after I moved to New Hampshire. I had become urbanized and sedentary since the days when I slept with skunks, and I had turned inward. For several years I spent my days leaning above a strange desk, a green door on stilts, which was so high that to sit at it I bought a barstool upholstered in brown leatherette. Besides, the entire Northeast seemed like 12 the inside of a house to me, the sky small and oddly lit, as if by an electric bulb. The sun did not pop over the great trees for hours—and then went down so soon. I was suspicious of Eastern land: the undramatic loveliness, the small scale, the lack of sky to watch, the way the weather sneaked up without enough warning.

The woods themselves seemed bogus at first—every inch of the ground turned over more than once, and even in the second growth of old pines so much human evidence. Rock walls ran everywhere, grown through and tumbled, as if the dead still had claims they imposed. The unkillable and fiercely contorted trees of old orchards, those revenants, spooked me when I walked in the woods. The blasted limbs spread a white lace cold as fire in the spring, and the odor of the blossoms was furiously spectral, sweet. When I stood beneath the canopies that hummed and shook with bees, I heard voices, other voices, and I did not understand what they were saying, where they had come from, what drove them into this earth. 13

Then, as often happens to sparring adversaries in 1940s movies, I fell in love. 14

After a few years of living in the country, the impulse to simply *get outside* hit me, strengthened, and became again a habit of thought, a reason for storytelling, an uneasy impatience with walls and roads. At first, when I had that urge, I had to get into a car and drive fifteen hundred miles before I was back in a place that I defined as *out*. The West, or the edge of it anyway, the great level patchwork of chemically treated fields and tortured grazing land, was the outside I had internalized. In the rich Red River Valley, where the valuable cropland is practically measured in inches, environmental areas are defined and proudly pointed out as stretches of roadway where the ditches are not mowed. Deer and pheasants survive in shelter belts—rows of Russian olive, plum, sometimes evergreen—planted at the edges of fields. The former tall-grass prairie has now become a collection of mechanized gardens tended by an array of air-conditioned farm implements and bearing an increasing amount of pesticide and herbicide in each black teaspoon of dirt. Nevertheless, no amount of reality changed the fact that I still *thought* of eastern North Dakota as wild. 15

In time, though, *out* became outside my door in New England. By walking across the road and sitting in my little writing house—a place surrounded by trees, thick plumes of grass, jets of ferns, and 16 banks of touch-me-not—or just by looking out a screen door or window, I started to notice what there was to see. In time, the smothering woods that had always seemed part of northeastern civilization—more an inside than an outside, more like a friendly garden—revealed themselves as forceful and complex. The growth of plants, the lush celebratory springs made a grasslands person drunk. The world turned dazzling green, the hills rode like comfortable and flowing animals. Everywhere there was the sound of water moving.

And yet, even though I finally grew closer to these woods, on 17
some days I still wanted to tear them from before my eyes.

I wanted to *see*. Where I grew up, our house looked out on the 18
western horizon. I could see horizon when I played. I could see it when I walked to school. It was always there, a line beyond everything, a simple line of changing shades and colors that ringed the town, a vast place. That was it. Down at the end of every grid of streets: vastness. Out the windows of the high school: vastness. From the drive-in theater where I went parking in a purple Duster: vast distance. That is why, on lovely New England days when everything should have been all right—a fall day, for instance, when the earth had risen through the air in patches and the sky lowered, dim and warm—I fell sick with longing for the horizon. I wanted the clean line, the simple line, the clouds marching over it in feathered masses. I suffered from horizon sickness. But it sounds crazy for a grown woman to throw herself at the sky, and the thing is, I wanted to get well. And so to compensate for horizon sickness, for the great longing that seemed both romantically German and pragmatically Chippewa in origin, I found solace in trees.

Trees are a changing landscape of sound—and the sound I grew 19
attached to, possible only near large deciduous forests, was the great hushed roar of thousands and millions of leaves brushing and touching one another. Windy days were like sitting just out of sight of an ocean, the great magnetic ocean of wind. All around me, I watched the trees tossing, their heads bending. At times the movement seemed passionate, as though they were flung together in an eager embrace, caressing each other, branch to branch. If there is a vegetative soul, an animating power that all things share, there must be great rejoicing out there on windy days, ecstasy, for trees move so slowly on calm days. At least it seems that way to us. On days of high wind they move so freely it must give them a cellular pleasure close to terror.

Unused to walking in the woods, I did not realize that trees dropped branches—often large ones—or that there was any possible danger in going out on windy days, drawn by the natural drama. There was a white pine I loved, a tree of the size foresters call *overgrown,* a waste, a thing made of long-since harvestable material. The tree was so big that three people couldn't reach around it. Standing at the bottom, craning back, fingers clenched in grooves of bark, I held on as the crown of the tree roared and beat the air a hundred feet above. The movement was frantic, the soft-needled branches long and supple. I thought of a woman tossing, anchored in passion: calm one instant, full-throated the next, hair vast and dark, shedding the piercing, fresh oil of broken needles. I went to visit her often, and walked onward, farther, though it was not so far at all, and then one day I reached the fence. 20

Chain-link in places, chicken wire, sagging X wire, barbed wire on top, jerry-built with tipped-out poles and uncertain corners nailed to log posts and growing trees, still it seemed impermeable and solid. Behind it, there were trees for miles: large trees, grown trees, big pines. I walked up to the fence, looked within, and could see elk moving. Suave, imponderable, magnificently dumb, they lurched and floated through the dim air. 21

I was on the edge of a game park, a rich man's huge wilderness, probably the largest parcel of protected land in western New Hampshire, certainly the largest privately owned piece I knew about. At forty square miles—25,000 acres—it was bigger than my mother's home reservation. And it had the oddest fence around it that I'd ever seen, the longest and the tackiest. Though partially electrified, the side closest to our house was so piddling that an elk could easily have tossed it apart. Certainly a half-ton wild boar, the condensed and living version of a tank, could have strolled right through. But then animals, much like most humans, don't charge through fences unless they have sound reasons. As I soon found out, because I naturally grew fascinated with the place, there were many more animals trying to get into the park than out, and they couldn't have cared less about ending up in a hunter's stew pot. 22

These were not wild animals, the elk—since they were grained at feeding stations, how could they be? They were not domesticated either, however, for beyond the no-hunt boundaries they fled and vanished. They were game. Since there is no sport in shooting feedlot 23 steers, these animals—still harboring wild traits and therefore more challenging to kill—were maintained to provide blood pleasure for the members of the Blue Mountain Forest Association.

As I walked away from the fence that day, I was of two minds about the place—and I am still. Shooting animals inside fences, no matter how big the area they have to hide in, seems abominable and silly. And yet, I was glad for that wilderness. Though secretly managed and off limits to me, it was the source of flocks of evening grosbeaks and pine siskins, of wild turkey, ravens, and grouse, of Eastern coyote, oxygen-rich air, foxes, goldfinches, skunk, and bears that tunneled in and out. 24

I had dreamed of this place in Valley City, or it had dreamed me. There was affinity here, beyond any explanation I could offer, so I didn't try. I continued to visit the tracts of big trees, and on deep nights—windy nights, especially when it stormed—I liked to fall asleep imagining details. I saw the great crowns touching, heard the raving sound of wind and thriving, knocking cries as the blackest of ravens flung themselves across acres upon indifferent acres of tossing, old-growth pine. I could fall asleep picturing how, below that dark air, taproots thrust into a deeper blankness, drinking the powerful rain. 25

Or was it so only in my dreams? The park, known locally as Corbin's Park, after its founder, Austin Corbin, is knit together of land and farmsteads he bought in the late nineteenth century from 275 individuals. Among the first animals released there, before the place became a hunting club, were thirty buffalo, remnants of the vast Western herds. Their presence piqued the interest of Ernest Harold Bayne, a conservation-minded local journalist, who attempted to break a pair of buffalo calves to the yoke. He exhibited them at county fairs and even knit mittens out of buffalo wool, hoping to convince the skeptical of their usefulness. His work inspired sympathy, if not a trend for buffalo yarn, and collective zeal for the salvation of the buffalo grew until by 1915 the American Bison Society, of which Bayne was secretary, helped form government reserves that eventually more than doubled the herds that remained. 26

The buffalo dream seems to have been the park's most noble hour. Since that time it has been the haunt of wealthy hunting enthusiasts. 27

The owner of Ruger Arms currently inhabits the stunning, butter-yellow original Corbin mansion and would like to buy the whole park for his exclusive use, or so local gossip has it.

For some months I walked the boundary admiring the tangled landscape, at least all that I could see. After my first apprehension, I ignored the fence. I walked along it as if it simply did not exist, as if I really were part of that place which lay just beyond my reach. The British psychotherapist Adam Phillips has examined obstacles from several different angles, attempting to define their emotional use. "It is impossible to imagine desire without obstacles," he writes, "and wherever we find something to be an obstacle we are at the same time desiring something. It is part of the fascination of the Oedipus story in particular, and perhaps narrative in general, that we and the heroes and heroines of our fictions never know whether obstacles create desire or desire creates obstacles." He goes on to characterize the Unconscious, our dream world, as a place without obstacles: "A good question to ask of a dream is: What are the obstacles that have been removed to make this extraordinary scene possible?" 28

My dream, however, was about obstacles still in place. The fence was the main component, the defining characteristic of the forbidden territory that I watched but could not enter or experience. The obstacles that we overcome define us. We are composed of hurdles we set up to pace our headlong needs, to control our desires, or against which to measure our growth. "Without obstacles," Phillips writes, "the notion of development is inconceivable. There would be nothing to master." 29

Walking along the boundary of the park no longer satisfied me. The preciousness and deceptive stability of that fence began to rankle. Longing filled me. I wanted to brush against the old pine bark and pass beyond the ridge, to see specifically what was there: what Blue Mountain, what empty views, what lavender hillside, what old cellar holes, what unlikely animals. I was filled with poacher's lust, except I wanted only to smell the air. The linked web restraining me began to grate, and I started to look for weak spots, holes, places where the rough wire sagged. From the moment I began to see the fence as permeable, it became something to overcome. I returned time after time—partly to see if I could spot anyone on the other side, partly because I knew I must trespass. 30

Then, one clear, midwinter morning, in the middle of a half-hearted thaw, I walked along the fence until I came to a place that 31 looked shaky—and was. I went through. There were no trails that I could see, and I knew I needed to stay away from any perimeter roads or snowmobile paths, as well as from the feeding stations where the animals congregated. I wanted to see the animals, but only from a distance. Of course, as I walked on, leaving a trail easily backtracked, I encountered no animals at all. Still, the terrain was beautiful, the columns of pine tall and satisfyingly heavy, the patches of oak and elderly maple from an occasional farmstead knotted and patient. I was satisfied, and sometime in the early afternoon, I decided to turn back and head toward the fence again. Skirting a low, boggy area that teemed with wild turkey tracks, heading toward the edge of a deadfall of trashed dead branches and brush, I stared too hard into the sun, and stumbled.

In a half crouch, I looked straight into the face of a boar, massive 32
as a boulder. Cornfed, razor-tusked, alert, sensitive ears pricked, it edged slightly backward into the convening shadows. Two ice picks of light gleamed from its shrouded, tiny eyes, impossible to read. Beyond the rock of its shoulder, I saw more: a sow and three cinnamon-brown farrows crossing a small field of glare snow, lit by dazzling sun. The young skittered along, lumps of muscled fat on tiny hooves. They reminded me of snowsuited toddlers on new skates. When they were out of sight the boar melted through the brush after them, leaving not a snapped twig or crushed leaf in his wake.

I almost didn't breathe in the silence, letting the fact of that pres- 33
ence settle before I retraced my own tracks.

Since then, I've been to the game park via front gates, driven 34
down the avenues of tough old trees, and seen herds of wild pigs and elk meandering past the residence of the gamekeeper. A no-hunting zone exists around the house, where the animals are almost tame. But I've been told by privileged hunters that just beyond that invisible boundary they vanish, becoming suddenly and preternaturally elusive.

There is something in me that resists the notion of fair use of 35
this land if the only alternative is to have it cut up, sold off in lots, condominiumized. Yet the dumb fervor of the place depresses me—the wilderness locked up and managed but not for its sake; the animals imported and cultivated to give pleasure through their deaths. All animals, that is, except for skunks.

Not worth hunting, inedible except to old trappers like my uncle 36
Ben Gourneau, who boiled his skunk with onions in three changes

of water, skunks pass in and out of Corbin's Park without hindrance, without concern. They live off the corn in the feeding cribs (or the mice it draws), off the garbage of my rural neighbors, off bugs and frogs and grubs. They nudge their way onto our back porch for cat food, and even when disturbed they do not, ever, hurry. It's easy to get near a skunk, even to capture one. When skunks become a nuisance, people either shoot them or catch them in crates, cardboard boxes, Havahart traps, plastic garbage barrels.

Natives of the upper Connecticut River valley have neatly solved the problem of what to do with such catches. They hoist their trapped mustelid into the back of a pickup truck and cart the animal across the river to the neighboring state—New Hampshire to Vermont, Vermont to New Hampshire—before releasing it. The skunk population is estimated as about even on both sides. 37

We should take comfort from the skunk, an arrogant creature so pleased with its own devices that it never runs from harm, just turns its back in total confidence. If I were an animal, I'd choose to be a skunk: live fearlessly, eat anything, gestate my young in just two months, and fall into a state of dreaming torpor when the cold bit hard. Wherever I went, I'd leave my sloppy tracks. I wouldn't walk so much as putter, destinationless, in a serene belligerence—past hunters, past death overhead, past death all around. 38

Gordon Grice

Caught in the Widow's Web

A collector of spiders, Gordon Grice is the editor of *The Ogalala Review*, published in Guyman, Oklahoma. "Caught in the Widow's Web," reprinted here from *Harper's Magazine*, appeared in longer form in the Fall 1995 issue of *The High Plains Literary Review* under the title "The Black Widow."

I hunt black widows. When I find one, I capture it. I have found them in discarded wheels and tires and under railroad ties. I have found them in house foundations and cellars, in automotive shops and toolsheds, in water meters and rock gardens, against fences and in cinder-block walls. 1

Black widows have the ugliest webs of any spider, messy-looking tangles in the corners and bends of things and under logs and debris. Often the widow's web is littered with leaves. Beneath it lie the husks of consumed insects, their antennae stiff as gargoyle horns; on them and the surrounding ground are splashes of the spider's white urine, which looks like bird guano and smells of ammonia even at a distance of several feet. 2

This fetid material draws scavengers—ants, sow bugs, crickets, roaches, and so on—which become tangled in vertical strands of silk reaching from the ground up into the web. The widow climbs down and throws gummy silk onto this new prey. When the insect is seriously tangled but still struggling, the widow cautiously descends and bites it, usually on a leg joint. This is a killing bite; it pumps poison into the victim. As the creature dies, the widow delivers still more bites, injecting substances that liquefy the organs. Finally it settles down to suck the liquefied innards out of the prey, changing position two or three times to get it all. 3

Widows reportedly eat mice, toads, tarantulas—anything that 4 wanders into that remarkable web. I have never witnessed a widow performing a gustatory act of that magnitude, but I have seen them eat scarab beetles heavy as pecans, carabid beetles strong enough to prey on wolf spiders, cockroaches more than an inch long, and hundreds of other arthropods of various sizes.

Many widows will eat as much as opportunity allows. One aggressive female I raised had an abdomen a little bigger than a pea. She snared a huge cockroach and spent several hours subduing it, then three days consuming it. Her abdomen swelled to the size of a largish marble, its glossy black stretching to a tight red-brown. With a different widow, I decided to see whether that appetite really was insatiable. I collected dozens of large crickets and grasshoppers and began to drop them into her web at a rate of one every three or four hours. After catching and devouring her tenth victim, this bloated widow fell from her web, landing on her back. She remained in this position for hours, making only feeble attempts to move. Then she died. 5

The first thing people ask when they hear about my fascination with the widow is why I am not afraid. The truth is that my fascination is rooted in fear. 6

I have childhood memories that partly account for this. When I was six my mother took my sister and me into the cellar of our farmhouse and told us to watch as she killed a widow. With great ceremony she produced a long stick (I am tempted to say a ten-foot pole) and, narrating her technique in exactly the hushed voice she used for discussing religion or sex, went to work. Her flashlight beam found a point halfway up the cement wall where two marbles hung together—one a crisp white, the other a shiny black. My mother ran her stick through the dirty silver web around them. As it tore it sounded like the crackling of paper in fire. The black marble rose on thin legs to fight off the intruder. My mother smashed the widow onto the stick and carried it up into the light. It was still kicking its remaining legs. Mom scraped it against the floor, grinding it into a paste. Then she returned for the white marble—the widow's egg sac. This, too, came to an abrasive end. 7

My mother's stated purpose was to teach us how to recognize and deal with a dangerous creature that we would probably encounter on the farm. But, of course, we also took away the understanding that widows were actively malevolent, that they waited in dark places 8 to ambush us, that they were worthy of ritual disposition, like an enemy whose death is not sufficient but must be followed by the murder of his children and the salting of his land and whose unclean remains must not touch our hands.

The odd thing is that so *many* people, some of whom presumably 9
did not first encounter the widow in such an atmosphere of mystic reverence, hold the widow in awe. Various friends have told me that the widow's bite is always fatal to humans—in fact, it almost never is. I have heard told for truth that goods imported from the Orient are likely to be infested with widows and that women with bouffant hairdos have died of widow infestation. Any contradiction of such tales is received as if it were a proclamation of atheism.

We project our archetypal terrors onto the widow. It is black; it 10
avoids the light; it is a voracious carnivore. Its red markings suggest blood. The female's habit of eating her lovers invites a strangely sexual discomfort; the widow becomes an emblem for a man's fear of extending himself into the blood and darkness of a woman, something like the legendary Eskimo vampire that takes the form of a fanged vagina.

The widow's venom is, of course, a sound reason for fear. The 11
venom contains a neurotoxin that can produce sweats, vomiting, swelling, convulsions, and dozens of other symptoms. The variation in symptoms from one person to the next is remarkable. The constant is pain. A useful question for a doctor trying to diagnose an uncertain case: "Is this the worst pain you've ever felt?" A "yes" suggests a diagnosis of black widow bite. Occasionally people die from widow bites. The very young and the very old are especially vulnerable. Some people seem to die not from the venom but from the infection that may follow: because of its habitat, the widow carries dangerous microbes.

Researchers once hypothesized that the virulence of the venom 12
was necessary for killing beetles of the scarabaeidae family. This family contains thousands of species, including the June beetle and the famous dung beetle that the Egyptians thought immortal. All the scarabs have thick, strong bodies and unusually tough exoskeletons, and many of them are common prey for the widow. The tough hide was supposed to require a particularly nasty venom. As it turns out, the venom is thousands of times more virulent than necessary for this purpose.

No one has ever offered a sufficient explanation for the dangerous venom. It provides no evolutionary advantages: all of the widow's prey would find lesser toxins fatal, and there is no particular benefit in killing or harming larger animals. A widow that bites a human being or other large animal is likely to be killed. 13

Natural selection favors the inheritance of useful characteristics that arise from random mutation and tends to extinguish disadvantageous traits. All other characteristics, the ones that neither help nor hinder survival, are preserved or extinguished at random as mutation links them with useful or harmful traits. Many people—even many scientists—assume that every animal is elegantly engineered for its ecological niche, that every bit of an animal's anatomy and behavior has a functional explanation. This assumption is false. Evolution sometimes produces flowers of natural evil—traits that are neither functional nor vestigial but utterly pointless. 14

We want the world to be an ordered room, but in a corner of that room there hangs an untidy web. Here the analytical mind finds an irreducible mystery, a motiveless evil in nature; here the scientist's vision of evil comes to match the vision of a God-fearing country woman with a ten-foot pole. No idea of the cosmos as elegant design accounts for the widow. No idea of a benevolent God is comfortable in a world with the widow. She hangs in her web, that marvel of design, and defies reason. 15

A Letter from E. B. White

In a letter dated January 22, 1984, E. B. White responded as follows to questions from the editor about the composition of his "Once More to the Lake," an essay that has become a modern classic:

I'm not an expert on what goes on under my hood, but I'll try to answer your questions.

When I wrote "Once More to the Lake," I was living year round in this place on the coast of Maine and contributing a monthly department to Harper's. I had spent many summers as a boy on Great Pond—one of the Belgrade Lakes. It's only about 75 miles from here and one day I felt an urge to revisit the lake and have a week of freshwater life, which is very different from saltwater. So I went over with my small son and we did some fishing. I simply started with a desire to see again and experience again what I had seen and experienced as a boy. During our stay over there, the "idea of time" naturally insinuated itself into my thoughts, because my son was the age I had been in the previous life at the lake, and so I felt a sort of mixed-up identity. I don't recall whether I had the title from the start. Probably not. I don't believe the title had anything to do with the composing process. The "process" is probably every bit as mysterious to me as it is to some of your students—if that will make them feel any better. As for the revising I did, it was probably quite a lot. I always revise the hell out of everything. It's the only way I know how to write. I came up with the "chilling ending" simply because I was describing a bodily sensation of my own. When my son drew on his wet bathing trunks, it was as though I were drawing them on myself. I was old enough to feel the chill of death. I guess.

Sorry I can't be more explicit. Writing, for me, is simply a matter of trying to find out and report what's going on in my head and get it down on paper. I haven't any devices, shortcuts, or tricks.

GLOSSARY

ABSTRACT General, having to do with essences and ideas: Liberty, truth, and beauty are abstract concepts. Most writers depend upon abstractions to some degree; however, abstractions that are not fleshed out with vivid particulars are not likely to hold a reader's interest. See CONCRETE.

ALLUSION A passing reference, especially to a work of literature. When feminist Lindsy Van Gelder put forth the "modest proposal" that words of feminine gender be used whenever English traditionally uses masculine words, she had in mind Jonathan Swift's essay by that title (Essays for Further Reading). This single brief reference carries the weight of Swift's entire essay behind it, humorously implying that the idea being advanced is about as modest as Swift's tongue-in-cheek proposal that Ireland eat its children as a ready food supply for a poor country. Allusions, therefore, are an efficient means of enlarging the scope and implications of a statement. They work best, of course, when the refer to works most readers are likely to know.

ANALOGY A comparison that reveals a primary object or event by likening it to a secondary one, often more familiar than the first. In expository writing, analogies are used as aids to explanation and as organizing devices. In a persuasive essay, the author may argue that what is true in one case is also true in the similar case that he is advancing. An argument "by analogy" is only as strong as the terms of the analogy are similar. For examples of analogies and a discussion of their kinship with metaphors, see the introduction to Chapter 7.

APPEAL TO EMOTION, TO ETHICS, and TO REASON See MODES OF PERSUASION.

ARGUMENTATION See PERSUASION.

CAUSE AND EFFECT A strategy of exposition. Writing a cause and effect essay is much like constructing a persuasive argument; it is a form of reasoning that carries the reader step by step through a proof. Instead of "proving" the validity of the author's reasoning in order to move the reader to action, however, an essay in cause and effect is concerned with analyzing why an event occurred and with tracing its consequences. See the introduction to Chapter 4 for further discussion of this strategy.

CLASSIFICATION A strategy of exposition that places an object (or person) within a group of similar objects and then focuses on the characteristics distinguishing it from others in the group. Classification is a mode of organizing an essay as well as a means of obtaining knowledge. The introduction to Chapter 2 defines this strategy in detail.

CLICHÉ A tired expression that has lost its original power to surprise because of overuse: *We came in on a wing and a prayer; The quarterback turned the tables and saved the day.*

COMPARISON AND CONTRAST A strategy of expository writing that explores the similarities and differences between two persons, places, things, or ideas. It differs from description in that it makes statements or propositions about its subjects. The introduction to Chapter 6 defines this kind of expository essay in some detail.

CONCRETE Definite, particular, capable of being perceived directly. Opposed to *abstract*. *Rose, Mississippi, pinch* are more concrete words than *flower, river, touch*. Five-miles-per-hour is a more concrete idea than slowness. It is a good practice, as a rule, to make your essays as concrete as possible, even when you are writing on a general topic. For example, if you are defining an ideal wife or husband, cite specific wives or husbands you have known or heard about.

CONNOTATIONS The implied meanings of a word; its overtones and associations over and above its literal, dictionary meaning. The strict meaning of home, for example, is "the place where one lives"; but the word connotes comfort, security, and love. The first word in each of the following pairs is the more neutral word; the second carries richer connotations: *like / adore; clothes / garb; fast / fleet; shy / coy; stout / obese; move about / skulk; interested / obsessed.* See DENOTATION.

DEDUCTION A form of logical reasoning or explaining that proceeds from general premises to specific conclusions. For example, from the general premises that all men are mortal and that Socrates is a man, we can deduce that Socrates is mortal. See the introduction to Chapter 9 for more examples.

DEDUCTIVE See DEDUCTION.

DEFINITION A basic strategy of expository writing. Definitions set forth the essential meaning or properties of a thing or idea. "Extended" definitions enlarge upon that basic meaning by analyzing the qualities, recalling the history, explaining the purpose, or giving synonyms of whatever is being defined. Extended definitions often draw upon such other strategies of exposition as classification, comparison and contrast, and process analysis. See the introduction to Chapter 5 for a full treatment of definition.

DENOTATION The basic dictionary meaning of a word without any of its associated meanings. The denotation of *home,* for example, is simply "the place where one lives." See CONNOTATIONS.

DESCRIPTION One of the four traditional modes of discourse. Description appeals to the senses: it tells how a person, place, thing, or idea looks, feels, sounds, smells, or tastes. "Scientific" description reports these qualities; "evocative" description recreates them. See the introduction to Chapter 8 for an extended definition of the descriptive mode.

DICTION Word choice. Mark Twain was talking about diction when he said that the difference between the almost right word and the right word is the difference "between the lightning bug and the lightning." "Standard" diction is defined by dictionaries and other authorities as the language that educated native speakers of English use in their formal writing. Some other Levels of Diction are as follows; when you find one of these labels attached to words or phrases in your dictionary, avoid them in your own formal writing:

Nonstandard: Words like ain't that would never be used by an educated speaker who was trying to impress a stranger.

Informal (or Colloquial): The language of conversation among those who write standard edited English. I am crazy about you, Virginia, is informal rather than nonstandard.

Slang: Either the figurative language of a specialized group (moll, gat, heist) or fashionable coined words (boondoggle, weirdo) and extended meanings (dead soldier for an empty bottle; garbage for nonsense). Slang words often pass quickly into standard English or just as quickly fade away.

Obsolete: Terms like pantaloons and palfrey (saddle horse) that were once standard but are no longer used.

Regional (or Dialectal): For example, remuda, meaning a herd of riding horses, is used only in the Southwest.

ETYMOLOGY A word history or the practice of tracing such histories. The modern English word *march,* for example, is derived from the French *marcher* ("to walk"), which in turn is derived from the Latin word *marcus* ("a hammer"). The etymological definition of *march* is thus "to walk with a measured tread, like the rhythmic pounding of a hammer." In most dictionaries, the derivation, or etymology, of a word is explained in parentheses or brackets before the first definition is given.

EXPOSITION One of the four modes of discourse. Expository writing is informative writing. It explains or gives directions. All the items in this glossary are written in the expository mode; and most of the practical prose that you write in the coming years will be—e.g., papers and examinations, job applications, business reports, insurance claims, your last will and testament. See the Introduction for a discussion of how exposition is related to the other modes of discourse.

EXPOSITORY See EXPOSITION.

FIGURES OF SPEECH Colorful words and phrases used in a nonliteral sense. Some of the most common figures of speech are:

Simile: A stated comparison, usually with *like* or *as*: *He stood like a rock.*

Metaphor: A comparison that equates two objects without the use of a stated connecting word: *Throughout the battle, Sergeant Phillips was a rock.*

Metonymy: The use of one word or name in place of another commonly associated with it. *The White House* [for the president] *awarded the sergeant a medal.*

Personification: Assigning human traits to nonhuman objects: *The very walls have ears.*

Hyperbole: Conscious exaggeration: *The mountain reached to the sky.*

Understatement: The opposite of hyperbole, a conscious playing down: *After forty days of climbing the mountain, we felt that we had made a start.*

Rhetorical Question: A question to which the author either expects no answer or answers himself: *Why climb the mountain? Because it is there.*

HYPERBOLE Exaggeration. See FIGURES OF SPEECH.

INDUCTION A form of logical reasoning or explaining that proceeds from specific examples to general principles. As a rule, an inductive argument is only as valid as its examples are representative. See the introduction to Chapter 9.

INDUCTIVE See INDUCTION.

IRONY An ironic statement implies a way of looking at the subject that is different (not necessarily opposite) from the stated way. For example, when Russell Baker writes in "A Nice Place to Visit" (Chapter 6) that Toronto "seems hopelessly bogged down in civilization," what he implies is that New Yorkers define "civilization" in an uncivilized way. His apparent attack on Canadian manners is really a swipe at American ill-manneredness. We should be bogged down in such crudity, he is saying. Irony of situation, as opposed to *verbal* irony, occurs when events in real life or in a narrative turn out differently than the characters or people had expected. It was ironic that Hitler, with his dream of world domination, committed suicide in the end.

METAPHOR A direct comparison that identifies one thing with another. See FIGURES OF SPEECH.

MODES OF DISCOURSE Means or forms of writing or speaking. The four traditional modes of discourse are Narration, Exposition, Description, and Persuasion. This book is organized around these four modes. Chapter 1 gives examples of narration. Exposition is explained in Chapters 2–7; description, in Chapter 8; and persuasion (and argumentation), in Chapters 9 and 10.

MODES OF PERSUASION There are three traditional modes (or means) of persuading an audience to action or belief: the appeal to reason, the appeal to emotion, and the appeal to ethics. When applying the first of these, a writer convinces the reader by the force of logic; he or she constructs an argument which the reader finds to be correct or valid. When appealing to emotion, the writer tries to excite in the reader the same emotions the writer felt upon first considering the proposition he or she is advancing or some other emotion that will dispose the reader to accept that proposition. The appeal to ethics is an appeal to the reader's sense of what constitutes upright behavior. The writer convinces the reader that the writer is a good person who deserves to be heeded because of his or her admirable character. See the introductions to Chapters 9 and 10 for detailed discussions of these three modes.

NARRATION One of the four traditional modes of discourse. An accounting of actions and events that have befallen someone or something. Because narration is essentially story-telling, it is the mode most often used in fiction; however, it is also an important element in nonfictional writing and speaking. The opening of Lincoln's Gettysburg Address, for example, is in the narrative mode: "Fourscore and seven years ago our fathers brought forth on this continent a new nation. . . ."

PERSON The aspect of grammar that describes the person speaking, spoken to, or spoken about in a sentence or paragraph. There are three persons: first (I or we), second (you), and third (he, she, it, and they). See also POINT OF VIEW.

PERSONIFICATION Attributing human characteristics to the nonhuman. See FIGURES OF SPEECH.

PERSUASION The art of moving an audience to action or belief. According to traditional definitions, a writer can persuade a reader in one of three ways: by appealing to his or her reason, emotions, or sense of ethics. (See MODES OF PERSUASION.) *Argumentation,* as the term is understood in this book, is the form of persuasion that emphasizes the first of these appeals. An argument may be more concerned with pursuing a line of reasoning or stating the issued raised by a problem than with inciting someone to action. Nevertheless, an argument must persuade us that what it says is not only true but worthwhile; it must move us to believe if not to act. For a full explanation of persuasion and argumentation, see the introductions to Chapters 9 and 10.

PERSUASIVE ARGUMENT See PERSUASION.

PLOT An aspect of narrative. Plot is the sequence of events in a story. It therefore has more to do with actions rather than ideas.

POINT OF VIEW The vantage from which a story is told or an account given. Point of view is often described according to the grammatical person of a narrative. An "I" narrative, for example, is told from the "first person" point of view. A narrative that refers to "he" or "she" is told from the "third person" point of view. If the speaker of a third-person narrative seems to know everything about his or her subject, including their thoughts, the point of view is also "omniscient"; if the speaker's knowledge is incomplete, the point of view is third-person "limited." Sometimes point of view is described simply by characterizing the speaker of an essay.

PROCESS ANALYSIS A form of expository writing that breaks a process into its component operations or that gives directions. Most "How To" essays are essays in process analysis: how to grow cotton; how to operate a fork lift; how to avoid shark bite. Process analyses are usually divided into stages or steps arranged in chronological order. They differ from narratives in that they tell how something functions rather than what happens to something or someone. See the introduction to Chapter 3 for further discussion of this expository technique.

RHETORIC The art of using language effectively in speech and in writing. The term originally belonged to oratory, and it implies the presence of both a speaker (or writer) and a listener (or reader). This book is a collection of the rhetorical techniques and strategies that some successful writers have found helpful for communicating effectively with an audience.

RHETORICAL QUESTION A question that is really a statement. See FIGURES OF SPEECH.

SATIRE A form of writing that attacks a person or practice in hopes of improving either. For example, in "A Modest Proposal" (Essays For Further Reading), Jonathan Swift satirizes the materialism that had reduced his native Ireland to extreme poverty. His intent was to point out the greed of even his poorest countrymen and thereby shame them all into looking out for the public welfare instead of exploiting the country's last resources. This desire to correct vices and follies distinguishes *satire* from *sarcasm*, which is intended primarily to wound. See also IRONY.

SATIRIZE See SATIRE.

SIMILE A comparison that likens one thing to another. See FIGURES OF SPEECH.

SLANG Popular language that often originates in the speech of a particular group or subculture. See DICTION.

SYNTAX The interrelationship among words. In the sentence, *The police chased the woman who had beaten her dog,* the phrase *the woman who had beaten her dog* is the "direct object." This term describes the syntax of the phrase because it defines the function of the phrase within the context of the entire sentence. In a larger sense, syntax refers to the total network of relationships, including meanings, among words in a discourse.

TENSE The time aspect of verbs. In the sentence, *He took the money and ran,* the past-tense forms indicate that the taking and running occurred at an earlier time than the writer's telling about those actions. There are six basic tenses in English: past, present, future, and the perfect forms of these three: past perfect, present perfect, and future perfect. (Here "perfect" means completed. An action in the future perfect—*He will have left,* for example—will be completed in the future before another stated future action: *He will have left before the police arrive.*) In writing, it is a good idea not to switch tenses unnecessarily. If you start an essay in the past tense, stick to that tense unless the sense of your remarks requires a change: *He took the money, but the police will catch him.*

TONE An author's revealed attitude toward his subject or audience: sympathy, longing, amusement, shock, sarcasm—the range is endless. When analyzing the tone of a passage, consider what quality of a voice you should assume for reading it aloud.

TOPIC SENTENCE The sentence in a paragraph that comes closest to stating the topic of the paragraph as a whole. The topic sentence is often the first sentence, but it may appear anywhere in the paragraph. Some paragraphs do not have clear-cut topic sentences, especially if they function chiefly to link preceding paragraphs with those to follow.

TRANSITION The act of passing from one topic (or aspect of a topic) to another; the word, phrase, sentence, or paragraph that accomplishes such a passage. For an excellent example, see paragraph 5 of Alexander Petrunkevitch's "The Spider and the Wasp" in Chapter 3. Polished transitions are necessary if an essay is to be carefully organized and developed.

UNDERSTATEMENT A verbal playing down or softening for humorous or ironic effect. See FIGURES OF SPEECH.

INDEX